Urban MĀORI

The Prime Minister is welcomed to Hoani Waititi marae at Waitangi Day celebrations, 2017.
Courtesy Te Whānau o Waipareira

Urban MĀORI
The Second Great Migration

Bradford Haami
for Te Whānau o Waipareira

Oratia

This book is dedicated to my wife Selina and our daughter Zeo. It is also written in memory of my dear friend Jason Hotere, who was raised in Auckland, travelled the world, impacted many, and passed away suddenly in 2017. Moe mai e te hoa i roto i te rangimārie o tō atua. Arohanui atu ki te whānau pani ki a Tatiana, Taimane me Kiana.

Published for Te Whānau o Waipareira Trust by Oratia Books, Oratia Media Ltd, 783 West Coast Road, Oratia, Auckland 0604, New Zealand (www.oratia.co.nz)

Copyright © 2018 Te Whānau o Waipareira Trust
Text copyright © 2018 Bradford Haami

The copyright holders assert their moral rights in the work.

This book is copyright. Except for the purposes of fair reviewing, no part of this publication may be reproduced or transmitted in any form or by any means, whether electronic, digital or mechanical, including photocopying, recording, any digital or computerised format, or any information storage and retrieval system, including by any means via the Internet, without permission in writing from the publisher. Infringers of copyright render themselves liable to prosecution.

ISBN 978-0-947506-28-5

Front cover: Renata whānau (see profile, page 255), courtesy Renata whānau, image by Inspire Photography, Wellington.
Back cover: top left, Ngā Tūmanako kapa haka at Hoani Waititi marae, Auckland, courtesy of Reikura Kahi and Ngā Tūmanako; top right, Te Whānau o Waipareira painting by Robyn Kahukiwa, 1998, courtesy of Te Whānau o Waipareira Trust; lower, opening of Hoani Waititi marae, photographer unknown, 1980. Glen Eden Print Collection, GLEN-P-024, Auckland Libraries, West Auckland Research Centre.

Cover design: Cheryl Smith, Macarn Design

Printed in China

Contents

	Foreword *by John Tamihere*	7
	Acknowledgements	9
1	Ngā Heke Māori: Māori Migration	13
2	Te Au o Te Awa: The River Current	29
3	Tūranga Hou: A New Standing Place	49
4	Akoranga Mahi-ā-rehe: Trade Training	66
5	Te Whakahiato: The Rise of the Collective	82
6	Tau Whare: Laying Down Roots	101
7	Whakatū Marae: The Urban Marae	116
8	Ngā Piki me ngā Heke: Highs and Lows	132
9	Iwitanga Hou: Retribalisation	154
10	Mana Mātāwaka: The Urban Authorities	174
11	Noho Tāwāhi: Māori in Australia	198
12	Hokinga ki te Kāinga: Returning Home	217
13	Iti Oneone Hou: The New Morsel of Soil	237
	Endnotes	259
	Bibliography	288
	Index	302

Foreword

In the romantic rush to redefine and reclaim the way of the Māori, through developing and rebuilding iwitanga, we can never forget this great, urban migration.

It was urban Māori activism that provided the impetus for public recognition of matters Māori — whether it was the land march, the petition for our language, the first kohanga reo, the first kura kaupapa, or the first Māori side to represent our people in a World Cup.

This outstanding legacy of a people placed under great stress, with a government policy to assimilate them and turn them into brown folk that act like nice white folk, is a challenge worth telling. More importantly, it was a challenge that had to be overcome.

We have thousands of Māori, now buried in public cemeteries away from their tribal lands, who need to have their story told. We need their grandchildren to know the difficulties and challenges that confronted their ancestors. This book tells the sacrifices made and the obstacles overcome.

It is a tribute to Māori that our culture has survived. Urban Māori had to evolve and develop new tikanga. We had to develop new marae that celebrated our tribal diversity but did not wallow in our tribal differences.

We have never lost our spirit to defend our rights and our land — to be Māori. Having re-enlivened our spirit and belief in ourselves, our next great migration will be to break out of the socio-economic deprivation we presently occupy. That breakout is underway, and the grandchildren of those in this book will complete it.

John Tamihere
Chief Executive Officer, Te Whānau o Waipareira
Tāmaki-makaurau, October 2017

Acknowledgements

Urban Māori — The Second Great Migration recounts Māori peoples' migration from their rural, tribal landscapes to new urban environments around New Zealand and abroad. Māori traditional and contemporary history is the story of migration, and that includes the great twentieth-century urban migration of Māori people to the towns and cities, a modern-day phenomenon regarded as the fastest urban migration by any people group in the world.[1] Prior to World War II it was estimated 90% of Māori lived in rural areas. However, by 1966 62% of the Māori population lived in urban centres,[2] and by 1970 that grew to 80%. By 2013 it was recorded 84% of Māori lived in urban areas, a quarter of that population living in Auckland, New Zealand's largest city. At this time one in six people of Māori descent did not know their tribal affiliations, with many regarding themselves as 'urban Māori'.[3]

It was the recognition that this story had not been told in one volume that led Te Whānau o Waipareira Trust to commission Oratia Books to publish this work, and Oratia in turn to invite me to write it. I acknowledge the Trust for their conceptualisation and commissioning vision.

The opening chapter of this book comments on the nature of migration and the push–pull factors that influence the movement of people. It introduces the reader to the facts of Māori internal migration, pan-tribalism and adaptation to new environments. Each subsequent chapter loosely explores a decade from 1940 to 2010, recounting key events and narratives of those periods that were influenced by factors such as urbanisation, assimilation and later retribalisation. Specific chapters describe crucial developments that arose almost simultaneously out of urbanisation — such as the Māori trade-training courses of the 1960s, the rise of Māori collectives like the Māori Women's Welfare League, the Urban Māori Authorities and the establishment of urban marae. This narrative flow stretches overseas to comment on Māori in Australia and also investigates the phenomenon of urban families returning home to reconnect with their tribal roots. The conclusion comments on the maintenance of a future Māori identity that transcends place, whether it be rural, urban or overseas.

I have approached this kaupapa as a general overview of Māori urbanisation that offers a context for the migration of Māori to the city and abroad. Woven through the historical narrative are profiles of individuals and whānau, recounting their own migration journeys to the cities since World War II and their diverse experiences of urban life. In contrast to the wealth of academic material available on Māori urbanisation and its impacts, this book seeks to draw on these works but to offer new insights into the realities of urban Māori lives. My own experience, having moved from Whakatāne to Australia in my teens and then living in Auckland for more than 30 years, has informed my perspective on urban life. It has also enabled me access to my community of Māori from different tribes, generations and walks of life, many of whom are active participants in Te Whānau o Waipareira. This work has an unashamedly urban Māori voice, often leaning towards a West Auckland Māori narrative.

For their assistance in the research and writing of *Urban Māori*, I would like to acknowledge Waipareira and the Wai Research team for advice and access to their research resources. I am grateful to the many whānau members I was able to interview for allowing their family journeys, experiences and thoughts on urban life to be included in this publication. Your stories and images add colour to the picture painted in this narrative. I have drawn heavily on seminal works about Māori and urbanisation by scholars including Dr Ranginui Walker, Dame Joan Metge, Dr Mason Durie, Dr Roger Maaka, Professor Atholl Anderson, Dr Aroha Harris, Dame Judith Binney, Melissa Williams and Erin Keenan. Peter Dowling, Anna Fomison and Carolyn Lagahetau of Oratia Books have been a great support to me in the process of writing this work. I salute my family, who had to put up with me becoming a recluse over an intense period of reading, researching and writing to complete this work on such a complex subject.

The disruption of urban migration led to both negative consequences and positive adaptation. This book seeks to delve into the disruption of urban migration, to highlight the negatives, but more to emphasize the innovations that emerged out of Māori adaptation to modern migration and urban living.

This work is by no means a definitive history of Māori and urbanisation: it is merely a glimpse into the huge diversity of stories about the Māori experience in Te Ao Hurihuri, this changing world — much of which is yet to be discovered and uncovered.

Me āta haria mai te iti oneone i kapua mai Hawaiki.

Let us carefully carry in the hollow of our hands the small morsel of soil from Hawaiki.

Kia tau te mauri,

Bradford Haami
Auckland/Tāmaki-makaurau, June 2017

Chapter 1

Ngā Heke Māori

Māori Migration

The first great migration in traditional Māori history occurred around 800 years ago when ancestors intentionally voyaged over 3000 kilometres across Te Moananui-a-Kiwa (the Pacific Ocean), in unfamiliar conditions, to arrive in Aotearoa New Zealand. It was one of the last habitable land masses to be settled by humans.[1] Migratory canoe traditions recount the departure of ancestors from the sacred homeland of Hawaiki and other associated places such as Te Tihi-o-Manono, Motutapu, Wawautea, Rangiātea, Parinuiterā, Waerota, Matuaterā, Tawhiti-nui-a-rua and Patu-nui-o-āio at the edge of the sky.[2] Historians pinpoint Eastern Polynesian islands as the origin of Māori ancestors who arrived, explored and settled permanently in these newfound locales.[3] The traditions also feature return journeys to Hawaiki to obtain special emblems and precious delicacies needed in the new land. 'Problems of hunger, boundary disputes, personal feuds and warfare' are presented by traditional accounts as reasons for sailing into the vast ocean to find new homes.[4] Over-population and prophetic dreams were other causes for seeking new lands to settle.[5]

Not only did the ancestors carry food, plants and material possessions with them, they brought intellectual luggage and a world view that was implanted in the new land. The *iti oneone i kapua mai Hawaiki* (the small morsel of soil carried from Hawaiki), representing 'Hawaiki itself', was fixed into the new landscape as a mauri (life force). Through these mauri, ancestors could access the ancient homeland. The people had to adapt to the whenua hou (new land), its flora and fauna, and a completely new climate. The environment soon shaped their culture as Māori. The early migrant population grew to an estimated 90–100,000 people by the late eighteenth century.[7]

The *Tākitimu* waka tradition is one of many examples of a multi-generational migration of ancestors who voyaged from Hawaiki and settled the land from Te Tai Tokerau in the north to Te Waipounamu in the south. When *Tākitimu* arrived in the northern regions of Aotearoa at Rangaunu Harbour, which was described as a 'truly fertile land', its chief leader Tamatea was unable to secure settlement rights to this land. Tamatea and his people sailed to Aurere (Doubtless Bay) and continued past the famous reef known as Nukutaurua, arriving eventually at Tauranga in the Bay of Plenty.[8] Here some of the family of Tamatea established themselves at Mangatawa. Three generations later a family dispute between two brothers, Whaene and Kahungunu, saw Kahungunu leave the region and make his way to Whakatāne, and then on to Ōpōtiki, Whangarā, Tūranga and Whareongaonga, finally settling at Te Mahia with his famous wife Rongomaiwahine from this region. Eventually the grand- and great-grand-children of Kahungunu and Rongomaiwahine, in the time of Rakaihikuroa, Tāraia and Te Aomatarahi, migrated southwards again, conquering the lands from Wairoa to Waimārama and further on to Wairarapa.[9] All of the East Coast peoples from Te Mahia to the Wairarapa recognise Kahungunu as one of many prominent eponymous ancestors.[10]

Tribal histories are full of internal migration stories. Many groups of people shifted from their settlements annually due to the seasonal harvest of resources and to protect their territorial lands, resources and sacred places.[11] Other times hapū groups shifted to completely new environments, often within other tribal boundaries. Like the voyaging ancestors, there were circumstances that led to these movements, often leading groups of people to seek refuge elsewhere with relatives. At Te Awanga near Cape Kidnappers, the cursing remarks of Tamariki towards his younger relatives, over the wrongful distribution of whale meat for his son, led to an offense that saw nearly all of the people of the Cape Kidnappers region migrate permanently to the Wairarapa. Generations later in the same region, Ngāti Putanoa of Wairoa were defeated in battle by the famous ancestor Tapuwae, and shifted to Waimārama as refugees, some say under

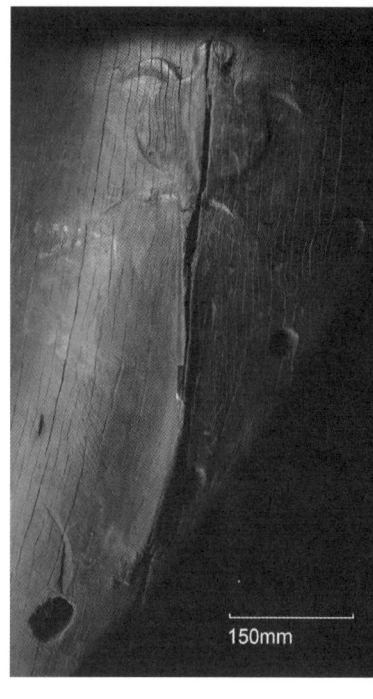

This section of a 600-year-old canoe hull, found at the Anaweka estuary on the South Island's West Coast, has been carved with a sea turtle in raised relief. The turtle design is a rarity in pre-European Māori art but not unknown. This find makes a strong connection between New Zealand Māori and tropical East Polynesian voyagers, who revered these seafaring creatures.

Courtesy of Dilys Johns, Conservation, The University of Auckland

the invitation of a relative. According to custom, these immigrants to the region were accepted by the presiding chiefs and gifted rights to lands and resources, sometimes jointly with the mana whenua (authority over land), provided their first fruits of the seasons were offered to the original giver.[12] These amalgamations were often solidified by arranged marriages between the migrants and the local mana whenua. Their children became the symbols of any peaceful agreement and became the takawaenga (mediators) for maintaining future peace.[13]

For South Island iwi Ngāi Tahu, the migration story across the land began from Wairoa on the east coast of the North Island and ended at Rakiura (Stewart Island). Dealing with family frictions and facing tribal opposition along the way, these ancestors journeyed 1600 kilometres to their final destination.[14] Migration was a potent catalyst for the naming of hapū (sub-tribes). As the migrating hapū travelled further south over time, away from the original ancestor they were named after, new names were eventually coined by split-off groups, taken from younger distinguished ancestors within the same lineage.[15] They joined other related hapū and other iwi to form new communities and new identities. This led to numerous hapū names, with more than a hundred recorded amongst only 2000 Ngāi Tahu in 1840.[16]

Colonial realities

In post-European times, the migration of tribes within New Zealand continued. For instance, after conflicts with other tribes in the Waikato, Ngāti Toa migrated south from Kawhia in 1820 with hundreds of people to Taranaki and on to Kapiti Island. The first part of the migration to Taranaki was known as Te Heke Tahutahu Ahi (The Fire-lighting Migration), recalling an incident where many fires were lit to give their enemies the impression of a larger body of people.[17] This heke was led by formidable leaders Te Pehi, Te Rangihaeata and Te Rauparaha, who encouraged the people to shift to the Kapiti region, where there was an abundance of resources and land, and greater opportunity to trade with Pākehā for guns.[18] The second stage of this arduous migration to Kapiti was named Te Heke Taramoa (The Bramble Bush Migration) after the obstacles the people had to overcome reaching their final destination. Similarly, after a polite invite by Te Rauparaha and certain inducements, Ngāti Raukawa decided to migrate from Maungatautari to the Kapiti Coast in 1828. A number of southern migrations by Ngāti Raukawa occurred, named Te Heke Whirinui, Te Heke Kariritahi and Te Heke Mairaro. Te Ahu Karamū led the first migration, Nepia Taratoa the second migration and Te Whatanui the third.[19] It has been intimated that Te Whatanui left Maungatautari due to a combination of grief from inland conflicts, and the attractions of a new place, including the promise of seafood in abundance.[20]

The land wars of the 1860s also saw the 'forced' movement of people into new territories. Below Mt Taranaki is Parihaka, a famous village that survives as a symbol of passive resistance and also as an example of a nineteenth-century pan-tribal community. It was in this village that many tribal groups, disaffected from their whenua due to the land wars, migrated here to become part of a pan-tribal community, all living together under a new order of society. Te Whiti o Rongomai, Tohu Kakahi and other whānau established Parihaka in the mid-1860s, after moving from the coastal village of Warea to seek refuge from constant attack by British forces.[21]

For 15 years Parihaka flourished to become the largest Māori settlement in the country.[22] The messages conveyed by the village strategic leaders, Te Whiti o Rongomai and Tohu Kakahi, attracted tribal groups from all over the country who were 'facing the impact of land confiscation and the reality of surviving without their ancestral lands'.[23] The new principles of the community were based on renouncing violence and status divisions, but empowering people to work together as a self-sufficient community under equality. Parihaka was described then, as "industrious, law-abiding, moral and hospitable", and the papakāinga swelled to 2000 with 1000 more arriving at monthly gatherings to hear the leaders speak. Many saw it as a "new Jerusalem".[24]

While tribes within the village had their own autonomy, they all contributed and subscribed to the over-arching kaupapa set down by the Parihaka leaders. In a painful series of events, Te Whiti and Tohu's dream of a self-sufficient village based on peace was destabilised by invading colonial troops, who confronted 2500 peaceful villagers sitting on the marae in November 1881. The troops imprisoned the Parihaka leaders without trial, and evicted 1500 men, women and children to their original tribal areas. The village was then systematically demolished.[25] On 9 June 2017 the Crown publicly apologised for the atrocities committed during the sacking of Parihaka and offered a compensation package as a settlement for the grievances of the past. Today Parihaka stands as a living testimony to a new envisioned Māori world, which was halted for a time but is to be rejuvenated.

The Kīngitanga and Rātana movements also influenced pan-Māori gatherings of iwi and hapū, who not only maintained their own autonomy, but also deliberately decided to align with these powerful prophetic-religious and political movements, as they seemed extremely relevant to the plight of the people at the time. One of the foundations of Wiremu Tahupōtiki Rātana's faith was unity through a pan-Māori ideology as opposed to tribal affiliations.[26] The original 39-acre land block where the Rātana village now stands originally belonged to the Rātana family. His message of unity through aroha (love) and news of his faith healings drew whānau and hapū from all over the country, many wishing to remove themselves from tribal land dissensions. The people came to reside in the pā (village), which soon became a permanent settlement of shacks, roads and shops,[27] later upgraded with better housing facilities and a church.

Although whānau groups who migrated to the settlement camped in tribal groupings in the village, they were committed to Rātana's vision of settling old tribal divisions between each other, embracing the 'māramatanga' (the enlightenment of Ihoa),[28] and taking on the name 'morehu' (remnant, broken) representing the survivors of the ancestors from the trauma of colonisation.[29] According to Dr Roger Maaka, Ratana's success didn't result in detribalisation but offered a viable alternative expressed through "prophecy and metaphor, ritual and organisation".[30] By 1926, he had 11,000 adherents, nearly 19% of the Māori population.[31]

A gathering in front of Te Manuao in the 1930s at Rātana Pā.
Usmar, Julie, Photographs and reproductions relating to Ratana. Ref: PAColl-3095-1. Alexander Turnbull Library, Wellington, New Zealand

Māori sought to support or seek the advantages of being part of these new forms of community. The migration and resettlement of people into these new territories forced the adaptation to new conditions, new environments and new ways of living, often producing modified tikanga and a modified identity. Pan-tribal groupings of whānau lived either permanently in residence in the new lands or occupied the new space for a short time until the reason to amalgamate no longer applied. Nowhere else has the combination of all these conditions been more realised than with the massive urban migration of Māori people from their rural tribal papakāinga to the cities after World War II.

Today this group of people is labelled Urban Māori.

A great migration

This great movement of people was recorded in the 1950s at the rate of 1% per annum, or 1600 people, leaving the hinterlands each year[32] and later grew to 10% per annum between 1961 and 1966.[33] The 1901 census records reported the number of solely Māori ('half-caste' or more) stood at 45,549. Fifty years later, in 1951, the number of 'those of Māori descent' tripled to 134,862.[34] In 1926, only 9% of the Māori population lived in the cities and boroughs,[35] with 90% of the Māori population still living in rural areas before World War II. Between 1936 and 1945 the Māori percentage of those living in urban areas, designated as a community of more than 5000 people, grew to 26%.[36] That trickle became a torrent as a second wave of migrants pushed urban Māori numbers to 35% in 1956 and ten years later to 62% in 1966.[37] That same year it was revealed 19% of Māori lived in Auckland, 8% in Wellington-Manawatū and 11% in the whole of Northland.[38] By 1970 that percentage of the Māori urban population grew to 80%.[39]

Based on these significant numbers, showing the progressive migration of Māori people to the city over the time span of 44 years (1926-1970), Māori became an urbanised people. One commentator ventured to say Māori were 'no longer a purely tribal people'.[40] The reality of living in a rural environment, where people operated within the social structure of iwi and hapū, changed completely after the urban shift that occurred after World War II;[41] this was something the cities were not expecting or even prepared for at the time. In 2013, 84% of Māori lived in urban areas, a quarter of those choosing to live in Auckland, New Zealand's largest city.[42]

The terms 'drift' or 'trickle', commonly used to describe this phenomenon, do not fully represent what occurred; at first a trickle but it became more like a tsunami.[43] The word 'drift' does not reflect the fact that Māori made conscious and deliberate organised decisions to migrate. The 'pull' to the city in search of 'work, money and pleasure'[44] was strong, but so too was the force of the 'push' away from the rural regions due to the unsustainable earning power of tribal land.[45] In 1939 it was recognised Sir Apirana Ngata's earlier land development schemes of the 1920s, where tribal lands were developed into farms and worked by other tribal farmers, would only support a quarter of the Māori population then. Twenty years on it was reported if all remnant Māori lands were to be developed, no more than 4000 farms would be operational for an estimated Māori population of a quarter of a million.[46] The rising population presented a problem where the diminishing of a Māori land base could not sustain employment for Māori and people would have to migrate to the cities to find work.[47] Additionally, the de-valuation of Māoritanga was manifest through the idea of setting aside one's Māori identity for a Pākehā education that would allow the next generation to live comfortably in a Pākehā-orientated world. Whānau divisions, harsh domestic conditions and in some cases the heavy presence of kēhua (ghosts), mākutu (curses) and tapu (restrictions) were more personal reasons for moving.

Sir Paul Reeves wrote how his mother, who grew up on the 'edge of the pa', made a 'conscious decision' in 1921 to move to the city for work, away from 'her home and her Māori relatives to a situation where she could not do Māori things in a Māori way'.[48] Māori were introduced to a cash economy to which they had to adjust and needed to learn skills to survive in this system. While Government policy encouraged assimilation and integration into a Pākehā way of life, the fact that individual young Māori women and men, and later families, made personal 'choices' to move is a factor that cannot be diminished in any way. Between 1942 and 1969, the strongest response to urbanisation and integration came from Māori women who were charged by the state with guiding Māori men into becoming 'ideal' Māori citizens.[49]

During the 1960s, young Māori women flocked to the cities looking for employment opportunities. Hostels run by the United Māori Mission in Auckland city became a safe place for Māori to stay.

Courtesy of United Māori Mission

Joan Metge's study of Māori urbanisation in Auckland revealed a complex pattern of migration where half of her sample of whānau went directly from a tribal district to the city, another third shifted between rural areas before going to a major city, and the rest travelled to the city via intermediary small towns.[50] Those small towns included Whāngarei, Rotorua, Gisborne or Whanganui. People in Auckland tended to congregate in the central city suburbs of Grafton, Newton, Grey Lynn, Freemans Bay.[51] Auckland as the destination of choice grew to 330,000 people in 1951 and by 1966 there was a population of 550,00, with a third of New Zealand residing here over the next ten years.[52] There were always 'go to' homes, where key whānau houses became gateways for visiting tribal relations who were transitioning into the cities.[53]

As the momentum grew accommodation became overcrowded and families eventually shifted to newly built subdivisions like Avondale, Glen Innes, Ōtara, Māngere, Glen Eden and Te Atatū, or Porirua and Wainuiomata in Wellington. The Department of Māori Affairs tried to alleviate the congestion by expanding its housing programme from 700 in 1960 to 2000 in 1967. These homes built in the cities followed a policy where Māori were 'pepper-potted' among Pākehā homes — in some cases one Māori dwelling to a block of Pākehā houses — in the interests of integration.[54] Young men attending Māori Trade Training stayed in church-run city hostels and were organised into teams to build the Māori Affairs homes. Since 1959, thousands of Māori male graduates have learned a building trade skill and entered the workforce. In contrast to this, Māori also obtained rental housing through the State Advances Corporation, which did not have a pepper-potting policy.[55]

Adapting identities

Families who made the shift maintained connections with their elders and family 'back-home' in a variety of ways. With whānau back-home still tending farms and gardens, it was common for trailer-loads of rīwai (potatoes), kūmara (sweet potatoes), vegetables, fruit, kaimoana (seafood) and meat to be sent to relations in the city. In return, foods and commodities easily purchased in the city were sent back-home, often with funds for gatherings and family upkeep. Most families made regular trips back-home. Carpooling was a common cost-sharing option. However, the cost of transport became a major factor for many families who could not make regular trips back, particularly when transporting a tūpāpaku (deceased relative) home to a tribal burial. Many first-generation migrant Māori who arrived in the city were poorly educated but worked hard in the labour force, but never expected to stay too long. After earning enough money and offering the children a better education, there was a common thought of returning back-home to the family farm or to the original homestead at some time. This was a fervent goal for many of the first and second generations of city migrants. However, few reached that aspiration in their lifetime and most never made that transition home. The notion of 'home' or 'back-home' places for Māori refers to locations, including the present location, where parents, grandparents and ancestors derived their descent. It is usually a place with boundaries, named boundary markers, a marae or a number of marae representing a number of hapū and families. For the children and grandchildren of the first city migrants, who still dwell in the city permanently, the notion of returning back-home is still a common desire. The urban landscape is where many migrant families tried to re-create the 'village-style back-home' but in a new setting, and could be considered simply an extension of back-home.

It became necessary to adjust to new tikanga and redefine whānau (family), hapū and more particularly iwi (tribe) in an urban context. This should not be surprising, as this dynamic has been occurring among Māori for hundreds of years. Whānau carried their māramataka knowledge and the associated tikanga for planting and harvest of various foods and adapted them to the new city landscape. The custom of the distribution of kai (food) between relations was extended to pan-Māori enclaves of families in the suburbs.[56] Also, the collective whanaungatanga (relationships) extended beyond just kin-based relationships, and became central to the capacity building that occurred in the city to organise Māori under different models of community. New forms of whānau, not based on whakapapa (geneaology), evolved in the city. For example the 'workplace whānau' was a particular kind of connectedness among a group of people in the workplace, which included other ethnicities, genders and occupations.[57] The churches, hotels, sports organisations and the workspace became places where strong long-term non-kin relations were fostered.

The decision to shift from the papakāinga to an urban landscape saw second- and third-generation Māori migrants become culturally dislocated, living in a state of detribalisation and discontent.[58] This was substantiated by census statistics for 2013 that showed one in six people with Māori descent did not know their tribal affiliations, with many regarding themselves as 'urban Māori'.[59] On the whole the major criticism of urban migration is that it was a ploy by successive governments to assimilate Māori to become Pākehā and aspire to the modern Pākehā lifestyle. This brought about disconnection to tribal communalism and whānau ties to land. A house in the city with a small patch of grass for a flower bed or a vegetable garden became the new family tūrangawaewae (place to stand).

The label 'urban Māori' has elicited a variety of responses. Many city-based Māori embrace the term and see it as reflecting their new social reality. Others resist its sometimes derogatory use by Māori who have not left home and re-categorise the term 'urban' as 'multiple',

The Māori Affairs Trade Training programme, run between 1959 and 1981, saw hundreds of young Māori men leave their rural homes to attend the city training schools. These young trainees were boarding at Gillies Hostel in Auckland in 1979. Many of the trainees found good employment, married in the cities and progressed to run their own businesses.

Courtesy of United Māori Mission

'co-existing', and 'interacting' concepts of home.[60] Others prefer to be known simply as Māori or whānau Māori living in a city location.

With the increase in Māori populations in the cities, the need for a marae-style gathering space became crucial. This saw the creation of community centres or the use of halls to cater for the cultural rituals associated with births, weddings and tangihanga, so often carried out inadequately in the smaller suburban homes. The Auckland Maori Community Centre became that very gathering place from the 1940s — it was the face of urban Māori. This was progressively followed by the emergence of secular, pan-Māori urban marae. This innovation has seen many new marae established throughout New Zealand's urban centres, extending to church congregations as well as secondary and tertiary institutes. The founding of these marae was not without conflict over mana whenua rights and tensions between inter-tribal world views, but they represent a symbol of Māori cultural maintenance in the urban milieu. The urban marae and the variations of its organised structures are a 'testament to the adaptability of the Māori and the vigour of their cultural renaissance'.[61]

The urban environment has become a hotbed for the creation of new innovative forms of councils, social networks and institutions. It further created the conditions for the rise of Māori protest and an alternative way of being Māori.[62] However, the emergence of Urban Māori Authorities like Te Whānau o Waipareira Trust challenged the status quo of the iwi development system, in search of their own autonomous recognition as an iwi in an urban world. By 2008, Te Whānau o Waipareira were servicing the social needs of 15,000 households of pan-tribal Māori and non-Māori.[63] For many the notion of urban Māori is non-existent. As one leader put it, 'There is no such thing as urban Māori, never has been and never will be.'[64] In other words, they are all tribal and should be identified with their iwi back-home.

Māori migration to the urban centres was, as Melissa Williams puts it, "a 'life-course' and an inter-generational process of 'cultural negotiation'."[65] It is considered to be the 'most accelerated shift for a national population anywhere'.[66] It was 'persistent and irreversible'[67] and has became an 'unmarshalled force' not only towards New Zealand urban centres but also now to Australia, where an estimated one in six Māori now live.[68] This has redefined what it means to be Māori[69] and begat a new and dynamic mātāwaka (pan-tribal) culture.[70]

Ella and Mia Henry, Auckland

Ella Henry celebrates her 61st birthday in 2015 with her daughter, Mia Henry-Teirney.
Courtesy of Mia Henry Teirney

Dr Ella Henry is a well-known face in Māori academia and film production circles. A senior lecturer in Te Ara Poutama at Auckland University of Technology, she has extensively studied Māori women in leadership and Māori entrepreneurship, and taught Māori media, co-operative education and Māori business.

She has lived in the city since she was six years old. Her parents' introduction to city life occurred during their courtship in 1935. "Dad was trying to be flash and he took my mother to the city. Because they had no family living in Auckland they had to stay down at the 'in-town' pā, called Waipapa." They married in 1936.

"Mum was a 'half-caste' and spoke no Māori. Her father was an Irish storeman who married a Māori woman and together they had nine children. Mum said they were told by their mother to marry Pākehā," Ella explains. But Ella's mother Martha was disobedient and married Sam Henry who, as she told Ella, was Māori through and through. "He was a reo speaker and lived as a tūturu Māori." Sam was a mechanic who had joined the military in 1939 as an engineer and was stationed in Wellington. At that time the couple already had three children and the family still lived in Northland. Sam would return to the family on furlough once a year. By the end of the war the couple had six children. "We lived in Ahipara, then at Kaitaia, where everyone was whānau. Mum was always home," Ella remembers.

As a child Ella had the freedom to walk into any home; she lived in "a village, with lots of family time".

Ella, born in 1954, was nine years younger than her closest sibling. All of her siblings moved to the cities during the 1950s because of the lack of work in Kaitaia. Ella's parents realised they too would need to move if they were to see their mokopuna, and relocated to New Lynn in West Auckland. Her parents took up employment at the local factories, alongside other family members. "Mum and my sisters worked at Crown Lynn Potteries, my sisters' husbands were employed at Amalgamated Brick and Pipe, and Dad was at the Astley Tannery." Ella's extended family planted roots in both West Auckland and Ōtara.

"I grew up around my dad and his Māori mates who all spoke Māori. They didn't need to prove they were Māori, they just were — whereas Mum came from a family who wanted to be Pākehā to fit in," Ella says.

Ella always felt different in the city. Being at a new school she soon became aware she was different — she was brown and didn't have flash clothes or shoes. With everyone at work early in the morning, there were no village aunties to look out for her. "I'd come home after school and everyone was still at the factory. It was quite a lonely time for me and probably led me to going completely off the rails," Ella says. She sees her life from age 7 to 16 as traumatic and just a blur.

"While visiting a Pākehā primary-school friend's house, I sat out on the back step while everyone else had milk and biscuits inside the house. I felt I couldn't enter a white person's house. This is something I internalised about Māori and Pākehā relationships: we were taught to be respectful to them," she says. Ella was a model student at intermediate. "I wanted to be what my parents wanted me to be and that was a 'good Māori'. But Auckland was uncomfortable for me. The city was a dangerous place for young Māori who didn't know who they were. I was the only one at home and the village wasn't there anymore."

Her low self-esteem became the root of a spiral of self-destruction that began when she reached 15. She escaped into a world of sex, drugs and rock 'n' roll.[71] "I went out with a Highway 61 gang guy who introduced me to hard drugs, which was fabulous at the time, and I did everything you would do to keep on those drugs. I saw Led Zeppelin live and worked at Levis Nightclub." Due to her drug abuse, at age 17 Ella was sent to a psychiatric unit at Oakley Hospital. "When friends died of drug overdoses and alcohol, I knew I had to get away. I left for Australia and broke my father's heart," she remembers. He died two months after she left New Zealand, in 1975; he lay at Mahurehure marae in Point Chevalier, Auckland.

Between 1974 and 1979, she was in an abusive relationship. She returned to New Zealand and stayed with friends in the South Island. Interpol police tracked her down to Moonlight Creek and took her to Christchurch to identify friends who had been murdered by Mr Asia. That was a turning point in Ella's life.

She returned to Australia and worked on the prawn trawlers in the Gulf of Carpentaria for two seasons. In 1981 she sailed with a friend on a yacht to South Africa, where she lived in Cape Town as an honorary white. "I wasn't an African, and I learned a lot about racism while I was living in South Africa," Ella reveals. She was in South Africa at the same time protests against the South African rugby tour occurred in New Zealand. "We heard nothing in South Africa about what was going on in New Zealand until I returned to London," she states.

She returned home in 1984 to find friends and whānau involved in land rights, joining Māori protests and studying. In 1986 she started university, completing two degrees in 1990 and 1995, the first in her lineage to obtain a university education and a degree. Today, Ella is a forceful voice for Māori and women's rights, all proclaimed with a strong wit, a sense of humour and a smile. She has been a strong advocate for the work of Waipareira Trust in West Auckland, where her mother was a foundational kāhui kaumātua member.

Recently Ella took her three grown-up daughters on a road trip to reconnect with her marae and her urupa in the north. "At all the marae and urupa I belong to, even where my parents are buried at Waimahana, I realised I am a visitor to those places now and I'm an urban Māori. Those places are not my home. So I have decided I will live and die here in Auckland, but my children can decide where they want to be," she proclaims.

Ella's second daughter, Mia, is currently a Producer Intern for Jump Film and Television. "I got into this because Mum and others were in Ngā Aho Whakaari (Māori in Film and Television) for 20 years." Mia has a strong desire to help people through the medium of film and television and to tell stories with a social impact on a large scale. She has produced a pilot episode for a web series, and a short film. Born in 1990 at Waitakere Hospital, Mia attended a local kōhanga reo unit and later a bilingual school, until she reached intermediate. Growing up, she was conscious of being raised in a Māori environment, but has also been mindful of her Irish and Croatian ties. "We weren't one or the other," she says. "I feel I'm deeply connected as a Māori woman who can speak Māori and who has a lot of empathy towards Māori issues."

She has a strong connection with both Waimahana of Ngāti Kahu ki Whangaroa, where her grandparents are buried, and Avondale in Auckland, where she grew up. "Waimahana is where back-home is, but where my family is, that is home. Once you are urbanised, then that's home. My cousins feel Ōtara is their home and they've been there for three generations," she explains.

Mia sees herself as urban Māori or, as others call her, a 'townie brownie'. "I guess being urban Māori means somebody who has grown up urban and can survive within that environment. I didn't grow up in the country so I couldn't handle it probably, whereas I know every bit of Auckland," she says. She feels a definite divide between urban and iwi Māori, "but I think that comes from not understanding each other's challenges. I think it's important for us to remember the past histories of where we came from and how people were led here and struggled. I know my grandparents were poor for a long time and so too were my parents and I acknowledge that," she says, "but many of our rural relatives think we're rich because we're urban."

"My mum made a conscious decision to pursue academia for us, so we would have a better opportunity in life." Mia went to university and has graduated from AUT with a Bachelor of Business. "This has given me an understanding of the world and how to process information and broaden my preparation to live in this global environment. If we'd grown up in Waimahana we would all be more connected as a family to our whakapapa and to our elders as well. But I think there's opportunities in the city — I have my reo and tikanga and live in an urban world. I'd say I'm privileged and that comes from my parents' decisions to place us in this environment."

Ella has strong views about the tension that exists between iwi and urban Māori. "Urban Māori is a made-up term, it became a social phenomenon — a way of being — with a huge population in this state. We as a people have been urbanising for a hundred years and it is not going away so we had better understand it, it's a part of who and what we are as Māori." She sees urban Māori as 'Māori at a different address'. She is adamant that "the opposing forces between urban and iwi; being those who are urban, those who never left back-home and those who have recently returned home, start to define who is more Māori than the other, or who has a greater quality of Māoriness. At the end of the day we all have an obligation for a better world for our people, where our kids feel comfortable in their skin and bones, no matter how they choose to be Māori."

Chapter 2

Te Au o Te Awa

The River Current

In 1901 only 3% of the Māori population lived in the largest urban city of Auckland. The majority still lived in self-sufficient rural environments, operating within the communal societal structures of local iwi and hapū. The iwi or tribe was the largest effective political group linked to a particular territory. Within that landscape, iwi were composed of a number of hapū of expanded whānau or families, who could number anywhere from 200 to 300 people. All were linked by whakapapa as kin and were effective as political units created to defend territory.[1] The marae associated with iwi and hapū are rich in ancestral memories, and stand on the land as a tūrangawaewae for the families linked to it. The marae was central to all community activities, rituals and tikanga. It is the central meeting place of a tribal community, traditionally made up of a marae ātea (an open courtyard), wharenui (meeting house), wharekai (dining hall) and an ablutions block.

The coastal or inland territories of the tribes sustained the people for generations. Seasonal resources were strongly protected by hapū who harvested using strict rules and timeframes. These were self-sufficient communities. Embedded in the place names of these environments were the histories of seasonal migrations of ancestors. It was common practice for families and hapū to migrate seasonally, moving around the territories. They would pack up and leave one area, moving to another far-off area to maintain relationships with tribal kin.

Speaking of the people of Panguru, Melissa Williams says migration stories preserved a history of mobility that had been inscribed into the region's mountains, harbour and valleys — defining and reinforcing the relationship between people, land and resources.[2]

The effects of colonisation and the loss of land through confiscations, government policy and the demand for sales, changed the tribal landscape forever. Māori were introduced to the world of the cash economy, on which they became reliant. From the middle of the

Two boys digging for kauri gum. Much of the Māori population in the north had entered the cash society working as labourers in the gumfields, road-making, forestry and also farming. By the 1930s, much of this work had ceased and people became poor. The limited land and resources were soon unable to sustain Māori families, leading to an almost mass exodus from the rural regions to the towns and city centres.
Ref: 1/1-009779-G, Alexander Turnbull Library, Wellington, New Zealand./records/22894970

nineteenth century, the push and pull of internal and global economic and political forces caused Māori people to scatter from their rural tribal territories into urban centres, looking for 'work, money and pleasure'. Impoverishment and disease depleted the resources of rural communities and spelt a bleak future for those left with lands on which to make a living. As early as the 1870s Māori began to leave their communities in search of work.[3] From 1926, and for the next 40 years, the strong currents of circumstance meant a trickling flow of migration became a raging torrent.

This movement drastically altered New Zealand race relations. Māori were predominantly isolated in the rural districts, while Pākehā lived in the towns and cities and 'had scarcely even seen a Māori let alone know any'.[4]

Migration stories

The Anania whānau shifted from Northland to Auckland in 1956, where they lived in Grafton and Newton. Kathrine Christensen (nee Anania) remembers that prior to settling in Auckland, the family was always on the move around Northland, following her father Walter Anania wherever he was able to find work. "We arrived to Auckland in the dark," Kathrine remembers. Family elders in Rawene "were afraid for us", but on reaching Grafton, Kathrine found the city a fascinating place and she felt no fear.[5]

The Makiha family are originally from Waimā and Tāheke. Rereata Makiha recollects how his family moved from Tinopai to places all over the Kaipara Harbour area, working in farming and forestry. Families earned multiple incomes using a mixed farming model and everyone provided for one other. People had access to land, waterways and fisheries. Everyone used ancestral māramataka (lunar calendars) to govern gardening and fishing activities. Matu Makiha, Rereata's father, became a minister and was posted to Waimā and then later to Manurewa in Auckland. Soon the entire family became permanent residents in Auckland. The home communities were built on firm bonds between families and hapū and those bonds remained strong when people shifted to the cities. They provided for each other: those in the city returned with city foods; those in the rural regions would send local produce to whānau in the city. There was a kin-based economy of exchange among the people, an economy that is almost forgotten these days, Rereata says.[6] Rereata began working in forestry at Tokoroa and later in the freezing works at Southdown, Penrose.

As a child, Kelly Renata lived in the Urewera forest. His father Luckie decided to leave Tuai for Wellington in search of work. Kelly remembers sleeping in the car at night in Wellington until his father found a hostel in which the family could stay. Luckie quickly secured employment, which came with a home. Kelly and his family have lived in the Hutt Valley for three generations.[7]

These migration testimonies reflect the complexity of migration patterns Māori individuals and families established in the early- to mid-twentieth century. In the 1960s, Joan Metge's seminal work on Māori urbanisation revealed three paths by which rural Māori families travelled to reach the cities. Families travelled directly from their tribal area to the city, or shifted from one rural region to another before heading for a major city. Another group moved through small towns and cities until finally settling in the larger cities.[8]

For the last half of the nineteenth century it was commonly believed the Māori people were a 'dying race' and they were about to become extinct.[9] With poor health, high mortality rates and the population of Māori falling to 45,849 in 1900, it became a commonly held view that the only way for Māori to survive would be to assimilate into the much larger European-descent population. Numbers of Europeans in rural districts exploded during the nineteenth century, but increasing Pākehā urbanisation occurred in the twentieth century due to a growing urban-based economy. By World War I, more than half of the Pākehā population were urban dwellers.[10]

Living standards in Māori communities were harsh. Colonisation and its effects had rendered self-sustaining communities into dependent ones, often isolated from the new economic and political realities of the dominion.

A political response

Movements such as the Repudiation Movement of 1870, and later the Kōtahitanga Movement of the 1890s, tried to improve Māori lives and debated vigorously the issues involved coming to terms with Pākehā society.[11] A new breed of Māori leaders was emerging. Māui Pōmare, Te Rangihiroa Peter Buck, James Carroll, Wi Pere, Hone Heke and Apirana Ngata pushed to improve Māori living conditions and also urged Māori to retain their lands by developing them.[12] The notion of developing and utilising land to keep it from the Crown and land sellers was something previous Māori leaders desired, but the lack of capital was a major issue. Apirana Ngata described the living conditions of these communities.

> There are Māori communities which are satisfied to live in minimal reserves, where they grow the vegetables they require, from which they make seasonal excursions into the labour field to obtain the minimum resource for the purchase of clothes and food, and where they [live a country life] between periods of employment.[13]

Graham Butterworth gives a telling description of the state of Māori living in the 1920s.

> ... the Māori standard of living did not even approximate to that of the European. Māoris, at least in the Auckland province, were still largely Māori speaking, often with only a limited command of written and even spoken English. They were poorly educated, partly because of the lack of proper educational facilities — few, in fact even reached Standard 6 and fewer still went on to Māori secondary schools. Their main economic importance was as a source of labour to farmers, particularly for their seasonal peaks, and as unskilled labour in the timber industry and on rural 15 public works projects. Most Māoris lived in out-of-the-way villages with only limited social contact with European society.[14]

After years of aggressive land sales and the confiscation of Māori lands as a consequence of the Land Wars of the 1860s, by 1919 there were 1,996,805 hectares of land left in Māori ownership. Only 755,280 hectares were actually held by the owners, the rest was held by Pākehā leaseholders.[15] Māori leader and politician Sir Apirana Ngata saw an opportunity to economically develop the remaining Māori rural land to help curb the reality of severe Māori impoverishment. He embarked on a programme of encouraging Māori to develop their tribal land, which had multiple owners. From 1922, Ngata used state funds and initiated schemes throughout the country, at any place he could find underdeveloped Māori land and a willing community. Ultimately providing work for unemployed men and their families, the land would be utilised as a farm so it had to be cleared, ploughed, grassed, fenced and stocked.[16]

The land was inadequately connected to the rest of the economy as it was less fertile and less developed. By the 1950s, the land development schemes that had been designed to create prosperity for Māori, "particularly the small dairy units developed under Apirana Ngata's scheme", were not economically viable or able to sustain rapidly growing communities.[17] According to one account, only 54 of the 500 residents of the Te Rarawa community at Ahipara in the Far North made a living working for the nine full-time farmers in the area. It wasn't enough.[18]

In 1940, Professor Horace Belshaw observed that the existing freehold land, if fully developed, would establish 5000 farms supporting 20,000 people, only one-quarter of the population then, leaving 60,000 unprovided for, even if the population did not increase.[19] Belshaw concluded that "this was a picture of a people whose land resources were inadequate" and "no tribe had sufficient land to support its people". He expected Māori would find work in other rural activities, believing Māori would not urbanise easily; he thought Māori were "less capable of prolonged and continuous [work] effort" and were "less responsible in European work". He also noted that Māori were "not interested in commerce and [is] less efficient in the professions or callings requiring abstract thinking".[20]

Those projections couldn't have been further from reality. One popular opinion held by Pākehā was that Māori were not suited to living "their lives in crowded towns".[21] Another view believed Māori to be backward-looking and not interested in progress, which was false.[22]

By 1926 the Māori population had grown to 63,670,[23] of which 90% lived in rural regions. However, in reviewing the statistics, Brian Easton reveals 84% of Māori were classified as rural and up to 15% were defined as living in urban towns close to their papakāinga, where 5000 people or more were living.[24] On the night of the 1926 census, 70% of the Māori population lived in the greater Auckland region north of Taupō, with 434 Māori residing in Wellington and 1162 Māori living in Auckland.[25] The largest Māori urban centres of that time were Rotorua, Gisborne, Napier and Whanganui, which were to become transition towns for people shifting to the bigger cities. For the quarter of a century following 1926, Māori began to move away from land-based industries because the land could not employ them. Outdated agricultural techniques were swiftly replaced with new farming methods that reduced intensive labour, and those living in the rural subsistence economies were being displaced.[26]

The trickle had begun, but the effects of the Depression put a stay on that movement. In the 1930s, the people of Hokianga were described as "impoverished and demoralised".[27]

Opportunities for income were few. Large amounts of funds from the sale of lands were well and truly gone — most good land was already in European hands by now and all the millable timber had been removed, the kauri gum industry had ceased and the impact of the Great Depression meant a shortage of money and huge cuts in casual labour.[28] Dame Whina Cooper was well aware of these conditions for the people of Panguru and in 1934 she spoke of their poverty to the Royal Commission on Native Affairs.

> … the people were very poor. Most of them were road-making, gum-digging and bush-felling. … They had no money to go on the land. After the timber was worked out and the gum-digging became unprofitable, the people became poorer than ever. They were living in shacks and did not have any land in which to plant a few kumaras or other vegetables … some of them went round to [Pākehā] farmers and did a lot of work. They even asked for a bit of mutton and things like that in order to feed their children.[29]

War and the city

Besides land issues the influence of internal forces such as the government economic policy and external global pressures of trade and war, not least for Māori, there existed strong elements of change for all New Zealanders. Over a period of 100 years, Māori had entered a capitalist society and customary patterns of living were slowly abandoned. Māori invested in local industry and employment, generating a reliance on waged work. Add to this the rapidly increasing Māori population and decreasing infant mortality, and growing pressure on limited land resources to produce and provide.[30] These circumstances provided strong incentives for farming families to try their luck in the towns and cities. This created a progressive depopulation of the home papakāinga, which made the rural communities even less economically viable.[31] The shift to urban areas by individuals and whānau, who migrated through a range of pathways, has created a diverse picture of Māori urban migration.

The advent of World War II provided an additional external pull of rural Māori towards the cities. Sir Apirana Ngata urged Māori to enlist for military service to raise morale and mana in the eyes of the Pākehā. Māori participation in the war was what Ngata described as "the price of citizenship". There was a mobilisation of men into the 28th Māori Battalion. They were organised into tribal units, modelled on the Pioneer Battalion of the Great War. This fostered a brief resurgence of tribal organisation, but this was, in the future, countered by the urbanisation phenomenon at home.[32] On the home front, young Māori who were ineligible for enlistment in the military service were mobilised by the Native Department under the Manpower Act.

Out of the formation of the Māori Battalion, the Māori War Effort Organisation (MWEO) emerged in 1942. The MWEO's first task was to list Māori recruits for the war. This organisation was

Colonel James Henare, Eruera Tirikatene wearing a kākahu huruhuru (feather cloak), Walter Nash and Peter Fraser leading the 28th Māori Battalion through Wellington on its return from World War II.

Pascoe, John Dobree, 1908–72, photographic albums, prints and negatives. Ref: PAColl-0783-2-0651, Alexander Turnbull Library, Wellington, New Zealand

wholly Māori and involved all tribes. It became the largest Māori organisation ever established, with 315 tribal committees formed, including 41 tribal executives that were divided into 21 zones.[33] Through the recruitment process, MWEO encouraged vital food production for wartime. The committees were given responsibilities for registering and control of Māori 'manpower'.[34] From an estimated population of 95,225 in 1942, the MWEO rallied 17,000 Māori into the military services and 10,000 into essential industries.[35] It was a first: Māori were participating in mainstream New Zealand on their own terms,[36] while Māori saw it as "the greatest thing" since "the signing of the Treaty of Waitangi".[37] Few of the 'essential industries' were close to Māori rural homes. The majority of these war effort industries drew workers to the towns and cities such as Auckland, Hamilton or Wellington. MWEO became a bridge between the rural world and the city urban environment.

Initially 20- and 21-year-old women were 'manpowered' to contribute to the war effort industry. This was eventually expanded to encompass all between the ages of 18-40, single or married.[38] Young Māori men and women were 'manpowered' into industries and factories or on to farms. They were drawn and enlisted to city-based services. Prominent Māori writer Mihipeka Edwards remembers how "when the war broke out most of the girls from up-country were Manpowered. There was a big influx of young people to Wellington to do the war work."[39] One voluntary welfare officer from the Ngāti Pōneke Committee in Wellington reported that some 300 young women, most of whom worked in hotels and restaurants, were dwelling in the poorest city areas and with the gravest social issues. It was a similar situation in Auckland.[40] This attracted the attention of MWEO, who aided the appointment of women welfare officers in the cities and towns. The officers assisted the young Māori women to gain and improve their employment and accommodation conditions.[41]

Some young Māori found lodgings with relatives who were already stationed in the city, while others had to find alternative accommodation. Those in rural areas generally opposed the loss of their young women, specifically those who could work on the farms as aides or helpers to farmers' wives and mothers with children. Some parents found the working schedule coupled with childcare harsh, so much so that some children were placed in orphanages until the war was over.

Three generations of Māori at a vegetable production project near Levin in 1943, a project created as part of the Māori War Effort. These volunteers were working under the direction of the Māori War Effort Organisation, set up to organise recruitment and patriotic activities among Māori during World War II. The organisation also played a welfare role with young Māori working in towns and cities and provided a working model for the Māori Women's Welfare League.
Ref: 1/4-000258-F. Alexander Turnbull Library, Wellington, New Zealand

The National Service Department urged girls to find their own board. In Wellington the Young Women's Christian Association (YWCA) and hostels for transients were two options for accommodation. There was a growing need for boarding facilities for workers moving to the city.

Meanwhile Māori elders perceived the city as an unsafe place. Māori tribal committees steadily opposed their young women being drawn to these so-called 'vile' cities.[42] Elders were concerned about the young women's welfare in a troop-ridden city where Māori women were "chasing them [soldiers] like mad" and falling into trouble.[43] In Hamilton, some were living on the streets, which Princess Te Puea deplored. With her support, the girls' hostel Te Rāhui Wahine Hostel was established in Hamilton in 1945 (see Chapter 4).

Hostels for young Māori women emerged in the cities not only as a place to live but also as a sanctuary that provided protection from

Atareta Rennie plays the piano while fellow boarders work on handcrafts at the Pendennis Māori Girls' Hostel in Thorndon, Wellington, in 1954. The hostel was home to several generations of young Māori women who had moved to the city from their rural homes.

Ref: ½-040753-F, photographer: T. Ransfield. Alexander Turnbull Library, Wellington, New Zealand

a dangerous city environment. The Māori hostels for young women (and later men) were established in the main centres as gateways into an urban life. In 1943 the National Service Department appointed Māori officers to act as guardians and friends in the larger towns and city centres and as a liaison with "their own people".[44] These officers helped the young women stand against the difficulties of life so they could avoid being exploited by employers and accommodation managers.[45] For some of these young women, it was the first time they'd met Pākehā. The influx of Māori into the city hostels meant racist attitudes were exposed, with objections to Māori and Pākehā sharing hostel accommodation.[46]

The 1945 Māori Social and Economic Advancement Act was intended to give the MWEO a permanent form that established the tribal committees into tribal executives. They had limited self-governance and the extremely wider brief of improving the social, economic and moral well-being of the people. By 1949 there were 63 tribal executives and 381 committees.[47] According to Tipi Ropiha, the under-secretary to the Minister of Native Affairs, their aim was the "full integration of the Māori race into the social and economic structure of the country".[48] The emphasis was on "social education", "good citizenship" and "steering Māori along the path of modernity without neglecting their cultural needs".[49]

Many Māori who had served in the war effort did not return to their tribal areas to live permanently as was expected.[50] Returned servicemen from the 28th Māori Battalion searched for work in different localities in the towns and cities, but the highest employment that most able leaders of the battalion could find was with the Department of Māori Affairs, or in teaching.[51] The scattering of servicemen to urban locales is said to have prevented the regrowth of tribal sentiment "gaining any political advantage".[52] The loss of Māori men in the wars also contributed to the loss of potential future Māori leadership.

The desire for better living standards, work and higher wages, other than what was available in the country, were drawcards for shifting to the cities.[53] This is not to take away from other complex reasons individuals and families chose to migrate. For instance, a number of families shifted to the city because their children needed medical care.[54] Education and the opportunity to grow in the Pākehā world became paramount. Parents who were punished for speaking their own language and had 'Pākehā superiority' drilled in to them stopped speaking their native tongue and did not re-tell their family histories to their children. People believed shifting to the city to learn how to live in the Pākehā world would give their children a better opportunity to survive in the new and changing world. Others left their home environments to free themselves from alcohol, violence and mākutu (curses).[55] While interaction with the realm of taniwha (water spirit) and wairua poke (haunting spirits) was a norm in Māori society, many didn't want their children and mokopuna (grandchild) subjected to the fearful world of kēhua (ghost, spirit) and the tapu restrictions of the old marae.[56]

The push and pull effects of urban Māori migration did not occur solely in the larger city centres. The growth of industry in or near provincial towns like Rotorua, Kawerau, Tokoroa, Gisborne, Hastings and as far south as Ashburton, Invercargill and Bluff attracted Māori from other tribal areas to shift to these towns for employment and eventually permanent settlement. Pan-iwi communities developed and many married into local families, becoming integral to the make-up of these towns and contributing strongly to the development of these communities. This urbanisation to the provincial towns and then to the larger cities played out differently in each region. Communities were affected differently and responded to the circumstances in distinct ways.

Gisborne's position and its port made the town an urban centre on the North Island's East Coast. As the commercial and administrative centre for the East Cape region, Gisborne and its agricultural, horticultural, dairy, meat and wool industries attracted droves of East Coast Māori families. In 1901 the population of Gisborne was 2737. This number increased in 1926 to 15,000 and in 1955 Gisborne became a city (20,000 or more), with Māori numbers rising to 3000 by 1961. By 1976 the total population had reached 30,000. This urban swell saw pressure placed on the local Ngāti Oneone tribe of Kaitī, Wainui and Okitū, who experienced adverse affects of exclusion from decisions on local development.[57]

In 1936 the urban Māori population had grown to 17% and by 1945 a quarter of all Māori lived in urban centres.[58] In Wellington the population increased from 589 to 1200, illustrating that people were dispersing from their mana whenua environments and spreading into city suburbs in a similar dispersion pattern to non-Māori.[59] In Auckland city, Māori migrants were drawn to suburbs where there were affordable lodgings that were close to the central city, workplaces and entertainment. Freemans Bay, Grafton, Herne Bay, Ponsonby and Grey Lynn became home for hundreds of Māori. Auckland had the highest urban population after the war, followed by Wellington, the Hutt, Christchurch and Dunedin. Concentrated manufacturing increased in the main centres, which meant there was plenty of work and wages that were above the national average. Between 1936 and 1945, the Māori proportion of workers in manufacturing rose from 4% to 18% as a result of wartime "manpowering".[60]

The Wellington experience

Seeking another 'Māori face' in the foreign cityscape, like Wellington, was a reality for many Māori. There were individuals and families from related iwi who, often through personal connections, gathered in enclaves bound by streets and suburbs, not by mountain ranges, creeks and coastline. 'Go to' or 'stop in' homes known as 'whare Māori' became the norm in the city, with an open-door policy to care and nurture visiting whānau. These were homes in the city where tribal relatives from the rural regions could visit and congregate, usually at one key family's home. As these families began to extend their tent pegs beyond their own tribal enclaves, they began to connect with other diverse tribal people in close vicinity to where they set up their own homes, forming non-kin-related "urban whānau"[61] and new community whakapapa.

In the absence of a marae in Wellington, Hapi and Ripeka Love offered their home, known as Taumata, at Korokoro in Lower Hutt for iwi to gather and carry out traditional functions and hospitality.[62] There was always the desire for a marae to be established there to demonstrate the long-term connections of Taranaki whānui to the Wellington region.

The 1890 census recorded only 250 Māori in the Hutt valley. This represented a mobile Māori population who came to the area for seasonal employment. In 1901 Māori travellers from Horowhenua were living in the Hutt and cutting flax. These were not long-term settlements but seasonal sojourns into the region that occurred from the 1880s and into the twentieth century.[63]

The mobile nature of whānau, hapū and iwi was a common phenomenon that led to the mass migration of the 1950s, which was a migration with a major difference: it was primarily for permanent settlement. As early as 1918 in the Hutt Valley, a group known as Ngā Pani o Te Whanganui a Tara (The Orphans of Te Whanganui a Tara) formed to take up the cause of Māori in the district, to teach te Reo Māori and support Māori in sport.[64] Their patron was Sir Māui Pōmare. Even though this group included members of the local iwi, the word 'orphan' indicates a sentiment of urban Māori feeling distanced from their original homes.[65] In 1932 the group was superseded by a new executive named Te Rōpū o Whanganui a Tara, who discussed acquiring their own 'kāinga'. The rōpū was gifted land on which to build a marae, raising funds for the marae through concerts and contributions from organisations such as The Taranaki Trust Board. Te Tatau O Te Pō marae, was opened in 1933. Arguably the first traditional urban marae in Wellington, it was built by iwi who were conscious of pan-tribal Māori living in the city.[66] It fulfilled the valuable purpose of welcoming visiting Māori while prioritising the status of mana whenua.[67]

In 1926 the census recorded 216 Māori in the Wellington and Hutt Valley area out of a population of 98,893.⁶⁸ By 1945 Wellington City had a total population of 123,771 with 780 Māori recorded there, but the number rose to 1200 when including the wider Wellington districts.⁶⁹ Māori who entered the region in the early decades of the twentieth century were overwhelmed by the large numbers of Europeans and felt dislocation, loneliness and culture shock, so would seek "pan-iwi fellowship with other Māori".⁷⁰ This led to the formation of groups such as Ngāti Pōneke, where a shared Māoritanga (being Māori) could be expressed by iwi and migrant Māori.

For Vera Warmington (later Morgan), who moved to Wellington from Waimā, Hokianga, in the 1930s for work in the Government Buildings tearooms, Ngāti Pōneke became whānau. It was 'a home away from home' in a Pākehā world where she says she felt lonely and lost.⁷¹ Without Ngāti Pōneke, Witerena Harris also says she would

Ngāti Pōneke Cultural Group, Wellington.
Ref: ½-045021-G9. Alexander Turnbull Library, Wellington, New Zealand/records/22628767

have been 'a lost person'. However, supporting this pan-iwi group also brought her into conflict with her own Te Arawa people.[72]

Led by Kingi Te Ahoaho Tahiwi, Ngāti Pōneke was established in 1937 and staged its first public performance in 1938. Miria Pōmare played a leading role in the club; her contribution was pivotal in fundraising for Māori troops and aiding the welfare of Māori in hospital.[73] In September 1944 the club secured a 20-year lease of the Red Cross Building on Lambton Quay to use as a Māori community hall. The Ngāti Pōneke Hall was a place for the retention of Māori culture and for bringing Māori and Pākehā closer together.[74] Like the Auckland Maori Community Centre, hundreds of Māori joined the Ngāti Pōneke club or attended the whānau dances on the weekends. A wide range of Māori groups used the hall. This eventually progressed into the building of Pipitea marae in the central city at Thorndon, which was opened in 1980 and became a permanent home for Ngāti Pōneke.

The Māori leaders who attended the 1939 Young Māori Leaders' Conference held in Auckland expressed their growing concern with the movement of their people to the city. They proposed a social and cultural centre in Auckland, discussion groups, adult education and even the establishment of an 'urban marae'.[75] Twenty years later, at the Young Māori Leaders' Conference in Auckland in 1959, the same issues were raised with the added question of whether Māori could preserve their own culture while 'participating fully in the economy and culture of the Pākehā'. Elders believed the primacy of their people's Māoritanga should supersede the duties of their business interests. In speaking about Māori housing in Pākehā neighbourhoods, the consensus among the elders was Māori should "disperse their houses among the Pākehā houses". They also believed Māori should continue to live in their own concentrated settlements around a traditional marae.[76]

While the sentiment of the elders was valid then and even now, the irreversible tsunami of Māori flowing to the city for "work, money and pleasure", and the young people's desire for a new kind of lifestyle, became a compelling yet unpopular answer to the elders' concerns.

The people spoke with their feet.

Anania Whānau, Auckland Central/Glen Innes

Kathrine Christensen (nee Anania), with her brother Wynn Anania (centre) and cousin May Johnson (right), meeting in Papatoetoe in 2016.

Courtesy of Bradford Haami

The Anania whānau shifted from Northland to Auckland in 1956, where they found lodgings in a boarding house on Cobden Street, Newton Gully, off Karangahape Road. It was a strange and terrifying world compared to life in the Hokianga. The cars, the roading, the buildings and the density of people presented Walter and Kate Anania and their children with a new world to discover and, later, to overcome.

Walter had continuously searched for employment in the gumfields, forestry or other forms of labour, so he was away from home for long periods. "We never saw our father. Mum decided to shift to Rangi Point in the Hokianga due to the lack of water on the land in Kaihū and then on to Te Karaka," Kathrine remembers. "We moved again, to Waiwhatawhata and then, with three horses, me, Mum and my elder sisters Frances and Venus, we relocated to Ōmāpere and later to Rawene, where Dad had a more permanent position operating the ferries or launches across the Hokianga Harbour for Jim Subritzky."

Kathrine's brother Wynn was born in Rawene and it was there she attended high school.

Her parents seldom spoke te Reo Māori around the children. "The hurt from being punished for speaking their own language must have been strong. Mum and Dad never spoke Māori to us at all, only when visitors arrived. They wanted us to learn the Pākehā language and ways first," Kathrine recalls. "However, the

Catholic Church services were in both Māori and Latin languages. Any cultural activities such as kōrero, poi, waiata, and learning tāniko weaving, were taught to us by the convent nuns. We could perform and weave but we were never taught what anything meant. Our parents never talked to us about those things."

The family shifted to Auckland where Walter had found more permanent employment. Fifteen-year-old Kathrine viewed Auckland like it was "Buckingham Palace. You could get lost in the huge place." The Ananias shifted into a number of boarding houses in the inner city: Cobden Road in Newton, Kari Street in Grafton and then to 79 Grafton Road, a haven for migrant Māori. Interestingly, their home spaces were close to the Symonds Street cemetery, where Kathrine's mother Kate's ancestor, Judge Fredrick Manning, was buried. The inner city of Auckland from Grafton to Freemans Bay, College Hill, Ponsonby and over to Newton, was stacked with boarding houses filled with Māori, and later, Pacific peoples.

The Anania home became a point for the gathering of hundreds of whānau. The communal tikanga continued in the city — whānau shared their earnings with each other, and food such as meat from the freezing works, shellfish from Ōrere Point or eels taken from the Ako-o-te-Tui and Waipāruru streams in Grafton Gully, were distributed among them. Kaanga pirau (rotten corn) and kina (sea urchin) were still treated traditionally, stored in a stream's running water. "There was never any feeling of danger for us in the city, we were never afraid," says Kathrine. The Māori Community Centre at Freemans Bay was the place to be on Friday nights. She remembers it as a place where everyone met their relatives of a similar age, sang and danced all night, without the interference of alcohol she remembers.

Living in a cash economy meant working to pay the bills, something Walter and Kate Anania were staunch about. They were also adamant about not being in debt. Their strong work ethic gave Kathrine and Wynn a strong resolve to work hard. Kathrine found a job at the hospital as a ward's maid. It was here she eventually met her American husband, who she married in 1962. They left for America in 1964 when Kathrine was 24 years old.

Wynn was ten years old at the time Kathrine left for America. Wynn's life took a completely different trajectory. He'd follow his dad everywhere. Every day he'd ride his bike to the Astor Pub at the corner of Symonds Street and Newton Road to meet his father after work. Walter would give Wynn money to take home, then join the men crowded into the public bars, drinking until 6 o'clock closing. The culture of drinking as much as you could before closing became a constant among working men.

Wynn, Kathrine and their cousin, May Johnson, believe poverty wasn't initially prevalent among Māori. "Everyone rallied together in those days, families and relatives moved together in big numbers, there was always a bed to sleep in somewhere and they always distributed their kai and no one went hungry."

Despite there being food on the table and a roof over their heads, conflict between his parents over the lack of money in the house compounded the situation, says Wynn. Occasionally Wynn would return from school to find no one home. One day he found a note on the table from his mother saying she had gone to the hospital. "She had admitted herself into Ward 10 at Auckland Hospital — that was the mental health ward." At a later date she was admitted to Oakley Mental Hospital for shock treatment. This was usual for Wynn's mother. "We never knew why she went to the hospital. There was no stigma associated with this," Wynn says.

He admits these situations disrupted his schooling. Wynn's early school days at St Benedict's Catholic Primary School (off Symonds Street, Newton) were spent with children from northern Māori Catholic families: the Toko, Campbell and Whittaker kids. Later he attended Seddon High School, now Western Springs College, where he says there were Pacific Island kids as big as men. "They had already formed themselves into pseudo-gangs of boys," he says. Wynn excelled in sports, which made him acceptable to the Pacific Island boys, and he made friends for life.

Wynn remembers how disappointed his parents were when two policemen arrived at their home and accused him of stealing bikes. "One of my friends narked on me. I was the scapegoat who ended up at a hearing in the Children's Court and let off with a warning," he laughs. He remembers there were crews of kids meeting everywhere in the central city. Wynn and his inner-city friends began drinking alcohol from the ages of 13 and 14. Older family members of friends would purchase alcohol for the young people.

Auckland City Mission in Airedale Road, off Queen Street, ran Friday night dances for young people. From age 12 Wynn would sneak down to these dances, often taking part in brawls with the Pacific Island boys. This is where he earned a reputation as a scrapper. The city gangs were The Nigs, The Apaches, MC5s, Kelston Sharks and the Boot Hill Boys from Ōrākei. "Scrapping was the way guys showed their strength. This culture was based on being a good scrapper — not showing any weakness," Wynn says.

Due to the demolition of homes in Grafton and other areas, the family shifted into a Māori state house on Hurstwood Place, Glen Innes in 1968. Wynn attended Tāmaki College, which had a large Māori roll due to the movement of Māori families out of the inner-city slums into newly formed suburbs such as Glen Innes. Wynn met a lot of relatives his age at this school. There wasn't much to do except to roam around the parties in the local area. New crews were constantly forming. "One of my cousins was in a gang called The Freaks based in Newmarket, and another cousin was in the motorcycle gang, the Glen Innes Saints," he says.

The snooker hall at Glen Innes was where Wynn mixed with other young people and whānau of his age. He was also attracted to the music scene. Māori family bands would practise in their garages and perform at socials. At one of these band practices, someone made a comment to Wynn that he shouldn't go down to the Oriental as there were too many 'head hunters' there. The Oriental became a fight club, where men who were cut down in a fight were kicked in the head by fighters wearing heavy boots — giving rise to the term 'head hunter'.

Wynn thought that was a great name for a crew and he and Carl Hartwell designed a patch with this name. Pretty soon the Head Hunters grew into a Glen Innes-based gang made up of family members from the Toko, Abraham, Daniels and Pirini whānau and other youth, mostly from Tāmaki College. They gained a reputation as fighters, challenging local men and taking on 'big boys' such as the Hells Angels.

"We became a lethal crew. Terrible things occurred in these days. We had a good time as young guys, holding territory — they were pretty crazy days," Wynn says. "I lived by my wits by watching my dad." Wynn did time in prison for "terrorising the eastern suburbs", he says.

In his thirties he drifted away from the gang culture to a new way of life. His local community elected him on to the Maungarei Marae Committee, where he served by running Maccess and PEP training courses for youth, slowly curbing the flow of kids into the gangs. He became involved in Māori rugby league alongside ex-Māori coach Tom 'Lummy' Newton and he continued his passion for music by managing local bands.

In 1990 Wynn served the eastern community on a number of projects, where he worked with John Tamihere. In more recent years he has worked with Willie Jackson on local ventures for other urban Māori communities. The Urban Māori Authorities such as MUMA and Waipareira are essential organisations that service the health needs of Māori in the city. "They are the only organisations looking out for Māori in the city and they have become a one-stop-shop lifesaver to many," he insists. He strongly supports the role of Urban Māori Authorities that provide healthcare to urban Māori. In his parents' day there were no Māori service providers available and nothing to bridge the gap between the move from rural to city life or vice versa.

Wynn's family migration symbolises the plight of many Māori: shifting from a simple rural bliss to a city-life filled with opportunities and traps. The Anania whānau engaged in both the opportunities of city life and the pitfalls of suburbia, and endure today to tell their story.

Chapter 3

Tūranga Hou

A New Standing Place

Through the 1940s and 1950s, more and more Māori made first attempts to integrate into the new urban context. For many the destination was Auckland, a place that has long attracted migrants due to its rich resources and strategic location – its desirability embodied in the name Tāmaki Herenga Waka, or 'Tāmaki Gatherer of Canoes'. Tāmaki is linked to the histories of many iwi throughout New Zealand, and from the 1950s onwards the tribal links multiplied. Much of the flow came to central-city lands that included the Waikuta (College Hill) and Tunamau (Franklin Road) streams and the renowned bay called Waikōkota (Freemans Bay), into which these surrounds flowed. The area was described in the late 1880s as having 'beauty and calm',[1] and as a 'fairy beachland'.[2] By the mid-twentieth century, however, the bay had been reclaimed and formed the basis of Victoria Park, and the landscape was built up. Surrounded by large-scale industry, dotted with overcrowded wooden houses on tiny sections in narrow dirt streets,[3] the area was in 1946 described as a rat-infested slum and deteriorating residential district.[4] A 1950 council planning report noted:

> There is an invasion of factories into decadent wooden houses, and factories built of permanent materials cheek by jowl

with the tiny cottages where the enjoyment of light and air is menaced.[5]

Such was the environment of shanty huts, dilapidated houses and old commercial buildings[6] that many Māori entered when they flocked to the city. Conditions may not have been much worse where they had come from, but now they also had to navigate landlord-tenant relations, which were not governed by law.[7] Despite the derelict and poor environment of low rents and close proximity to work, Māori created a tight-knit community with an amazing camaraderie.[8] At the same time as large-scale migration was also beginning from the Pacific Islands, Auckland became home to the largest urban Māori population.[9] And for many whānau Māori moving, this would be a permanent shift.

Kathrine Christensen (née Anania) and her family were drawn to the city by her father's search for work, and were obliged to settle in less-than-healthy inner-city conditions as they sought to carve out a

Young Māori woman on the production line at the Taniwha Products Ltd soap factory, Westfield, c.1955.

Sparrow Industrial Pictures Ltd. Auckland Libraries, Footprints 03749; photograph reproduced courtesy of Otahuhu Historical Society

new life. Kathrine recalls that the "place we rented was filled with rats due to the rubbish heaps on empty lots.[10] In those days Ponsonby was run down and it wasn't a pleasant place to stay, it was dangerous, with all the two-storey houses overcrowded with people." Housing was indeed a major issue, especially in Wellington and Auckland. Since 1944 Māori housing in suburbs such as Panmure were identified as horrendous. Rent prices for Māori were exorbitant, even in the most rundown areas of the city.[11] Urban growth increased competition for places to live. The combined population of Wellington and the Hutt Valley jumped from 200,000 in 1951 to almost 290,000 in 1966, with much of the growth occurring in the state-housing suburbs in the Hutt Valley and the new suburbs further along the coast.[12] Similarly, Auckland housed a population of 330,000 in 1951 that exploded to 550,000 in 1966 — a third of New Zealand lived in Auckland and there were no signs of population growth slowing down.[13]

While two-way movement between the country and towns was considerable, especially between the three regions of Waikato, Bay of Plenty and Hawke's Bay,[14] Auckland was the preferred city for more permanent relocation. A migration chain was created: whānau and friends who had already settled in Auckland during the war years provided an open door for relatives to enter the city environment. 'Employment and enjoyment' were important factors in moving to the city, but whānau connections between back-home and the city were a major encouragement to move.[15] Māori were drawn to cheaper housing in the inner-city suburbs of Grafton, Newton, Ponsonby, Grey Lynn and Freemans Bay. An indication of the concentration of Māori who chose to live in central Auckland was reported in 1963, with an estimated 14,000 Māori dwelling within a four-mile radius of the Central City Post Office, "with almost half coming from areas other than Northland".[16]

Assimilation and integration

Since the mid-nineteenth century, New Zealand's Native Policy had sought to assimilate Māori into a European cultural mainstream. The post-war urban movement seemed to present an opportunity to accelerate that assimilation.[17] The government had long encouraged replacing so-called 'archaic' traditional structures "with modern European behaviours and sensibilities": this renewal was seen as a "gift to the native peoples".[18] Dan Morrow's study of Māori and modernity, reiterates Sir Apirana Ngata and Te Rangihiroa Sir Peter Buck's positions that the reconciliation of Māori with the material aspirations and standards of European New Zealand did not suggest "turning Māori into Pākehā".[19] Morrow describes how Ngata rejected complete cultural assimilation, and instead believed that tribalism could co-exist and even encourage individual economic success, and that the fusion of modernity and tradition was central to a positive trajectory for Māori.[20] Nevertheless in the 1950s and 1960s, as Morrow points out, government policy remained essentially assimilationist "in its conviction that the ultimate merging of Māori and Pākehā into a single, Pākehā-orientated national culture, was both desirable and inevitable".[21]

Later *The Hunn Report*, published in 1961, highlighted social issues facing Māori in the city, including a 'statistic blackout' of Māori in higher levels of education, meaning most worked in labour-orientated employment, making them vulnerable to economic changes. However, the major thrust of the report solidified the ideas of assimilation and modernisation, recommending New Zealand move beyond 'assimilation' to the trend of 'integration' and 'relocation', where the mixing of Pākehā and Māori would truly create "one nation wherein Māori culture remains distinct".[22] In reality this indicated Pākehā dominance over a 'detribalised' Māori minority.[23] The report made it clear that Māori should not seek to claim too much cultural difference.[24]

The Department of Māori Affairs, commonly known as 'Māori Affairs', was a major actor in the assisting and implementation of integration. Māori Affairs welfare officers worked closely with Māori and tribal committees, and later with branches of the Māori Women's Welfare League, to visit stressed families who were wrestling with the demands of the new urban environment.

From 1960, Māori Affairs applied further impetus for urbanisation by initiating a Māori urban relocation programme. Māori families were encouraged to put aside their self-sufficiency and subsistence living in the rural regions to move to the towns and cities for work — not only the major centres but also secondary cities like Whangārei, Gisborne and Levin. The Department aimed to expand its housing programme from 700 in 1960 to 2000 by 1967.[25] Under the scheme, by 1965 Māori Affairs had relocated 399 families and assisted 485 other families to find work or accommodation.[26]

In keeping with the official line, the Department encouraged Māori

A view of small, run-down, inner-city houses in the foreground and a new block of apartments on Grey's Avenue, central Auckland. From the 1950s, this was the central Auckland environment to which Māori families shifted. It is estimated that 14,000 Māori lived in the vicinity of these buildings.

Sparrow Industrial Pictures Ltd, Auckland Museum, PH-NEG-4068C

to apply for houses and assimilate into urban life by engaging in the policy of 'pepper-potting'. Pepper-potting was the planned dispersal of Māori among Pākehā-filled suburbs in the hope of encouraging integration and avoiding ghetto formation.[27] An allowance of one Māori nuclear-family unit per block of Pākehā families appeared to be the maximum before white flight set in and property prices tumbled.[28] It was common practice for low-income Māori families to capitalise on their family benefits by arranging an advance to use as a deposit on a Māori Affairs house — this was called 'capitalisation'.

The government's key lending agency, the State Advances Corporation, preferred to lend money to Māori who lived in the 'Pākehā Way', that is, as a nuclear family rather than an extended family. Some Māori chose to take the state-house option so they were not forced into pepper-potted housing. Others preferred to tolerate sub-standard living conditions rather than live in an all-Pākehā community. Māori families soon began to cluster in enclaves, in areas where there was cheaper housing.[29] This sometimes gave rise to the idea that Māori were aiming for separatism.[30]

Housing options in the city were limited by racism. It was difficult for Māori to find good rental homes or to purchase city houses. Eruera

Stirling recounted how his wife Amiria approached a real estate agent about a home they were interested in buying in Herne Bay. She was twice told that the home had been sold, yet it continued to be advertised in the newspaper. Amiria approached a Pākehā friend to negotiate the purchase and he secured the home on Mercer Road in the Stirling name.[31]

The notion of buying a house to secure a stable future in the city for themselves and their descendants was problematic for Māori. It required a long-term commitment to the city; that meant putting down roots, which many elders resisted. 'This is not our home' was a common thought among first-generation migrants who always planned to return home to their tribal lands — their true tūrangawaewae, the standing place where one gains the authority to belong.[32] Owning a home in the city had implications beyond simply finding a place to live. Melissa Williams states this was an option designed "to replace an impractical Māori attachment to their land, and the rights of tribal membership that it bestowed, with urban '[t]urangawaewae based on home ownership'".[33] Government policies were created to break down the remaining facets of Māori society that were blocking full integration into mainstream society. This included "tribalism and the Māori attachment understood through the concept of tūrangawaewae" and "the continuation of specific Māori cultural norms that differentiated Māori from Pākehā".[34] Placing whānau Māori in a single dwelling emphasised the importance of the single nuclear family, while pepper-potting underlined an individualism that Māori adopted, but sought to reconcile with whakapapa and kinship links. Despite the ideal of the singular family being in direct contrast to the open-home policy of most Māori, there were those who delighted in dispersed city living where they could gain privacy from frequent visitors, parties and boozing.

Megan Woods' research into the role of gender in the urbanisation and integration of Māori into suburban life reveals how the State supported women in encouraging their husbands, families, hostel charges, boyfriends and friends to become good citizens in an integrated urban world.[35] As homemakers, Māori women carried the burden of ensuring their family was considered a 'good neighbour' and that they were 'house proud'. Presenting a 'good image', particularly in the maintenance of one's home and gardens, was essential in promoting good race relations. Pākehā New Zealanders had little contact with Māori so it was essential that Pākehā would know the worth of Māori through these standards.³⁶ The Department of Māori Affairs stressed to Māori homeowners that they should not place washing on the fence line or hang it in the front porch. The clothesline should be in the back yard, along with a garden set aside for vegetables. The front of the home was the correct place for a tidy flower garden, designed to project a good image to Pākehā.

As early as 1948, one member of Parliament suggested linking social security with attaining Pākehā standards of domestic respectability.³⁷ By 1950 suggestions were made to Māori Affairs that prize money be offered to create a competitive environment among Māori to keep their homes and marae respectable.³⁸ The Department, with the Māori Women's Welfare League, ran a series of best-kept home and garden competitions. These were ideal opportunities for Māori to beautify their homes, but more to prove to Pākehā how capable they could be at reaching high standards of domesticity. In one competition the winner received a framed picture of "Mrs Whyte's 'temple' ideal of femininity and domesticity, her own home and garden".³⁹

Despite pepper-potting and the promotion of 'standards', Māori continued to use traditional gardening techniques. Many Māori couldn't see the point of flower gardens, but were intent on supplying extended whānau and even Pākehā neighbours with produce from their more communally based maara-gardens. Auckland's inner city became a hive of industry, with traditional food-gathering techniques and tikanga carried out to meet the needs of everyone. It was common for earnings and food to be shared. Shellfish from Ōrere Point or eels taken from the Ako-o-te-Tui and Waipāruru streams in Grafton Gully were distributed between families, just like back-home. Kaanga pirau (rotten corn) and kina were still treated traditionally by being kept in the running waters of inner-city streams.⁴⁰

The Makiha family, who shifted to Manurewa, adapted their northern west coast māramataka (seasonal lunar calendar) to the local area to read the seasonal cycles for growing food and tracking the appearance of fish and eels. When visiting the local inner waterways to check the migration of eels it was common to meet other Māori families, usually relatives, applying their own māramataka to the same area for the same reason.⁴¹ Whanaungatanga and manaakitanga were still strong values for Māori living in the city. This meant large numbers of relatives visited each other's homes, something mistaken by Pākehā neighbours as 'overcrowding with visitors'. Kathrine Anania and her cousin May Johnson remember that "families and relatives moved together in big numbers around the city, there was always a bed to sleep in somewhere, and the people always distributed their kai. No one was poor or hungry as far as we could see."[42] But practices of food gathering to supplement an earned income became more occasional and soon gave way to the purchase of food in the marketplace.[43]

The world of work

Jobs were easy to find — whether in factories, post offices or service industries, the demand for labour seemed insatiable to impressionable young Māori. In 1961 the magazine *Te Ao Hou* featured a group of young Māori women shifting from Wairoa to Wellington. The writer advised the young women about the realities of city life.

> It's easier for young Māoris to settle in the city if they have a responsible adult person there to guide them, and help them over such difficult problems as accommodation … Life in the city is not easy: you have to work regularly, be careful with money, accommodation often gives trouble, and friends and relatives often find themselves in difficulties you have to help them out of.[44]

Amos Softgoods, which was searching for labour, recruited the 12 women from their schools. Lena Manuel, the Māori Welfare Officer in Wairoa, short-listed suitable girls with good school qualifications and the 12 were selected for the available positions. The personnel manager, Mr White, informed the girls about the work, paid for their travel arrangements and promised the parents that their daughters would be well trained and looked after.[45]

On arriving in Wellington, Mr White advanced the young women two weeks' wages and found the girls hostel accommodation. The dressmaking factory where they were trained and then employed was in Kilbirnie. More elaborate dress designs were carried out in the city factory, where some of the women went when their skills reached the required level.

The company paid for further training for the women, and sought new accommodation when their first hostel lost its appeal. Finding accommodation for young Māori proved a problem for the company, until suitable hostel lodgings at Pendennis Māori Girls' Hostel were found.⁴⁶ Hostels run by or employed by companies for their workers were common. Many Māori who left their rural homes began their working careers living in these hostels.

While Māori began to enjoy higher incomes, more social services, better health and a higher standard of living, life in a total cash economy meant families used to subsistence activities had to adjust to the idea of working to meet the needs of rent, time-payments, hire purchases, electricity, rates and mortgages. Once committed to this system, the migrants were permanently integrated into the Pākehā economic system.⁴⁷ Accommodation, alcohol, cash and the ease of purchasing household comforts were traps for rural people unfamiliar with the money system. Many Māori living beyond their means were ensnared by 'a pile of debts and judgement summonses'.⁴⁸ The North Shore Māori Tribal Committee cited financial difficulties, with some families unable to pay their debts, as a real concern and a "universal problem". In 1961, Tupi Puriri commented how:

> … big firms like Maple Furnishers, Smiths and Browns, etc … who operate a form of Hire Purchase system, opened up an unlimited amount of credit to people moving from the back-blocks to the city, who were mainly unsophisticated.⁴⁹

Māori were rarely encouraged to achieve high levels of education in secondary schools. This confined many urban Māori with limited qualifications to unskilled or semi-skilled employment in agriculture, the building trade, factories, freezing works, road maintenance, transport and general labouring.⁵⁰ In 1956 only 7% of Māori held professional, managerial or clerical positions, compared to 27% of non-Māori.⁵¹ Despite this Māori earned relatively good wages, particularly in construction and at the freezing works. Added to these wages were family benefits, which improved Māori incomes. Unfortunately, a lack of educational qualifications made Māori particularly vulnerable to the economic changes that occurred in the mid-1970s when unskilled workers, of which Māori were over represented, were first to lose their jobs.⁵²

Maintaining the culture

Whānau elders either stayed in the city or regularly travelled back and forth from the rural kāinga to ensure the city-based whānau had a good start in the initial stages of urban settlement,[53] if only to 'keep an eye' on the grandchildren to continue that sense of community.[54] Other elders took trailer-loads of food to their city whānau to ensure they had enough, a practice that continued in some families for many years. Melissa Williams records that parents and grandparents of the young urban Māori population from Panguru were instrumental in initiating the transformation of the inner-city landscape into a familiar home-place for their children. They reinforced the values of their Panguru upbringing, encouraging their families to gain work, live in better homes and seek a higher standard of living. Secondly, they shepherded cultural values of whakapapa, whānau rights and obligations, and maintaining church ties as a framework by which Māori community networks could be developed.[55] Te Whakapono (the Catholic faith), and in particular the connection with the Mill Hill Order, was a strong uniting force for Panguru Māori in the city. This connection gave rise to the emergence of communal leisure sites and later Te Unga Waka, the Auckland Māori Catholic Centre/marae in Epsom in 1966.[56]

Generally speaking, the expected departure from the so-called 'archaic' established tribal social structures did not necessarily occur when Māori moved to Auckland.[57] While rural-urban relationships were maintained, whakapapa links to other hapū kin quickly became apparent, as did the locations of other whānau homes, making available a "broad support network".[58] Living in close proximity to a mix of Māori tribal people who were "just like us but not" meant broadening the meaning of whānau beyond the borders of hapū- and iwi-based kin to encompass a wider shared Māori experience.[59] Soon, new dynamic networks were formed that were not necessarily kin or tribe based. These networks, once derived from hapū and iwi membership within tribal territories, were based on Māori neighbourhood enclaves, church congregations, hostel communities, workplace-whānau, welfare-based groups, sports team relationships and later, pan-Māori marae. While tribal recognition was evident,[60] these relationships extended beyond kin to include ethnic, gender and multi-tribal bonds, so much so that it was commonly thought by city dwellers that "there was no such thing as tribalism, everyone regarded themselves as just Māori".[61] Kin relationships were always a given, but non-kin-based whānau were to become a more regular form of relationship derived out of the urban experience.

Perhaps the most visible expression of urban Māori was the famous

Tūranga Hou 59

A crowd seated inside the Auckland Māori Community Centre,
a popular meeting place for Māori living in Auckland city.
Auckland Museum, PH-NEG-H2021

Auckland Māori Community Centre on the corner of Halsey and Fanshawe streets. It became the face of urban Māori in Auckland. The centre was based in a building that carried a peppercorn lease, and was governed by a trust made up of representatives of the Department of Māori Affairs, Auckland Rotary Clubs, the Waitematā Tribal Executive, the Māori Women's Welfare League and the 28th Māori Battalion Association.[62] In 1948 the venue was firmly established as a favourite for community dances, socials concert parties, tangi and cultural gatherings. It assumed the role of Auckland's only urban marae and became the first point of contact for newly arrived Māori to the city and those who were homesick.[63] Hoani Waititi, a well-known Māori educationalist, was a compére for many of the concerts. Young people could rock and roll and hear the up-and-coming contemporary Māori performers such as the Howard Morrison Quartet, the Quin Tikis, the Hi Fives, Kiri Te Kanawa and Prince Tui Teka,[64] without the influence of alcohol.[65] Everyone knew where to go to get a boil-up, rēwana bread, kaimoana and a cup of tea.[66]

Young adults would meet in the city, sometimes en masse, to engage with relatives in Grey Lynn, Ponsonby, College Hill, Freemans Bay, Newton and Grafton, but primarily for the young people to follow the flow of entertainment. Life was full of excitement.

With the movement of people to the suburbs and the building of other marae, the Auckland Māori Community Centre was no longer a vital element on the Auckland Māori scene.[67] After the Community Centre era, the young people followed the entertainment to other venues, and preferably to see their cousins.[68] One of the popular Māori bands of the day was The Radars. Six o'clock closing of hotels ceased in 1967, and venues such as The Gluepot on Ponsonby Road began to use live entertainment to attract patrons. Their first resident band was The Radars, a quartet of blind singers and partially blind musicians who originally formed at the Auckland Institute for the Blind.[69] For seven years The Radars entertained audiences, as well as backing visiting artists such as Billy T. James, Rim D. Paul, George Tumahai and others. They played to full houses on Friday and Saturday nights, packed with whānau who followed their movements. The band took a rest when bigger acts such as Prince Tui Teka and The Volcanics visited. Their run at the hotel ended in 1976 when other Māori acts moved in to take their place — until the end of 1977, when everything changed and a more New Zealand rock sound prevailed.[70] The Mon Marte, Peter Pan Club, Picassos and the Great Northern Hotel were all places frequented by the Māori populace following the flow of music and dance.

In 1966 this inner-city haven was 21% Pacific and 19% Māori.[71] However, by 1986 the population of Māori and Pacific people had diminished to 24% due to the slum clearances of Freemans Bay, the motorway developments in Grafton and Newton and the inner-city commercial developments of the 1960s. Hundreds of Māori dwellings were demolished, forcing further 'scattering of kin' out of Ponsonby,

Newtown, Grafton, Freemans Bay and Grey Lynn[72] to new suburbs in Glen Innes, Northcote, Ōtara, Māngere and later Te Atatū and Henderson. In Wellington similar estates were built at Porirua, Hutt Valley and Wainuiomata.[73] The planning of new housing subdivisions saw a one-third mix of each of private, state and group houses.[74]

The growth of Ōtara

Many Māori found themselves living in Ōtara. Over the years Ōtara has been publicly scrutinised both positively and negatively, but more often in a negative light. Stereotypical media headlines have included, for example, 'Ōtara; City without a Soul'.[75] In the 1950s Ōtara was still largely a rural area. It was chosen as the location for a large state housing development, the first project of its kind in New Zealand. The community, complete with industrial, commercial and ancillary services, was planned and created from the late 1940s and took over a decade to build.[76] Originally the abode of the Ngāi Tai, who now reside at Maraetai, the plan for modern Ōtara was a triangular block bordered by the Tāmaki River and the Ōtara Creek in the north, the southern motorway to the west, East Tāmaki Road in the east and Puhinui Road to the west. This suburb arose at a time when Auckland was suffering a housing shortage.

Ōtara's flat topography and close proximity to the southern motorway made it a desirable site, and 1200 acres were purchased for the project at $900 per acre.[77] Developed by the Ministry of Works and signed over to the Manukau County in 1958, the first houses were built on the western side of the motorway at the Wymondley Block in 1958–59. This coincided with the urban renewal programme of the inner city, something Ranginui Walker described as unfortunate, as Ōtara became a dumping ground for the "derelicts of Auckland".[78]

In 1957 there were 108 houses and by 1969 some 3724 units had been constructed.[79] In 1961 the census recorded a population of 1660 and by 1969 it had increased to well over 21,000. Pākehā represented 65% of Ōtara's population in 1965, while Māori and Pacific peoples represented 38%. Five years later, the Pākehā percentage was down to 57%.[80] According to one source, the Lands and Survey Department described Ōtara as an example of what not to do in a major housing development. It lacked amenities, kindergartens, trees and parks, and there was little to occupy the suburb's growing population of children from low-income households.[81]

Ranginui Walker's 1970 thesis study of Māori adjustment to urban living focused on first-generation Māori living in Ōtara. He interviewed whānau who had recently settled in Ōtara, including one family who had shifted here from inner-city Grafton in 1964.

> We lived in a flat in Grafton. Nobody wanted a Māori with kids. The best we could do was one room at £3/10- [$7] a week where we lived and cooked. Six couples shared the bathroom. There were rats every-where. Washing was difficult and had to be done in the basement where we carried hot water down two flights of stairs. We were glad to have a roof over ourselves. I didn't care about the name Ōtara, it's just the same as anywhere else. Whose fault is it? We didn't plan it. I've got to know everyone else now, we like it here.[82]

At the time of Ranginui Walker's research, it was estimated some 6000 Māori and 2000 Pacific Islanders were living in Ōtara. He mentions a survey of 100 homes that identified the two highest tribal

State housing in Ōtara, South Auckland, 1967.
Fairfax Media, Auckland Libraries Footprints 00086

groups represented were Ngāpuhi and Tainui, with only 4% of the spouses having spent their childhoods in Auckland. The rest were raised in rural kāinga associated with at least one marae.[83]

After questioning a number of first-generation adult Māori from the Ōtara community, Walker believed that a common neo-urban Māori sub-culture was emerging that distinguished them from Pākehā.[84] He listed the elements of this sub-culture as: early socialisation in a rural Māori community; affiliation to one or more marae; an early life characterised by economic depression, poor housing, cash cropping, farming or seasonal labour, caring for younger siblings and traditional Māori food preference; kin-based life marked by the sharing of food and property; an acquaintance with Māori death custom; observation of hui and marae etiquette; respect for elders; belief in tapu and other spiritual phenomenon; and a commitment to religion.[85]

Maintaining an assured and continued distinct Māori lifestyle in the urban milieu was a dominant issue for Walker. He came to the conclusion that close proximity to Pākehā sharpened a minority group's identity. He proposed that a new pan-Māori identity was emerging out of the experience of urbanisation at Ōtara,[86] and that Māori in Ōtara were still very much committed to their Māori identity.[87]

This was an indication of the state of the majority of Māori living in the city. They had once lived in a community where kinship was a major cohesive factor. In the metropolis they took on a tūranga hou (a new standing place) — transplanting rural institutions to the urban environment with the establishment of voluntary, civic, cultural, religious, sports and arts and crafts clubs, many of which were adaptations of traditional structures.[88] State-sponsored structures were also to emerge that would support transition to the urban setting for Māori by means of hostels and trade training. As we will see in the next chapter, these too would take on a character reflective of the kin-based structures of traditional Māori communities.

The Rudolph Family, West Auckland

Judy Rudolph was four years old when her whānau migrated to Auckland in 1955 from Kaikohe, Northland. Her mother Motau Komene was from Kohewhata marae at Kaikohe but was brought up in Tinopai. Many of her immediate family had died in the early tuberculosis epidemic. She married Waru Rudolph from Te Hāpua, and after becoming parents, they decided their two children would need to embrace the Pākehā world to survive. They agreed never to speak their native language in front of their children. Motau was keen on education but Waru didn't really care too much about it. Together they made the move to the city to offer a better way of life for their children.

"Our father Waru was labouring in Kaikohe but he decided to seek better work in Auckland. We arrived in Auckland in 1955 to Dad's nephews' home in Caroline Street, Ponsonby. There were a great number of Māori living here then," Judy says. "Even our grandmother, Mum's mother, lived in Auckland at Pompallier Terrace with her second husband, a Pākehā." Waru worked at the wharf for a number of years but moved in to bricklaying. He followed the usual path of working men who 'occasionally' drank immediately after working hours. As far as Judy can recollect, her father was never violent towards the family. "He was the softie of the two," she claims. "They were both country people and they found it hard to integrate in to city life."

They were able to buy a home thanks in part to an unusual government scheme. A subsidy was available if they accommodated a reformed prisoner into their home. The house was worth £8000. The family shifted into a new home in Valdale Road in Henderson, West Auckland, "where we lived with an old Pākehā man, an ex-prisoner", Judy says. This old man stayed with the family, but was removed when it was discovered he was being abusive. Despite this, the government continued their promise to pay off the house. "That's how we got our home," Judy declares.

Valdale Road was surrounded by fruit orchards, vineyards and a dairy milkbar close by, run by a Pākehā family. The Rudolph whānau was the only Māori family in their street as they were part of the government's 'pepper-potting' scheme that sought to place Māori families into Pākehā communities so they could be integrated into mainstream society. In fact, Judy says, the family didn't mix at all and kept to themselves. "We were told not to worry about what others said. We didn't know we were brown until someone made a racist remark against the kids and Mum had to tell us we were brown and Māori," Judy laughs.

The children attended Pomaria Primary School from 1960, the year the school opened, making the Rudolph children founding members. Waru and Motau had

11 children including Caroline, who was a deaf mute with an IHC disability. "We spent most of our lives caring for her," Judy says. Motau did all the baking in the house, played the piano and the ukulele and encouraged the children to waiata, specifically on a Monday night, which was family night. "Dad adored his whānau and spent all his life close to us and to Mum," Judy remembers.

Much of their community engagement was in a Māori context. "Mum loved to attend the gatherings at the Māori Community Centre where they could dance, but more to meet up with their relations. Mum loved it. Relatives such as Jack Wihongi and others all lived locally as well." Motau joined the local Māori Women's Welfare League team on Swanson Road. League members were involved with fundraising for Hoani Waititi marae and the children would follow their mother to meetings with social worker Betty Walk, who strongly supported the marae.

"Mum and Dad and all our family regretted losing our Māoritanga. We've all tried to learn our reo. It doesn't mean we don't understand tikanga," Judy reflects. The pull to return home grew strong for both Motau and Waru, who always thought about returning to Kaikohe, but they realised to go back home without their children and mokopuna would have been a strain for them. They couldn't resource the return home and there was a sense it would be hard for whānau to visit them back home. However, they told their children they wanted to lie at their home in Auckland when they died and be buried back-home in Kaikohe. In the 1980s Motau began to search her whakapapa. "She'd travel the country finding her relations," Judy remembers.

Both Motau and Waru passed away within five weeks of each other in 1990. Despite calls from Uncle Haki Wihongi to bring them both to lie at Hoani Waititi, the whānau declined and acted out their parents' wishes to lie at their Auckland homestead and to bury them in Kaikohe.

"Looking back, they were successful in giving us all an education and giving us opportunities for life. We've all done well with the tools our parents left us. Many of us want to shift home, but we are so conditioned to earning and needing to earn; there is little work back home as well and no papakāinga-type housing available for us," Judy says.

All of Motau and Waru's children and mokopuna were raised in Auckland and all except one continue to live in a city environment. Only recently has one of their children, Pauline Rudolph, returned home to Kaikohe in 2016. She is the first of the family to move home to their original papakāinga and she now works for social services in the area.

As far as Judy is concerned, there is no doubt: "Our parents made the right decisions for their time."

Chapter 4 | Akoranga Mahi-ā-rehe

Trade Training

The strong association between the employment training programmes designed for Māori and the urban hostels that accommodated hundreds of Māori in the cities of Auckland, Hamilton, Wellington and Christchurch, played a significant role in establishing young Māori into the urban centres.

After World War II, the Māori hostel became a crucial avenue for the "organised drift to the city".[1] The National Government of 1949 financially supported the provision of more Māori hostels, but the state realised it could not carry the entire burden of the hostels. In 1951 Cabinet approved a pound-for-pound subsidy scheme to establish hostels in conjunction with church or welfare organisations. In 1948, of the 173 spaces available to Māori in the hostels, Māori girls took 79% of the places.[2] By 1953 there were six new hostels and 155 spaces available, of which 60% were Māori girls and 38% boys.[3] Up until 1966 Māori women between the ages of 15 and 24 were still the largest Māori migrant group.

One woman who has spent most of her life involved in the hostels and training is Kathy Eruera of Te Whānau-a-Apanui. In 1972 at the age of 17, Kathy boarded a bus alone from Edgecumbe to find work in Wellington. She had passed School Certificate in English, home economics, typing and bookkeeping, and she had her Sixth Form Certificate from Edgecumbe College, but she had no desire to go to university or teachers' training college. Her mother, Hinewai, felt she should apply for the pre-employment programme under Māori Affairs and encouraged Kathy to travel to the hostel in Wellington to "go find a good job in the Pākehā world".[4] Kathy followed her mother's advice.

In Wellington Kathy and other young Māori women from the eastern Bay of Plenty were housed in a "flash" three-storey Methodist Church Hostel in Berhampore. Kathy loved having her own bed; she and her sister had shared a bed back home. Kathy and the other 28 girls attended a six-week course at the Wellington Polytech to learn how to dress, walk and talk properly in preparation for attending a job interview. "We were rough-as country bumpkins; we didn't know there was such a thing as talking correctly to get a job," she laughs. Shaking hands was the most difficult rudiment of Pākehā etiquette for Kathy: "I was ready to greet my boss with a kiss, as was Māori custom." A very shy Kathy was also apprehensive about making direct eye contact with a boss, something the girls were taught was important. The girls came from a world where it was disrespectful to look elders directly in the eyes. She suffered from homesickness and her only communication with whānau was by letter.

She was encouraged to apply for a position as a junior typist with the South British Insurance Company. "A man from the company extended his hand to me and I shook it and remembered not to kiss him," she remembers. The interview went well and she was offered the job, starting the following week. She sent some of her income home to her parents, and continued to live in the hostel for the next year, until she shifted to Petone. She remained in Wellington until 1976, when she transferred to work in Auckland, and boarded there at Hepburn Street Girls Hostel. She later shifted to Australia for a period of time, and gave birth to a daughter there. She eventually returned to Auckland where she continued to work as an office typist/receptionist until 1996, when Bob Joyce of United Māori Mission employed her as manager of her former place of residence, the Hepburn Street Hostel. This hostel housed university students and working girls then.

Today in 2017, Kathy is the matron at Lovelock Hostel, Auckland, where young Māori and Pacific Island girls participate in hostel life in

Whaea Kathy Eruera (back row, third from left) and her hostel girls from the 2016 Inzone Education student intake at Papakura Marae, 2016.
Courtesy of Bradford Haami

conjunction with the Inzone Education Programme. It seems Kathy's whānau were called to nurture young women and men in the cities. Her parents Paddy and Hinewai Eruera took a rest from farming at Whakatāne to act as manager and matron of the Trentham Hostel in Wellington, caring for the Māori trade trainees for 15 years, until 1981.

The trade-training path

For 20,000 young Māori,[5] hostel life and attending trade-training schools from the late 1950s into the early 1980s was an adventure and an opportunity to not only escape the mundane life at home of "getting up at 5 every morning to milk the cows",[6] but to learn a trade, gain a qualification and find employment.

In 1959 the Department of Māori Affairs launched its trade-training school initiative in conjunction with technical institutes in the city, starting with ten boys recruited for carpentry. By 1966 there were 144 boys each year, learning seven different trades at centres in

Auckland, Lower Hutt and Christchurch.[7] Initially, carpentry was offered in Auckland in 1959, followed by a second course in 1961 at Gracefield in Lower Hutt, and a third at Weedons in Christchurch in 1962. In 1966, 150 houses had been built by the trainees and onsold to Māori families.[8] In 1962, courses in plumbing and electrical wiring were started and opportunities for motor mechanics opened in Auckland in 1963.

Māori welfare officers frequented the rural schools to recommend Māori students to attend trade-training programmes in Auckland, Wellington or Christchurch, depending on their school results. During the 1950s and 1960s, trade training of Māori male youth in order that they secure employment was a priority that had consequences for the rural communities. For example, in 1967, of the 52 Ngata Memorial College graduates in Ruatoria, only 16 remained local, while the rest moved away for training or employment. This became a pattern that repeated every year.[9]

Finding accommodation in the cities for the trainees was essential. Under a subsidy payable to approved church or welfare organisations, from 1951 the Department of Māori Affairs sponsored hostels in the main centres.[10] Some of the hostels provided accommodation for young, single Māori girls during wartime and into the 1960s. At these hostels, the young women would be "trained and educated in the principles of right living".[11] For young Māori men, the combination of the Māori hostels and trade training ventures throughout the country contributed to the emergence of a new breed of skilled Māori. By 1968, primarily because of the trade-training schools, 1129 Māori were housed in urban hostels but now 65% were boys and 35% were young Māori women.[12]

Colin Campbell, originally of Ngāti Porou, was part of one of the last intakes to the training schools between 1979 and 1981. He boarded at Tiraroa Hostel on Owens Road, Auckland. He recalls:

> For the rural boys, it was hard — it took about 3 or 4 months to adjust just from being away from home. They were shy, afraid to ask questions, thinking they were dumb and not up to it, but the tutors were good and encouraged the boys to ask questions. They were whakamā and everyone got over that and their confidence was built up after five months. There were boys who spoke Māori and they trained us in waiata and we had inter-hostel singing competitions and we had to meet at the church

to compete. We were told if we failed we'd be kicked out — we wanted to make it.[13]

He continues, revealing how the hostel-trainee experience changed the boys' lives.

> The hostels put a focus in us, it didn't mean we were losing who we were but it gave us more life tools. If we were at home on the pā we'd just be drinking and doing nothing, what's the point of that? We all passed and enjoyed ourselves to the point where 20 of us in our team still hold the record for putting up a 30-storey building — a floor every two weeks, boxing, framing and pouring concrete and shear walling — on the corner of Queen Street and Custom Street. We did a few buildings in Queen Street. We didn't have to talk much, we all knew what to do.[14]

The earliest combined hostel/trade-training facility was in Christchurch, and it appears it originated out of a visit by three South Island elders to Ngāruawāhia in 1949. Reverend Wera Couch of Rāpaki, Joe Moss from Ōtākou and Reverend W.E. Falkingham of the Christchurch Methodist mission, arrived at Tūrangawaewae marae at Ngāruawāhia to support the Rātana movement's visit to Princess Te Puea's marae. On this visit the South Islanders were impressed by the establishment of Te Rāhui Wahine Hostel for girls, which had been operating in Hamilton since 1945.

Heeni Wharemaru, a past matron at Te Rāhui Wahine, recounts how the influx of American servicemen training for combat in New Zealand posed a problem for Tainui elders and church officials, who were mutually concerned about "our own" young women, who were "chasing them like mad" and getting into trouble.[15] She remembers how Reverend Arthur John Seamer, a well-known Methodist minister, conceived the idea of creating a youth hostel in an appropriate city for these young women. Under Māori supervision, those staying at the hostel would be given the opportunity to attend secondary and tertiary education.[16]

With Princess Te Puea's blessing the church purchased a two-storey building in Bryce Street, Hamilton, and set it up as a hostel for Māori girls.[17] During the war years, women from the outlying districts would travel to Hamilton to give food, Anzac biscuits, cakes and clothing to their whānau in the 28th Māori Battalion. After they had delivered their gifts and produce, the women would have no accommodation, sleeping anywhere they could, under hedges or in parks. It was a necessity deplored by Te Puea.[18] At the time, the cityscape was perceived as morally evil and as a place of "rotten temptations", which was dangerous and seductive to young Māori women.[19]

Te Rāhui Wahine was a place of refuge where young Māori women were protected and given access to good education. They were living in a conservative city that had no experience with Māori: employers there had not yet begun to employ Māori.[20]

This hostel concept strongly resonated with the Christchurch visitors, and Joe Moss approached the Methodist Mission in 1951 about a similar home for young Māori women in difficult situations in their city. The Methodist Church purchased a property at 238 Stanmore Road in the eastern suburb of Richmond through their Māori Mission Department, with an added subsidy from the government. The homestead was originally run as a hostel by a Christchurch firm who not longer required the property for its original use.[21]

The hostel was opened in 1953 and named Rehua by Henare Aratumahina Jacobs, after one of the higher levels of the Māori heavens.[22] Initially it was home for 14 girls from Rotorua, the King Country, Christchurch and other places.[23] Joe and Taka Moss (nee Ellison) were the first master and matron for the hostel. However, the success of the home was short lived as they could not keep the beds full and the exercise proved to be uneconomical.[24]

A new idea was formed during a discussion with the Minister of Māori Affairs: could the hostel be used as a home for boys who were training in a trade? There had been a new push from the government to house young Māori male apprentices and workers in the cities, a matter that overrode the "desire to protect young women".[25]

The Department of Māori Affairs suggested that young Māori women were more able to cope in urban environments than their male counterparts, meaning they were in less need of hostel care.[26] New Zealand was moving toward an economic boom during the 1940s, creating a demand for skilled tradesmen. The "State turned its attention to encouraging the urbanisation of young Māori men to take up apprenticeships and enter trade training."[27]

The move to Christchurch

A relationship between Ngāi Tahu elders and the local technical school gave rise to the availability of trade training for young Māori men in Christchurch. An envoy from Christchurch was sent to Te Mahia on the East Coast in the North Island to speak with Māori elders and enquire about recruiting their young boys to Christchurch to learn one of three trades offered by the technical institute. The trades were carpentry, painting and mechanics. The East Coast elders agreed to the idea and boys were organised for recruitment by Emarina (Lena) Manuel, the Māori Welfare Officer for that region.[28]

With support from Māori Affairs, the first 18 boys from the North Island and two from the South became residents at the Rehua Stanmore Road hostel. The combination of church-based hostel accommodation and trade training was the first of its kind. The boys were expected to train for five years; accommodation in the hostels was only available for two years to allow space for new intakes of trainees. The boys would have to find their own accommodation after their two years had passed. It was expected the boys would return to their home communities as tradesmen and men of faith.[29]

Christchurch was a foreign landscape for the boys, who saw "very few, if any, Māori faces in Christchurch".[30] It was rare to find Māori in the city. However, the 1945 census showed 589 Māori lived in Christchurch. Over the following 30 years the Māori population soared more than tenfold. The Ngāi Tahu villages of Tuahiwi, Taumutu, Rāpaki, Ōnuku, Wairewa and Koukourarata were on the outskirts of the city, but after World War II, increasing numbers of Ngāi Tahu sought employment in Christchurch city. The influx of Ngāi Tahu into Christchurch contributed to a post-war increase in Māori population alongside the "steady stream of migrants from the North Island" who arrived to work as seasonal labourers and trade trainees.[31]

Few of the trade trainees had travelled outside of their home regions, but some had already experienced boarding school, which gave them a taste of mixing with other Māori. It was regarded as a big deal and an opportunity. In Christchurch "we'd spot a brown face and automatically move towards each other", one of the students remembers. "However, we'd have to be careful who we called Māori and Pākehā as some Ngāi Tahu looked very Pākehā to us." Venturing into the city was an experience for many of the boys. They

Barry Baker (second left, standing) and other boys from Taumarunui who were selected for the Māori trade-training scheme. They are about to board the train for Christchurch in 1970.

Courtesy of Barry Baker

were greeted by a "sea of bikes"; everyone rode bikes in the city.[32] Most Pākehā had had little to do with any Māori, while many of the North Island boys had never met a Pākehā. Some of the boys were invited to Pākehā homes for dinner, creating strong bonds with those families "and their daughters", while others had unpleasant experiences. Befriending Pākehā was unheard of among some of the boys and their families who came from regions such as Gisborne, where relations between the two races were practically non-existent.[33]

While on the course the boys earned a wage, paid rent and

saved to buy clothes and their own bikes.[34] The close-knit whānau of young men created an environment where those who were doing well coached the others. Culture, church and sport were strong components of life at the hostels. Boys participated in inter-hostel rugby games and later played club rugby, and they took part in Māori concert parties that travelled throughout the South Island fundraising for the accommodation and training. One group of boys was invited to perform to packed houses alongside well-known Ngāi Tahu figure Te Ari Pitama's culture group at the Civic Theatre.[35]

Terry Ryan was privileged to be housed at Rehua, where he slept with others in little army huts on the ātea (outer court). "We were all one big happy family doing things together," he says. It was a world with no television and the telephone was toll-barred. Letter writing was the main mode of communication and the mailman was the most popular person among the boys. "A lot of the boys suffered from homesickness, so letters and gifts from family were a godsend," Terry comments. "You couldn't just get on a bus to go home from here — it was a long way back to the North Island." Sunday roast meals were the best meal of the week, and church was a priority on Sundays. "Often we'd go down to the city centre to see the action. Pākehā folk would come in to town from all over the place to see a Māori boy, who was probably the first Māori they had actually seen."[36] It was described by some as a bit of "a sideshow" when Pākehā would drive past the hostel to get a glimpse of the Māori boys.[37]

In 1957 the committee that presided over the hostel decided to sell the property and acquire new premises on Springfield Road, St Albans. The need for accommodation to house the growing interest in this scheme meant adding new buildings to the property. Additional boarding facilities were built in 1958, taking the number of beds to 31, but soon another 12 beds were needed.[38] The original wooden hostel was named Te Maire by Mrs Hinerua Couch (nee Riwai), after the early Methodist missionary, Rawiri Te Maire.[39]

In 1958 the idea of building a recreation hall arose. Later, this idea developed into designing a Māori meeting house to "keep the boys in touch with art and culture of their race" and also to "serve as an admirable centre for Christian work among the Māoris of the South Island".[40] Reverend Falkingham felt the boys needed a hall that should have a Māori carving inside, but some of the local Māori women advised him to "do it right".[41]

When asked, the boys themselves voted to build a marae rather than a gymnasium. Plans to carve a meeting house began in 1958 and soon a pan-tribal house representing the tribes of the trade-trainee boys became a reality. With voluntary labour from the hostel boys and materials donated by local businesses, a semblance of a house began to take shape. Henare Paikea Toka was installed as the master carver. Local women weaved the tukutuku panels, while the boys painted the kōwhaiwhai on the rafters.[42] The marae was opened as a carved house in 1960 by the Waikato people, led by Princess Piki, and named Te Whatu Manawa Māoritanga o Rehua. It was only fitting Waikato should officiate the tapu-lifting ceremony as it was in the Waikato, while being hosted by Te Puea, that the idea for the hostel had been formulated.[43]

In the 1960s other hostels under church management emerged in Christchurch. There was Te Kaihanga Māori Boys' Hostel (Anglican) in Riccarton, which opened in 1962, Te Aranga Hostel (Catholic), and for the girls there was Roseneath (Presbyterian). Despite the influx of pan-iwi Māori into the schemes in Christchurch, the urban Māori population had only reached 1.9% in 1971.[44] Most Māori were still migrating to Auckland, Wellington and the Hutt.

Hostels then and now

In Auckland between 1943 and 1970, more than 16 hostels had operated with the express purpose of "settling young migrants into the city in a moral, homely environment while they trained or worked".[45] Many of those hostels were managed or owned by religious organisations such as the United Māori Mission (UMM). The UMM was a missionary organisation launched in 1936 to reach Māori communities.[46]

The association between UMM and the Auckland hostels is attributed to Sister Jessie Alexander, a Presbyterian deaconess and an accomplished linguist who had worked with Māori people since 1913. She lived among the followers of Te Kooti and the prophet Rua on the East Coast for many years.[47] In 1938 she saw many young Māori women occupying the cities, at "a loose-end", living rough in the slum areas of the city, down at the wharves. She saw the women wandering streets that were teeming with soldiers, during blackouts and curfews, "earning a living" in a way she felt were "bad conditions". Something needed to be done "to help a Māori girl towards good citizenship".[48]

Māori trade trainees at work in Auckland.
Courtesy of United Māori Mission

Sister Jessie sought to answer the invasion of letters from anxious mothers pleading with her to "care for their daughters who had come to Auckland and knew little of city life".[49] She was adamant a Christian home in the city for Māori girls was "well overdue". This would be a home away from home, where the women could be taught, guided and entertained into "a more wholesome way".[50] In response she had obtained a hostel for 12 resident girls in Union Street. It was opened in 1940 and dedicated with the name Te Kāinga Rangimarie (The House of Peace).[51] Very quickly, Sister Jessie realised their service needed to be expanded.[52]

Impressed with her work, in 1944 G.R. Mason, Minister of Native Affairs, purchased the large Presbyterian Manse at 29 Hepburn Street, Ponsonby. Two years later he purchased 89 Gillies Avenue, Newmarket for the same purpose. The Union Street premises were eventually sold and replaced with the purchase of another property at 60 Shelley Beach Road in Herne Bay.[53] The hostels were affectionately known as "Heppy", "Gillies" and "Shelly".[54] Gillies Avenue, which was owned by the Māori Trustee and leased to UMM, became the new boys hostel at the time; the other two were for young Māori women. It was UMM's brief to cater for the "spiritual, social and material requirements" of the young people.[55]

In 1966 the hostels in operation in Auckland housed 180 beds.[56] There were new homes such as the Owens Road Hostel, where 50 boys could be accommodated. This hostel was purchased by the Department of Māori Affairs and leased to UMM, while Domett Avenue Hostel and Dominion Road were owned and operated by the Presbyterian Church.[57]

In Lower Hutt, Wellington trainees were provided with accommodation at the Trentham Immigration Hostel, stationed next to the Trentham Military Base. It too was administered by the Department of Māori Affairs.

Amid the hostel environments, youth saw new opportunities, new ways of living, and formed many new relationships, many of which resulted in marriages. Few of the boys returned home to reside with their families again.[58] While something of Māori culture and tikanga of a previous generation may have been lost in this environment, many of the trainees maintained their whakapapa links with whānau and never lost their natural manaaki tangata and whanaungatanga ways.[59]

In November 1981 funding for the 77 trade-training schemes was scrapped by the government of the day, a decision many of the older boys of the time still feel was regrettable. This forced the closure or repurchasing of many of the hostels. Rehua Hostel in Christchurch could not be closed because it had been redesignated as a marae, which is still its core function today.

Today the modern version of this movement is expressed at Rehua marae through the scheme He Toki ki te Rika: Inspiring Māori Leadership in Training, maintaining the legacy and success of the old days. According to Norm Dewes, modern-day trade-training schemes are modular — compartmentalised — whereas the original trade-training courses taught the boys how to build a complete house.[60] Sadly, the Christchurch earthquake of 2011 saw the destruction of a number of the hostels, but Rehua marae still stands as a memorial to that history.[61] Courses based here made a difference to many Māori in their transition from the countryside to the South Island's major city. Importantly, the courses offered a foot on the ladder into employment for the young Māori participants. According to Roger Maaka, the Māori trade trainees in Christchurch went on to represent the highest number of self-employed Māori in New Zealand.[62]

The hostel experience led to the meeting of young Māori men and women in the city, resulting in many marriages. This is the wedding of Dave and Janice Ruka.
Courtesy of United Māori Mission

In Auckland, Whaea Kathy Eruera, a past tenant of the women's hostels in both Trentham and Auckland, is currently the senior matron for the girls at Lovelock Hostel, Mount Eden, Auckland. The Inzone Education Programme is a contemporary extension of the past hostel and educational training schemes. Inzone seeks to offer opportunities for Māori and Pacific Island boys and girls to attend high-performance state schools such as Auckland Boys Grammar and Epsom Girls Grammar, by establishing hostel accommodation within these school zones for successful applicants.

The students are from outside the school zones and many are from disadvantaged homes. Initiated in 2005 under the umbrella of the UMM, the programme is now under an independent trust, The Inzone Education Foundation. The programme continues to provide a positive whānau-orientated, culturally appropriate home base and education-focused environment designed to maximise the students' capacity to succeed academically, and to also enjoy sports and cultural co-curricular activities. Faith and kaupapa Māori are still the core drivers that underpin the foundations' work.[63]

Barry Baker, Christchurch

Barry Baker and his wife Helen at their home in Christchurch, 2016.
Courtesy of Bradford Haami

Barry Baker hails from Taumarunui but has lived in Christchurch for 46 years. He was brought up in a number of mill settlements including Manunui, Moerangi, and Taumarunui; wherever his father Jim's work happened to be was where the family went.

Barry is the sixth of 13 siblings. He was brought up around Taumarunui, after his family shifted there from Northland for employment. Barry fondly remembers the settlements they lived in, as they were all like villages. "We all lived in each other's homes." His father died in 1962 when he was nine. Barry's mother, Mary, worked a number of jobs to pay off the cost of a Māori Affairs home in Taumarunui. His oldest brother, Len, took on the mentoring role their father would have performed.

Barry lived with his Uncle Colin at Hauhungaroa, where he attended Tongariro High School for two years. It was here Archie Taiaroa, the Māori Welfare/vocation guidance officer at the time, recruited Barry to join other local boys to attend trade training in Christchurch. "That's where the boys from Taumarunui all went. My brother Fred did the mechanic training in Christchurch in 1968. This appealed to me — an adventure, my big OE," Barry remembers. "I remember a one-armed Pākehā Australian guy turned up at my Uncle Gilbert's at Moerangi to meet me. He was an ex-air force pilot in the war but now was in charge of pastoral care at the hostel. He travelled the country to meet every boy before we came to Christchurch. He was an amazing man." This man was Bill Cox.[64]

In 1970 the boys left Taumarunui on the train, caught a ship to Lyttelton Harbour and took another train to Christchurch. Mick Hughes, a Māori Affairs representative, met the boys and guided them to three buses divided into carpenters for Te Kaihanga hostel, mechanics for Te Aranga, and painters at Rehua. "I was heading to Te Kaihanga hostel. We travelled down Moorhouse Road, it was absolutely amazing, everyone appeared to own a bicycle. We travelled to 34 Hansons Lane, which was in the old Ballantyne family homestead, where we met Bill Cox again, which was comforting.

"The carpenters spent two years in residence, which meant on our arrival there were boys starting their second year. The second-year boys already knew the ropes and Bill utilised them initially in paving the way for all the newbies." Bill Cox, with Bill and Mary Davis, created a whānau-orientated environment. Kapa haka, rugby and church events featured in the early days and were the platform for lifelong friendships between the boys.

"Bill Cox was tenacious about empowering young men to make decisions about their well-being. We had a social committee, a council and a law-and-order committee," recalls Barry. "Training was in an air force warehouse in Weedons that had been transformed into a training centre for bricklayers and builders. And we spent most of that year doing theory with a basic introduction to practical building under the tutorage of Trevor Marsh, Robin Sides, Bert Helm and Ken Cooper, and Bob Coulters for the bricklayers. The second year was practical building on Māori Affairs' homes. We were split into four gangs of six boys under the supervision of Māori Affairs tutors Dave Townsend, Ted Hill, Ray Caully and Jim Ponsonby.

"The trade training brought out the competitive edge in each gang trying to outdo each other.

During the school holidays we were placed with builders for practical experience out in the real world. I was placed with cottage builder Doug Timperley. On completion of our two years, we generally ended up working with the builder we had a placement with. My builder (Doug) was a bit unconventional and paid everyone the same wage and that arrived in the form of a cheque. In the early 1970s they were hard to get cashed. I would go to Bruce Hills menswear to cash it, having to buy a shirt each time," Bill laughs. "One positive thing about the trade training of the time was how big companies like Fletchers valued the quality of the graduates of the scheme and would take many of them on. They were great days, we were young, fit and created a comradeship between us all that has endured for 46 years."

The boys at Te Kaihanga had a strong kapa haka team, tutored by Hori Brennan and old boys Tommy Reihana and Harry Williams. There was always rivalry between the hostels in both kapa haka and rugby. After two years in Te Kaihanga, Barry left and flatted with others for a few years. "In that time many of us met our future partners." Barry finished training in 1973 and continued in the trade. He worked as a furniture mover then went for a job in the prisons, where he worked for 24 years. At the same time he was still actively involved with the hostels, coaching rugby and performing administration tasks and the running of Rehua marae. When the hostel system closed, Barry was vocal about it. "Trade training was an investment, but we all worked and paid our taxes to New Zealand," he states. "It cost $360,000 to run a hostel and trade training a year, and instead they built a new 60-bed youth prison that cost three million to build and three million to run. Where do our kids go now? They're high on the suicide list. The hostels exposed us to diversity and whanaungatanga. I believe pastoral care and mentoring was the key to the success of our guys, many of whom run their own businesses now."

In leaving home, Barry came to see the importance of his own culture, tikanga and identity, something he believes in and has tried to impart to the youth in the prison and to his own children. "My children saw their dad go to work but many of our whānau at home didn't. Kids from the north would come and stay with us to work and I'd try and tap into their passion. The trade-training schools tapped into the potential of our youth."

His wish is one day to head back to Taumarunui, but Christchurch has been his home for 46 years with his wife Helen, his children and now his mokopuna. His mokopuna and his strong sentimental love for Christchurch holds him there for the present.

Chapter 5

Te Whakahiato

The Rise of the Collective

Ella Henry's memories of back-home in Ahipara and Kaitaia are of a village where every Māori home was her home, where there was freedom and safety among the myriad of aunties and uncles. Home was a collection of safe places and she knew everyone as blood family.[1] Historian Aroha Harris describes this way of life as "a collection of safe places networked by blood relations among whom adults shared responsibilities for all children — theirs and others. Young children were unquestionably and unconditionally 'whangaied' [fed, adopted, nurtured] by grandparents and other relatives."[2] She continues:

> Homegrown processes were instituted for disciplining and educating young people, which might include their being sent to live temporarily with relatives while attending school or in the aftermath of disputes in the home. Home was also a cooperative place. The spoils of hunting and fishing were distributed among the wider whānau ... Communities fundraised to rebuild and maintain marae, and co-operated in their farming and gardening endeavours ... despite the lure of an independent life in the exciting city, the strong sense of Māori community and belonging ... could be difficult to leave.[3]

This description was the state of the world Ella remembers as a child. That world quickly changed for her when the family shifted to New Lynn in Auckland — there were no more familiar homes in close proximity to visit. The hours her parents and elder siblings worked in the local factories meant Ella was left alone to organise her own day with nowhere to visit as familiar, safe, kin-based homes. This had consequences for her life and spun her in to a trajectory of "lost-ness" for a time (see profile, page 27).

Poata Eruera of Glen Eden had a similar experience when his family moved from Ōtangaroa in the north to Auckland. His sister had suffered an accident and fallen into a coma. The family shifted from Raurimu near Taumarunui to Grafton in Auckland to be closer to her hospital care. Poata's father had seen a morepork on his axe the Sunday of the accident and believed it to be a bad omen.[4]

Poata and his brothers were eventually sent back north to be cared for by whānau. Three years later, in 1961, Poata rejoined his immediate whānau in a very small house on College Hill, Freemans Bay, in Auckland. He felt his life was "in turmoil". "It was scary," Poata says. Coming from a one-roomed schoolhouse where all the other pupils were whānau, to Napier Street Primary School where he had no family, was a shock. "Māori bullying and the strapping [at school] of kids was rife. It was something I'd never witnessed before," he says. He found peace and solace when his mother would take him to the Leys Institute Library on St Mary's Road, Ponsonby. He'd never seen so many books before. The adventure, drama, imagination and provocation of the reading and writing world has remained with him and influenced his own writing career.

The family eventually shifted into a new state house at Northcote, near Hāto Petera Māori boys' school, although Poata and his brothers didn't qualify to attend the school. Poata and his family were living in a neighbourhood of pan-tribal Māori and mixed races.[5] There were no immediate whānau nearby as most were still back home. Instead, the Eruera family reached out to extended whānau throughout the city, particularly at the Auckland Māori Community Centre. Poata says, "We were always there." At one point Poata remembers being sent back to his father's people at Tinopai to be taught tribal whakapapa and history by his Uncle Henare Toka. The visits stopped when it became apparent Poata did not have the capacity to hold the knowledge that was being imparted.

In the city, maintaining whānau connections took many forms.

For some city-dwelling whānau, intentionally gathering for lunch once a month kept the wider family in touch with each other and fulfilled the need to maintain an ongoing form of whanaungatanga.[6] For Poata, the Auckland Māori Community Centre played that role. It was where the Eruera family found other whānau in Northcote to mix with. The advent of television in the 1960s created another reason for gatherings: the whānau would gather weekly at the home of whoever had a television set to watch shows such as *Bonanza*.[7]

Both Ella and Poata see their childhood journeys to the city as traumatic and both were affected by the changes in different ways. The experiences of Māori living in the city and the underlying drive for integration impacted on the dynamics of whānau living and tribal connectivity, but crucially on Māori identity and world view.

At an Auckland leaders' conference in 1963, Harry Dansey pinpointed the issue of identity and "being Māori in Auckland", suggesting people would have to choose "whether to be a Māori with all its cultural implications, whether to be what is in effect a brown Pākehā, or whether to strike a balance between the two".[8] There was a definite adjustment into the Pākehā world taking place. In writing about learning the Pākehā way, Arapera Blank uses the ancient phrase "whakarerea iho te kakau o te hoe" (put aside the handle of the paddle) to describe the departure from the Māori norms of life and "getting accustomed to civilisation".[9]

Collective initiative

For many whānau their urban experience was exciting and beneficial. There were new opportunities for education and employment, the engagement with comforts and technologies of modernity, and new relationships were formed with other Māori tribes, Pākehā, Pacific peoples and other ethnic groups. This led to racial conflict but also saw cross-cultural relationships emerge and develop into inter-racial marriages. In the early whaling era of New Zealand, many Pākehā–Māori marriages were forged between Pākehā men and Māori women, from which a large section of the Māori population are now descended. However, between 1940 and 1960 there was an increased proportion of mixed marriages, particularly between Māori men and Pākehā women, and predominantly between those in a younger age group.[10] Soon, inter-marriage between Pacific peoples and Māori would be common. Māori elders were concerned about inter-marriage between other tribes and non-Māori. As one elder put it, he didn't want his mokopuna to have "any bloody bugger's blood".[11]

For some Māori whānau, city life became glaringly detrimental. For others it was a more subtle progression. The notion of the village or of a collective of homes as safe havens for blood relatives changed dramatically. This concept was either adapted or transferred to suit, or was in many cases totally lost. The loss and disconnection from whānau, hapū and the iwi collective brought with it negative consequences, but also presented Māori in the city with opportunities to reshape and adapt their own social indigenous structures to new environments. A new mobile generation, now living outside of the confines of their elders, tribal boundaries and their religious mentors, found freedom in the city, but were ill-equipped to handle the independence. Soon, moral standards dropped and the children came into conflict with the law, and its consequences. The Māori male offending rate (3.5%) in 1958 was three times higher than Pākehā (1.5%). By 1968, 40.1% of Māori boys and 16.7% of Māori girls had appeared in the court system.[12]

Pan-tribal voluntary church organisations, cultural clubs, sports clubs, family and tribal organisations, Māori committees, Māori councils, Māori Women's Welfare League and other emerging social agencies became key to the cultural and social adjustment of Māori to urban life. Ranginui Walker identified three major developmental tasks Māori migrants to the city needed to undertake in adjusting to the urban lifestyle, namely, survival skills in the cash economy, transplanting their culture into the cityscape, and the development of political structures and strategies for dealing with a metropolitan society.[13]

Māori attempts to recreate pan-Māori structures to cope with these adjustments came in the form of "Māori Committees", which emulated early tribal committees. The Māori War Effort Organisation (MWEO) of the 1940s mobilised tribal committees to raise produce and funds for the war effort. Afterwards, MWEO refocused its attention to the welfare of the Māori people. They advised the National Service Department that they should select welfare and liaison officers (all women) to work with the tribal and executive committees in assisting Māori with social and economic problems. In 1945, 400 leaders representing 30 tribes made a plea to the government to maintain this organisation for the future of Māori development. In due course a compromise between the government and MWEO was reached, in the form of the Māori Social and Economic Act 1945. Under the Act, tribal committees and executives were placed under the auspices of the Department of Māori Affairs as the vehicle for the government to deal with Māori issues. The department was now committed to co-operating with Māori, which would have been unthinkable in the pre-war years. Māori experienced a love/hate relationship with this department that had evolved from the paternalistic voice of the government.[14]

In 1946 a Welfare Division was developed from within the Department of Māori Affairs. Welfare officers were selected to co-operate with Māori organisations to aid in the improvement of Māori living standards and direct them "in the essentials of good citizenship and civic responsibility".[15] Rangi Royal of Ngāti Raukawa, a former land developer supervisor and B Company commander, managed 34 welfare officers in the department. These officers were working with some 381 tribal committees. By 1949 they had handled some 10,000 cases.[16] Māori women's welfare committees were formed and grew rapidly. The experience of Māori women in these committees and those in the Country Women's Institute and the Māori Health League, combined with growing urbanisation, motivated Māori women to establish a forum of their own to articulate Māori health and social needs.[17]

In 1951, with the aid of Rangi Royal, the women rebranded themselves as the Māori Women's Welfare League at a pivotal meeting of delegates held at the Ngāti Pōneke Hall. A national executive council was formed and Whina Cooper of Panguru was elected president, with Mira Petricevich as secretary. The league's role was to promote fellowship and understanding between Māori and Pākehā and to instil in Māori mothers the care of home and children, and to encourage Māori arts[18] and "perpetuate the Māori culture".[19] The constitution and its goals matched the integration philosophies underpinning government policy on family, motherhood and being Māori.

Whina Cooper was tasked with establishing branches and district councils. The league grew quickly, so much so that by 1956 there were 300 branches, 88 district councils and 4000 members. The Māori Women's Welfare League became whānau for many women living in the city. Some of these women had no close relatives or elders nearby so those at the league became whānau, and they looked out for the needs of each other's families. Hine Poa of the Hutt Valley in

'Soccer success' at Ōtara, 1981. Māori were drawn to urban sports clubs to engage in physical activity. Sports teams also offered the opportunity to mix in a new pan-tribal, multi-cultural whānau environment.

Fairfax Media, Auckland Libraries Footprints 00413

Wellington said the league women of her area "became a backbone for each other … they became my brothers and sisters and carers … it's continued right through to our grandkids."[20]

In Ōtara there were seven registered branches, each allocated a zone under the influence of a president. When a new branch was formed, territory would be allocated to it, with boundaries set at local district council meetings.[21] Each of these league branches had a specific vision. Te Rongopai branch of the league was a collective of Māori mothers led by President (Mrs) Fue. Their focus was the promotion of the day-care centre to foster interaction with Pākehā.[22] Local fundraising events saw the formation of Te Rongopai Junior Welfare League to encourage youth membership. The East Tamaki Women's Welfare League was comprised of middle-aged women speakers of the reo but business was conducted in English. Members contributed to a "distress cupboard" where food was donated to be distributed to needy people in the community. Cartons of tinned goods from local businesses were added to the collection, which was open to anyone in the community: Māori, Pākehā or Pacific Islander. The president cited one needy case they visited where:

... the man was off work. The mother had only one tin of Milo, which she was feeding to the baby. She had one piece of dry bread, which she was saving for the children when they came back from school.[23]

There was a strong need to reach out. This branch also took an interest in helping to provide children of needy families with books and school uniforms.[24] Another branch of the league was the Ōtara West Māori Women's Welfare League, started in 1967.

Māori language in schools and culturally responsive hospital services were among the issues for which league members advocated. Whina Cooper was particularly pointed towards the poor housing conditions of Māori in Freemans Bay, Auckland. The league challenged the Department of Māori Affairs' housing programme and, after painstakingly walking the streets of Freemans Bay surveying Māori homes, it produced a report highlighting the extent of overcrowding that was prevalent among Māori. Whina organised the Waitematā councils to walk the streets and knock on doors. At one house she visited, a family of 16 was living in a four-room house with one leaky room. In one room there were 16 children playing on the bare boards.[25] Another hovel in Nelson Street consisted of six rooms housing 30 people. In another, a family consisting of a pregnant woman, her husband and five children lived in one room, had one bed between them and cooked on a Primus stove.[26] The league's overcrowding report and the atrocious slum conditions urban Māori were living in both surprised and placed pressure on the Department of Māori Affairs and the Housing Corporation to step up their housing initiatives.[27]

The Auckland City Council, Māori Affairs and the Housing Corporation made some amends, demolishing the slums of Freemans Bay and building new houses for Māori at a rate of 100 houses more per year. By the end of the decade "most Māori families in Auckland were adequately housed".[28] In Whina Cooper's annual report for 1957, she highlighted the widespread activities of the league in the areas of housing, rest homes, foster homes for welfare children, health, education, arts and crafts and the upgrading of marae facilities.[29]

The voluntary Māori Wardens emerged simultaneously with the Māori Women's Welfare League. Arising out of the provisions of the 1945 Act, operations were regulated by the Māori Welfare Act of 1962 (and changes in 1974). Following in the footsteps of past

The Māori Wardens volunteer services have a proud history of protecting and keeping Māori communities safe. Their role has broadened over the years to include interceding and liaising on issues of health and safety, education, youth assistance and whānau support in the wider community. These members are from the Waitematā Māori Wardens team. The team are with leaders Jack (centre back) and Evelyn Taumaunu (centre front) at a TelstraClear Centre event in Manukau City, Auckland.

Courtesy of Jack and Evelyn Taumaunu

moral law enforcers such as the Ringatū pirihimana, Rātana kātipa, and particularly the Kīngitanga waatene formulated by Te Puea, the warders were seen as "crucial components of their communities' fight against crime and disorder".[30] Wardens were nominated by tribal and later Māori committees to "enforce local law and order to keep people out of trouble".[31] Their work was primarily to assist Māori to adapt to city life, carrying out this work in a manner that reflected local community wishes. They promoted respect for law and order to prevent crime and defuse hostilities before the police arrived to a scene. Drunkenness and disorderly conduct were given special attention by the wardens, who carried out their duties in the spirit of manaaki (kindness), aroha (love) and rangimarie (peace).[32]

Mission organisations of the Anglican, Catholic, Presbyterian and Methodist churches, along with the traditional Rātana and Ringatū faiths, and new religious groups, formed to create a sense of kin and non-kin community, fostering youth clubs, culture groups and sports. Many churches recognised the plight of migrant Māori and established social services to assist integration. The Ōtara Māori Catholic Society believed the gathering of people and maintaining cultural integrity was central to the church. The Catholic Church's recognition of biculturalism provided a better way than "integration on Pākehā terms".[33] John Walters realised there were many Rātana followers in Ōtara but there was no minister. After his daytime job as a concrete factory worker, he was a Rātana minister. Rātana church services were run in private homes until the congregation had grown enough to hire the East Tamaki Hall. One hundred people, the majority being under 16 years of age, attended services regularly, but there were 500 followers in Ōtara at the time.[34]

In 1959 the Māori Evangelical Fellowship (MEF) was founded during a meeting in Avondale of like-minded Māori; they aimed to form churches that ministered to the spiritual needs of Māori by encouraging Māori leadership and full responsibility in the government of the church. Soon branches emerged in East, West, North and South Auckland.[35] The Ōtara branch began in 1965 with Pastor Te Rito, who became well respected for his welfare work in the area. He was eventually elected to the Māori Committee and later was the chair of the local marae steering committee.[36] Darlene Evans, whose father was a founding member of MEF, was happy that sports was a big part of church life for those Māori "who were naturally gifted in sports. The people of the various churches would gather to play rugby, netball, basketball, and table tennis which was huge amongst the people and we'd all meet on Labour Weekend."[37] These Auckland gatherings would see hundreds of Māori members co-operate in MEF church activities.[38] According to Ranginui Walker, the affiliation to the church outside of tribal areas served to "replace the kinship system of the rural marae".[39]

Communities of Māori involved in cultural performing arts played a pivotal role in gathering young and old people living in urban communities to maintain their reo, tikanga and culture, and to express their identity and whanaungatanga. Peta Awatere and Anne Tia ran the Aotearoa Folklore Society, with members from various clubs around Auckland, at a local primary school. In association with the Ōtara Māori Committee, the society's sessions tutored young people in action song, poi, haka, kawa o te marae, whaikōrero and arts and crafts. The aim was "to teach the young person to be a good

Māori, sure of his worth as a person and the richness of his own culture and traditions".[40] The society had to move out of the district, to the disappointment of the Ōtara Māori Committee chairman, who became convinced of the need for a marae in Ōtara.[41]

Many of these culture clubs were made up of pan-tribal members of the urban communities, with Pacific Island and Pākehā friends and families becoming members as well. The emergence of pan-tribalism as an ideology was a direct outcome of urbanisation and was further reiterated by culture clubs, which became crucial for the transmission of culture, instilling discipline and formality into the lives of young people and fundraising to build their local urban marae.

Te Rōpū Manutaki (who were eventually based at Hoani Waititi marae in West Auckland), Te Wero o te Whakapono (The Auckland Māori Anglican Club) at Tātai Hono marae, Ngāti Pōneke of Pipitea marae in central Wellington, and Māwai Hakona of Ōrongomai marae in Upper Hutt, were teams of pan-tribal Māori who performed concerts to fundraise for the building of their respective marae. These 'culture clubs' were fundamental to sustaining Māori cultural continuity in an urban world. Today, Māori performing arts is a key

Kapa haka teams were essential to the revitalisation of culture in Māori communities and fundraising for the building of marae. Te Roopu Manutaki are a prominent group on the competition circuit. They have played a pivotal role for maintenance of culture in West Auckland and fundraising for the building of Hoani Waititi marae. This image shows Te Roopu Manutaki as the winners of the 1971 Auckland District Māori Cultural Competitions.

Reproduced from *Te Whānau: A Celebration of Te Whānau o Waipareira*, 2001, courtesy of Te Whānau o Waipareira Trust

vehicle for the expression and maintenance of identity for both urban and rural Māori. Te Waka Huia performing arts club leaders Bub and Pimia Wehi established this rōpū in the 1980s, primarily to create a new form of a communal village for urban Māori youth and designed to maintain the members' "cultural identity in suburban Auckland".[42]

Melissa Williams tells of at least 13 Panguru families settled in Te Atatū, West Auckland. They engaged with a wider Māori community that rose dramatically from 125 to 766 people between 1956 and 1966. She records that this population consisted of pioneering Māori leadership and collective Māori activity, which assisted in the overall long-term community development of "Māori West Auckland".[43] It could be posited that urban pan-Māori creative foresight and vision birthed significant traditionally adapted innovations in politics, culture, education and health from the whānau Māori enclaves to the suburbs, the cities and throughout the nation.

Kuia Ereti Letty Brown, originally from Te Araroa and of Ngāti Porou and Te Whānau a Apanui, was encouraged by her parents to board a bus and leave home to further her education. Reluctantly, she caught a bus to Auckland at the age of 18 where she met with other family whom she didn't know very well. She was soon mixing with a collection of Māori social networks linked to work and to the Auckland Maori Community Centre.[44] Letty raised her family in West Auckland during the 1960s. She sought to gather people together to meet her vision to "raise a confident Māori family immersed in the cultural imperatives of her own tribal upbringing".[45] She played a pivotal role in establishing a weekly Māori session at a local play centre in a bid to attract Māori mothers to bring their children to preschool. However, she found Māori were too embarrassed or suspicious of Pākehā to bring their children to the play centre. Parents and staff of the play centre were shocked at her analysis of the situation, but after a lot of discussion, her sessions were established as one of the first of their kind. The session became known as the Waipareira Playcentre.[46] It eventually "snowballed with the support of Māori women to the establishment of a Māori language and arts programme; a branch of the Māori Women's Welfare League; the Māori culture group, Manutaki; a Māori committee; and the eventual establishment of Hoani Waititi marae in 1980".[47] In 2016 Letty received the first honorary doctorate of its kind from Unitec Institute of Technology for her work in early childcare. The doctorate was bestowed on her at Hoani Waititi marae, an urban marae that she and many other kaumātua and kuia were responsible for establishing and where her mokopuna were taught in their own reo and culture.⁴⁸

Hoani Waititi marae

The culmination of the rise of urban pan-Māori collectives like those with which Letty and others were involved saw the emergence of urban-based marae such as West Auckland's Hoani Waititi marae. This marae is probably the most well-known urban pan-tribal marae and houses kōhanga reo, kura kaupapa, wānanga and kaumātua units. It has been the home marae for generations of young urban Māori, their elders and parents seeking to establish a haven, a village or a kāinga to foster their language, culture and identity. It is well used by the urban Māori community it serves. The meeting house is Ngā Tūmanako and the marae is dedicated to the memory of Hoani Waititi, the Māori language educationalist and a strong advocate for urban Māori. Hoani was involved with the original Auckland Maori Community Centre. He passed away in 1965 at the age of 30. He was a catalyst for change.

The ceremonial welcome at the opening of Hoani Waititi marae, West Auckland, 1980.
Photographer unknown, 1980. Glen Eden Print Collection, GLEN-P-022, Auckland Libraries, West Auckland Research Centre, Waitakere Library

The enthusiasm of the local West Auckland Māori community was the driving force behind the establishment of Hoani Waititi marae. In the 1950s and 1960s, the West Auckland suburbs of Te Atatū, Rānui and Henderson were flooded with Māori, mostly from the north and some from Ngāti Porou. Community leader, academic and politician Dr Pita Sharples says, "Many were lost in the new urban culture. The change from the rural to an urban way of life was a huge culture shock."[49] The lack of a marae meant families held tangihanga in their homes, which many felt inappropriate. Pākehā neighbours would ring the police to break up 'the party next door' and conflicts would arise.[50]

The impetus for a marae in West Auckland arose from whānau Māori in the area who were involved in committees such as the Māori Welfare committee, the Māori Women's Welfare League, culture groups, the Māori Council Ground Committee, a Māori kindergarten and a Māori play centre. Some say the idea emerged as early as 1963.[51] The people tried to figure out ways to recreate a sense of identity and belonging in the city and suburban setting.[52] As Mavis Tuoro of West Auckland explains, the unification of these organisations was due to the "desire to continue our culture and tradition in the cities. We wanted to recreate whānau, hapū and iwi structures for our people in the city."[53]

According to Arapeta Awatere, a District Māori Welfare Officer in Auckland, the project was initially spearheaded by the Waipareira Māori Women's Welfare League, with fundraising originally planned by Mrs Mavis Tuoro, Mrs Tuini Hakaraia, Mrs Titewhai Harawira and Arapeta Awatere.[54] In 1967 the Western Districts Marae Campaign Committee was formed and people began to bake cakes, run bottle drives, hold dances, compete in walkathons and runathons, and organise housie and raffles to fundraise for a marae for the local Māori community. In 1968 Te Rōpū Manutaki Culture Club was created and aided the fundraising. While there was overwhelming excitement for the project, not all the people agreed with the idea; many still adhered to their own tribal marae 'back-home' as their associated place of identity, while others who were tribally orientated contributed to the fundraising and attended the opening, but never associated with the marae because they felt it wasn't theirs.

The original site for a marae was sought at Te Atatū Peninsula, but this did not eventuate. Another site, on Parrs Cross Road, was located.[55] When Letty Brown and Mavis Tuoro went to look at the eight acres of land proposed for the marae, their hearts sank at the state of the property. It was covered in rubbish, mud and trees. However, it was cleared by many periodic detention workers, who were led by Dennis Hansen. Pine Taiapa, the famous Ngāti Porou master carver, blessed the property. Many years later, Pine and his brother Hone were to work on the carvings for the marae.[56] Others, such as Don Rameka, were integral to the establishment and building of the marae. Don was also well known for spiritually cleansing the newly urbanised local lands of kēhua (ghosts) so they could be inhabited.

The wharekai, named Te Aroha, was built in 1976; the wharenui, named Ngā Tūmanako (the aspirations), and Hoani Waititi were opened in 1980, with 18,000 people attending the ceremony. The stance of the people in the region was to set aside any tribal affiliations to create a multi-tribal, pan-Māori unity among themselves. "Once it was built, I committed my entire life to this place," said Tuini Hākaraia. She believed the name 'Hoani Waititi' was appropriate for the marae because the purpose of the marae was to continue in his

Prime Minister David Lange with Pita Sharples and Sir Paul Reeves at the opening of the new classrooms for Te Kura o Hoani Waititi.
Hanly, Gil, 1934–, photographer, Auckland Museum, PH-2015-2-GH1099A-2

footsteps, educating children in the ways of the Pākehā and to teach Māori. Her hope was that the children would go home and influence their parents "who haven't got time to be Māori", she said. "Hoani Waititi has gone to the people through their children."⁵⁷

Under Pita Sharples' leadership, a kōhanga reo was established at the marae. With children from the kōhanga graduating to school level and the possibility of them losing their reo in the mainstream school system, in 1985 the local people responded by building the first Kura Kaupapa Māori at Hoani Waititi. In 1993, the secondary school Te Wharekura o Hoani Waititi was established.⁵⁸ Today the marae and the school complex hosts five kapa haka teams: Te Rōpū Manutaki, Te Rautahi, Ngā Tūmanako, Te Wharekura o Hoani Waititi, and Puawai — Te Kura o Hoani Waititi. The marae also offers a number of family social assistance initiatives, a drug rehabilitation programme, restorative justice hui, and a marae-based youth course.⁵⁹ Waitangi Day celebrations have become a huge local affair in association with Te Whānau o Waipareira.

Hoani Waititi marae was "the first urban marae built in Auckland on the non-tribal secular principle of an elective committee". That

Hoani Retimana Waititi (1926–65) was raised among his people at Whangapāraoa in the Eastern Bay of Plenty. He trained as a school teacher and became a prominent Māori language teacher, educator and cultural advocate, especially for urban Māori.
Courtesy of Ans Westra

same principle has been the impetus for the establishment of other West Auckland school marae such as Kākāriki (Green Bay High School), Kōtuku (Rutherford College), Pānuku marae (Henderson High School) and Mahanahana marae (Massey High School).

In aspiring to cater for the cultural and welfare needs of West Auckland Māori, Hoani Waititi marae and the social agency Te Whānau o Waipareira Trust (Waipareira Trust) became strongly linked. As one kaumātua said, "He mahi nā Te Whānau o Waipareira Trust, he mahi anō tā Hoani Waititi marae, ka whakapiri ēnei rōpū mō ngā wā ake tonu atu" (The work of The Family of Waipareira Trust and the activities of Hoani Waititi marae are inseparable for ever).[60] Hoani Waititi marae served to unify and provide a focus for Māori in West Auckland.[61]

The collectives of West Auckland as detailed in the Waitangi Tribumal report 414 were grass-roots community organisations of non-tribal associations formed, as one kaumātua stated, "to advance and promote tikanga Māori, te Reo, Business, Horticulture, Health, Education and other social needs in a holistic way".[62] Māori health manager and Waipareira trustee Naida Pou observed these Māori committees advocated for families in the courts voluntarily and initiated family group conferences in the mid-1970s well before they became formalised in law under the Children, Young Persons, and their Families Act 1989.[63] Urban pan-tribal organisations contributed greatly to initiatives that influenced social and health policy and Māori cultural development throughout New Zealand.

Hutana Whānau, Auckland

Brothers Steve and Greg Hutana of Henderson, Auckland, 2017.
Courtesy of Steve Hutana

Steve Hutana lives in Henderson, West Auckland, where he was born and raised. He has a young family and is a lecturer in architecture at Unitec Institute of Technology.

The Hutana whānau were early migrants to Auckland city. Steve's grandmother Teo Raiti Taumaunu of Whangarā, grandfather Rupena Hutana of Tokomaru Bay and their four children shifted to the city with a contingent of other East Coast families between 1935 and 1937. Their move was primarily to find better employment. Teo Raiti and Rupena changed their names to Joey and Reuben Newton (as an acknowledgement of Newton Road), perceiving that Pākehā names would garner them easier entry into accommodation and employment. Reuben soon found work on the roads, laying down the Papakura Highway extension.

Joey was a strong supporter of the Māori Women's Welfare League and later the Māori Wardens. A fluent Māori speaker, she used to tell her husband to "speak English" to her if he wanted to insult her. She was an avid traveller, often returning to the East Coast. As a member of the Country Women's Association she travelled the world on ocean cruises, where she would be given a platform to speak as an ambassador for Māoridom. She sold produce from her gardens to raise funds for her overseas journeys. Reuben loved his rugby, drank beer and worked hard.

Steve's father, Alwyne Hutana, was two years old when his parents decided to shift to Auckland. The third of four sons, Alwyne had not heard Māori spoken in his home in Auckland but he was sent to Te Aute Māori Boys College in the

Hawke's Bay. Alwyne was conscripted into compulsory military training, where he was stationed at South Head camp at Devonport. He later entered the workforce as a spray painter, where he became one of New Zealand's top workers in this profession. He eventually landed a position at the Nissan Datsun factory at Wiri, which lasted a few years. Nissan had a policy not to promote Māori. "It was plain discrimination," Steve proclaims. "Pākehā workers were promoted before my father, and many wouldn't take the position because they recognised Dad was the best. Dad eventually quit, but that racist attitude affected him, it seemed to follow him around."

Alwyne met Patricia, Steve's mum, at a party in Australia, from where both returned to New Zealand in 1968. Joey gave her home to Alwyne, where the couple lived for a while. Alwyne would frequent the Howick RSA to drink with local Māori and they all gravitated into a heavy drinking culture. "There were continuous long hours of drinking. It seems the pub became their marae," Steve says.

As far as Steve can remember, his father was drunk every day. In 1974 Alwyne sold the Howick home to buy a house in Glen Eden. He continued to work and drink hard. His routine was to catch a bus from Waikumete Cemetery to Wiri, where he worked with solvents all day, and drink six nights a week at the Westwood Hotel in Kelston. Life was tough for the kids — it was volatile. "Dad was a massive Lion Red drinker and Mum drank spirits. They drank three litres of alcohol a day, every day except Mondays. Mum was aggressive and our lives were not normal," Steve remembers.

Food was sparse. "We were poor. The fridge was full of Lion Red: some of the bottles had a teaspoon in them to stop it going flat. The bulk of our food was cabbage with scraps like kidneys, livers — hard livers — and vinegar to flavour it. Lunch was whatever fruit we could pinch from the trees on the way to school. Breakfast was Weetbix with tomato sauce. I was lucky as my neighbour friend Anaru never ever had a kai," Steve recounts. "I remember walking in to other people's homes to eat their ice cream from their freezer because I was hungry.

"I'd fight a lot at school so I was sent to a health camp for six weeks where there were a lot of other Māori and Pacific kids. It was good as this gave us a break from our abusive homes," Steve says. "I failed every subject at school."

Steve and his siblings had little if any Māori connection in their lives. Alwyne took the kids to the opening of Hoani Waititi marae, where Steve remembers his father knowing a lot of people. Steve marvelled at the 19 hangi that were laid out to feed the people who had come to the opening. Another time, when the march led by Whina Cooper came across the Auckland Harbour Bridge, Steve saw his father go berserk. "He didn't agree with the march because local elders had advised the people at a hui not to support the activists in the march. He was against it," Steve says.

In 1981 Alwyne's mother Joey, Steve's grandmother, died in Palmerston North. She was returned back-home to Tokomaru Bay to be buried. Three months later her husband Reuben Hutana remarried, to his childhood sweetheart, but died three months into the marriage. He gifted all his first wife's lands to the second wife, leaving Steve's father Alwyne no inheritance. Alwyne was heartbroken.

To add salt to the wound, Alwyne also lost his job. He was unemployed and on a benefit for the next three years; he couldn't get a job so he worked on PEP schemes. He eventually died in a paddock, of alcohol poisoning, on Lincoln Road, Henderson, aged 48. Alwyne's three siblings also died of alcohol-related diseases, all of them before the age of 60.

Steve and his two brothers and sister were compensated for the loss of their father's inheritance when their Uncle Jack Hutana left an inheritance to Steve and another cousin. Steve sold his share, compensated his siblings and purchased a home in West Auckland for his family. Today Steve owns two homes, one for his family and another for his mother.

The urban world was not kind to the Hutana family, but for Steve, who always had a hatred of the consequences of alcohol, he and his siblings have managed to survive against the odds. Steve is married to Kelly and together they have three children; he is also involved in faith-based ministries that have been a saving grace for him.

Trying to recover a connection to his Māoritanga and to his papakāinga roots in Tokomaru Bay has been extremely difficult, especially as Steve has had no one to accompany him home. "We lost the richness of who my grandmother was and her cultural values," Steve says. "Moving from the marae was detrimental to us, now being three generations of urban dwellers. When I went back to Tokomaru to try and connect, it was very hard; whānau in Auckland had lost the value of their own identity and couldn't see the point in making reconnection. The people didn't know who we were any more. Neverthless, the Hutana house was still standing on the beach — this helped to re-establish a link back-home for us." He adds, "Without my grandmother or any of the elders around now, there is nothing to connect us to the land, the marae, the people, to the atua and our Māoritanga. We have had to start all over again."

Chapter 6

Tau Whare

Laying Down Roots

The marae, which includes the land where the whare tipuna (ancestral meeting house) and the wharekai (dining hall) stand, is the focal point of Māori community life. Sir Apirana Ngata, the father of the modern-day cultural renaissance, believed the meeting house was the essential symbol of Māori identity.[1] The marae is intimately linked to the local tribal landscape and to its people. It is the very essence of the people's "genealogical identity to the surrounding lands".[2] Sir James Henare of Te Tai Tokerau made the telling statement, "Te iwi marae kore, ehara, te marae iwi kore, he moumou" (a people without a marae are nothing and a marae without people is a waste).[3] Paul Tapsell writes, "The house genealogically reinforces the prestige of the *tangata whenua* (home people — descendants of specific ancestral lands) and leaves the *manuhiri* (non-kin group visitors) in no doubt as to who is in charge at all times, within the *marae* space."[4]

The marae is the place where the tribal community meets to talk, and perform weddings, tangihanga, church, community activities, and ceremonial events that are usual for any Māori community. Hospitality is a central ingredient in the complex interactions between groups and individuals on the marae; the marae is the place where those who are part of that community can express the fullness of Māori hospitality.

A lack of marae in the city meant that migrants had been unable to live in a Māori way. According to one review, in 1971 there were only six marae in Auckland to cater for the needs of 44,300 Māori, a huge contrast to 70 marae available for 8000 people on the East Coast.[5] The overcrowding and limited access had an impact on the people's association to marae. With work schedules taking priority and 70% of the Māori population aged under 25, visits and active involvement in marae was low. However, this did not deter Māori from carrying out the same rural processes of birth, death and marriage, and adapting to their city environments. State houses were turned into 'little marae' for tangihanga, where rooms were cleared for the tūpāpaku to lie inside. Customary hospitality was provided by temporary outdoor cooking facilities.[6] For some the dignity of the tangihanga was lost because it was not held on a marae. Further to this, overcrowding became a local authority health issue.[7]

Attendees at the 1939 Young Māori Leaders Conference acknowledged the future urbanisation of their people. Showing foresight, they recommended the establishment of urban marae.[8] In due course 'urban marae' were designed and built throughout New Zealand in the main city centres, aiming to cater for the cultural needs of Māori immigrants and to maintain their cultural identity, but mostly without whakapapa links to the land. In establishing urban marae, city Māori managed to "reconcile their new urban environment with the [cultural] attachments of their past, with neither being to the exclusion of the other".[9]

Dr Ranginui Walker envisaged the urban marae to be the most "powerful cultural statement the Māori has made in modern times".[10] He described the urban marae as the place where "the ultimate conjunction" of Māori and Pākehā occurred.[11] In 1982 he also commented on the resistance of Pākehā to the building of urban marae. The grounds of some of the objections appeared to be based on ignorance.[12] Some assumed the marae would attract undesirables, become 'booze barns', create a road hazard, or bring gangs into the area. These attitudes were nothing but "alarmist in the extreme", Dr Walker wrote.[13] He described the purpose and workings of the marae and the responsibilities of the marae committees:

> … marae are places of refuge for our people and provide facilities to enable us to continue with our own way of life within the total structure of our own terms and values. We need our marae for a host of reasons,

that we may rise tall in oratory,
that we may weep for our dead,
that we may pray to our God,
that we may have our feasts,
that we may house our guests,
that we may have our meetings,
that we may have our weddings,
that we may have our reunions,
that we may sing,
that we may dance,
and that we may learn our history
and then know the richness of life
and the proud heritage which is only ours.[14]

Cultural spaces

As discussed in chapter 3, many first-generation elders who had shifted to the cities with their families were not prepared to purchase a house or to sanction the building of a marae in a city location. It was commonly felt purchasing a house or building a marae in the city meant putting down roots, and burying their dead on foreign soil. They thought, "we're not staying here because we're not from here, we will go back home after a time." This was a common strategy for not losing connection to the lands back home.[15]

Nevertheless, Māori who stayed in the city wanted cultural spaces specific to their needs. Communal halls in the city centre served the needs of 'quasi-tribes' such as Ngāti Pōneke in Wellington and Ngāti Akarana in Auckland. However, these were only temporary solutions.[16] Perhaps the most famous of these communal gathering places, to become a strong impetus for the concept of the 'urban marae', was the hugely popular Auckland Maori Community Centre. The centre quickly became the face of Māori in Auckland. The old army barracks next to Victoria Park on Fanshawe Street in Freemans Bay were converted and became the Auckland Maori Community Centre. The centre opened in June 1949 as a pan-tribal Māori social and cultural centre. Puti Tipene Watene advocated this kind of centre. The former New Zealand Rugby League team captain arranged housing for Māori in the city, and helped establish the community centre in 1948. Northern Māori MP Tapihana Paraire Paikea and Prime Minister Peter Fraser opened the centre.

Mayor John Allum attended the opening and declared the centre to be a place where Māori should be encouraged to "develop along the lines of their own culture and traditions and to accept their share of responsibility".[17]

The centre hosted a mix of informal and formal events, such as dances, hui and tangi (funerals). It was run by a trust, made up of representatives from the Māori Women's Welfare League, the Waitematā Tribal Committee, the Department of Māori Affairs, Rotary and the RSA, who wanted the centre to be a place for the young people "to relax and enjoy each other's company".[18]

The Waitematā Tribal Executive was a pan-tribal body, which included members of the Onehunga, Ihumatao and Māngere tribal committee that acted on behalf of migrant Māori and tangata whenua on the Auckland isthmus.[19] Kaumātua of the calibre of Eruera and Amiria Stirling of Te Tairawhiti, Anne Tia (a devout Rātana), and Tūmanako Reweti of Ngāti Whātua were strong advocates of ensuring urban Māori would not forget their connections, their

Dancing at the Auckland Māori Community Centre, 1962.
O.039605 Te Papa Museum, Ans Westra

identity or the maintenance of their reo and tikanga. A carving and tukutuku school was run and Māori culture and history was kept alive at the centre.[20] The centre also housed a performing culture club, and it quickly became the place to meet. It was the "face of Auckland Māori"[21] and became "the most tangible symbol of Māori belonging in Auckland".[22]

For entertainer Wi Wharekura, an original member of the Howard Morrison Quartet, the centre was a home away from home, a place where Māori from all over New Zealand but now living in Auckland "could hang out and just have a good time being Māori".[23] "There were football events at Victoria Park with strong Māori players and after the games they'd cross the road to the centre for a big Māori kai. People like the famous Waka Nathan and Mac Herewini came out of teams based around the centre," he says.

On Friday night all communities were welcome and those evenings were set aside for special events. Saturdays were reserved for private functions, but Sundays were for the young people, where after 1 p.m. they could let their hair down. These were afternoons for table tennis, indoor bowls, and drop-ins by football and basketball players. By 5 p.m. everyone was looking forward to the pork bones and watercress coming out of the kitchen. "Every brown person in Auckland knew when this kai was on the table," Wi remembers fondly. There were performances by Māori clubs such as Maranga (run by Arapeta Awatere) and Rangimarie (the Catholic Māori Culture group), and entertainers from throughout the Māori world.

Twice-yearly talent quests were staged, where aspiring Māori entertainers stood to show off their talent and make a name for themselves. Howard Morrison, Kiri Te Kanawa and the Māori Hi Fives played at the centre.[24] Anzac Te Oka, Dusky Nepia and the Playdates with Danny and Paul Robinson, Toko Pompey, Ike Metekingi, Ray Paparoa, Kahu Pineaha, Pumi Taituha, Robbie Ratana, Ben Tawhiti, the Te Kiwis, the Cook whānau from which Marsh Cook became an original member of the Quin Tikis, and Weasel Taiaroa, all emerged on the performing stage at the centre. The centre was the starting place for many soon-to-be-famous Māori entertainers.[26] "Entrepreneurs would walk in to the centre and just take their pick," Wi says.[27]

The centre had strict rules that didn't include rock 'n' roll. As a result, when this genre of music became popular the centre lost much of its patronage to other clubs. When the centre relaxed its formalwear and music rules, the young people returned and the house was full again within three months.²⁸

It was a gathering place for whānau coming from different parts of New Zealand. It was also a crucial space where Māori, Pacific and Pākehā relationships were fostered, resulting in many elopements and marriages.

On the occasion of the death of educationalist Hoani Retimana Waititi in 1965, special permission was sought from the city council so he could lie in state there.²⁹ Thousands of mourners came to show their respect for Hoani, who had passed away at the young age of 39. Due to restrictions on the use of the centre for ceremony and tangihanga, this produced heated discussions between tribal Māori on the trust board. It was common for community halls and private homes to be used because of the lack of marae, but these premises were inadequate for tangihanga. House doors, steps and windows were removed and sometimes the caskets were turned sideways to fit the tūpāpaku inside to accommodate for the needs of a whānau in mourning.³⁰

This was an indication that "Auckland Māori needed a marae to which they all belonged".³¹ The Akarana Marae Society, chaired by Eruera Stirling and based at the centre, sought to build a marae on six acres of land purchased by Maharaia Winiata and others in New Lynn. Carved poupou were created and funds were raised to maintain the land, but the New Lynn Council had designated the land as industrial and refused to sanction the project.³² It was decided to offer the carvings for a new marae being built at Māngere. King Koroki sent his people to collect the carvings and they were installed into Te Puea house at Māngere.³³

Weaving a tukutuku panel for Ngāti Ōtara Marae, 1981.
Fairfax Media, Auckland Libraries, Footprints 00402

Marae development advances

Urban marae emerged out of the agitation of Māori communities to find a space to stand. Sir Hugh Kawharu wrote about how the Auckland Maori Community Centre gave young Māori a place for amusement but thwarted "any effort at self-expression in a truly Māori way" and lacked the sanctity of a marae.[34] While a marae and the carved meeting house would serve traditional Māori cultural needs, the function of urban marae would have to reflect the desires of the newly formed urban organisations.[35] As a result a number of new forms of marae eventuated. These marae take the form of the taura here (binding rope) urban kinship-based marae, the secular pan-Māori/pan-tribal marae, church-based marae, and the multi-cultural marae. It can be argued that marae-a-kura (secondary school marae) and the tertiary institute marae need to be included in this category as well.

Marae facilities were built by tangata whenua who were engulfed by the urban sprawl. Te Puea marae at Māngere, which became prominent in 2016 for its open door policy to Auckland's homeless, was foreseen as early as 1933 with a gift of one acre of land by Mrs Te Paea Rewha.[36] King Koroki donated £4000 to the building fund and the Onehunga, Māngere, Ihumatao, and Waitematā Māori committees joined to spearhead fundraising for the project.[37] The marae opened in 1965, before a crowd of 4000 people,[38] and was at the time the only traditional kinship-based marae (Waikato) with an open door to all migrant tribes based in Auckland.[39]

Similarly, the taura here (binding ropes) groups are tribal members in the city who maintain tribal links to their iwi homelands through an intermediary organisation. Auckland is where the largest population of Ngāpuhi tribal members and their whānau reside, outside of their tribal territory. One report estimates Ngāpuhi tribal numbers of 20,000 live in Manukau City and 10,000 reside in Waitakere.[40] Te Taura Here ki Manurewa and Te Taura Here o Ngā Puhi ki Waitakere are two urban taura here or takiwā groups of Ngāpuhi members who relate back to their iwi organisation in Te Tai Tokerau. Piringatahi marae at Westhaven is a Ngāpuhi taura here marae. The Tūhoe tribe based at Te Tira Hou marae in Panmure, and the Ngāti Awa people of Mataatua marae in Māngere are also taura here groups that claim strong association to their respective tribes.

Communities in the city suburbs and housing estates initiated pan-tribal marae. This was the origin of the secular non-tribal-specific marae, commonly termed 'Ngā Hau e Whā' (Four Winds: multi-tribal) marae that embraced many tribal members and often, other ethnicities.

Hoani Waititi marae in West Auckland is probably the most widely known marae of this type, while Ngāti Pōneke, Maraeroa and Ōrongomai represent this form in the Wellington region.

Ngā Hau e Whā National Marae in Christchurch was originally envisioned by the people who formed the 'National Marae Association of Ōtautahi' after World War II.[41] The administrative body was first incorporated as a 'national' marae in 1961. An action group led by Rongo Nihoniho sought land and compliance to build a 'national' marae, which stirred up mass opposition.[42] Ngāi Tahu were initially unaccepting of the project. The local Aranui community were also opposed and lodged nearly 180 complaints to the then Christchurch City Council.[43] Despite the difficulties, the marae was opened by Koro Wetere in May of 1990 as Ngā Hau e Whā National Marae. It had a unique focus in that it was dedicated to embracing all Māori and all ethnicities of the world. Local youth that were unemployed, homeless, addicts or glue-sniffers were gathered on the site and nurtured by elders to help create the artwork for the whare. Named Aoraki, the whare was considered the biggest house of its kind in New Zealand.[44] In 2004 the marae was eventually placed under the guardianship-management of Te Rūnanga o Ngā Matā Waka Urban Māori Authority for Te Wai Pounamu.[45]

Other similar mātāwaka marae were established within rural tribal areas where many Māori from other tribal regions travelled to work at the freezing works, railways, seasonal work or shearing. Te Aranga marae at Flaxmere near Hastings, Pukemokimoki marae in Napier and the Waipukurau Community marae all stand in a Ngāti Kahungunu-dominated landscape representing all iwi and whānau.[46] Kirikiriroa marae in Hamilton was borne out of the efforts of an urban Māori group, Ngāti Hamutana (the people of Hamilton). The marae opened in 1984 under the sanction of Te Ariki Dame Atairangikaahu and the Kīngitanga. A marae-based urban rūnanga was established in 1988 under the name Te Rūnanga o Kirikiriroa. It has become the recognised voice of urban Māori living in Hamilton.[47]

Other urban marae were built by church organisations to care for the needs of the pan-tribal Māori congregations. Māori religious groups created their own Māori sectors in the city, based primarily on Te Whakapono faith as the central basis of kinship. This applied to Anglican, Catholic, Presbyterian, Brethren or Latter Day Saints. The entry of Pā Henare Tate of Motuti into the Catholic priesthood in 1962 triggered a massive fundraising drive that mobilised whānau from the Hokianga region and Auckland city central. Funds raised for the ordination spilled into the construction of Te Unga Waka at Epsom in 1966.[48] This was a centre for Catholic Māori but was viewed by affiliated Māori as their Auckland marae.[49]

The Māori Catholic Societies built their own centre, Te Whaiora marae at Ōtara, which was used from 1973 but opened fully in 1977, and the success of this centre is testament to the success of this form of marae.[50] Similarly, the Anglican Māori Mission on Khyber Pass in Auckland was established under the Auckland Māori Mission in 1967 due to a dwindling Pākehā congregation and the burden of maintaining the 1884 church. Sir Kingi Ihaka became the first Auckland Māori Missioner, creating a two-pronged approach to the premises — worship in the church and the work of cultural restoration through cultural events in the hall, which eventually became the wharenui named Tātai Hono.[51]

Some urban Māori communities also considered multi-cultural or multi-racial marae to include other immigrant ethnicities living in close proximity. Māori in Ōtara attempted to create a multi-racial marae. Ranginui Walker studied this kaupapa and commented that a "marae is a Māori institution, [so] a multiracial marae is a contradiction in terms".[52] After intense discussion it was decided to abandon the concept because of the lack of support from the local Māori people — a mere 30 out of 6000 people supported the idea.[53] Eventually, a newly formed committee pushed to build a Māori marae.

In more recent times marae have been established at secondary schools and tertiary institutes, primarily to recognise the place of Māoritanga in New Zealand.[54] The first of these secondary school marae, which arose from the desire of local Māori teachers, was Kākāriki, opened in 1978 at Green Bay High School in West Auckland. It was followed closely by Kōtuku marae at Rutherford High School, Paunuku marae at Henderson High School and Mahanahana marae at Massey High School. All of these marae are in close proximity to one another. The first tertiary college marae was Te Kupenga o te Mātauranga meeting house, which was opened in September of 1980 on the Palmerston North Teachers' College campus. Tānia Ka'ai recalls the concerted drive by Māori teacher-educators from

Governor-General Sir Bernard Fergusson with Mr Pei Te Hurinui Jones and Lady Fergusson at the opening of Te Puea Memorial Marae, Mangere, 13 November 1965.

Fairfax Media, Auckland Libraries, Footprints 02755

the mid-1970s to establish marae to enable teaching based on Māori pedagogy.[55]

Te Tumu Herenga Waka marae at Victoria University was the first university marae, opened in 1986. Today, there are more than 100 marae-a-kura (mainstream secondary school marae), and the five North Island universities have marae. Otago University does not have a marae due to a restriction put in place by the South Island tribal executive Te Runanga o Ngāi Tahu, who are opposed to educational institutional marae.[56] The current Te Tumu complex at Otago University operates as a functioning marae where the transmission of indigenous knowledge occurs but powhiri, karanga and tangihanga are prohibited.[57] Te Kōpū Mānia o Kirikiriroa at Waikato Institute of Technology in Hamilton and Te Noho Kōtahitanga at Unitec Institute of Technology in Auckland stand as other examples of tertiary campus marae and wharenui that are utilised as places of learning and promotion of reo and tikanga.

More recently, marae settings have also appeared within commercial organisations such as Television New Zealand. Here, the Māori Programmes Department, under Ernie Leonard, set aside a space named Te Rau Aroha as a marae to cater for hui, manaakitanga, and Māori tikanga. Before returning Ernie Leonard's tūpāpaku back to Awahou in Rotorua for his tangi, his body lay at Te Rau Aroha for a day. In 2005 there were 31 urban marae operating in Auckland alone, including church-based and education institution were affiliated marae.⁵⁸ In 2009, nationwide there was an estimated 1300 marae in urban, iwi and institutional settings.⁵⁹

The invasion of pan-tribal Māori and the rise of urban marae have been cause for tension with local tangata whenua, who claim tribal authority of the city landscape. The building of non-tribal marae within a specific kin group's tribal territory is a new experience. Ngāti Whātua of Auckland and Ngāi Tahu of Christchurch, as the tangata whenua of their respective regions, were exposed to this new urban innovation in their territories. In Auckland, the immigrant Māori population far outnumbered tangata whenua. In 1968, Ian Hugh Kawharu estimated 30,000 Māori migrants living in greater Auckland, while only 250 tangata whenua of Ngāti Whātua o Orakei were residing on the hill surrounding Ōkahu Bay.⁶⁰

For Ngāti Whātua, after the continual loss of 'inalienable' lands to the Crown since 1869, the last ten acres of their land was taken in 1950, enforced by the Public Works Act. The papakāinga and marae named Te Puru o Tāmaki were demolished. The people were subsequently relocated to the suburb of Ōrākei as tenants in rented houses.⁶¹ This effectively erased Ngāti Whātua from their ancestral landscape, except for a quarter of an acre that included a cemetery and chapel. The loss prevented Ngāti Whātua from asserting their tangata whenua status over wider Auckland, leaving a Crown-induced vacuum of tangata whenua.⁶² Immigrant Māori were flooding into the city and the mana whenua were subjugated.⁶³ In later years it would be that very urban migration that "reinforced among the people of Ngāti Whātua their tribal identity and customary tangata whenua rights".⁶⁴

Children from Favona Primary School take a break during a live-in at Te Puea Memorial Marae, Mangere.
Fairfax Media, Auckland Libraries, Footprints 00291

In 1991, tribal mana was restored by legislation, and with the redevelopment of Tumutumuwhenua marae. But by then, tens of thousands of non-kin Māori migrants to Auckland had created new places of identity for themselves. The census for 1991 recorded the Ngāti Whātua population as just over 9300, while Auckland's Māori population was more than 25,000.[65] According to Paul Tapsell, both Te Unga Waka and Hoani Waititi marae came to prominence in Auckland when there was a lack of a formal Ngāti Whātua presence.[66]

Similarly, but under different circumstances, in 1960 the pan-tribal Rehua marae was initiated as a recreation hall for North Island Māori trade trainees boarding at an inner city Christchurch hostel. The idea seemed to encroach on the mana of the Ngāi Tahu tribe's 97-year-old vision to have their own marae in the city. While Ngāi Tahu supported the concept, not everyone agreed with its premise.[67] With the closure of the Māori Affairs trade-training courses in 1981, Ngāi Tahu have retained the mana whenua over Rehua marae and the hostel up to the present day.

Despite these inter-tribal tensions, the convergence of urbanisation and the strong desire for the continuation of Māori culture and ways of life forced the innovation of urban marae as a provision for a new Māori identity built primarily on a new paradigm — a non-kin-based, pan-tribal sense of community.

Anaru Roberts, Auckland

Anaru Roberts standing in front of the family home at Kay Road, Panmure, where his grandparents first moved to in 1947 and where he spent his childhood.
Courtesy of Bradford Haami

Anaru Roberts lives in West Auckland and is employed by the District Health Board as a cultural liaison officer at Greenlane Hospital. His whānau have lived in Tāmaki-makaurau, where Anaru was born, for over 70 years. He recounts how his grandparents, Te Huhu Rota Kōpua (Peter) of Ariuru and Whakaara Irihapeti Te Rure (Ara) of Waiparapara, left Tokomaru Bay on the East Coast to find work and settle permanently in Auckland in the 1940s. His grandfather came to Auckland first and after a year, sent for the family. They found lodgings on Airedale Street, in the central city. The Salvation Army were a great support to the whānau, showing them a generosity that has never been forgotten.

Peter and Ara eventually shifted into a new two-storey state house at number 8 Kay Road, Panmure, around 1947. The house remained their family home for the next 44 years. Some of the houses in the street belonged to Māori families, but most were owned by Pākehā. Two doors down from the Kōpua home was the Roberts/Rapata whānau of Ngāpuhi, who had been living there for about a year. Another of Anaru's uncles lived in the house between the two families.

Anaru's father, Hohaia Rapata (Joe), fell in love with Yvonne Raiha Kōpua and jumped the fence to number 8. They had four children, including Anaru. Each grandmother on Kay Road claimed two children. These children were raised intermittently with their respective kuia, two doors apart from each other, while the parents went to work. Joe was a foreman at a plastics factory and Yvonne worked in administration for Air New Zealand.

"I remember every day we'd go to school, where I'd meet my siblings out on the street and we'd compare last night's dinner and our school lunches," Anaru says with a grin. "Our two grandmothers' worlds were different. My grandmother Ara [Ngāti Porou] had silverware and tablecloths on the table and my [Ngāpuhi] grandmother had newspaper and plain knives and forks on the table. We loved them both."

The families in the street, and particularly the women, worked for the Alex Harvey Industries in Mt Wellington and the men appear to have had employment spread throughout the city. Anaru's grandfather worked for a company in Penrose that laid down tarseal for new roads and highways. It was common for the men to wear rags around their nose and mouth as a safeguard from the fumes while mixing and laying miles of tarseal. "This is what the family believe killed him in the end — he wasn't a smoker and he died of lung cancer," Anaru says.

"We were a simple working-class family. We didn't have any academic qualifications or any luxuries, although we were the first family to purchase a black-and-white television in our street," Anaru recalls. "I remember the cousins back-home regarded us as wealthy city folk. We didn't really have much, but we didn't lack for anything either."

Life on the East Coast was considered tough. Anaru remembers the old bach at Tokomaru Bay, named Kiore Whatenga, as where his grandmother Ara once lived with 12 other people, including Tuini Ngawai. On return trips back-home, whoever arrived first had to dig a new long drop. By comparison, Auckland homes were very comfortable. Number 8 Kay Road became the 'go to' house for Tokomaru-ites visiting Auckland. "If you were from Tokomaru Bay, no one was ever turned away. It was always a big deal for whanaunga coming to the city," he says.

Ara was a fervent Māori Women's Welfare League supporter and rallied to the meetings at the local Panmure community hall (which eventually became the Tūhoe marae Te Tira Hou). The whānau were strong supporters of Ruapotaka marae in Glen Innes. On the weekends, whānau would go to the Auckland Maori Community Centre for the 'culture groups' (kapa haka).

Ara and her daughter Puau Te Moananui-a-Kiwa loved to sing. Ara was related to Tuini Ngawai and Ngoi Pewhairangi, the two most famous female composers from the East Coast whose songs were popular during and after the war years. It is no surprise to find Ara and her daughter Puau as original performers in Tuini's famous Te Hokowhitu-a-Tū culture team from Tokomaru Bay, which assisted Tā Apirana Ngata in his recruiting efforts for men to join the 28th Māori Battalion. In Auckland, Ara and Puau joined the New Zealand Māori Theatre Trust Chorus led by Inia Te Wiata, with Peter and Isobel Cowan, Joshua Gardiner and Robin Ruakere as the backing group.

"Māori language was spoken by both my grandmothers continuously, but specifically to us kids when we were being disciplined. My paternal grandmother gave me lessons in the reo for practical things," Anaru remembers. His Aunt Puau became well known and loved by the urban families in the district, so much so that the community dedicated the first Kura Kaupapa Māori in the region to Anaru's aunt and named it Te Kura Kaupapa Māori o Puau Te Moananui-a-Kiwa.

Ara and Peter returned home to the East Coast often to attend tangi, and there was always a three-week holiday over the Christmas period to maintain the bonds to home. When Ara and Peter passed away, busloads of people arrived at Kay Road to accompany their tūpāpaku to the East Coast to their final resting places. "All the elders that passed away on this street were returned to their own papakāinga urupa," Anaru says.

Anaru was sent to St Stephens Māori Boys College in South Auckland to instil something of his culture into his life. "I was shy to be Māori. I was raised to be pro-European. I went to St Stephens from year nine to learn something of being Māori," he says. "Most of those boys from that school are quite prominent men in the Māori world. Coming from the city, I was influenced by all these guys."

"At age 20 I went to Australia with my Aunt Puau to help establish a marae in Sydney with Wi Huata. Aunt Puau had made relationships with this community while travelling with the Māori Theatre Trust." Anaru decided to stay in Sydney. He had no intentions of returning to New Zealand. At the Bondi Hotel he met Huria Robens from Wairarapa and, after living in Bondi for three years, the couple travelled through Europe and settled in London, where Huria fell pregnant. She insisted all of their children must be born in New Zealand and attend kōhanga reo. At first Anaru disagreed with Huria's view; he was resistant and didn't see the value of Māori culture.

The couple returned to Kay Road for a while. They soon shifted to Masterton where their children Irihapeti, Te Korou and Puau were raised in total immersion kōhanga and kura. Anaru and Huria attended Victoria University Māori Studies to rejuvenate the reo and tikanga within their own lives. In 2006 the family returned to Auckland for employment, but also to send their children to Hoani Waititi Kura Kaupapa.

Anaru has come full circle and now works as a cultural advisor to advocate for cultural awareness when dealing with Māori patients. "I think the majority of Māori I work with have lost their identity because of their poverty. I don't see too many urban Māori who are successful. Life is all about what they can afford, which isn't much," he says.

In contrast to what he sees in his daily work, Anaru is satisfied with the decisions he and Huria have made to instil a strong cultural commitment in their children so they can move easily in both the Māori and the urban worlds. Irihapeti, their eldest daughter, says: "Knowing our Māori identity has given us a great foundation to maintain who we are and to take hold of what the world has to offer us." Irihapeti is an itinerant contractor for Māori organisations and in 2017 she was involved in campaign management for The Māori Party. Te Korou teaches Māori language at Hoani Waititi Kura and for Te Wānanga o Aotearoa's Pīnakitanga ki te Reo Kairangi programme. Anaru and Huria's youngest daughter Puau is currently a qualified chef at a restaurant in West Auckland, and seeks to advance her career overseas.

Chapter 7 | **Whakatū Marae**

The Urban Marae

This chapter profiles the stories and circumstances of some of the urban marae in New Zealand (marae hou, or new marae). Their stories reveal the strong urgency Māori felt to maintain some "cultural continuity" in a foreign space and "in the face of dominating Pākehā in New Zealand".[1] The story of Hoani Waititi marae in West Auckland has already been told in chapter 5.

Rehua marae (1960), Christchurch

Rehua marae in Christchurch in the South Island is most likely the first urban marae built in New Zealand. The concept of Rehua marae emerged out of the need to build a recreation hall for the Māori trade trainees living on site at Rehua Hostel, Springfield Road, in 1958. The site was originally a puna (water gathering area) for the inhabitants of Puari Pā located in the city, hence the name Springfield.[2] The hostel, originally opened in April 1957, was named Rehua by Henare Jacobs after one of the higher levels of the Māori heavens.[3] Rehua had been the name for the hostel on Stanmore Road and was carried over to the new site.

The notion of a recreation hall soon morphed into a wish for a meeting house designed to "keep the boys in touch with art and culture of their race, but will also serve as an admirable centre for

Christian work among the Māoris of the South Island".[4] Reverend Falkingham, the boys' supervisor, felt they needed a hall that should have a Māori carving inside, but some of the local Ngāi Tahu women, namely Matt Carroll (nee Rehu), Hiria Rennie (of Ratana Pā), Mata Newson (nee Tirikatene) and others, spurned the idea of having one token carving in the building — they said, "Do it right".[5]

The planning of a carved house began in 1958. Ngāi Tahu elders were invited by the Christchurch Central Mission Board of Management to co-operate in "safeguarding the sacred traditions associated with such a building".[6] In the early years Rehua was supported by Wellington-based Māori welfare officers and was embraced by local Canterbury kaumātua Jo Karetai, Whetu Pitama and Riki Ellison. The Ngāi Tahu Trust Board supported the Mission in the building and the opening of the new meeting house, approving a grant to Wera Couch, who represented the group.[7]

The Ngāi Tahu elders who sat as an advisory to this kaupapa were Wera Couch, Eruera Tirikatene, Riki Ellison, Jo Karetai, Jim Manahi, Waha Stirling, Rua Rakena and the only female on a Māori council then, Tokomaru Ryan.[8] However, while Ngāi Tahu saw this as a positive move for the city, they did not perceive the building would be an "official marae" or a "Ngāi Tahu space".[9] Since 1857 Ngāi Tahu had desired that their own house be erected on their own space in Christchurch. It has been an ongoing negotiation with provincial governments and councils that has never been realised.[10] The emergence of a multi-iwi marae on the doorstep of Ngāi Tahu was not a dream that all Ngāi Tahu supported.[11]

At a meeting at Rāpaki in 1959 it was agreed that Rehua should be a pan-tribal house that would incorporate the whakapapa of all the boys who lived on the premises. The marae was built with voluntary labour. The hostel boys laid the foundations and local businesses donated materials. The tōtara logs for the carved poupou and epa came from Okains Bay farmer Murray Thacker, and one log was donated from the East Coast of the North Island.

Out of Wera Couch's connection to Te Waiata Choir, a travelling Māori choir that performed during the war years, came an acceptance by fellow performer and master carver Henare Paikea Toka to be master carver on the project. Master wharenui builder Pine Taiapa also became involved, while the tukutuku work was crafted by women from Rāpaki, Taumutu, Wairewa and Ōtautahi. Moke Couch and Henry Stewart were in charge of the kowhaiwhai patterns, which were painted by the hostel boys. The boys felt a South Island pattern needed to be included and the elders sanctioned the use of a stylised kiwi-embryo pattern that originated from a painted rock at Shepherds Creek on the Waitaki River.[12]

The tapu of the completed house was lifted in 1960 by the Waikato people, led by Princess Piki. Because the initial idea for the hostel originated from a visit to the Waikato with Te Puea, it was only fitting Waikato should officiate the tapu-lifting ceremony.[13] The house was named Te Whatu Manawa Māoritanga o Rehua. Later that day Prime Minister Walter Nash opened the house, accompanied by other officials including Sir Eruera Tirikatene.[14] There were 5000 people who attended the opening. Te Whatu Manawa Māoritanga o Rehua was the first house said to represent all tribes in New Zealand, and to be built on land designated as Pākehā land for general purposes.[15]

In 1977 a wharekai was built alongside Rehua and named after the Ngāi Tahu ancestress Hemo-ki-te-Raki. The next year, title to the property was transferred to Rehua Marae Trust Board under Ngāi Tahu control.[16] Today the complex functions as a marae with an attached health and social agency and a modernised trade-skill programme known as He Toki Ki Te Rika.

Mataatua marae (1978), Māngere, Auckland

The urban Ngāti Awa marae named Mataatua is situated in the centre of Māngere township, Auckland. The buildings, a wharenui and a wharekai, were opened in 1978,[17] with a kōhanga reo added later.

The origins of this marae stemmed from the 1950s, when a group of predominantly Ngāti Awa Māori created a rugby club in Ponsonby. The Mataatua Society was formed as a place where Ngāti Awa people could meet and socialise among themselves and with people from other tribes.[18] 'Go to' homes such as that of Bob and Emma Mate in Murdoch Road in Grey Lynn was where Whakatāne people gathered when in the city.[19] However, under the heavy burden of hosting visiting sports teams and whānau, it was decided to begin fundraising to build a marae. Tuhoe had opened Te Honoa-a-te-Kiore house at Te Tira Hou marae in Panmure in 1973. Ngāti Awa felt it pertinent to build a house to cater for the influx of other Mataatua people into the city.[20]

Stanley Pio Keepa of Ngāti Awa was a real estate agent living in Howick. He was the leader of the fundraising committee for the

Mataatua Marae in Mangere was built to cater for the needs of Ngāti Awa people from the Bay of Plenty region living in Auckland.

Fairfax Media, Auckland Libraries, Footprints 00290

Mataatua Society, and helped secure land and finance for the project. The local council offered land for the marae and the Department of Māori Affairs offered the Mataatua Society a deal for the construction of the buildings: for every two dollars the society raised the Department would contribute a dollar.[21] The piece of land at 17 Killington Crescent in Māngere was within Tainui tribal territory and permission was sought from Te Arikinui Dame Te Atairangikaahu to build a marae there. Permission was granted and the funds were raised in a very short time due to a loan offered by Pio Keepa.[22]

The Mataatua marae founding members held meetings with Te Rūnanga o Ngāti Awa from Whakatāne at various stages of building, and during those hui the names for the urban hapū, wharekai, and wharenui were chosen. Ngāti Awa-ki-Tamaki would be the hapū, Awanuiarangi would be the wharenui, and Tuteiere, another Ngāti Awa ancestor, was the name of the wharekai. Urban Mataatua members were now a taura here (binding rope) organisation, joined to their iwi mother ship. The marae was opened in 1978 in the presence of Te Arikinui Dame Te Atairangikaahu and Ngāti Awa of Whakatane. A kōhanga reo was added to the marae.[23] Hirini Moko Mead commented on the importance of the formation of Ngāti Awa-ki-Tāmaki to Ngāti Awa as an iwi:

> For this group the act of building a marae, paying for it and managing it every day for several years is proof of their ability to be hapū.[24]

Additionally, Mataatua marae has adopted the words of Te Kooti spoken in 1893 as its own whakataukī. The words reflect the holistic purpose of the marae:

> *Mataatua hangaia e koutou he tāwharau*
> To provide shelter for Mataatua peoples

These words encapsulate the mission and purpose of Mataatua marae as a shelter or refuge for its people.[25] The marae was created to fulfil the needs of urban Ngāti Awa people, to establish a meeting place for the people and to house visiting whānau. There was also a strong desire to create a tūrangawaewae for the children of the founding members.[26]

Attracting more Ngāti Awa active members to the marae is an issue of sustainability. The Auckland population of Ngāti Awa is estimated at 2688 members, but the active membership involved in the daily running of the marae totals less than a hundred.[27] Despite the local hire charges for the marae premises, it is recognised that measures to encourage non-participant Mataatua-Ngāti Awa people are needed for the future viability of the marae and the maintenance of Ngāti Awa identity within the urban environment.

Awataha marae, North Shore, Auckland

Awataha marae stands alongside the motorway at Te Raki Pae Whenua, on Auckland's North Shore. It is recognisable from the northern motorway by the Native American totem pole that stands on the marae ātea looking over the Waitematā Harbour.

The initial notion for establishing a marae on the North Shore occurred in 1961 at a meeting of the North Shore Tribal Committee (NSTC). In 1974 the NSTC commented on the census data showing the North Shore population was 107,000, of which 2989 were Māori, with 15% under the age of 15. It was deemed critical that something be built to cater for the needs of Māori in the area. The North Shore Māori Committee responded to a city council question as to who the tangata whenua were for the marae with the following statement:

> In view of the mixed tribal population interspersed throughout the North Shore, and in the best interests of all peoples, perhaps an idealistic approach to the project is the concern of an Associated group of Different Tribes.[28]

A meeting to gather support for the marae was held between the Minister of Māori Affairs and tangata whenua groups comprising Ngāti Paoa, Ngāti Mahuta, Ngāti Maru, Ngāti Tamaterā, Ngāti Whanaunga, Ngāpuhi and Kawerau-a-Maki. It was agreed that a marae needed to be built to cater for Māori families in the region.

In 1986 land was eventually made available to lease for the purposes of housing a marae. In 1988 the organising committee was renamed the Awataha Marae Incorporated Society. It had taken 25 years for the vision to begin to be realised. Waiwharariki (the North Shore branch of the Māori Women's Welfare League) were strong advocates for the marae and they began fundraising.

The Awataha marae project booklet of 1987 was designed to raise public awareness of the venture. The marae was presented as a place of "inter-cultural communion"[29] where "Pākehā could meet Māori on Māori terms and come to a better understanding of what it means to have a bicultural society".[30] The North Shore marae community was comprised of Māori, Pākehā and many other ethnic peoples. The Awataha elders believed in the notion of collaborative bicultural and cross-cultural partnerships as a fundamental way for Māori to successfully move forward into the future, while retaining firm ties to Māori culture and knowledge.[31]

The marae buildings were built on Crown land in Northcote and administered by the Awataha Marae Incorporated Society. Awataha was designated by the Auckland City Council as a Māori purpose zone where Māori people who had lived for generations on the North Shore could come together.[32]

The ritual blessing of the land occurred in 1987 and fundraising began in 1988. Over $2 million was raised, enabling the building of the administrative block and the kaumātua houses in 1990, followed by the raising up of the whare tipuna named Tane Whakapiripiri in 1992. The North Shore Māori Committee adopted the "open kawa" (open ceremonial rules) of the Kawerau-a-Maki tribe of the region for Awataha. At a dawn ceremony in 1992 a mauri stone from the Waitakere Ranges, gifted by Kawerau-a-Maki, was laid into the ground by kaumātua Pat Ruka to symbolise the life force of the tribe. A kura kaupapa was eventually opened in 1994[33] and since then portions of the marae premises have been leased or rented for community services. In 2005 the services offered included Te Puna Hauora Health Clinic and a childcare centre, Te Kura Kaupapa o Te Raki Paewhenua, a number of counsellors and a full-time Māori wardens' space.

The progressive decisions of the kaumātua and kuia council, who were interested in creating new traditions rather than staying stagnant, meant the marae was marred by conflict. When the elders embraced gender equality and allowed women to speak from the paepae at the 1990 opening of the administration block, local Māori boycotted the ceremony.[34] However, due to bureaucratic restrictions and the lack of human resources, Awataha decided not to hold tangihanga (funerals) here, a decision contrary to usual Māori marae protocol. No tūpāpaku has lay inside the uncompleted wharenui to date, but selected tangihanga have been held in the seminar room.[35] The discontent in the local Māori community over this decision continues over not being able to have deceased whānau members, many of whom contributed to the building of the marae, lie in state there. In response to having nowhere in the region to hold tangihanga, another marae named Uruamo was proposed for Beach Haven.[36]

Frances Waaka leads a group called Uruamo Maranga Ake and she says, "6615 Māori live in Beach Haven and 17,073 altogether on the North Shore. The group sought to build a functional community marae as 'a place to be Māori' and for 'the normalisation of Māori'."[37] As at late 2017, this marae is still in process.

Te Raki Paewhenua Kōmiti Māori published a pamphlet in 2017 claiming there is still no marae of which the wider community feels an integral part, and they have called the Awataha Marae Incorporated Society (AMI) to account.[38] The frustration is now generational, says kōmiti member Raewyn Harrison.[39] Because a request for a special general meeting between the AMI and the Kōmiti Māori was not granted, the Kōmiti called for a very public and visual peaceful protest in June 2017 to force their point.[40] In supporting their cause the Kōmiti Māori quoted a statement by Sir James Henare when the marae was originally established:

> There are several urban marae to the east, to the west and to the south of Auckland and rural marae to the North, but none on the North Shore — serving a large Māori population and the community in general.[41]

Taking these issues into account and the fact that the wharenui still stands uncompleted today (2017), Awataha marae is still to fulfil the dreams of its community and realise its full potential for Māori on the North Shore.

Ngāti Pōneke and Pipitea marae (1980), Wellington

Pipitea marae in central Wellington was established in 1980. The origin of the marae arises out of the formation of the Ngāti Pōneke Young Māori Club, which began as early as 1937.

A Māori church service, led by Temuera Tokoaitua of Rangiātea church in Ōtaki, had been planned for St Thomas's Anglican church in Newtown, Wellington. The service was organised to cater for the spiritual needs of young Māori who had migrated to Wellington to find work. A choir for the service was organised by Kingi Tahiwi. It comprised seven members at the original rehearsal, where hīmene (hymns) and action songs written by Apirana Ngata were performed. The Ngāti Pōneke Young Māori Club was birthed out of the Māori Mission Society.[42] It grew and new songs were composed by Kingi Tahiwi on banjo, with Jock McEwen on piano. In 1938 the club gave its first concert at the Wellington Town Hall in aid of the Sir James Carroll memorial at Wairoa. Kingi Tahiwi led the men and Miriama Heketa led the women. The club was strongly supported by Sir Apirana Ngata and Lady Pōmare.[43] It continued to grow and perform at many functions, including the annual Māori Picnic in Upper Hutt, held at a time when there were only 400 Māori in Wellington.[44]

Wellington was the first colonial town to emerge among Māori in the 1840s. Soon, Māori "disappeared from the streets of Wellington". By the 1930s just a few hundred lived in the greater urban area and newcomers spoke about wandering the streets looking for another Māori face.[45]

For many, Ngāti Pōneke became a "lifeline to which we all clung" and encouraged pride in "our heritage", in an era where Māori communalism was regarded by Pākeha with disdain.⁴⁶ In the mid-1940s Ngāti Pōneke participated in providing services for the war effort. Kingi Tahiwi demanded high standards to prove their equality with urban Pākehā.⁴⁷ In 1944 Prime Minister Peter Fraser allowed Ngāti Pōneke to make use of the Red Cross building at the north end of Lambton Quay. The Ngāti Pōneke Māori Association was established to manage the building and it became the central city Māori community hall. In the early 1970s the club decided to build a marae. Land at Thorndon was given by the Crown for this kaupapa. The proposed name of Pipitea originated from the name of the original pā (which was where Wellington Girl's College now

Crowds gather around the meeting house at the dawn opening of Pipitea marae, Thorndon Quay, Wellington, 31 May 1980.

Dominion Post, photographic negatives and prints of the *Evening Post* and *Dominion* newspapers. Ref: EP/1980/1751/19a-F, Alexander Turnbull Library, Wellington, New Zealand/records/23225306

stands).⁴⁸ A fundraising committee was formed and in 1978 Jock McEwen was asked by Ralph Love to take charge of the design and carvings for the marae, with the aid of other carvers and trade trainees.⁴⁹ The house, named Te Upoko o Te Ika a Māui, was opened at a dawn ceremony on 31 May 1980. Subsequently, the marae has helped transplant Māori culture into the urban milieu.⁵⁰

In 2009 the Port Nicholson Block Settlement Trust and the Ngāti Pōneke Māori Association Incorporated created a partnership, offering the marae for use by all, a place at which all iwi and races can meet.⁵¹

Ōrongomai marae (1976), Upper Hutt

The idea of an urban marae in Upper Hutt was sparked by conversations between the women of Māwai Hakona Culture Group and the Awakairangi branch of the Māori Women's Welfare League, in particular with regard to having a place in the valley to take their loved ones who had passed away.⁵² In 1957 Upper Hutt was a small village consisting of one general store and nine grocery stores.⁵³ Fundraising began in 1966, with Tuesday night housie. When Jock McEwen learned about the idea in 1967, he and Hera Dovey Katene-Hovath, the leader of the Māwai Hakona Culture Group, began to assist in realising the full potential of a pan-tribal house. Jock though the house should be called Ōrongomai, which was the original name of the area. "This was a little-tried concept, with no guarantee of success."⁵⁴ It was decided that two-thirds of any fundraising takings should go into the marae fund, and one-third to the organising groups: the Rimutaka Māori Committee and the Māwai Hakona Cultural Group.⁵⁵

From 1969 Māwai Hakona performed at a number of fundraising events, including the opening of the Upper Hutt Civic Centre in 1969 and the Queen Carnival in 1970. Raffles, concerts, a film evening, market days, a chess match and a public demonstration of knitting, karate and gymnastics all contributed to the fundraising effort. It was a community affair with the army, prisoners, police and companies such as Dunlop and General Motors contributing to the marae.⁵⁶ The city council offered a one-acre (40-hectare) site on the corner of Ward Street and Fergusson Drive at Trentham Memorial Park but local residents objected. The current site, on the corner of Park Street and Railway Avenue, was purchased in 1972. In September 1975 a

The whare whakairo at Ōrongomai marae was opened in the Hutt Valley in May 1989 and officiated by Sir Kingi Ihaka.
http://uhcl.recollect.co.nz/nodes/view/11832, Ref: 1989 05 30 1

dedication of the land was held at the marae.[57] The wharekai was the first building completed, officially opened by Governor-General Sir Denis Blundell on 22 August 1976 and named Rongomai. In 1982 the local community began a kōhanga reo in one of the rooms.[58]

It wasn't until 1989 that the whare whakairo (carved house) was officially opened by Sir Kingi Ihaka. The house was named Kahukura and displayed 50 carved pou and poupou.[59] The carvings represented different tribal areas, as well as Polynesia and Pākehā. Jock McEwen helped establish and carve the whare whakairo. He thought that the test of "whether this was a 'real' marae was if tangi were held here".[60] The house began to be used for tangihanga by the community. Although Jock felt that the people of the community would retain a special attachment to their home marae, he did think that eventually urban marae would be regarded as equal to or more important and that this was a natural consequence of Māori living city lives.[61]

The marae has made strides. The *Upper Hutt Leader* records that a women's health centre was opened on 23 March 1992. In July of 1995 the marae was negotiating to buy council houses at 5 and 7 Railway Avenue, and sought 2000 square feet of space for their training operations and office space. They were running secretarial, catering, and pathways to development courses. The marae soon established a kōhanga reo. In January 2005 the first four Ōrongomai marae Bachelor of Mātauranga Māori (Māori studies) students graduated from a programme run in conjunction with Te Wānanga o Raukawa of Ōtaki.[62]

Kākāriki marae (1978), Green Bay High School, West Auckland

In 1972 a petition asking for Māori to be taught in all schools provided an impetus for te Reo Māori to enter the classroom. It also set the scene for a marae to be built on school grounds in recognition of the value of Māoritanga in New Zealand education.[63] As part of the wider kaupapa of cultural regeneration, Kākāriki marae was established in 1978 as the first marae-a-kura ('mainstream' school marae), built at Green Bay High School in West Auckland.[64]

Pat Heremia and Rā Kōhere were the driving forces behind the building of the marae, but a local family culture club formed in 1968 was the impetus for the original kaupapa. Pat saw the two main functions of the marae as creating an opportunity for the people of all nationalities to experience Māori culture and providing a meaningful context for the teaching of Māori language.[65] It was a radical innovation at the time. In 1980 the *New Zealand Herald* reported on the pōwhiri for third-form students at the school, something that has subsequently become common practice at secondary schools throughout the country.[66] In 1982, Oriwa Ormsby and Judy Cooper opened a kōhanga reo next to the marae, which was originally named Te Aniwaniwa Te Kōhanga Reo. Since then the kōhanga has had a number of administrations and name changes. In 2009 the unit relocated to Glen Eden and was renamed Te Kōhanga Reo o Kākāriki.

Hui, tangihanga, wānanga and the youth justice-based marae tribunal have been held at this marae. Kākāriki has also been used as a film set for the 2007 British-Māori television comedy *The Man Who Lost His Head*, starring Martin Clunes and Nicola Kāwana.[67] In 2012 Kākāriki marae was redeveloped as a whare akoranga (a house of learning) to fit in with the school's forward progression as a twenty-first century New Zealand learning environment.

According to a Ministry of Education report, in 2000 there were 99 marae-a-kura in New Zealand secondary schools. Their existence recognises the value of Māori education in schools and as "a way to better engage with parents, whānau and community".[68]

Tertiary education institutes followed suit, with the first tertiary college meeting house opened in 1980 on the campus of the Palmerston North Teachers' College and named Te Mātauranga. The first university marae, Te Tumu Herenga Waka, opened in 1986 at Victoria University, Wellington.

Hokowhitu Ria, Rehua Hostel, Christchurch

Former Māori Trade Trainee Hokowhitu Ria and his wife Glenda at their home in Christchurch, 2016.

Courtesy Hokowhitu Ria

When Hokowhitu (Hoko) Ria set foot on Christchurch soil in 1959, he knew the city would be his home for many years. That was nearly 57 years ago.

Brought up on the coast near Gisborne, Hoko remembers most of his childhood days were spent at Manutuke or Waihīrere with his grandparents, in the kumara garden doing tasks such as planting, weeding and harvesting. "Mahi kai was our life, right from the age of 4 to 15," he says. He was the only boy in the family of seven sisters. "My dad was a very strict man, a fighter. He did all the cooking, gardening and washing — he was a perfectionist. But he very rarely spoke to us, he just grunted," Hoko remembers. The reo was rarely spoken to Hoko and his siblings. The marae was tapu for the children. "We were never allowed on the marae, we had to just sit in the wharekai and wait till someone asked us to do something," he says. When the men asked him to work in the kitchen he'd follow them. That's how he learned to butcher meat.

There was very little love between Hoko and his father, Arikihana Ria. "I learned to take his beatings and to just hold in my tears and not to cry," he laments. "Added to that, the garden was filled with kēhua [ghosts], I could smell them." One day when Hoko was in the field working, his father asked him, "Do you want go to work at either Auckland, Wellington or Christchurch?" Hoko blurted out, "Christchurch!" Subsequently, an unannounced taxi came to collect Hoko. He and his parents took a silent trip to the train station. Hoko had little idea of where he was going, but "I was happy and I didn't care where I was going". He stepped on to the train on his own, but found company with three others from Gisborne. As they travelled further south, other boys going to Christchurch boarded the train. From Wellington the boys went by boat to Lyttelton. When Hoko stepped onto the wharf, he felt his life had a new beginning. One of his friends commented, "No more hidings!" I said, 'No, I'm gonna dish it out now.' In those days I didn't know about forgiveness, I had so much hate inside of me."

Eight Māori boys from the East Coast were transported to Rehua hostel on Springfield Road in Christchurch to begin their trade training. They were one of the earliest groups of recruits. Hoko wanted to be a mechanic but "I got the sheet metal trade", he says. The trade training was for five years with a weekly payment of £1-14-9, which was considered a lot of money in those days.

In the hostel the boys never asked each other where they were from. Hoko says, "We were just brothers, Māori to Māori, all one." The matron of the house, Mrs Rennie, insisted the boys speak Māori at the dinner table. Dinner was followed by kapa haka. "That was a way of keeping our Māoritanga alive because we were so far away from home," Hoko recounts. "None of us were homesick then, we were having too much of a good time."

The Methodist church managed the hostel, and attending church services was compulsory. Hoko remembers going to church with the boys in shorts, singlets and bare feet. The boys sat at the back. "In the middle of a hymn we sang with all our strength and the whole church turned around to look at us. The minister just smiled at us," Hoko laughs. After the service the minister thanked the boys but asked them to wear shirts next time.

Christchurch was huge compared to Gisborne. "There was more to do here than in Gisborne. It was a city of bikes and cars had to give way to them," Hoko says. The lack of brown faces in Christchurch was noticeable. "I remember writing letters to Mum to tell her how Pākehā here would look at us and start a conversation with us Māori. My mother didn't believe me because no Pākehā talked with Māori in Gisborne — they were racist."

The Methodist Mission travelled through the country raising funds for a recreation hall for the boys. "The hall was eventually built as a marae," Hoko says. "We laid the boxing and the concrete for the foundation of that house, then we were rewarded with lovely pork bones and puha." Hoko was intrigued when famous master carvers Henare Toka and Pine Taiapa arrived to carve the meeting house. "Kuia and kaumātua from all over the motu used to come to the marae.

Then Ngāi Tahu claimed the house. Despite this, many of us kept long-term ties to Rehua, running the house and joining the Te Whatu Manawa kapa haka team," Hoko says.

After 14 months Hoko shifted out of the hostel to find a flat with friends. He finished his time at A&T Burt's sheet metal business and returned home to Gisborne for a short time. Eventually he returned to Christchurch, which he considered home: "I realised I'm from Gisborne but my home was Rehua." He began a job as an engineer at Hamilton's Jet Boats, where he worked for 21 years. He later found work with the council as a labourer, which he did for 27 years until he retired at the age of 70. During that time he was involved in building many of the high-rise buildings in Christchurch, including the hospital.

In this time Hoko and his first wife purchased their first home from Māori Affairs. "They had been building Māori Affairs' homes all over Christchurch and the capitalisation of the family benefit became the way to pay off our mortgage," Hoko says. The marriage ended and the home was sold. Today, Hoko is remarried and he and his wife Glenda own a freehold house in Crawford Street.

For Hoko, the trade-training school gave the boys a glimpse of a new lifestyle and taught them new life skills. "We worked hard and drank hard, like our parents," he says, "but all the boys did well out of our time in those early days."

Chapter 8

Ngā Piki me ngā Heke

Highs and Lows

The initiative and spirit that enabled the construction of urban marae reflected a positive establishment of roots in the city. Marae enabled a continuation of tikanga, a focus for community, and a haven for those in need. Those negative factors were unfortunately mounting for many who had made the move to the cities, and for the following generations. As Brian Easton makes clear in "Māori Meets More Market", Māori were increasingly represented at the wrong end of the socioeconomic spectrum, in disproportionate numbers in the statistics on poverty, welfare dependency, gang membership, crime and incarceration.[1] These lows can be balanced against the energetic and committed responses the community made to their situation. Alongside the challenges, this chapter explores the positive response achieved by Māori wardens, activists and pioneers in fields such as kura kaupapa Māori (Māori-language immersion schools) and Māori health initiatives.

Welfare officers

Māori Affairs welfare officers were among the first ports of call for new arrivals in the cities. They were to become a "friend, counsellor and guide" to Māori families and youth, assisting them into the new culture or the Pākehā society.[2] Since 1969 the number of welfare officers increased to 33 in Auckland, Wellington and Hamilton.[3] In a 1973 speech to the Māori Welfare Officer's Association, the Minister of Māori Affairs, Matiu Rata, acknowledged the work of the officers, which encompassed "any matter which promotes the welfare and progress of the Māori and Island people either as individuals or groups".[4] He reiterated the officers' role in the community.

> The work of welfare officers has called for enthusiasm, courage, initiative, energy, patience, tact and an understanding of the Māori people and their aspirations, the capacity to influence leadership and, above all, common sense. I am aware also that your work will continue to be, as in the past, to encourage and assist in matters of housing, education, vocational training, trade training, health and physical welfare, law and order — to name but a few facets. Undoubtedly, this work will continue for some years yet, but the prime role of officers is to work with groups on community development in an effort to prevent casework arising.[5]

Up until the 1970s the city had offered Māori full employment and lifetime security. This scenario was slowly changing as urban environments became "sites of unemployment, welfare dependency and insecurity".[6] This was the state of affairs for generations of Māori families over the next 20 years. In 1990, the average income of Māori households had decayed to 20% below the average New Zealander's income.[7]

The process of urbanisation exacted a high price from city-born children. Cultural loss, dislocation from tribal origins and disenfranchisement from the customary ways of parents and grandparents meant the family unit was cut off and disorganised.[8] This disorganisation was associated with the notion of detribalisation, which was identified with 'culture contact', integration and the process of colonisation in the 1960s.[9] However, while many urban-based Māori had detached from their tribal roots, there were many first-wave urban Māori (and reaching into subsequent generations) who never detribalised but adapted their tribal outlooks into the new environment.

Generally speaking, city-born Māori grew up in a new world with little or no knowledge of cultural values, cultural pride or who they were as Māori. 'Being Māori' was derived from the activities and experiences of Māori family units existing in urban neighbourhoods. These issues were "further compounded by the difficulties with socio-economic adjustment".[10] Sir Pita Sharples, one of the founders of Hoani Waititi urban marae, describes the social problems he observed among Māori who came to live in Auckland in the 1950s and 1960s.

> The change from the rural to an urban way of life was a huge culture shock. So many families were soon run down and the children were in trouble. They were broke, they had their power and water cut off, they owed rates and stuff like this. The discipline of the city was totally different from the discipline of the country. So there were huge problems.[11]

The *Puao-te-ata-tū* report of 1988 highlighted the disproportionately high numbers of Māori in the welfare system, since the establishment of the Department of Social Welfare, compared with the general population.[12] It stated that many of the youth appearing before the police and in the welfare system "brought with them histories of substandard housing, health deficiencies, abysmal education records, and an inability to break out of the ranks of the unemployed".[13] The report reiterated that the relative socio-economic status between Māori and non-Māori had remained unchanged for many decades. Education and economic underachievement by Māori were reflected in increased crime rates, poor infant and life expectancy, high unemployment and low incomes. *Puao-te-ata-tū* stressed that 62% of Māori left secondary school without passing at least one subject of School Certificate, compared to 28% of non-Māori. The report continued by highlighting that only 45% of Māori owned their own homes (with or without mortgage), and 50% rented compared to 73% non-Māori owning and 24% renting. The median income disparity between Māori and non-Māori was $2039 per annum; and 50% of prison admissions were Māori.[14] These statistics were cause for great concern and highlighted the underlying issues Māori welfare officers faced in the field.

Ngāmaru Raerino was a welfare officer during the 1970s; he worked for three years in Rotorua, three years in Wellington and nine years in Auckland. He says Rotorua was considered an urban centre where people from Ruatahuna, Reporua, Rotoiti, Tokoroa, Te Puke and more locally from Awahou had to move. The people shifted to districts such as Western Heights, Ford Block and Ngāpuna. In 1976 Ngāmaru shifted to Auckland, where the issues of dislocation were heightened.

The Puao-te-ata-tū social welfare report (1988) revolutionised the way Māori were treated by the Department of Social Welfare, recommending the placement of care back in the hands of Māori and iwi.
Courtesy of Bradford Haami

Families could not sustain a living on lands they could not build on by law and these people were placed into state or pepper-potted housing in the towns. Integration didn't work, it grouped a whole lot of Māori and Pākehā people from low socio-economic backgrounds; peoples who were unemployed and needed welfare benefits and assistance to go into the houses. Most couldn't afford to keep the houses going. So what happened, they went in with nothing and came out with no money. As a welfare officer we were to help people from depressed areas or rural folk living in dilapidated housing to live in the towns and to maintain their houses. Papakāinga (ancestral settlement) living people didn't know how to live in close proximity to other people. A lot of them came from houses that had no electricity or running water — they drew water from streams and wells ... People lit fires in stoves to cook or were breaking wood from floors and walls for fires.[15]

Ngāmaru was involved in having to chase up "crucial mortgage defaulters". "There was a lot of defaulting on mortgages, but you couldn't just throw people out into the streets ... but we had to force the sale of houses."[16] By one account, nearly two-thirds of the housing mortgages administered by the Māori Affairs during the 1970s were in arrears.[17] Rereata Makiha was also a welfare officer for Māori Affairs in Auckland from 1972 to 1987.

> I was in charge of a team of school teachers in South Auckland — we could tell at the end of the year what every Māori kid was going to do, apprenticeships or leave school … we tracked them to help them out. If they moved to a different district, we'd contact officers down the line to follow them up. We were looking at the skill of the whole then, but the system became more individualised. We'd take the ratbag Māori kids off the streets and run camps for them, take them scrub cutting down on a farm in the Waikato for a number of weeks. The kids needed straight talking — most of them were homeless — they didn't want to stay home because of the abuse in their own homes. We worked alongside Māori Women's Welfare League, the Māori Wardens, the Māori Council. Families weren't open to co-operating with us as welfare officers, they felt we were interfering. Only the old people welcomed us.[18]

Rereata was part of the J-teams (Joint teams) made up of police, social welfare, Māori Affairs and the churches, who had combined to help combat the rise of gangs in the 1970s. As he remembers, "When the fights hit the fan, the police would stand their ground. There were knife fights, you name it."[19]

Anne Tia, Betty Walk, Agnes Tuisamoa, Jim and Mere Ransfield, Eddie McLoud and Letty Brown, and Fred Ellis, affectionately known as 'The Royal Family', assumed legendary status in their roles as social workers in their neighbourhoods of Freemans Bay and Ponsonby. This team were first-generation Māori migrants who operated together, catering to the needs of the homeless, the poor and prisoners. They all shared in kaumātua Eruera Stirling's belief that it was vital for Māori to remain connected to their traditional culture.[20]

Ani (Anne) Ngaropera Tia, a devout Rātana and originally from Poroporo papakāinga at Te Hāpua, arrived in Auckland during World War II. She learned to speak English at her job at a chocolate factory in Parnell. Ani became a central figure in the running of the Auckland Maori Community Centre. In 1969 she was asked by her culture club leader, Peta Awatere, to assist him in organising culture groups among the inmates at Mt Eden Prison, where he was incarcerated for murder. Ani taught Māori culture at Mt Eden, Paremoremo maximum and medium prisons for 23 years.[21] Out of this voluntary work, she trained as a social worker and ran an open home for the homeless and for prisoners who had nowhere to go when released. Eventually she and her family moved into the Auckland Maori Community Centre, where she created a branch of the Māori Women's Welfare League, worked as a project supervisor for a works-skills programme and acted as a surrogate grandmother for the homeless in the night.[22]

Betty Walk came to Auckland during World War II and became increasingly concerned about the rising homelessness, Māori youth crime, and the plight of ex-prisoners. Through the Māori Women's Welfare League, she set up hostels for migrant Māori and ex-prisoners and used her own home as a refuge for troubled youth. She was involved in the establishment of homes under the Arohanui Trust that were used to house ex-prisoners, unemployed and troubled youth in a home-like whānau environment. The residents paid board and obeyed house rules, including a ban on alcohol and drugs. In the years she contributed to the community she "helped get the support they needed to achieve their potential".[23] Betty inspired others such as Fred Ellis, an ex-prisoner, to take up community work.[24]

Letty Brown and Eddie McLoud of Māori Affairs operated a halfway home for the homeless next to Betty's Te Arohanui House on Hopetown Street. Letty and Eddie stood in the courts for the underprivileged and set up a Māori language nest to impart te Reo Māori, hope and whānau ideals to those young people. All of these volunteers had learned from their elders that they were ethically compelled to feed and serve the underprivileged.[25]

Alcohol and its aftermath

The Māori wardens' involvement with the liquor trade saw them patrol local hotels for unruly patrons and underage drinking. With little authority, these volunteers relied on tact and the art of persuasion to carry out their duties. Often the actions of the wardens were governed by what they saw as right, without any reference to the law.[26] The impacts of alcohol among Māori grew as Māori urbanisation increased, especially with hotel opening hours extending to 10 o'clock from 1968.[27] The onus of restricting drunkenness and disorderly behaviour was a statutory obligation of liquor licensees and hoteliers, but they preferred to transfer this responsibility to the wardens to save themselves trouble and expense.[28] The wardens were faced with the dilemma of patrolling and imposing sanctions on public drinking and its often aggressive consequences. Their predicament lay in the fact that they were enforcing a moral code on a legitimate, normalised and socially tolerated activity.[29] Alcohol was integral to societal obligations of hospitality, and the bar room or local tavern had become the "substitute marae".[30]

Alcohol has been an issue for Māori and their leaders for over a century. In the mid-nineteenth century the leaders tried to curb the effects of alcohol on their communities. In 1874 Haimona Te Aoterangi and 167 others petitioned Parliament to put laws in place against this "nākahi nui" (great snake) alcohol which "impoverishes us" and "turns the intelligent men of the Māori race into fools".[31] In 1884 Ngāti Maniapoto persuaded the government to declare the King Country a dry area. Racist laws such as the Alcoholic Liquor Sales Amendment Act 1895 prevented Māori women, unless married to a European, from buying alcohol, and the Licensing Amendment Act 1904 did not allow Māori men to buy alcohol in most of the

Two men on a Dominion Breweries bottling line. Readily available alcohol became a huge concern for Māori elders, who labelled it nākahi nui: a great snake.

Auckland Museum, PH-NEG-70A (iii)

North Island.[32] In 1915–16, nearly 160,000 New Zealanders signed petitions calling for 6 o'clock closing, which was made permanent in 1918. The law restricted the opening hours of public drinking places in a bid to increase the efficiency of the workforce.[33] It became normal practice for Māori working men to join their non-Māori colleagues at the pub after work "to drink as much beer as they could before the so-called 'supping up' time of 15 minutes was announced".[34]

According to one account, 250 people at a tangi consumed 1700 bottles of alcohol over 36 hours.[35] For some, heavy alcohol consumption and family abuse were core reasons to leave for the city and look for something better.[36] However, the opportunities for drinking were heightened by the massive Māori migration to the cities.[37] Fiction writers detailed the new drinking opportunities available to Māori during the post-war move to the cities. In her recollection of the end of the 1950s, Mihi Edwards wrote in her autobiography about the despair and drinking then prevalent in Māori lives.

> If it takes me all of my life, I think, I am going to remind the Pākehā what he has done to us. My sister is being dragged into the bowels of despair through drink. The kids are exposed to all the violence and swearing, caused through booze, and I suppose will grow up thinking it a way of normal life, repeating what their parents are doing, belting their wives and then their children as well. They do not know any other way to behave.[38]

Alan Duff's controversial novel, *Once Were Warriors* (1990), portrayed terrible images of alcohol and violence in Māori society through the lives of Jake and Beth Heke.

> It's not toughness we need anymore, it's — it's — shaking her head.
> So what is it we need, O solver of the world's problems? Beer! Hahaha!
> Laughing. Rocking back and forth with it. And drowning another glass in one long, sweet increasingly mindless pull.[39]

After hours, people sought out the rugby clubs or the dedicated 'sly grog' homes where alcohol could be purchased or consumed on site, outside of the law. Sometimes a taxi was ordered to go and pick up alcohol from a 'sly grogger' on behalf of Māori who at the time were unable to purchase alcohol from public outlets. Each district had these kind of premises, often called 'The Club' and known to everybody. One Auckland premises run by a Māori family acted as a club where gangs would converge with local punters to continue drinking. The premises were open every day and alcohol and drugs were always available. There were good and horrific times in this space, which often made the neighbours shiver. At one time the neighbourhood petitioned to have the sly groggers removed.[40]

There was a "crisis in Māori drinking because of major breakdowns in Māori community patterns."[41] For some families, alcohol was considered a "staple diet"[42] and even "more important than bread and milk".[43] Social workers Mavis Tuoro and Connie Hanna of West Auckland named the major social issue among Māori as "the alcohol abuse of Māori men in the local pubs" and the spending of money on alcohol.[44] By the time Māori Affairs arrived to assist these families, they were already in arrears with their mortgages and falling apart.

While the average daily consumption of alcohol was the same for Māori and non-Māori, about a quarter of Māori did not drink at all and those who did drink did so less frequently than non-Māori. However, Māori consumed more.[45]

Alcohol was one of a number of components that fuelled the breakdown of whānau in the rural regions, towns and city. For the Marshall family (profiled later in this chapter), estrangement from tribal origins and a parental break-up precipitated a family move to the city. However, it was alcohol that played a large part in sending the children's lives into despair. Alcohol supplanted paying rent, electricity and food, forcing the children to live on the streets of Auckland searching for sustenance, shelter and safety. Abuse, dysfunction and gangs became the norm in a world saturated with alcohol. It has taken years for members of the Marshall family to break free from the cycle of alcohol-related circumstances and dysfunction to find some semblance of whānau safety.

The growth of gangs

As the 6 o'clock closing ban was removed in the late 1960s, Māori and multi-ethnic gangs began to emerge and became an enduring feature of New Zealand society.[46] The first hint of emerging youth gangs in New Zealand occurred when the 'teddy boys', the 'bodgies' and the 'milkbar cowboys' appeared in the 1950s out of "informal youth associations due to rapid urbanisation".[47] These gangs were initially comprised of adolescent European males. However, at least 41 teenage gangs emerged in Auckland and 17 in Wellington.[48] With the arrival of the Hells Angels Motorcycle Club in Auckland, who were affiliated with the American gang of the same name, the formal gang structure of a leader, a sergeant-of-arms and a code of conduct began to emerge.

A Polynesian gang culture also developed in the 1960s, after Pacific migration began to increase, something Poata Eruera and Wynn Anania witnessed occurring in the schools. However, it was Māori urban migration that proved to be more significant in the development of Māori gangs. The Friday night dances in the city became the place where young people gathered to challenge each other and find a Kingpin.[49] The combination of city kid bicycle gangs, the tough guy image that was portrayed in the pubs, and the rise of snooker halls, combined with a socially challenging environment, saw new forms of identities arise. Gangs were neighbourhood and patch-name specific.[50] Key factors in the increase of gang membership among colonised people include alienation of land, loss of language and culture, forced assimilation and acculturation, unemployment, poverty, alcohol and drug abuse.

In his book *Patched,* Jarrod Gilbert gives a clear compounded picture of the impacts of social forces on "multiple marginality", relegating low socio-economic minorities to society's fringes. He says:

> The process of marginalisation continues with the breakdown of formal and informal controls ... Families, under stress, in poor jobs and in deficient housing, fail to provide adequate supervision. The problems are exacerbated by failure at school due to language difficulties and 'culturally insensitive and ethnocentric curriculum'. Youths facing similar circumstances cling together and have negative experiences with law enforcement, creating hostile attitudes and a rejection of mainstream social norms. At that point they commit to alternative street rules and identity, often by joining a gang.[51]

Māori were prevalent in all the emergent gangs such as Black Power, the Boot Hill Boys, the Head Hunters, the Highway 61s, the Mongrel Mob, and the Storm Troopers. Connie Hanna, an experienced Māori Affairs worker from Auckland, shared how the gang members were the children of Māori urban migrants of the 1960s and "They were the product of the breakdown of whānau links in the cities," she said.⁵²

Perhaps the ultimate manifestation of cultural disenfranchisement was exemplified in the Mongrel Mob gang's manifesto. The Mob, New Zealand's largest gang, did not recognise ethnicity, language or any form of duty to New Zealand as a nation. Being Māori meant nothing to members (although the majority of members were Māori); the patch and their 'dog culture' ruled.⁵³ No one identified as tribal, ethnic or from anywhere specific in the early days of the gang, and anyone could join to give their allegiance to their patch (a bulldog wearing a German helmet).⁵⁴ Recognition of tā moko and culture is only a recent idea.

Tuhoe 'Bruno' Isaac, an ex-leader of the Mongrel Mob, recalls that members were guys brought up "in welfare homes and borstals, reared in dysfunctional families and abused as youngsters".⁵⁵ Members came from homes without encouragement or any vision for the future. "We became disenfranchised non-citizens and we embraced that to the fullest."⁵⁶ Rawiri Taonui and Greg Newbold have written that

Gang leaders at a summit meeting with politician Matiu Rata in 1981.

Evening Post (newspaper, 1865–2002), photographic negatives and prints of the *Evening Post*, Ref: 35 mm-01430-35a, Alexander Turnbull Library, Wellington/http://natlib.govt.nz/records/22779506

A group of young Māori members of Ngā Tamatoa on the steps of Parliament in 1972. Back row, left to right: Toro Waaka (Ngāti Kahungunu), John Ohia (Ngāi Te Rangi, Ngāti Pūkenga), Paul Kotara (Ngāi Tahu), and Tame Iti (Ngāi Tūhoe). Front row, left to right: Orewa Barrett-Ohia (Ngāti Maniapoto), Rawiri Paratene (Ngāpuhi) and Tiata Witehira (Ngāpuhi).
Dominion Post (newspaper), photographic negatives and prints of the *Evening Post* and *Dominion* newspapers, Ref: EP/1972/5388/11a-F, Alexander Turnbull Library, Wellington/records/23069211

comradeship and rebellion were central to gang life in the 1950s, while crime was initially impulsive and petty until the 1970s, when Māori gangs received more prominence for their "high-profiled acts of violence", not seen on New Zealand streets before.[57] With as many as 3500 gang members in a national population of 4.3 million people, New Zealand is said to have more gangs per capita than many other countries.[58]

According to Rawiri Taonui, "Alienation paved the way for two roads: one without consciousness-raising [which] created Māori crime and gangs; a second built on conscientisation led to radical protest."[59] The 1970s was a decade characterised by protest, lobbying and a fight for justice, redress of past land grievances, recognition of the Treaty of Waitangi, the retention of Māori culture and language and the re-assertion of self-determination. Reaction to the continued integration of Māori into mainstream Pākehā society and the loss of culture was vehement. The Māori Affairs Amendment Act 1967, which introduced provision to change the remaining Māori lands under 'European' status, was dubbed the 'last land grab' and sparked a major Māori land rights movement that led to the 1975 Māori Land March.[60]

For language and rights

This set the stage for Māori activism and agitation for political change at a number of levels. The protest movement arose out of the experience of Māori youth in the city, concluding successive governments had manipulated their plight. Formed in 1970, Ngā Tamatoa, a group of young, educated and urbanised Māori, some unionists and other seasoned political activists, stood to "challenge the old guard of the 1950s and 1960s to face new choices and strategies for articulating Māori grievances and engaging with the state".[61]

The Eruera brothers, Taura and Poata, would meet other Ngā Tamatoa members in a hideout in Swanson. They say they joined the movement to "preserve and reinforce Māori identity rather than staying second-class citizens. The whole basis of the movement was the ratification of the Treaty of Waitangi and te Reo Māori," Poata says.[62] Further, they sought equal Māori representation, the return of confiscated land, correction of Pākehā bias in history books and Pākehā respect for Māori culture. Continued agitation by Ngā Tamatoa and other emergent groups on many fronts saw the eventual implementation of the Waitangi Tribunal Act in 1975, which led to the hearing of historical grievances back to 1840. The hearings were followed by Crown apologies, settlements and compensations, a process still under way for many tribes. By the 1980s, over 2300 historical petitions to government over land losses and related issues were still to be addressed.[63]

The reo was a priority for the members of Ngā Tamatoa, the majority of whom were non-speakers. They collected 30,000 signatures for a petition calling for the inclusion of the reo in schools. Members established the first kura reo (taking urban youth to rural marae to learn the reo from their elders), introduced the first Māori language day and secured a one-year teacher training course for native speakers.[64]

Government policy had excluded Māori language from schools and the number of Māori language speakers declined from 95% in 1900 to 5% in 1980. First-generation native speakers who migrated to the city often chose not to speak to their children in Māori, wishing to save their children from the grief of discrimination and castigation dished out to them during their own school days. Additionally, parents wanted their children to succeed in an English-speaking world and they decided to forgo their language and culture. Being away from traditional supports of kin and language communities compounded the issue. Many urban Māori could no longer sustain the language within their homes.[65] Richard Benton's research made it clear that by the 1970s, the Māori language played a marginal role in the upbringing of children. The passing of the present generation of Māori-speaking parents would create an era of a language without native speakers.[66]

The emergence of the Kōhanga Reo Language Nests, founded in urban Wellington at Wainuiomata in April 1982, created a movement that fundamentally shifted the demographics of Māori language speakers. Within three years 6000 children were being educated in their own language across 416 kōhanga reo nationwide.[67] Māori parents concerned about the loss of the reo in mainstream schools launched kura kaupapa Māori, total immersion secondary schools. By 1990 there were seven kura kaupapa Māori, primarily established in urban Auckland Māori communities.[68] By 2009 there were 73 kura kaupapa Māori, with just over 6000 students.[69]

With strong Māori language revitalisation efforts in the following years, te Reo Māori received official language status with the implementation of the Māori Language Act of 1987. The Māori Language Commission was established and later Te Māngai Paho was tasked with funding Māori language and culture programming for television and radio. Language revitalisation has had a prime space in the hearts of the people for many years. Today, efforts are also in place to seek the revitalisation of mātauranga Māori (Māori knowledge), which appears to have been left behind but is gaining traction.

Crucial health initiatives

Māori agitation for biculturalism, cultural recognition, treaty partnership and self-determination in the 1970s and 1980s reached into the belly of government agencies and colonial establishments. One little-known but significant development to emerge out of Māori agitation and the motivation to deal urgently with urban

Māori realities was the formation of a pan-tribal Kāhui Kaumatua Council in 1989 at Princess Mary Children's Hospital. This urban council of Māori representatives from all major tribal groupings living in Auckland, including Ngāti Whātua as tangata whenua, became responsible for cultural safety advice for the bicultural parent liaison officer at Princess Mary Hospital. It later became a conferred eldership and co-management partner for Māori health policy with the hospital board. Birthed out of pioneering Māori women from West Auckland, a gathering of urban Māori elders changed the face of the hospital system in Auckland; its influence has reached further afield around New Zealand.

In 1985 Auckland General Hospital Principal Nurse Mary Futter realised that hospital staff were "missing the point" when it came to caring for Māori patients, their families and acting in a culturally sensitive manner.[70] She recognised that there were cultural differences at play and it didn't matter how conscientious hospital staff clinically cared for clients, an unsatisfactory outcome for Māori seemed to prevail. One particular incident led to the beginning of change in the system. A young Māori mother had come to the hospital carrying her sick child. Barefoot and poorly dressed, she had been treated with disdain by staff and she left. Sadly, the child died. Nurse Futter was made aware of the event and she responded by helping to push open a door to cultural change in Princess Mary Hospital.[71]

She sought the advice of Dr Ranginui Walker and past race-relations conciliator Pita Sharples, who advised her to employ Māori in the system. This was imperative if the system wanted a favourable response from the Māori community. A Māori liaison position was mooted.

It was strongly recommended the hospital implement an acceptable education programme to deal with the issue of institutional racism to "pave the way" for a Māori appointment.[72] In 1987, race relations educator Karena Way filled the position, the first of its kind in the New Zealand health system. Under extreme pressure she organised and ran seminars for the Hospital Management Group and department heads on institutional racism, the Treaty of Waitangi and biculturalism.[73]

Hospitals in New Zealand had traditionally embraced English-based values, to the point that "there was little difference between a hospital in England and one in New Zealand."[74] Māori had an aversion to hospitals; they were not perceived as places where people regained health, instead they were regarded as institutes of illness and eventually death.⁷⁵ The *Puao-te-atatū* report called for a conscious effort to make institutions culturally inclusive in their character and more accommodating of cultural difference. Education on the topics of anti-racism, biculturalism and the Treaty of Waitangi was required to facilitate general acceptance by hospital staff of the coming changes in policy and practice.

Judith Amohaere Ngaropo (now Amohaere Tangitu), a resident of Te Atatū North, West Auckland, took the position as the Parent Liaison Officer at Princess Mary Hospital in 1987. Her role was to liaise with Māori families whose children entered the hospital. Travelling with the district nurse, Amohaere witnessed the conditions of Māori families living in poverty firsthand. The nurses, doctors and hospitals did not know how to create a connection with Māori families and their communities. They also had little desire to engage with Māori.⁷⁶

Parents wishing to be close to their ill children could not secure accommodation and were governed by the hospital's limiting visiting rules. Family members were found sleeping in their cars at the Auckland Domain, utilising public toilets for ablutions and the lily ponds to wash. Sometimes mothers hitchhiked from outlying districts as far away as Papakura, Pukekohe and Waiuku, to visit their ill children. They would have no clothes, no petrol, no food, no money, nowhere to sleep, and no friends or family with whom to connect. It was often a foreign world into which they entered. These circumstances became a deterrent for many families wishing to visit their children.

After alerting the hospital board to the situation, an empty ward was transformed into family accommodation and named Whānau House. Eventually the Auckland General Hospital followed suit and created a whānau room, which provided accommodation for families, initially free of charge. The room was modelled on the Princess Mary Hospital's Whānau House. The creation of these spaces was a breakthrough in the New Zealand health system.

Culturally appropriate care (or cultural safety) was recognised as essential to making the hospital a lot more amenable to the needs of Māori. In 1987 Irihapeti Ramsden assisted in the development of the controversial 'cultural safety' guidelines for the curriculum in safe nursing and midwifery education. This concept was later formalised in 1988, but it wasn't until 1991 that the Nursing Council of New Zealand made cultural safety a requirement in the state examinations for nurses and midwives. The guidelines, known as the kawa whakaruruhau, were written by Irihapeti Ramsden and finally adopted by the Nursing Council in 1992.[77]

Implementing cultural safety as part of training was a completely different process to rolling it into practice on the hospital floor. Amohaere felt this process needed a kaumātua council to guide this work. Kuia Mahia Wallace and kaumātua Toby Curtis and Canon John Tamahori supported this process and a Kāhui Kaumatua (Council of Māori Elders), a multi-tribal eldership from the Auckland region, was created and formalised in October 1989 as a dual-decision making body. The council was designed to sit alongside hospital management and provide cultural knowledge to the organisation that would assist in meeting the needs of the urban Māori population. These kaumātua had a great desire for the general upgrade of Māori health. Elders who participated in this pioneering council between 1989 and 1994) were Canon John Tamahori, Mahia Wallace, Toby Curtis, Te Pere Curtis, John Turei, Bill Tāpuke, Dave Mackey, Doc Wikiriwhi, Danny Tumahae, Ruby Gray, Brownie Williams, Rangi Matehaere, Thompson Tamehana, Ngarau Tupai, Amelia Oppenheim, Ihimaera Ihimaera, Eru Potaka Dewes, Dr Hone Kaa, Dave King, Celia Burkhart, Wally Te Ua and Mavis Tuoro.

The work of this collective led to the implementation of the first ever hospital accommodation for visiting families, the blessing of rooms, the colour coding of linen to delineate between that used for the body and food, appropriate understanding of tapu and noa in the context of nurturing patients, and the implementation of consents for the removal and disposal of body parts. A separate Māori health unit named Te Whānau Atawhai (The caring family) was eventually established on the 7th floor of Starship Hospital manned by kai-atawhai carers. Led by the Kāhui Kaumātua and managed by Amohaere, this unit provided "appropriate and effective Māori health services to improve the quality of life for Māori and all other people in Tāmaki Makau Rau."[78]

This Kāhui Kaumātua viewed themselves as a group of elders representing many tribes. They volunteered their services in the development of Te Whānau Atawhai, which aimed to cater for the needs of their pan-tribal people entering the hospitals. The kaupapa of Te Whānau Atawhai was "Whanaungatanga — awhi, manaaki, atawhai (Create a sense of family — embrace, support, care)."[79] The core principles of the unit were to implement and develop whānau practices within the healing process for patients and families, develop cultural awareness, strengthen relationships with the multi-disciplinary clinical teams, and provide a link to the community for ongoing support.[80] They strongly believed cultural safety should walk alongside clinical treatment and this was the responsibility of all health carers in the hospital system, not just Māori.[81] Te Whānau Atawhai opened the door for the future establishment of the *He Kamaka Oranga Māori Health Management 1994* policy and strategy, which set a new direction for Māori health development.

While the circumstances associated with urbanisation created negative impacts and destructive environments, it also generated responses where pan-tribal collectives penetrated culturally discriminating political institutes and government agencies to force change for the recognition of Māori culture, needs and rights.

Lianne Marshall, Pakuranga, Auckland

Lianne Marshall with her family at Pakuranga. Back row: Angie, Talia, Samaria, Dellas, Dinah, Front row: Kylah, Jaden, Lianne, Jadice.
Courtesy of Bradford Haami

Lianne was born in Stratford but her fondest memories of family are of their times in Taumarunui. Lianne's father Thomas was Tūhoe and her mother Doulene was Ngāpuhi. Doulene met Thomas while she was nursing him in Kaitaia Hospital. The two eloped and eventually landed in Taumarunui, where Thomas worked as a linesman. They had 12 children; Lianne was number nine.

The children had plenty of outdoor space in which to play, Lianne remembers. "We'd play all day and make sledges, build huts, climb trees, swim in the rivers, chase sheep, and gather up sheep's tails to cook in the fires." However, her parents' raised voices would pierce through the walls of their home and the undercurrent of alcohol and violence was an unwelcome part of family life. "Mum and Dad had a tumultuous, rocky relationship, which ended up with us leaving Taumarunui," she remembers. "One day, out of the blue, we were told to get ready. We're going on a big trip to Auckland, Mum told us." Lianne, five of her siblings and her mum boarded a train bound for Auckland, her eldest brother joining them later. "We thought it was exciting going to the big city. We were actually kicked out of home basically. While us kids thought it was an exciting adventure, the heartache and fear of an unknown future would have been huge for our mum."

Arriving in the city, the Marshalls found themselves at an aunt's place in Point Chevalier — there were already two adults and three kids in the small house. The safe space of the countryside was replaced with concrete walls, cars, highways and loneliness. "Life wasn't fun anymore and we felt we were intruding there at our aunt's home, we were like a bit of a nuisance," she says. "Understandably, a big family like ours overtaking another family's home caused bad vibes between Mum, her sister and my uncle — we could hear the arguments."

The Marshalls were able to secure a Māori Affairs grant to buy in Avondale. "I remember thinking this was a really flash house with a huge backyard. Basic furnishings were given to us by family and the house cost $10,000," Lianne says. "Mum had become an alcoholic and she'd drink with another single mum across the road. The neighbours would use all her money to buy alcohol and that meant there was no food and no power in the house. We'd walk the streets at night to steal. We just starved a lot." She remembers going to school with nothing to eat. "We'd rummage on the ground or in the bins at school for food, or steal our friends' lunches, something I always felt bad about."

There was a Pākehā whānau that lived next door who often fed the children. "We loved it there. They were missionaries who also taught us something of their Christian missions' world view," she says. Other times whānau would collect the children and take them on outings.

"Mum was also on prescription medication — Valium— just to cope with anxiety. To make it worse she got involved with spiritism," Lianne remembers. "Mum made several attempts to take her own life, either by swallowing all her Valium and trying to drink herself to oblivion, or by driving through busy intersections without stopping. She'd always be amazed to wake up the next morning still alive." Doulene's parents had passed on and, rejected by her whānau at Ahipara, she was the black sheep of the family. "There was nowhere else for us to go really," says Lianne. "I used to wish for a happy family because I never had one. I didn't know what a happy family looked like anyway."

Lianne's mum lost the Avondale house and the family were forced to shift. "We moved to New Lynn with Mum's niece. There were six in that family. They were a bit more accommodating and helped us get into a housing corporation home in Māngere," says Lianne. With the new house in Māngere came a stepfather — a Māori man from Northland. "He was fond of us, but there was abuse in a form I would rather not talk about. One by one the older brothers and sisters left home when they were 15, leaving just me and my youngest brother home alone." The neighbourhood in Māngere was mostly Māori with one Pākehā whanau next door. At school, Lianne was rebellious. "I was eventually kicked out in the middle of third form for abusing teachers, assaulting students, truancy and being under the influence of alcohol and drugs — I just didn't care. When the vice principal arrived at the house to see if everything was okay and to try and get an understanding of why I was 'acting out', my stepfather managed to squirm his way out of any further investigation. I used to wish I didn't exist," she says.

Lianne fell pregnant and her partner's parents helped raise the baby. "I had two children while in an abusive relationship. I endured regular beatings and often feared for my life. Alcohol, drugs and gang life became the norm," she says. "I was in this relationship for 10 years, until 1987, when my stepfather came back into mine and my sisters' lives again as a kind of rescuer," she says. "We separated ourselves from our abusive relationships and returned to the stepfather, who at this point was no longer with our mum; she had married another deadbeat. I found out the so-called rescuer continued his abuse, this time with my daughter, which was a big guilt trip for me. I moved out immediately. I don't know why our Māori men live in this vicious cycle of abuse and violence. Our brothers all went on to have stable, enduring marriages; I can't explain why the same upbringing affected us girls and we had opposite outcomes, I can't put my finger on it."

Everything changed when one of Lianne's sister's twin daughters was run over and killed in Māngere. "It was a wake-up call for all of us," she laments. "It made us look at our own lives and ask, 'Where are we going?' Our lives were so empty, everything looked so dark," she declares. "I didn't want to drink anymore. I didn't want to go to parties, I went to church instead. Finding faith was my escape out of a world of abuse." Around this time Lianne confronted her stepfather on his deathbed and, "I forgave him," she says. "He acknowledged me and the tears began to stream down his face before he died. It was a sweet end to a bitter story," she explains.

"I was not brought up with any Māori, any whakapapa, nothing, and that's something I get embarrassed about. I know a little but not enough to feel confident. I do wish I knew more. It's like we have been brought up in no-man's land, like we don't fit in with the Pākehā and the Māori, we live in that middle-ground," Lianne explains. When she married again the new family moved to the Bay of Plenty, close to her father's tribal home of Ruatoki. It was here Lianne felt, for the first time, that she was 'home'. Sadly though, she never made any real connection to her father's whānau. Lianne had six more children, each of whom spent most of their lives in this region. Abuse in her relationship soured the marriage and Lianne returned to Auckland, to more familiar surroundings.

In 2016 Lianne experienced a year of restoration and tragedy. Her mother Doulene passed away, but not without the healing of their relationship. This was overshadowed by the heart-rending death of her 21-year-old son Jonas Isaac Rika, who committed suicide at the end of the same year. Jonas was receiving treatment at an acute mental health unit at Middlemore Hospital in Otahuhu when he fled the hospital. He was missing for nearly six weeks.[82] He was found dead on the fence line of the hospital premises. Lianne considers the circumstances surrounding his care and his death are cases of negligence and two investigations into his death are under way.[83] Jonas' death spurred Lianne to an involvement in social work. "The city is good for study and work. It wasn't kind to us and it wasn't good for my son," she states.

Despite the highs and lows of her life, Lianne is a survivor and she is strong in her hope for a better life. "Otherwise what else is there?" she says. "One of the greatest lessons I have learned is this: we don't have to remain victims, it's all a matter of perspective and I would much rather be in the position of being an overcomer in the face of adversity." Lianne says she has always had a strong sense of resilience to survive. "When faced with a tough situation, I have always stood my ground. In my kids today I see resilience and in some I see vulnerability. I am extremely protective of my children and have had to resist the need to shield them as I know they need to learn to stand on their own two feet."

Chapter 9

Iwitanga Hou

Retribalisation

In the mid 1980s a new season of retribalisation arose throughout the nation, where iwi (tribes) were formalised by legislation and became a lot more visible in the civil life of modern New Zealand society. This was considered the beginnings of a form of tribal autonomy and cultural recognition by the Crown. However it also brought with it vehement division between iwi- and urban-affiliated Māori groups. This chapter explores the emergence of retribalisation and the impact it had on the urban pan-tribal communities.

In her thesis on migration in Northland, Ulrike Andres records how urbanisation continued through the 1970s and up until 1986, when the trend changed from a collective phenomenon to a predominantly more individual journey. Many Māori up to this period had become 'detribalised' or disconnected from their tribal identity for reasons driven by circumstance and choice, migratory push and pull factors, and the irrelevance of the tribal structure in the day-to-day lives of urban-based people. A tribal identity had become something more distant and nostalgic than an actual living way of being.

However, during the 1980s tribal identity was to take on a greater significance for Māori as radical changes in the public sector began to recognise iwi. A new cultural and political philosophy swept through the country that encouraged the re-establishment of formalised iwi networks and also saw the formation of new kinds of official urban Māori communities. The Iwi Authorities appeared on the political landscape alongside new social entities, aptly described as taura here kin groups living outside their iwi regions and mātāwaka or urban pan-tribal groups and organisations residing in another's tribal territory.

In 1978 the Department of Māori Affairs, under Kara Puketapu, introduced the Tū Tangata (Stand Tall) concept, aimed at assisting government and non-government agencies to acknowledge and recognise the strategies Māori communities might employ to prepare them for the future. Tū Tangata was a Māori development community programme that included kōkiri skills training, mātua whāngai, kōhanga reo, women's wānanga and business training, with an underlying philosophy of self-determination and self-reliance.[1] The Kōkiri Centre programmes emerged to facilitate the devolution of decision making to Māori communities. Kōkiri were set up in areas with high populations of Māori and provided an avenue for urban Māori communities to become self-reliant and to create a variety of educational and youth training programmes. Urban groups with kōkiri centres formed trusts and worked co-operatively with other groups to deliver social services to their communities. In this environment organisations such as Te Whānau o Waipareira Trust in West Auckland were born.[2]

The 1980s saw an explosion of Māori community-based networks in West Auckland. There were 56 Māori groups, including Te Atatū Māori Women's Welfare League, Waipareira Women's Welfare League, Māori Wardens, various marae committees, Kōhanga Reo, a kaumātua group, the soon-to-emerge Tū Tangata schemes, a kōkiri centre, and others, scattered throughout West Auckland.[3] Whaea Evelyn Taumaunu of Te Atatū North remembers attending an advertised meeting on the top floor of the Māori Affairs Building at Te Atatū North in February 1982. "People came out of the woodwork to discuss a way for the growing number of West Auckland Māori organisations and committees to communicate better with each other."[4] The top floor, the corridors and the lifts were jam-packed with people she recalls. The people wanted to collaborate in a more co-ordinated fashion to cater for the growing needs of the local Māori people.[5] She says "They had little control over the city's development and were stuck in a cycle of erratic funding with no real co-ordination of resources and skills."[6] Government funders did not favour small and loose groupings and it was recognised that a better structure was needed, one that wasn't competitive but collective.[7] They were all dealing with problems created by rapid urbanisation, problems that included decades of high unemployment, poor housing and low education.

Te Whānau o Waipareira

In July 1982 Connie Hanna of Māori Affairs called a meeting at Hoani Waititi marae. She informed the Māori community and government departments in the Waipareira area that a kōkiri unit would be created. Sixty people representing 23 different organisations attended that hui, and local Māori Women's Welfare League leader and school teacher June Mariu was elected as the Waipareira Community Management Group's first chairperson. Ossie Peri and Jerry Taingahue were co-vice-chairs. The management group included representatives from Māori Affairs, Social Welfare, departments of Labour and Justice and the police. The unit was established as one of seven in Auckland, the others being on the North Shore, Auckland City, Panmure, Ōtara, Māngere and Papakura.[8] In 1983 a resolution was passed to create Te Whānau o Waipareira as a charitable trust and on 24 August 1984, 20 trustees signed a deed to formally constitute Te Whānau o Waipareira Trust.[9]

June Mariu says Waipareira Trust was formed as "a good way of bringing people together who desired to make things happen for local Māori".[10] This holistic form of co-ordination became the strength of Te Whānau o Waipareira and its pathway to uplifting local Māori was "progressive unity".[11] This focus, translated as 'Kōkiritia i Roto i te Kōtahitanga' (progressively working in unity) was the foundational vision statement for this "sophisticated, pan-Māori, non-tangata whenua" urban identity.[12] As pioneers following a proactive and creative way, Te Whānau o Waipareira became a highly organised network of local, regional, national and international pan-Māori groups, "engaging astutely with the contracting environment brought about by the restructuring of government social services".[13]

Essential to Waipareira's make-up was Te Rōpū Kaumātua, formed early in the life of Te Whānau o Waipareira to support all the activities of the Trust. The rōpū was created to play a traditional role in an urban setting. John Tamihere remembers a period when Māori elders were being pushed to one side, and when the young activists

A gathering of pan-tribal kaumātua who aligned themselves with West Auckland's Māori Urban Authority, Te Whānau o Waipareira Trust.

Reproduced from *Te Whanau, A Celebration of Te Whānau o Waipareira*, 2001, courtesy of Te Whānau o Waipareira Trust

saw them as sell-outs. "They were never sell-outs. They just weren't skilled enough to defend themselves and articulate their views. They were quite mesmerised by the white man," John says.[14] When Waipareira was created John had realised there were numbers of elders who weren't being respected and honoured. He believed they needed the right to commune as they had when they were being brought up among their kin in their tribal homelands. "So I set up our Te Rōpū Kaumātua and called our elders together, anyone 65 and over in the West, to meet and share the stories of their upbringing. The beauty of Waipareira is that it's pan-tribal. We don't care what your tribe is. Or what your religious denomination might be … there's room for anyone. And having the elders there brought a serenity, a calmness, and a dignity that had been missing for some time."[15]

The elders were initially involved in helping people trace their whakapapa to the tribes, and "trips back to their homeland so aunties and uncles, who've lost contact with their whānau, can be reconnected".[16] The elders were available for tangi, hui, blessings for the opening of new projects, and representing Waipareira at events elsewhere. They visited prisoners and mentored young people on the brink of trouble with the law. On the marae the paepae was filled with kaumātua from numerous tribes, not just one iwi. The kaumātua were always kept busy and they were the role models for the young people at Waipareira. Their families often complained because they didn't have a babysitter anymore; their kaumātua were too busy. One Waipareira member said, "In some places in Māoridom the respect for the kaumātua has broken down, but here at Waipareira it is being reborn." For over 20 years the key role of Te Rōpū Kaumātua has been to support Waipareira whenever they are called.[17] Their work in the organisation is encapsulated in the proverb, "Nā te kaha me te aroha, ka mōhio mai mātou te wairua o tā rātou mahi (Their commitment and love for the people is a huge strength)."

With changes in the political climate in the late 1980s and into the 1990s, Te Whānau o Waipareira's profiles on the political and cultural stages were heightened. Despite some resentment from their iwi-affiliated cousins, the organisation became a critical provider of services and community development for the Māori they served in West Auckland.[18]

For Te Whānau o Waipareira and other emerging urban authorities and trusts, the political landscape of the 1980s and 1990s signalled a new phase of complexity and turmoil that would force change and division but also create an environment for innovation and reflection. The 1980s saw Māori find a new confidence, motivated by a new generation of educated leaders who began to make their presence known. Māori leaders who attended the atmosphere-changing 1984 Hui Taumata (Māori Economic Summit Conference) openly stated their desire to see Māori break free from the dependency cycle of government welfare schemes and take control of their own destiny.

Devolution and control

Self-control and self-determination were the primary desires of the people in a political environment where the fourth Labour government came to power touting free-market reforms. One result of this policy was the devolution of Māori Affairs. The control of the department's government-funded programmes was to be handed to Māori groups, primarily to tribal organisations. The government saw the re-establishment of the traditional iwi tribal structure "as an appropriate means of delivering government programmes to Māori people".[19] The Treaty of Waitangi Amendment Act 1985 supported this re-iwi-isation. The Act empowered the Waitangi Tribunal to investigate Treaty claims back to 1840, and it officially acknowledged tribal groups and territories that existed in 1840.[20] This retribalisation was about installing the iwi as the vehicle of self-determination.

The process of devolution and its effect on iwi, and the ramifications for the urban Māori voice, were profound. Māori Affairs was devolved to become the Ministry of Māori Policy (Manatū Māori) with the Iwi Transition Agency (Te Tira Ahu Iwi) set up to assist iwi in building their capacity and capability to enable them to deliver services to their people. This process was to be completed by 1994.

Many Māori saw devolution as an opportunity for greater participation and self-sufficiency, while others regarded it simply as the government abdicating its responsibilities for Māori affairs.[21] *Te Urupare Rangapū*, the Labour Party policy statement, was issued in 1988. It announced that the development of Iwi Authorities would be "fully operational" by 1994.

The Rūnanga a Iwi Act, originally the Iwi Empowerment Bill, followed close behind. The Labour Government adopted it in 1990 to help facilitate devolution and bring about the incorporation of iwi. The Act's crucial aim was to establish Iwi Authorities as rūnanga capable of running the department's programmes. The rūnanga would be accountable to the government.

It seemed at this stage of Māori development that the iwi would be given greater status. It was the primary social organisation in Māori society. Hirini Moko Mead explains that the basic meaning of the word iwi is derived from bone, which gives strength and form to a body. He says the characteristics of an iwi as a social group are that it claims and occupies a large estate of land that it defends. It is a political group that maintains alliances to many hapū whose members acknowledge descent from or whakapapa to a common ancestor. Mead reiterates that iwi stood like an independent nation that defended its lands and resources, and hapū were part of this collective. He records that an officer of the Department of Māori Affairs, Wishy Jaram, was seconded to the Wellington office to prepare a paper for the Rūnanga a Iwi Bill. After interviewing a number of people about the essential characteristics of iwi, some of his findings were listed in section 4 of the first draft of the Rūnanga a Iwi Act dated August 1990. These included:

- descent from (commonly acknowledged) tupuna

- o collective possession of a demonstrable cultural and historical identity, based on a shared body of traditional lore (this was struck out)
- o a developed political organisation with widely shared aspirations (struck out)
- o a structure of hapū (struck out and replaced with the single word hapū)
- o a network of functioning marae (struck out and replaced with the single word marae)
- o belonged historically to a (clearly delineated rohe) takiwā
- o continuous existence traditionally and widely acknowledged by other iwi (reworded but essential point maintained).[22]

The final Rūnanga a Iwi Act 1990 defined iwi in section 5, basing that definition on the preceding findings, with slight changes as indicated. Section 28 of the Act outlined the duties of an incorporated rūnanga: to look after the iwi members it represents; to register its members and identify where they live; and to acknowledge the right for other iwi in their takiwā to establish taura here groups or, as quoted in section 29, for its own members to set up taura here in other takiwā with the consultation of the iwi with mana whenua. The logical consequence of these developments was the establishment of constitutional tribal voices.

Tribes applied for status as accountable iwi rūnanga, who as applicants to the government, had to meet most if not all of these characteristics of iwi to participate in the economic reforms of the time, where greater responsibility and empowerment was supposedly devolved to tribal communities.[23] Seen as the re-establishment of iwi, within a decade Māori became major players in providing a range of services in the health, education, welfare and labour sectors that were previously run by the state or professional enclaves.[24] Out of this process came greater understanding of the tribes' position showing sizeable percentages of iwi members living outside the tribal territory whose status as members was unclear, and many tribes had large numbers of Māori with distant or no tribal affiliations residing in their regions.[25] Additionally, the urban centres, which were full of immigrant Māori communities, were often found to be in the majority; their presence threatened the identity and sovereignty of local tribes.[26]

The Rūnanga a Iwi Act was repealed by the incoming National

party and replaced with the Ka Awatea (It's a New Day) policy for Māori development. The policy focused on 'closing the gaps' in education, employment, economic development and health. The Iwi Transition Agency and the Ministry of Māori Affairs (Manatū Māori) were consolidated to become the Ministry of Māori Development, today called Te Puni Kōkiri. The momentum generated by these policies and the mobilisation of iwi was commonly referred to as iwi development.

Stephen Webster recorded 42 "acknowledged iwi" in 1974,[27] and as the 1990s rolled into the turn of the millennium some 95 distinct iwi were recorded.[28] By early 1998 there were about 55 iwi and, later that same year, 78 iwi were acknowledged by Te Ohu Kaimoana, the Fisheries Commission. By 2001 the government census recorded 95 distinct iwi.[29] Webster cited the promise of benefits derived from the importance given iwi in government policies, and later the qualification by the fisheries commission, for the increase in the number of registered iwi.[30] This major turnaround in numbers ran contrary to past governmental policies that had previously worked against tribalism. State agencies had previously labelled the pursuit of Māoriness as separatist.[31] Webster wrote that contemporary Māori kinship was now being "revitalized" in capitalist forms.[32] Others, such as Elizabeth Rata, postulated that colonialism and 'global capitalism' shaped the form of the contemporary tribe, which overwhelmed any legacy of the past. Rata saw retribalisation as an ideology that championed the tribe rather than the wider ethnic group (Māori).[33]

In 1994 Dr Roger Maaka questioned whether these policies really matched the realities of Māori society at the time, in his paper *The New Tribes: Conflicts and Continuities in the Social Organization of Urban Māori*. He identified two realities: one, that 80% of Māori lived outside of their iwi-based areas, and two, that 27.5% acknowledged no tribal affiliation. By restricting Māori advancement specifically to the tenets of autonomous 'iwi' development, Maaka questioned its appropriateness in light of current Māori realities, reckoning that the vision was flawed.[34] He questioned if the iwi was the most effective vehicle for development and concluded that the government policies did not take into account that the tribe as the fundamental social organisation of Māori society and the tribe as the fundamental essence of Māori identity had diverged as the twentieth century progressed.

Iwi and rūnanga: a Ngāti Kahungunu case study

Throughout the twentieth century the tribe's status as the primary organising force had changed. The majority of Māori who claimed affiliation to a tribe did not live and work in a tribal context. Dr Roger Maaka wasn't "arguing a case of tribal versus pan-Māori development, but that political organization must reflect social reality".[35] Ranginui Walker also criticised the revival of tribal structures as flawed because over 70% of Māori lived away from their tribal areas. It was clear to him that the devolution would deliver nothing to Māori living away from their tribal areas in the towns and cities unless they formed groups linked to their tribal rūnanga.[36]

One example of the complexities of creating the taura here and matāwaka groupings, and organising them formally in an urban context, is illustrated in the workings of the Ngāti Kahungunu council formulated in Christchurch. Maaka followed and recorded the activities of his Ngāti Kahungunu tribal relatives living within Ngāi Tahu territory in the South Island. They organised themselves into a taura here council and branched into supporting a matāwaka (pan-tribal) rūnanga in response to the changing cultural, political and economic landscape of the 1980s and 1990s.

Ngāti Kahungunu are situated on the East Coast of the North Island. Their tribal area covers a sizeable territory from Wairoa to the Wairarapa. They have a number of common ancestors connected to the Ngāi Tahu tangata whenua of the lower two-thirds of the South Island. Illustrious ancestors such as Uenuku, Paikea, Porourangi, Tahumakakanui, Tahupōtiki, Ira, Kahungunu, Whatumamoe, Tāmanuhiri, Tamawhakatina, Te Aomatarahi, Te Hikaraeroa, Tūmāpuhiarangi, Waipuha, Rokomaiwhaia and Tuputā are all found in the tribal histories and whakapapa of both Ngāti Kahungunu and Ngāi Tahu.

In 1980 Ngāti Kahungunu elders of Heretaunga called a meeting to explore creating an organisation to unify their Kahungunu people from Wairoa to Wairarapa.[37] The upshot was Te Rūnanganui o Ngāti Kahungunu (The Great Council of Ngāti Kahungunu). The desire for tribal mobilisation and unity, spearheaded by respected high-profile personalities and with the support of Kahungunu people, reflected the mood of the 1980s. In 1988 this rūnanga became an incorporated society and the official Iwi Authority, the voice of the tribe.[38] Te Okenga (Aussie) Huata's personal vision was to tap into the talents of Kahungunu people living away from home and to include them in the development of the tribe as a whole.[39] He encouraged Kahungunu people living outside of their North Island tribal region to form themselves into associations that would allow them to affiliate with Te Rūnanganui o Ngāti Kahungunu in Heretaunga.[40]

Ngāti Kahungunu people living in Christchurch responded in June of 1987 by formalising their kinship links. They created Te Rūnanganui o Ngāti Kahungunu ki Waitaha (The Ngāti Kahungunu Council of Canterbury), a taura here entity. Over the years many northern Ngāti Kahungunu people, including those from the trade-training era, had made the South Island their home. Ngāi Tahu members also married into and lived in Ngāti Kahungunu territories. According to statistics, by 1991 Ngāti Kahungunu-affiliated people made up 15% of the total Māori population in Christchurch.[41]

The Christchurch group would meet to learn Kahungunu karanga, oratory and waiata. In two years they established themselves as a visible social network in Christchurch. The group recognised their rūnanga needed to become a legal entity if it wished to fulfil any public community role. A constitution with objectives and membership rules was created, primarily to maintain and strengthen the links between Ngāti Kahungunu people living in Canterbury and the tribal organisations of the "home districts".[42] The Christchurch-based rūnanga was acknowledged as an official associate to Te Rūnanganui o Ngāti Kahungunu. Kahungunu people from throughout the South Island began to gather and in 1989 they formed a wider taura here council named Te Rūnanganui o Ngāti Kahungunu ki Te Waipounamu (The Council of Ngāti Kahungunu in the South Island).[43] This created a wider outreach for members of Ngāti Kahungunu in terms of becoming involved and getting to know each other.

In July 1987 at a pan-tribal meeting held in Christchurch, Māori Affairs stepped forward to discuss the implications for Māori when the devolution of its programmes to Māori groups capable of running them occurred. The Christchurch Kahungunu group were reluctant to become involved at that time as they were newly formed, but they elected two representatives to a new entity that was to become Te Rūnanga o Ngā Maata Waka (the faces of the canoes: Multi-tribal Council), representing the pan-tribal voice for the Māori community in Christchurch. According to Norm Dewes, an approach was also made by the late kaumātua Hōhua Tūtengaehe to consider setting up an urban Māori entity for those Māori who did not originate in Christchurch but lived there. The elders saw the need to create a unified voice and to find a vehicle to address the needs of urban Māori in Christchurch.[44] In 1989 Te Rūnanga o Ngā Maata Waka council was formalised and met under a new constitution.[45]

The reality of devolution meant accepting a workload, previously funded by the government, on a voluntary basis. This became apparent when the Kahungunu rūnanga had to deal with social problems without the resources of trained people or finances. During the devolution period of 1987–1990, both Māori Affairs and Mātua Whāngai began to refer clients to their individual tribal groups, but without any of the support promoted by the Iwi Transition Agency. Homeless Kahungunu people seeking assistance from Māori Affairs were referred to the newly formed rūnanga as if it were an extension of Social Welfare or of the Department of Māori Affairs. Sadly, the rūnanga had little if any finances or resources to be able to provide any real aid, except those gained through donations and its own fundraising. In this case the gap between theory and practicality appears fundamentally flawed. In the urban environment, the taura here were unable to carry out the social responsibilities for their own kin.[46]

Devolution went from discussion to policy within eight months and rūnanga members were required to attend a constant round of meetings to familiarise themselves with a flood of unfamiliar ideas and procedures. When the Rūnanga a Iwi Act was repealed, the drama caused interest in the Kahungunu rūnanga to wane. Roger Maaka reflects how the Kahungunu rūnanga was successful in making links among its own tribespeople, but was less successful on a number of other fronts. Out of an estimated population of 1300 Ngāti Kahungunu people in Christchurch, the maximum number of people they were able to attract was only a hundred. Also, establishing formal links with the home rūnanga, despite routine communication from the Christchurch group, was impractical because of geographical distance and the lack of support.

Out of the experience of this taura here group, Maaka concluded in 1994 that tribal identity in an urban takiwā would have "very little tangible effect on the daily life of its members". He suggested the urban taura here groups would stay active as social and cultural groups or as a support base for their delegates on pan-Māori organisations, but other than that "they would remain politically passive".[47] Maaka also noted that the lack of a home base or an effective communication network, giving access to a city-wide distribution of its members, were difficult factors to overcome. Creating an outpost far from the tribal home base and in another tribe's territory, he felt, was "too great an adjustment for the Māori psyche" at the time, as the traditional notions of respect "seemed to act against such a development".[48] These factors, along with the lack of government support, put their vision beyond their full capacity but continued to dwell in the hearts of the people.

Nevertheless, Ngāti Kahungunu rūnanga representatives took a leading role in the activities of Te Rūnanga o Ngā Maata Waka (Maata Waka) that was, like many organisations, formalised out of the Rūnanga a Iwi Act and the Iwi Transition Bill. This rūnanga included pan-tribal Māori members. At the time of its incorporation, Maata Waka was defined as 'the confederation of all tribes, all nations, all people'. Central to the philosophy of Maata Waka was a belief that everyone be recognised as a beneficiary of Te Tiriti o Waitangi and the intent of the Treaty should apply to all. By 1990 Maata Waka had evolved a system of portfolios covering areas of concern in the community, including education, employment, health, housing, justice, welfare and economic development.[49] However, just as Ngāti Kahungunu ki Waitaha received little support from the government, Maata Waka fell into the same position. There was an expectation that it could provide the kinds of social services Māori Affairs once provided. Requests for assistance overwhelmed the organisation, and its members realised it would be unable to achieve little. The organisation became moribund.[50] At a meeting called by Te Rūnanga o Ngā Taura Here o Whanganui-a-Tara, similar mātāwaka urban Māori groups from Auckland, Hamilton, Wellington and Christchurch attended. The common thread in group discussions was how 'iwi development' favoured the tangata whenua of the cities and rejected the needs of urban Māori who were the majority in the city environments.[51]

The establishment of Maata Waka brought to the surface tensions between Ngāi Tahu tangata whenua, despite senior Ngāi Tahu kaumātua being present at the Maata Waka meetings. The failure to invite Ngāi Tahu to the inaugural Maata Waka meeting called by Māori Affairs was an unfortunate mistake that cast a shadow over inter-organisation negotiations over the years. At a later Ngāi Tahu meeting, the raising of strong legal action against the presence of

Ngā Hau E Whā Marae in Aranui Christchurch has played a pivotal role in the civil and social affairs of the local urban community. Here District Court hearings are being held on the marae after the Christchurch earthquake in February of 2013.
Photograph by John Kirk-Anderson, courtesy of Fairfax NZ

any mātāwaka urban Māori authority was mooted.[52] Opposition to any other type of iwi authority other than Ngāi Tahu was repeatedly publicised. The 1990s was marred by vigorous jostling for position, particularly over the issues of the denial of mātāwaka representation at any top-level decision making, despite being numerically stronger, and the needs and aspirations of mātāwaka being determined by tangata whenua.[53] A working equilibrium was eventually found and Te Rūnanga o Ngā Maata Waka became the voice for non-Ngāi Tahu Māori in Christchurch.

Norm Dewes from Wairoa (Ngāti Kahungunu-Ngāti Porou) is an ex-trade training scheme graduate from Rehua Hostel. He has led Te Rūnanga o Ngā Maata Waka for over 25 years. Today, the Mātāwaka organisation has been the guardian-manager of the embattled Ngā

Hau e Whā National Marae in Christchurch since 2004. Under the mantle of Maata Waka the marae provides crucial social services for the local community and all New Zealanders.[54] Norm reflects on how the rūnanga arrived at where they stand now. "We laboured for years over the old mentality of 'them' — being Ngāi Tahu, and 'us' — urban Māori in Christchurch. We had to get rid of that idea. We know we are in Ngāi Tahu territory, in particular Ngāi Tūahuriri territory, and we have adopted a collaborative and unaggressive approach to work with the local iwi for the benefit of all. They have been gracious to us. So there is a need for mutual respect in our partnerships as Māori," he states.[55] Today he believes the biggest asset of the marae is "the relationship between the Maata Waka community, our families and with Ngāi Tahu".[56]

Finding ways to maintain the 14-acre property and economically realise the purpose of the 'national marae' with integrity has not been easy, Norm says. "The focus of the elders was to look after the unwashed, the unclean, the unwanted and the un-everything, to give them a chance and for those who are in prisons," he recalls. "Hence, we have been strongly involved in the fields of health, education, recreation, employment, entertainment, justice, road safety and community services to enhance our community and this country."[57] Because of the national focus of the marae set down by the founding elders, Norm sees the necessity to cater for the needs of everyone, including the growing immigrant population moving into Christchurch. More recently, after a long and laboured consent process with the Māori Land Court, the rūnanga is now involved in building affordable social housing units on marae property as part of relieving the current burden for housing in Canterbury, but more specifically to cater for the urgent need of accommodation for workers. This project will cater for 51 workers engaged in rebuilding Christchurch over the next few years.[58]

Urban Māori Authorities

The struggles and tensions experienced by Te Rūnanga o Ngāti Kahungunu ki Waitaha and Te Rūnanga o Ngā Maata Waka reflect the great efforts and toil of urban organisations of the likes of Te Whānau o Waipareira, the Manukau Urban Authority, Te Rūnanga o Te Upoko o te Ika, Te Rūnanga o Kirikiriroa, Te Rūnanga o Murihiku and others — to create an accepted and recognised voice to fulfil the new social needs of increasingly large numbers of Māori who now lived outside of their tribal homes, and who did not affiliate with their iwi.

The landmark event in the 1990s that motivated the urban authorities to collaborate for recognition of urban Māori was the allocation of proceeds from the fisheries settlement of 1992.

During the 1980s, fishing rights dominated the Waitangi Tribunal processes. Matiu Rata argued that the Crown had "exercised presumptive rights over customary Māori fisheries". This was the basis for the Muriwhenua Fisheries Claim.[59] The tribunal's Muriwhenua report and the Ngāi Tahu Sea Fisheries report precipitated the largest and most complicated of all Treaty settlements, and it negotiated the full and final settlement of all Māori commercial fishing claims.

The then National government offered Māori the 'Sealord Deal'. The Crown would assist Māori in the 50% purchase of the Sealords Fisheries company, and purchase 20% of the nation's fish quota for allocation among Māori tribes. The settlement was worth $170 million and provided for customary food-gathering rights.[60] In return, Māori were asked to cease Treaty-based claims to the country's fishing resources.[61] Amidst myriad controversy, through tribal leadership, Māori agreed to the settlement. The Sealord Deal was signed in September of 1992 and led to the Treaty of Waitangi (Fisheries Claims) Settlement Act. It was a pan-tribal settlement to benefit all Māori[62] and was considered a momentous occasion, representing the most significant shift of resources from the Crown to Māori.[63]

The iwi model was proposed as the paradigm to distribute quota and the proceeds from the assets. Distribution to iwi was to be carried out by a government-appointed Waitangi Fisheries Commission named Te Ohu Kaimoana. The public wrangling over the appropriate model of distribution to iwi saw the commission "bogged down for more than ten years devising a formula that would accommodate all Māori claims."[64] In line with the Rūnanga a Iwi Act, in devising an equitable and workable allocation formula, Te Ohu Kaimoana decided only traditional iwi would receive fishing quota, rejecting urban Māori.

'Distributive justice' was sought by urban Māori who considered their rights had been neglected by the deal, and challenged the official operating definition of 'iwi'.[65] Urban Māori who were not affiliated to an iwi, and Urban Māori Authorities failed to qualify for a share in the assets and reparations under the Commission's definition of iwi. Under Article 2 of the Treaty, iwi had exclusive rights to the resources they owned.[66] Representing the mātāwaka pan-Māori voice, Norm Dewes said, "We were not recognised by the government as having any real status."[67]

Dame Temuranga Batley-Jackson (formerly June Jackson) and other first-generation urban Māori with diverse backgrounds established the Manukau Urban Māori Authority (MUMA) in 1985 to represent the needs and interests of South Auckland urban Māori. With a strong portfolio of social services, MUMA has served the community with a 'by Māori for Māori' attitude for 27 years. June Jackson has sat on the parole board since 1986. She has been a fierce advocate for urban Māori and has always had 'amicable' differences with iwi.[68] Tania Rangiheuea records how June began a dialogue with government on the rights of urban Māori and, in 1991, she said:

> When I first started fighting with the Government over the right of urban Māori to share in resources set aside for Māori, I was on my own. I didn't care ... I'd look those iwi leaders straight in the eye and ask them who was caring for the people in the cities. Of course it was us.[69]

At the same time, a Māori lawyer by the name of John Tamihere was appointed chief executive of Waipareira Trust. Born in Auckland in 1959, Tamihere is of Ngāti Porou ki Hauraki and Whakatōhea descent, and after graduating with law and arts degrees from the University of Auckland had worked for Māori Affairs and in private practice. He was to bring the voice of the Waipareira collective to the forefront to fight for the rights of urban Māori. Te Whānau o Waipareira Trust joined forces with MUMA, along with Te Rūnanganui o Te Ūpoko o Te Ika and Te Rūnanga o Ngā Maata Waka to resist Te Ohu Kaimoana's allocation process excluding urban Māori. With the support of thousands, these Māori urban organisations began a long and arduous battle for the rights of urban Māori to be recognised alongside iwi.

Their battle was to become a war, not directly against Te Ohu Kaimoana, but against retribalisation or fundamental tribalism, a dictum that rejects what is not tribal and says you don't belong if you are manuhiri (visitors) or rāwaho (strangers). Retribalisation denied urban Māori rights to the benefits of Treaty of Waitangi settlements except through mandated tribal organisations, which were now the flagship for future Māori development. This presented a major barrier for mātāwaka peoples living in the cities or in the smaller provincial towns, where the majority of the Māori population had settled permanently. While many urban Māori recognised their own iwi status, the majority could not sustain a presence in both their tribal homelands and the urban centres. This created a real quandary as to who was going to care for the day-to-day needs of a large population of urban Māori living far away from their iwi-based centres.

Who would stand for their rights and cater for their needs?

Jim Ranginui, Kirikiriroa (Hamilton)

Jim Ranginui with his son Simon, daughter-in-law Hana and his mokopuna, James, Mārama and Ruby-Jade. Hamilton, December, 2016.

Courtesy of Bradford Haami

Jim Ranginui left his homeland of Waikaremoana in the Urewera forest when he was 18 and has lived away from home in urban situations for the past 52 years. He was one of the younger children of 11 siblings to Dave and Ani Ranginui. The family lived on whānau land at Tuai, Waikaremoana. His father ran dry stock on the land and drove freight trucks and buses to supplement their income. There was half an acre of land set aside for crops, a portion of which was always set aside for kai contribution for hui and tangi at the marae. Deer stalking and pig hunting added meat to the simple kai available and is still an essential and favourite activity for Jim and his whānau.

People were poor, Jim remembers, but the village community provided for everyone. Jim's branch of the Ranginui family were mihingare (Anglican, Church of England) and were influenced by the American Evangelist Billy Graham's message that swept through New Zealand and the Tūhoe region in 1959. Te Reo Māori was the home language until Jim attended school, where the children were prevented from speaking their own tongue.

Like many Tūhoe from his region, Jim was sent to Te Aute College in Pukehou, Hawke's Bay. "In the first two months at the school there was a 'breaking in' period of time — it was a school rule — you were prohibited from making any contact with whānau," Jim says. As a junior he faced brutal violence from senior bullies, who beat him in the cloak room. It was something he was not prepared for and had never before experienced. When some of the women staff who were Tūhoe informed his parents of Jim's ordeal, he was transferred to Lindisfarne College in Hastings, where there was no bullying. Later, Jim returned home to attend Wairoa College. At the behest of his father, he was recruited by Māori Welfare Officer Lena Manuel to attend a Māori trade-training course in Wellington.

At the Wairoa train station with his sisters and parents, Jim waited for the southern train to arrive. He knew nobody and had no knowledge of distance or the location of Wellington. For Jim it was another traumatic separation from family. He remembers his mother being devastated at seeing him leave. Jim's father was adamant he had to leave to find work — there was nothing at home and being Māori wasn't going to get him far. He was sure this was the right decision for his son. "I was petrified as I stepped on the train, I cried as the train left my family behind," Jim remembers.

Māori boys from all over the East Coast filled the two railcars. "Quickly the boys made friends," Jim says. "Pulling into Wellington was mind-boggling yet exciting." They were met by Ralph Love, a lovely man who transferred all the boys and their luggage to Trentham, where they were allocated shared huts at the hostel. The Māori Affairs Trade Training School was situated at Gracefields industrial area near Petone. Jim had to sleep in a small hut with another new boy, Harry Bradnock.

Initially Jim chose to be in the electricians' trade course, but he missed out on a place and was put into carpentry and joinery. The course was over three years and accommodation was provided for two years. In their third year, the boys had to find their own accommodation.

In the first two weeks the boys were tested to review their level of education. Jim knew he didn't pass. His friend Digger Ruru told him to ask the other boys to help him. Jim had seen the boys smoking and drinking to the point that their allowances were all spent by the end of the week, and he knew he would need to offer something to them in return for their help. He offered to lend the boys weekend money for their help. The boys took the trade and taught Jim every night. It took him two months to begin to comprehend what he was being taught. The results of his next tests showed the tutors he was more than capable of doing the study.

Jim always looked forward to the monthly visits by his parents. They would drive from Waikaremoana, towing a trailer of food for all of the boys. Other parents did the same and families would often plan to combine their visits. "The hākari we'd have were fantastic," Jim reminisces. One day Jim approached the army brigadier about converting an unused army barracks into a community marae. The brigadier agreed and the boys set to work refurbishing the premises. They renovated the space, fitted new furniture and installed a black-and-white television.

The local Upper Hutt Māori haka group, Māwai Hakona, led by Dovey Katene-Hovath, became a whāngai whānau for Jim and the boys. The group would include the boys on outings and make them feel part of the community whānau. Jim joined the haka team and performed with them around Wellington. It was his re-introduction to reo and tikanga.

In the second year the building trainees were separated into four teams and sent to Porirua, Mana, Wainui, Upper Hutt and Lower Hutt to build 'beautiful' Māori Affairs homes. The homes were created for the large influx of Māori families moving into the Wellington regions. "On completing each house we would plant a crop of potatoes to break in the soil for the new families entering the homes. We were building civilisation," Jim says.

In Jim's third year he moved out to flat with friends. He did his placement for six months with a joinery factory in Naenae, fitting houses in Porirua, Waikanae, Titahi Bay and Cannons Creek. The course was designed to be completed over four years, but Jim's year completed it in three years. He passed all of his exams. In 1968 Jim took a position in the Waikato with Bob Hynd for two years, building prefabs. In 1970 Jim met Margaret, an Irish woman, who became his wife. The couple were to have four children: Marcia, Simon, Mathew and Emily, all of whom were raised in Kirikiriroa, Hamilton.

Jim took on a lecturing position at Waikato Institute of Technology in Hamilton. He held the first Māori tutor position at the institute. Jim was on probation as a tutor for four years and was prohibited from teaching the Māori trade trainees. In 1975 he became the first full-time Māori tutor at Waikato Institute of Technology. Ten years would pass before another Māori was employed as a tutor. In 1978, due to a change in government policy, Jim was told he would train the Māori trade trainees. "I was much harder on our boys but supported them after hours with kai and tautoko," Jim says.

He says he was so busy he had little time to concentrate on tikanga or making connections with Tainui Waikato, until he opened a trainee course at Waahi Pā in Huntly and began a long-term connection with Dame Te Arikinui Te Atairangikaahu and her husband Whatumoana Paki.

Jim retired in 2004. He is proud of his children's achievements in education and their careers. They now have their own families. It would be years after his children had grown up that he would take a deeper interest in his Tūhoe identity. In 2016 he took his children and their families back to Waikaremoana to the opening of their Tūhoe Ruapani marae to rekindle that engagement. Some of his children are now working hard to re-discover their reo, which Jim did not pass on.

For Jim, the disadvantages of leaving home were greater than the advantages. "I lost the fluency of my Māoritanga but achieved education, professionalism and the skills of a trade. I had to leave home to obtain that, and my parents knew this," he says.

Jim believes whakapono (faith), whakapapa, aroha, tūmanako (hope) and whiwhi tohu mātauranga (receiving an education) are the main elements Māori living in the city need to maintain for their futures.

Chapter 10 | **Mana Mātāwaka**

The Urban Authorities

Since their establishment, the urban authorities have come to the notice of the public largely because of important litigations. They have become outspoken in their positions on New Zealand's cultural, economic and political stages. Their fight alongside iwi for recognition saw the urban voice rise to prominence. The Fisheries Commission Te Ohu Kaimoana managed the fisheries assets on behalf of all Māori and had decided the method of proportional distribution would be to divide the quota between iwi. Some tribes argued allocation should be made using the number of people affiliated to an iwi and others argued for distribution based on the length of coastline within a tribe's territory. Paul Meredith of the Mātāhauraki Research Institute wrote that iwi became the master narrative for constructing the identities and citizenship of Māori in the present, and urban Māori rose to "challenge that narrative".[1]

In West Auckland, Te Whānau o Waipareira were not prepared to accept the government's public policy favouring an iwi approach designed to accommodate all Māori interests and development strategies. John Tamihere commented, "The urban group said, 'We are Māori and we are in the cities. We make up a large bunch of Māori, so we want to be participating in this economic opportunity.' But that was denied."[2]

Waipareira were concerned that Māori who did not fall into a tribal category were given lesser status as Māori, and that urban Māori would be unlikely to benefit from the distribution of assets to iwi. This triggered a war of interpretation around the meaning of the word 'iwi' and its application with regard to non-kin-based Māori associations.[3] It was also argued that most of the social problems facing Māori occurred in the cities and that Urban Māori Authorities carried the responsibility for these people, not iwi. Additionally, many hapū with their own sovereignty over territory were also negatively affected by the revitalisation of iwi because they did not fit the criteria as a tribe.

The result was a series of legal proceedings that went all the way to the Privy Council in England. The Fisheries Commission filed in the High Court, seeking an order to prevent the Waitangi Tribunal from considering claims related to their allocation model. In response, Urban Māori Authorities compiled a register of urban individuals who had given the authorities a mandate to manage Treaty settlement assets on their behalf. When the case reached the Court of Appeal, over 10,000 people had signed the petition; within 12 days the signatures passed the 13,000 mark.[4] In 1996 the Court of Appeal ruled that urban Māori had a right to share in the assets, regardless of whether they could establish their ancestry to a particular iwi. The Court also ruled that the Fisheries Claims Settlement Act was a pan-Māori settlement.[5]

In 1997, however, Tainui, Ngāti Porou and the Treaty Tribes Coalition made an appeal to the Privy Council in England. The Council over-ruled the Court of Appeal's previous decision. The Council held that the question of who could be classed as iwi members fell outside the scope of the appeal and referred the matter back to the High Court to consider if "Te Ohu Kaimoana [was] obliged by statute to distribute to iwi and if so, in the context of the allocation scheme, does 'iwi' mean only traditional tribes?"[6] In 1998, the New Zealand High Court proceedings argued for either a positive answer to the question in favour of Te Ohu Kaimoana or a negative ruling. Some of the opinions from the evidence related to iwi included the following:

- A group that takes its source from the mana of a single ancestor to whom the group is genealogically connected.
- The removal of this element from the equation creates an entity of entirely different order.

- o Any group defined by any other factor cannot call themselves iwi.
- o If the question of whakapapa is destroyed we will be like that (swaggers, travellers) and lose our kin structure.
- o Urban groups fulfilled the function of the iwi in caring for the needs of Māori living in the city.
- o Prior to the 1700s, there were no "iwi" in the sense of tribes composed of hapu as "sub-tribes" and holding contiguous territory. Iwi in this sense have formed since then as an inseparable part of capitalism, settlement, and colonisation.
- o They (Urban Māori Authorities) regard traditional iwi as fossils ... the UMAs have become the colonisers of iwi.[7]

The Urban Māori Authorities did not contest the whānau/hapū/iwi paradigm so dominant in Māori society, but applauded the efforts of tribal leaders who had worked tirelessly to advance the interests of iwi. While challenging for what they perceived as their rights, the Urban Māori Authorities also legitimised traditional tribes living in traditional territories. In ruling, Justice Patterson determined that the Māori Fisheries Act as amended was clearly aimed at allocating assets "solely to iwi" and that "iwi does mean only tribes". If iwi required a whakapapa base, "then UMAs are not iwi". However, this did not preclude urban Māori who could affiliate to their iwi in the future, from securing those benefits. Tania Rangiheuea wrote, "The court's narrow conception of Māori culture and identity had recast Māori identity and Treaty discourse back into an archaic tribal tradition that had limited application to the modern-day realities of urban Māori dwellers."[8]

In 1999 the Court of Appeal dismissed Justice Patterson's decision. The three main litigants were Te Whānau o Waipareira Trust headed by the Honourable John Tamihere, the Manukau Urban Authority (MUMA) led by June Jackson, and Te Rūnanga o Ngā Maata Waka headed by Norm Dewes. In their bid to get a definitive statement of the meaning of iwi, the group twice fronted the Privy Council in England, took three High Court cases in New Zealand and three cases at the Courts of Appeal in New Zealand "at significant cost" to the Urban Māori Authorities. In 2000 the Fisheries Commission was revamped and June Mariu, chairwoman of Waipareira, and June Jackson, chairwoman of MUMA, became members of the Commission representing urban Māori.

Manukau Urban Māori Authority Marae and kura at Māngere, 2017.
Courtesy of Bradford Haami

Further legal action against Te Ohu Kaimoana was taken over the rights of urban Māori to have an opinion regarding a $20 million fund set aside 'for urban Māori' and administered by Te Pūtea Whakatupu Trust. The trust was formed in 2004 under the Māori Fisheries Act 2004, to promote education, training and research in fisheries' activities for Māori.[9] When a review of Te Pūtea Whakatupu Trust occurred in 2015, the National Urban Māori Authority (NUMA) sought further litigation. Willie Jackson of NUMA said, "There is $540 million in assets allocated for iwi, of which less than five percent is set aside to support the needs and aspirations of urban Māori … now Iwi are being told by TOKM [Te Ohu Kaimoana] to take it all. We can't allow that to happen."[10] He said NUMA was left with few options but to go back to the courts to ensure urban Māori were included as beneficiaries of the Māori fisheries settlement.[11] "We want fairness," Jackson said.[12] In July 2016 Judge Simon France ruled that urban Māori organisations were not provided adequate opportunity to present their views on a 2015 review proposing changes to Te Pūtea Whakatupu Trust."[13] "So now they have to consult with us,"

John Tamihere said.[14] Tamihere continued to provoke iwi leaders about fairness by reminding them, "That's ten percent of Māoridom endeavouring to control 90 percent of us."[15]

At the same time as the fisheries rounds were in legal process, another case related to the recognition of urban Māori rights and the definition of iwi came to the fore. After falling out with a unit of the Department of Social Welfare called the Community Funding Agency (CFA), Te Whānau o Waipareira (Waipareira) lodged a claim in 1993, led by kaumātua and the then Trust chairman Haki Wihongi, to the Waitangi Tribunal. Haki or 'Uncle Jack' was a strong advocate for urban Māori. Not only had he been involved with the Māori wardens and helped establish the national body, but he also instigated the Henderson Māori Committee, was associated with the Māori Council, involved himself with establishing Hoani Waititi marae and sat as the chairman and a founding trustee of Waipareira Trust. He had travelled to England as part of the urban Māori entourage to the Privy Council.[16]

His claim on behalf of Waipareira Trust alleged they were prejudiced by the CFA's policies and operations. The Trust alleged that the Crown had failed to recognise the special status of Waipareira as a Māori organisation and as a Treaty partner; had failed to consult and deal with Waipareira in accordance with the Crown's obligations under Article Two of the Treaty of Waitangi; denigrated Te Whānau o Waipareira; and trapped its beneficiaries in a state of dependency on the Government.[17]

The claim turned into a tangle of complicated legal arguments and evidence, fraught with philosophical differences based on the iwi-urban divide. At the heart of the case was a government agency preference for contracting with kin-based tribes or 'recognised iwi authorities', for which it applied a narrow definition influenced by the Department of Social Welfare initiative Te Puao-o-te-atatū (1988). John Tamihere said the claim was "essentially about fairness, due process and equality of opportunity".[18] Dr Pita Sharples supported the Trust, saying:

> Waipareira is the appropriate organisation to administer and deliver services ... amongst our people in West Auckland. We are better suited to know our needs and to deal with them than any government organisation. That is what the claim is saying.[19]

The Waitangi Tribunal assessed that the Department of Social Welfare held a particular importance to the views of iwi, which detracted from alternative views held by bodies such as Te Whānau o Waipareira.[20] In releasing the Waitangi Tribunal Report 414 in July 1988, the Tribunal upheld Waipareira's claim, rejecting the argument that only traditional iwi were the Crown's Treaty partners. The Treaty was for the protection of all Māori and not limited to traditional tribal communities.[21] This decision effectively confirmed Urban Māori Authorities as major parties in Māori politics.[22]

The Waipareira family

Waipareira never claimed to be an iwi, although John Tamihere provoked iwi leaders by calling the Trust "Ngāti Waipareira". It has never claimed for anything inherently associated with iwi rights or iwi inheritance and has never sought to usurp the status of iwi mana whenua. But neither did it want to be prejudiced by an ideology that dealt exclusively with kin-based bodies. It claimed that both non-tribal and kin-based Māori organisations should be recognised as having mana of their own, and that funding should be adequate for both to provide services to their respective communities.[23] It was more concerned with the Crown's recognition of 'pan-tribal whānau' in urban areas as a Treaty partner alongside iwi, and to support the right of urban Māori to organise and address their own problems in their own way using their own tikanga.[24]

The Waitangi Tribunal did not think Waipareira spoke for all West Auckland Māori, but they found Waipareira represented "a significant Māori community based predominantly in West Auckland" and was accountable to them. The Tribunal also found that Waipareira exercised its own distinct rangatiratanga in the delivery of social services,[25] but stopped short of referring to them as an iwi. Although the courts failed to deliver a favourable outcome for Urban Māori Authorities in the fisheries litigations, the Tribunal decision put Urban Māori Authorities on the Treaty agenda as a partner by way of Article Two of the Treaty of Waitangi.

Haki Wihongi's claim to the Tribunal painted an in-depth picture of the socio-economic state of the region and the activities of Waipareira from 1984 until 1993. The Trust's region encompassed the area from the Blockhouse Bay ridgeline to Point Chevalier and the territory east and west of this area as far north as Helensville.

Based on the 1991 census, the Māori population of the area was 28,800.²⁶ This was 11.5% of the whole population of Waitakere City. Henderson and Avondale had a 22% unemployment rate, exacerbated by the fact that only 6% of the Māori people were of working age and 75% of all incomes into Māori households in West Auckland came from welfare payments. The average Māori income was $12,000. Haki pointed out, "We make up 40% of the social work case load in the western district, we make up 45% of Correction Services, Justice Department work and 65% of police enquiry work ... the impact of these outrageous statistics is creating significant dysfunction in our communities."²⁷

He also profiled the Trust's activities. The Trust was the largest training provider in the West Auckland region offering second-chance education. They were the first organisation contracted to implement a significant primary preventative healthcare plan, which included a mobile service to children in need, bridging poor parenting and disadvantaged backgrounds. They ran a food co-operative and a social services division that catered for 30 cases a week of 'the most

John Tamihere was inducted as the CEO of Te Whānau o Waipareira at a ceremony at Hoani Waititi marae in 1991. Front row: Sam Waiti, Pita Sharples, John Tamihere, June Mariu and Sam Paniora.

Courtesy of Te Whānau o Waipareira Trust

dysfunctional families possible'. An Alternative Education Unit was established to upskill and mentor 30 Youth Justice referrals that were teenagers between the ages of 13 to 17.[28] Haki also outlined the Trust's proactive desires in the marketplace to secure, through its commercial arm, long-term sustainable employment for the members of its community.[29]

The Trust subsequently progressed from an organisation with zero funding in 1990 to having a net worth in 1997 of approximately $8 million.[30]

It was Waipareira's wish to create an iwi environment for urban people who could not trace their links to their traditional iwi, or who sought the comfort and solace of that environment in the city where they lived.[31]

Growth and consolidation

In response to the Tribunal's ruling, John Tamihere (the then CEO of Waipareira) and Willie Jackson, acting as an advocate for MUMA since 1996, set up Urban Māori Authority (UMA) Broadcasting in 1998 after securing the licence and assets held by Radio Aotearoa. Their vision was to develop broadcasting opportunities for urban Māori.[32] UMA Broadcasting grew to become the largest radio-broadcasting organisation in Auckland. It operates two stations, George FM and Radio Wātea (603).[33] In 2011 they were reaching a combined listening audience of 70,000 people.[34] In 1999 John Tamihere and Willie Jackson were both elected to parliament, where they continued to assist the progress of the Urban Māori Authorities.[35]

In 2003 a unified umbrella organisation for Urban Māori Authorities in Auckland (Waipareira and Manukau), Hamilton, Porirua and the South Island was formed. The National Urban Māori Authority (NUMA) sought to provide affiliate members with sustainable strategic policy and planning and service development advice, with the aim of co-ordinating and developing Urban Māori Authorities to achieve better outcomes for whānau.[36] Members of this group included Waipareira (West Auckland), MUMA (South Auckland), Te Rūnanga o Kirikiriroa (Hamilton) led by Mere Bazer, Te Rūnanga o Ngā Maata Waka led by Norm Dewes of Christchurch, Te Rūnanga o Te Ūpoko o Te Ika headed by Sharon Watene and Te Rūnanga o Murihiku (Invercargill) led by Witana Murray. The success of the urban authorities was due to the fact that various nonaffiliated Māori authorities applied to join NUMA as a model that suited their individual demands for Māori development.

By 2011 NUMA was the parent body of the Whānau Ora provider collective that included Waipareira, MUMA, Te Rūnanga o Kirikiriroa, and affiliates Te Kōhao Health (Hamilton), Te Roopu Awhina ki Porirua (Wellington), Te Rūnanga o Ngā Maata Waka (Christchurch) and Ōtāngarei Trust (Northland). The vision of Whānau Ora (well families) was negotiated into existence through the coalition agreement between the Māori Party and the National Party after the 2008 election. The concept takes an "interagency approach" to build the "capacity of all New Zealand families in need" through health and social service provision.[37] Dr Mason Durie notes that it was a response to evidence that a sector-based approach to caring for disadvantaged children was failing to generate sustainable solutions but had created a level of dependency.[38] Whānau Ora reflected the range of welfare policies tailored to Māori aspirations, building on the concerted efforts of the previous 20 years to improve Māori health and well-being and close deepening disparities. It was a "political articulation of flax-roots approaches to caring for and supporting whānau as a whole".[39] According to Te Puni Kōkiri, Whānau Ora devolved the delivery of its services to community-based commissioning agencies that worked with partners, providers and navigators to deliver customised support and services to whānau. Those partners and providers had to demonstrate competence in social, economic, cultural and environmental interventions as they might apply to families.[40]

The aim of NUMA was to bring Whānau Ora to all NUMA communities. According to one NUMA report, the collective provided 300 individual services and 705 staff to mātāwaka urban Māori (and non-Māori) populations in the members' regions.[41] In the 2006 census, of the 644,000 who identified as Māori, 137,133 lived in Auckland, 76,572 in the Waikato, 55,437 in Wellington and 36,669 in Christchurch, of which more than a third were under the age of 15.[42] Today, NUMA's members and affiliates make up an integral community of committed people who serve their regional communities.

MUMA's hub was Ngā Whare Wātea marae complex in Māngere, which comprised a whare whakairo (carved house), whare puni (small house), whare karakia (church) and wharekai (dining room). MUMA has had a long history upholding the rights and community guardianship of urban Māori living in South Auckland. From its Māngere base they provide high-need social, training and educational services for the Māngere-Ōtāhuhu area, which has a population spread of 14% Māori, 40% Pākehā, 27% Pasifika and 21% Asian. According to the 2013 census, incomes fell by 16% since the previous 2006 census and 33% of Māori and Pasifika tamariki lived in poor housing. The socio-economic index of deprivation (1–10: the higher the number the more deprivation) for central Māngere is 10.[43] MUMA engages with families using Māori values of manaakitanga (hospitality), aroha ki te tangata (love to all), mana tāne (empowering men), mana wāhine (empowering women) and provides a safe and secure environment for the delivery of its services to the community. In recent years MUMA has restructured so that its services operate as viable, self-sufficient and independent entities. It has progressed to running its own Whānau Ora services: whānau-centred services catering for the needs and aspirations of families; a food bank; school mentoring; employment; Huarahi Hou (restorative justice), a marae justice panel and a reintegration programme for low-risk criminal offenders. Wātea Funeral Services is also a special service based out of Ngā Whare Wātea. Attached to Radio Wātea is Radiowateanews. com and WāteaTV.com, distributors of news, views and issues.[44] MUMA also operates the Wātea Early Childcare Centre in Māngere and in 2015 opened Te Kura Māori o Wātea, a kaupapa Māori charter or partnership school.[45]

Te Rūnanga O Kirikiriroa (TROK) in Hamilton was established in the 1980s under the guidance of the late Te Arikinui Dame Te Atairangakaahu and the late Mayor Sir Ross Jansen. Wi Kuki Kiingi saw the opportunity to develop an 'urban' authority for Kirikiriroa marae. TROK was founded in the spirit and belief that Māori living in urban settings needed new ways to connect with and create their community. In the 20 years to follow TROK was able to develop a range of adult, youth and community services, and commercial enterprises.[46] CEO Mere Balzer and her team grew the charitable trust into the largest health and welfare provider for Māori in Hamilton.[47]

From 1988 Te Whānau o Waipareira was based out of an old police station in Henderson, Auckland. Maraea Brown was its CEO. As one Waipareira-ite said, "It was a hugely risky step for us because I can remember the Trust board sitting around and arguing about how we were going to pay for light bulbs and toilet paper."[48] By 1989

Waipareira was close to liquidation. John Tamihere arrived to audit the organisation and call the people to a vision. The board had 15 members who sat for three years. At the next annual AGM five new trustees were chosen, with one position always left for Ngāti Whātua as tangata whenua.⁴⁹ Through the 1990s the organisation grew in size and clientele as it developed its wrap-around services. Additional building sites had to be found to house its health, education and training services.

Te Whānau o Waipareira Trust team of Maraea Brown, Eddie Brown, Ricky Houghton, Heta Tobin, Reg Rātahi and Jack Wihongi.
Courtesy of Te Whānau o Waipareira Trust

Providing a social service was more than just a job, it was a task performed from the heart. As one staff member said, "Staff were prepared to say, 'Yeah, I'll take this kid'; a mainstream social agency would never be allowed to do that. It's not working out of procedures, it's working from the heart. And that's what social services is all about — working from the heart."[50] Another said, "I think we are like urban warriors seeking out the broken-hearted."[51] In 1999 the old courthouse in Henderson became Wai-Health, out of which all clinical and social services operated. Economic development was an important aspect to the organisation. Its corporate arm gave the Trust the ability to invest in property. The organisation purchased "50 percent of the Westgate Shopping Centre and 32 acres around its own marae".[52]

After serving as a Labour MP for two terms from 1999 to 2005, John Tamihere returned to lead Waipareira out of financial ruin. Staving off a financial crisis, the Trust sold off assets including the health clinic and its shares in Westland (Westgate Shopping Centre).[53] Tamihere's experience as a cabinet minister enriched his ability to be able to progress Waipareira out of the doldrums.[54]

The Trust's recovery is a testament to the 'strong bones' of the community.

By 2011 the Trust had been debt-free for a number of years, with a group revenue increase to $31 million.[55] Waipareira had undergone major restructuring, grouping its operations into three areas: Teina, services to the youth population under 25; Tuakana, services to the 25 and over population; and Tautoko, management, accounting, human resources and funding planning.[56] In January 2011, a landmark accomplishment for Waipareira was the shift into its new Whānau Ora Centre where a range of services were housed under one roof.

The building was opened with its new Whānau Tahi Navigator system installed. This IT project began in 2009 as a specially designed relationship management system via its Whānau Tahi development arm. It gave the Trust the ability to manage information across multiple sectors in health, education, justice, economics and social services in New Zealand. This innovative and outcomes-based tool offered providers a desired platform to meet funder, provider and family needs.[57]

In 2013 Waipareira launched a 25-year strategy with a vision to become Māori future makers, and champions for future generations. As the biggest provider of non-government services in West

Auckland, the Trust's strategic purpose was to see self-sufficient whānau[58] as leaders of change by encouraging high standards of education and health.[59] The plan identified research as a key area of development and signed a memorandum of understanding with Massey University that precipitated the launch of the Wai-Research arm of Waipareira. This unit's priority is to drive innovation that empowers whānau to prosper.[60] Its development arm, Whānau Tahi, also signed a memorandum of understanding with Microsoft and health information company Medtech.

With John Tamihere as its CEO, NUMA secured the role as the official commissioning agent for the North Island Whānau Ora health initiatives in 2014. The new Whānau Ora agency, Te Pou Matakana (TPM), is stationed at Te Whānau o Waipareira's whānau centre in Henderson, West Auckland.[61] There are three commissioning agencies throughout the country: Te Pou Matakana works with families in the North Island, Te Pūtahi o Te Waipounamu works with families in the South Island, and Pasifika Futures is dedicated to working with Pacific families across the country.[62] Two years into operation, TPM had contracted with 13 lead partners across six Māori regions nationally and engaged with 20,000 whānau.[63]

For the year 2015/16 Waipareira received 3725 new referrals, engaged with 7221 individual whānau members and achieved 3995 positive outcomes.[64] Te Whānau o Waipareira employs 200 full-time staff and has a large number of accredited volunteers.[65] The organisation's national and international partnerships are growing and their impact through innovative leadership is having an impact for urban Māori. John Tamihere says, "So the marae is Hoani Waititi, but the iwi is Waipareira. We don't have one eponymous ancestor as other iwi do, and rightly so. But we have, above all, our founding fathers and mothers from a range of tribes who brought us together to rejoice in our diversity and our tribalism rather than wallow in our differences … It's not about an either–or. It's about them (iwi) acknowledging that a second migration occurred. That the great marae, the great first kōhanga and kura and wharekura, came from the activism in urban Auckland … That's all we need. Then we need to move on."[66]

In 2014 a number of NUMA affiliates broke away to form Ngā Ngaru Rautahi (NNR) Aotearoa National Urban Authority Incorporated, a national urban authority. The organisation is a National Provider Collective made up of affiliate groups from

Auckland, Kirikiriroa and Te Waipounamu, and has a vision to "strengthen(ing) whānau aspirations".[67] NNR is seen as a National Value Network with a wide range of community services caring for all Māori in the regions. Originally a health service established in 1998, in 2014 NNR refocused its attention to broaden its range of services such as health, employment, education, justice, housing and social development. Each of the affiliates still stand as separate entities but they provide knowledge and support for each other. Chief Executive Officer Diane Tuari was the original settlor for the National Urban Māori Authority and was Deputy CEO of Waipareira Trust for several years. The Chair is Mere Balzer, CEO of Te Rūnanga o Kirikiriroa, and the current secretary is Norm Dewes, CEO of Te Rūnanga o Ngā Maata Waka of Christchurch. The founder is George Ngātai, CEO of the Whānau Ora Community Clinic, Manukau City and the Deputy Chair is Martin Kaipo, CEO of Te Hau Āwhiwhio o Ōtāngarei.[68]

Faith-based agencies

Numerous faith-based social service agencies working in the field of social and community service often engage with Māori clientele. These agencies are often motivated by the Christian ethics of service to community, to the lost, the widows and those in prison. Destiny Church, led by Brian and Hannah Tamaki in Auckland, with satellite churches throughout the country, has a social service outlook. In 2013 the church was recorded as having 6000 members,[69] of whom a considerable percentage were Māori. The church claimed Māori status in a number of ways. It declared itself an 'iwi-tapu' (a holy tribe), a spiritual tribe of God's people set aside as a chosen race, based on a scriptural premise from 1 Peter 2:9, which would in the end "be suited to rule the nation".[70] By drawing on the words iwi (tribe, people) and tapu (sacred, untouchable, set aside), the church placed itself firmly into a Māori tribe-like status, in recognition of Māori as tangata whenua. Destiny's iwi-tapu followed in the ways of earlier traditional communities such as the Hunga Whiriwhiri (Chosen People) of the Waikato,[71] Parihaka in Taranaki and Rātana Pā at Turakina, all who united their adherents through scripture or healing.

In 2008 Destiny Church sought to claim urban Māori authority status so they could serve Māori in their region who were disconnected from their iwi.⁷² Peter Lineham suggests some of the church members had lost their Māori identity and found it at Destiny, while others switched their allegiance from the marae to the house of Destiny.⁷³ In support of Destiny's proposal, Willie Jackson said, "Destiny has turned around thousands of Māori people's lives under the inspirational leadership of Brian Tamaki. Gangsters, fraudsters, drug dealers, you name it, they've had them and now Māori families are much better off."⁷⁴ Destiny's conservative position on issues such as gay rights and the role of women made the decision a controversial one. Despite opposition from all sectors, including directly from Prime Minister Helen Clark, Destiny was awarded UMA status in October 2008. Te Rūnanga a Iwi o Te Oranga Ake was incorporated to fulfil the function as the church's service provider arm.⁷⁵

In 2011 the church received Ministry of Social Development funding for four Community Max programmes for 79 youth in Auckland, Waikato and the Bay of Plenty to support them into full-time employment. Social services manager and church affiliate George Ngātai accused the government of discrimination because of its lack of funding in other areas, which Social Development minister Paula Bennett denied, saying the funding decisions were based on merit.⁷⁶ An ensuing application to fund a charter school was denied.⁷⁷ Te Oranga Ake has not yet become affiliated with NUMA.

Without ongoing governmental support, the pan-tribal church has needed to fund its own community social services programmes. For example, the iwi-tapu's "Man Up" programme was launched in 2015. "Man Up" is an Australasian programme created in response to the 'man problem' where men have failed to take responsibility for social problems that negatively impacted society. It is a self-funded 12-week social service programme for men wanting to face any issues they wish to resolve. The programme empowers men to become better fathers, husbands and leaders in their own whānau and communities.⁷⁸ It is currently 'going through the roof' in cities and small towns, attracting many gang members who relate strongly to the facilitators as well as finding themselves in a safe environment to share their stories.⁷⁹ "Man Up" has sought to reach out to the gangs of South Auckland and to help rehabilitate prisoners. A *Waikato Times* article reported that the programme had been banned by private prison operator Serco from the prison at Wiri.⁸⁰ At Easter 2017, Destiny held a rally, opening the church doors to patched gang members curious to hear their Easter Gospel message.⁸¹ Hundreds of people attended the gathering.

Pita Sharples, Eddie Kawiti, Logan Rupuha and Dame Whina Cooper, were all involved in advocating for the health and cultural well-being of urban Māori.

Reproduced from *Te Whanau, A Celebration of Te Whānau o Waipareira*, 2001, courtesy of Te Whānau o Waipareira Trust

Destiny Church's iwi-tapu is significant in its transformation of the lives of Māori in urban settings.[82]

At the heart of such organisations is the social, spiritual and economic well-being of Māori (and others) living in their respective cities and towns. They were and are crucial to supporting Māori who, were through no fault of their own, are unable to activate their tribal connections and draw down the benefits of iwi Treaty settlements or iwi social services. There are also Māori who do know their connections and opt to access the services offered by authorities such as Waipareira. One elder admits that the services he was able to access at Waipareira for his whānau over the last 18 years were of far greater benefit than those his own iwi have provided.[83]

Urban Māori Authorities in action

Nurturing and developing healthy Māori families is the core work of the Urban Māori Authorities. The already challenged social services are even more so when alcohol and drugs, in particular P-methamphetamine, are part of the problem. Testimonies of families caught in a web of social despair who have managed to find semblance of well-being through engagement with urban authorities is sobering. One compelling story is that of Cortez Olsen, for whom Waipareira's social services were a lifesaver.

Abandoned by her mother and raised by a solo father, Cortez says she has had to fend for herself most of her life. "My mum is just a lady and my dad instilled principles and values for our lives but we had no real family upbringing." Working to pay the bills, her father organised a friend to mind the children. The man abused Cortez for two years from age six and things worsened when the minder moved into the house. Cortez ran away and was placed in foster care. "I refused to go to the police, I ran away from them. I didn't attend counselling and no one believed my story. I ran down to Henderson scabbing money for alcohol and bus fares. I slept in cemeteries, schools, under the Henderson bridge, and at bus stops." She made her home at the New Lynn bus station. At 12 years old she was drinking meths and sniffing glue as a way of numbing her body to the elements so she could stay warm. "I ended up with a group of Pacific Island gang members in a two-bedroom flat. I'd watch them seduce girls with alcohol and rape them. I was caught warning the girls and had a brick thrown at my head and I was raped. I was no longer a respected part of the gang."

Cortez fell pregnant. "I was 14 and told my mother I was pregnant. I moved in with her. She immediately took me to have an abortion. I decided not to stay. A youth leader offered me a place and I'd turn up drunk, punching my own stomach, I was just out of control. But deep down I didn't want to be like my mum." Cortez eventually moved back in with her father and began to engage with Te Whānau o Waipareira, in particular attending doctor's appointments. "I didn't know anything about life skills then but the social services would awhi me and educate me how to be a mum. It felt like a real whānau. I ended up in a girls' home with Waipareira at Buscomb Avenue and when the baby was born in 1994, Waipareira was beside me during the labour and through to discharge at National Womens. I was then with Dad but under the care of Waipareira."

Mana Mātāwaka 191

This Robyn Kahukiwa painting depicts a new generation of Māori youth beneath an urban city landscape supported by Te Whānau o Waipareira Trust.

Courtesy of Te Whānau o Waipareira Trust

After moving around the country and falling into abusive relationships, Cortez moved back to Auckland with nothing. Soon she had three children to feed. One milestone she remembers well was the day her father came to apologise to her for not believing her story. She was 18. She inherited the Housing New Zealand home from her father but she couldn't afford to pay the rent. "I lived with no power, no money and no food. I was shoplifting, doing burglaries to feed my family. I'd go nightclubbing to steal people's bags for their money to feed us. I worked on construction sites while the girls were in Barnardos' care."

She found work at a poultry farm at Taupaki and stayed there for seven years. "I was working but it wasn't enough to cover rent, power and childcare so I lied and went on the benefit to cover my needs. I didn't know who Inland Revenue was, I just knew Work and Income. Coming of age, I had to join IRD because I was claiming for childcare and working for income. They prosecuted me for $25,000 because I was working and claiming the benefit. I was charged in court to repay this amount and do 150 hours community service. With Waipareira out of my life I was scared. No one tells you the procedures of the courts." The burdens of 'the system' and her lack of health and economic literacy became an enormous dilemma for Cortez when she entered the drug scene as a means to an end. "It was the only way of creating finance to feed the family and pay the bills," she says. She became a dealer. "I was homeless and living in a car with three kids. I had to create revenue. I went from a $100-a-week habit to paying $400–500 a day for my habit. My house was a one-stop shop. Soon I owed thousands. I went into my room and stayed there for six weeks — cold turkey — with a toaster to cook bread. The P-world had taken over my home. I cut everyone off and woke up a different person. I halted everything and paid my court bills and these days I'm free now," she says.

In 2007 her daughter Grace was struck with a physical condition labelled as a mental disorder by the hospitals; Cortez believed it was a physical and hormonal issue. Grace was placed under the care of Auckland Hospital in a paralytic state. She was on life support for a number of years. During this time Cortez was cleaning up her act while studying counselling at AUT, never abandoning her daughter. In 2016 Grace woke from her coma and today is living a normal life. "I've got big plans and big goals," Cortez says. "I have choices. I've learnt so much through this world and my studies have taught me about boundary setting with people. I'm good with money and I've learnt communication is key." Cortez does not see her story as tragic, but as a journey "I can build upon".[84]

The continued commitment for uplifting and supporting whānau can be seen in other testimonies like that of Corrin Phillips and her whānau. Engaging with Te Whānau o Waipareira's kaupapa Māori education programme, she was able to enrol her tamariki into an environment where she could see their self-confidence and passion for learning flourish.[85] Corrin developed her own skillset, which encouraged her to want to work. She had not worked before when she was offered a position as a child minder at Waipareira. Corrin's passion is for tamariki. She and her partner walked through the Incredible Years programme "where they triumphed in learning new ways to manage their tamariki".[86] Corrin says, "It's hard to explain the ways these programmes have changed our life."[87]

Pare Keiha and Paul Moon believe the presence of Urban Māori Authorities throughout the country is a testament to the fact that they fulfil the needs of the Māori communities they represent.[88] In their summation of the presence of Urban Māori Authorities, they conclude that the debate for or against them is unhelpful and unnecessary. They point out that Māori developmental aspirations may be enhanced by supporting Māori communities to develop and manage their own development needs.[89]

In 2001, then Mayor of Waitakere City Bob Harvey wrote about Te Whānau o Waipareira Trust: "A decade ago people in Henderson referred to the Trust as 'the Horis on the hill'. How things have changed. For me the Trust and the marae are at the very heart of this city, and maybe even the soul. Waitakere City revolves not around the shopping malls. Waipareira is the most remarkable vision of New Zealand. It is the face of Aotearoa in the new century. They went to the future first and said, 'This is how it could be.'"[90]

Taumaunu Whānau, Te Atatū North, Auckland

Evelyn and Jack Taumaunu at their home in Hamurana Place, Te Atatū North, Auckland.
Courtesy of the Taumaunu whānau

Jack and Evelyn Taumaunu and their family have lived in Hamurana Place at Te Atatū North, West Auckland, since the 1970s. The family have been strong cogs in the wheels of local Māori organisations, including at the local school marae, the Māori Women's Welfare League, Te Whānau o Waipareira Trust and the Waitematā Māori Wardens.

Jack is from Whangarā on the East Coast. He is an ex-Te Aute College student who worked in South Island freezing works before joining the army, where he served for eight years, touring in Borneo and Vietnam. He returned from military service and married Evelyn, who is from Whatawhata but was raised in Frankton, Hamilton. She was number 17 of 18 siblings and was raised in the Kiingitanga movement during the reigns of King Koroki and Te Arikinui Dame Te Atairangikaahu. She was used to the rituals of the Kīngitanga and serving in the wharekai at Tūrangawaewae.

After the couple were married in Christchurch, Evelyn, Jack and their children travelled to Kaitaia and Jack found a job at the Awanui Tavern after their vehicle broke down there. The family lived there for just under a year in an environment with seven other whānau made up of nine adults and 12 children. Jack later found employment as a travelling insurance salesman. The family travelled with him for 18 months until they found themselves in an Auckland rental property in 1970.

Jack then took a position working in the Dye House factory in Grey Lynn, where there were many other Māori employees. "We wanted to be in a place to raise our children our way and have a life that could be more meaningful," Evelyn says. "We chose this lifestyle." Renting a house in Kelston cost $10 a week. They earned $56 a week, which was a lot of money at that time. Evelyn remembers there were 28 houses in the street, of which six were home to Māori.

Through a Returned Serviceman's loan, Jack and Evelyn were able to purchase their home in Hamurana Street. The home cost $22,000 then and today it is freehold. With seven children to feed, Evelyn remembers, "I had no whānau here. There were all sorts of people in this street and 27 different nationalities — Fijian, Swedish, Dutch, Pākehā, Pacific Islanders, party people, churchgoers. It was a real mix that grew on you."

According to Evelyn's observations of the community, she witnessed waipiro (alcohol) getting in the way of whānau development; budgeting was an issue as pay packets all went on alcohol. "I saw all the suffering among the children." She would invite the children to her house to encourage them to bake biscuits with her. "That was my small contribution to the local whānau. You can worry and be concerned but you couldn't intervene as people didn't like you interfering with their lives, telling them how to bring up their kids."

The talk around the west at the time was all about the development of a new marae. "All the Māori in the west fell into this kaupapa, including us," Evelyn remembers. "To see that place when it was opened and sitting on our blanket watching the kapa haka with hundreds of people there — it was a proud moment. The marae was about the ability to identify with being Māori," she declares.

All the Taumaunu children went to Te Atatū Primary, the local intermediate and Rutherford High School, where they were engulfed in tikanga Māori. Youngest son Jarred 'Bumpa' was sent to Te Aute College to maintain the traditional link to the East Coast. Jack's father, Moni Taumaunu, had encouraged the whānau to continue the tradition of sending the boys to Te Aute, to which they agreed. Evelyn felt immense pride when she saw her children grow in their Māoritanga at Rutherford. Jarred says, "The kapa haka inside my brothers and sisters embedded that aroha for being Māori inside of them."

"It also comes back to the home environment first for the next generation to feel safe and secure in their identity," says Evelyn. "Ko Kōtuku te marae, ko Titirangi te maunga, ko Waitematā te awa' was their pepeha until they learned who they were in a wider tribal sense".

Jack and Evelyn are strong-minded, community-oriented people. They were basketball coaches, tennis coaches, sports referees and heavily involved in developing the local youth. "There were a lot of Māori involved in these events, they were real competitive. The other young people, whether they were Pacific

Islanders or Pākehā, they were all whangaied into the community of Te Ao Māori," says Jarred. "We treated everyone in our lives as Māori. We didn't care about who was Māori and who wasn't. They were all Aunty and Uncle to us. We learned the community whakapapa." Jarred remembers it was common for Samoan children to be involved in Māori kapa haka and for Māori to join the 'sasa dances'. "Kapa haka was the essence of whānau and te Reo," he says. "Entering the 'community whakapapa' meant everybody knew the parents of all the young people. There was an unspoken agreement that the community had free rein to correct misbehaving kids and inform the parents."

Evelyn met Whaea June Mariu at Rutherford College, where, in 1982, she had established Kotuku marae. June was involved with Hoani Waititi marae as well. "She had managed to organise Access and Maccess work schemes here via the Labour Department and Māori Affairs. There was machine knitting, sewing, catering, harakeke, tukutuku, carving, carpentry and music." After meeting June, Evelyn became involved at the kura. In March 1982 Evelyn joined the local Māori Women's Welfare League. "I met people such as Letty Brown, Mavis Tuoro, Claire Rogers, Coral Lavulavu, people who always made you feel welcome. However, I was curious as to where all the young people were, why aren't they helping? They didn't want to be involved with old people," she says.

One day Jack and Evelyn responded to an important message put in the local paper on the last Wednesday of February 1982. It called all the local Māori groups together. As Evelyn saw it, "People came out of the woodwork, it was a meeting to link all our connections. We met so we could share information: where our children were at, where we could learn the reo, what was the government saying, what could we do to reach a parity with non-Māori. People wanted to push for better education for our kids. We didn't want to be ignorant any more about what was going on around us." This was the origin of the well-known Te Whānau o Waipareira Trust.

She insists that education was all important. "It was paramount — we didn't want to see our children continually going into the justice system." She remembers Connie Hanna, Don Rameka, Tuini Hakaraia, June Mariu, Pita Sharples, Mavis Tuoro, Barney Tūpara, Tuck Nathan and Jack Wihongi rallying together to form what was to become Te Whānau o Waipareira. "The people never thought it would become what it has become today," Evelyn says. She became closely linked to Waipareira, as a board member and a director of aspects of the organisation such as Waitech, which became the largest Māori service and training provider in Auckland. "We wanted Waipareira to be a force to be known nationwide. We had programmes running all through Auckland City, Maungawhau, Māngere and Papakura. Put your hand up and do something about things in our community — don't just talk about it," Evelyn says. "We needed great leadership to be competitive, people who weren't scared to fight for the rights of Māori in social services, in education, in housing and social development. There was no real voice for Māori in West Auckland. With small cluster-voices it had little influence but when JT came he wasn't afraid and he wanted Māori to develop and have the same rights as others," she says.

Evelyn's children remember Te Whānau o Waipareira meetings being held at their home. For a younger generation, Waipareira was where they attended Waitech, an educational unit that ran training in mechanics, cooking, security and te Reo Māori. "I remember the Mai FM advertisement we thought was so cool: 'Waipareira take you higher, you know it when you feel it when you feel the vibe of Wai.' It was sung by Lapi Mariner," Jarred says. "Waipareira offered us health, education and youth development. We never saw anything bad emerge out of Waipareira." In 2014 Jarred was elected to the board of Te Whānau o Waipareira and sat alongside his mother, who was reappointed.

The family have also been involved in the Waitematā Māori Wardens for many years. Evelyn and Jack wanted to encourage youth involvement in the wardens and they developed the Waitematā Māori Wardens Trust in 2002. Jarred has continued his involvement with the wardens, recently marking 15 years of service with them. The teams patrol the West Auckland region for a minimum of 30 hours a week and provide passenger services support on trains, and do street beats in New Lynn, Henderson and Glen Eden.

The family have also been involved in programmes aimed at reducing the return of inmates to prison. "We entered the prisons to visit our own people," Jack says. "Some of our wardens emerged from the prisons and turned their lives around in the service. Manaaki ki te tangata, aroha ki te tangata: love the people is our whakataukī for the community." Jarred says, "When kids see the wardens they know we are going to talk and they know our status, we'll growl at them, they'll calm down and sit down. We earn the kids' respect — one respect for a warden is respect for all."

The whānau agree they were brought up as Aucklanders, not as 'urban Māori'. "We were raised in Tat North and we still call ourselves Aucklanders, but we know who we are," Jarred says. Their rural relatives often have a problem with Auckland because it's fast, and full of motorways and lots of cars. Often the 'brownie townies' are accused of being lazy, but the whānau says, "When many rural folk come here to work they find it hard, and realise those in the city work hard. Country life is about who you know whereas in the city there are a lot of processes before you can even get a job." Although they all admit that "if it wasn't for our upbringing we would be lost. Once you lose who you are, you lose that respect for identity, and then you go home to find your wairua."

Evelyn points out, "We've held all our 21sts in traditional ways here and had two whānau weddings. In the development of the kids' identity, we are a whānau at the end of the day who can say I'm a Māori who knows who I am and I am proud to be Māori."

Chapter 11

Noho Tāwāhi

Māori in Australia

Māori have been journeying to Australia since the beginning of the nineteenth century.[1] However, over the last 40 years there has been an almost mass migration of New Zealand-born Māori to Australia. Affectionately known as 'Mozzies', or blatantly referred to as 'Ngāti Kangaroo', 'Ngāti Skippy' or even 'plastic', these whānau have been 'pulled' overseas for many reasons including the climate, the 'bright lights', and the multi-cultural lifestyle in places such as Sydney, Melbourne and Queensland. The desire to be with whānau is a drawcard for many but the economic opportunities in the form of higher wages and better employment have probably been the biggest appeal for Māori.[2] For some, the move to Australia has given them relief from gangs, drugs and violence; domestic violence; traditional familial hierarchies; Pākehā prejudice; and has offered whānau greater opportunities to reach their potential. The flight of Māori to Australia is hard to ignore.

Prior to 1840, up to 1000 Māori had travelled to Sydney to trade, acquire new technology, and learn new ideas to disperse and teach back-home. Small numbers of Māori remained in Australia, until the 1960s when the "first signs of a significant trans-Tasman movement" saw thousands of Māori shift to the 'Red Continent' seeking new life and work opportunities in Sydney.[3] In an article on global migration, Māori academic Sidney Mead wrote about Māori leaving the country every year during the 1960s. He highlighted statistics showing that 290 people departed in 1960, increasing to 1750 in 1967.[4] Additionally, figures showed that each year larger numbers of Māori were leaving New Zealand than were returning. This development indicated the beginning of a new trend: "the movement of Māoris overseas".[5] In 1966 it was estimated 4000 Māori were in Australia.[6] Since then Māori have been leaving to make Australia their permanent home.

Prior to 1971, there were 1379 New Zealand-born Māori living in Australia, rising to 4445 between 1976 and 1980. Later, between 1986 and 1990, the number rose to 7638. The 1986 Australian Census, which introduced an ancestry question to the survey, showed that there were approximately 27,000 Māori overall living in Australia, and that there were more than three times as many Australian-born Māori than New Zealand-born Māori who were in the 65-plus age bracket.[7]

The 2001 census revealed that 35.5% of the estimated Māori population of 101,000 were in New South Wales, 29.7% in Queensland (19,000 in Brisbane alone), just under 14% in Victoria, and 6% in the other territories.[8] Based on the 79,000 of those resident Māori who knew how to answer the census question about their iwi affiliations, there were 20,000 Ngāpuhi, 12,500 Ngāti Porou, 11,500 Waikato, 10,000 Ngāti Kahungunu and 3000 Ngāi Tahu.[9] In a later report it has been estimated between 30,000 to 45,000 Ngāpuhi reside in Sydney and the Gold Coast.[10]

Ten years later in 2011, there were 128,430 people who identified themselves as having Māori ancestry living in Australia. Two-thirds of this population were born in New Zealand.[11] Based on this census, it was estimated that as many as one sixth of the Māori population lived in Australia and one in three Māori in Australia were born there, with 80% of this generation under the age of 25.[12] It was also estimated that 6.3% of those living in Australia spoke te Reo Māori in their homes.[13] Today, more Māori live in Southern Queensland than in 10 of New Zealand's 16 regions.[14]

The lure of Oz

Reasons for shifting to Australia have changed over the years, but employment and higher wages are significant factors. In 1969 Sidney Mead suggested Pākehā paternalism was a reason for Māori migration to Australia during the 1960s, the main two contributing factors being psychological and economic.[15] Mead proposed the psychological causes were based on trying to circumvent dominant Pākehā standards of life and values imposed on Māori.[16] He further commented that Māori sought employment opportunities overseas because of growing unemployment in New Zealand, coupled with a belief that the discriminatory attitudes of Pākehā employers did not place workers on equal terms.[17]

A 1998 survey of 1149 New Zealand-born Māori asking why they had moved to Australia revealed that in Australia they saw a better chance to get work or better jobs, they wanted to join family/whānau who were already there, they wished to start a new life, to pursue better opportunities, for the good weather, education, sports, or to depart from 'Māori politics' or negative experiences.[18] Māori wanted something better for their children.[19]

There is a range of anecdotal and personal circumstances that encouraged people to make the journey across the Tasman. Graeme Taiaroa, who relocated to Ipswich, Queensland with his children and grandchildren in 2015, recounts how some of his whānau shifted to Australia in the 1960s, after they had finished apprenticeships in the trade training schools in Christchurch. Waves of trade-training graduates from this era shifted to Australia for employment. Five generations of Taiaroa's whānau from Taumarunui have lived in Australia. Graeme's own children migrated to Ipswich for work, a better quality of life, but more importantly, to be able to buy their own homes. Despite saving for years and trying to buy their own homes in Auckland, the overpriced housing market made it almost impossible for these first-time 'Māori' purchasers to buy.[20] They have made the choice to shift and are now home owners, but in a different land.

Some men came to Australia to simply play rugby,[21] while others who had separated from their families tried to hide from paying child support for their children. Others left the abuse and violence of their community and home lives back in New Zealand. This sentiment was reflected in the film *Once Were Warriors*, which premiered at a private function to a packed Mermaid Waters Cinema on the Gold Coast in Queensland. Many Māori viewers were shocked at the film and left before the end of the screening. Others commented that the subject of the film was the reason they left New Zealand.[22]

In a recent article on the Māori-Australian dream, Ben Tua spoke about how he moved to Melbourne in 2009. Money was a big drawcard, but he was also keen to break away from the "status of Māori in New Zealand".[23] "There's a stigma against Māori in New Zealand but when they move to Australia that reputation isn't there," he says. "The reputation of Māoris in Australia in my mind is of hard workers; really reliable people. Whereas back home you're just a 'typical Māori'. You break free of that cast, your kids are going to have a better life and it continues on — you've broken the whole chain — so I guess it's a no-brainer." For Ben, the "plan was initially to go and earn money and come back, but that was six years ago".[24]

For many Māori the loss of employment opportunities in the freezing works or factory industries in New Zealand, where the majority of Māori were employed, was a major factor in their shift to Australia to find work, especially between 1984 and 2006.[25] Over the 15 years between 1984 and 1999 a third of these industries were closed and a fifth of all Māori workers were laid off.

Construction, mining, seasonal work, security, truck driving and entertainment were all areas Māori sought employment in Australia. Correction officers and the Australian army are also arenas Māori have sought to enter.[26] Shearers flooded the sheep sheds of Australia with their standard wide 86-mm combs (in contrast to the Australian pastoral regulation 64-mm comb). Māori favoured the 86-mm comb because it increased the number of sheep that could be shorn in a day; the Australians used their 64-mm comb to protect the fleece and the skin of the sheep.[27] The Australian wage packet provided a large increase. Māori shearers would fly from New Zealand to Australia once a year, to places as distant as Western Australia. Australian seasons offered more shearing days due to three lambing times: in New Zealand there were 100 days, Australia there were 224 days.[28] The heat of the conflict between Australian shearers and the New Zealanders over the latter's use of the 'immoral and repulsive' wide comb boiled over in 1983. The Australian Worker's Union supported the strike of local shearers throughout the country for 10 weeks. The dispute was resolved, with the allowance of wide combs for better productivity. The aftermath of this dispute lasted for over 10 years. Today, Māori are still notably involved in the shearing industry.

New Zealanders joining their workforce has always been a point of contention for some Australians. Popular media fuelled a perception that Kiwis, including Māori, were 'bludgers', taking their jobs. In his 2013 article 'Kiwi Bashing', Peter Mares wrote, "I came across a 1989 file note in which the New Zealand High Commission estimated that for every $1 in unemployment benefits paid to New Zealand citizens, the Australian government received more than $10 in tax revenues from New Zealanders who were working."[29]

Māori are recorded as being more likely to be in lower-skilled occupations or receive lower levels of income than others in Australia:[30] many working in construction, manufacturing and mining.[31] In three of the top five Māori occupations, Māori migrants earned higher incomes than the national average but earned less in higher-skilled jobs. One concern identified by a New Zealand demographics report concerning New Zealand-born Māori living in Australia, shows secondary and tertiary qualification levels and engagement with higher learning or upskilling was far lower than the more youthful generation of Australian-born Māori. This is a vulnerable situation for future financial security and well-being of Māori.[32] For instance, after 2001, the two most popular states Māori migrants were drawn to for work were Western Australia and Queensland. It has been recognised, if there were any future shocks in the mining or any other ancillary industries such as construction in Western Australia, this will have a disproportionately negative impact on Māori migrants there.[33] In saying that, one Māori resident in Alice Springs says there are many Māori in managerial positions within government agencies and social support services. They were able to work in Australia and upskill themselves at the same time.[34]

The Showbands

A sector of Māori society that found a niche overseas during the 1950s and 1960s, particularly in Australia, were Māori showbands. The mass migration of Māori musicians and showbands to Australia from the late 1950s and into the 1980s was due to that environment being more welcoming and more lucrative for talented Māori musicians.[35] "What began as a few dozen increased to hundreds," said Nuki Waaka, from the Mataatua district and one of the members of the Māori Volcanics.[36] The venues in New Zealand where the Māori showband style of music could be expressed were considered expensive, competitive and racist.[37] This led to Māori showbands seeking better opportunities overseas to perform and earn a living. Making their way to Australia became more financially lucrative and free of racial slurs.[38] Showband musician Robbie Ratana once jokingly said, "We had no money but we thought we were superstars, we did 9000 shows a week and thought we owned the streets," while Nuki Waaka saw Sydney as a "big city where the roads were paved with gold".[39]

One of the most famous entertainers of that era was Prince Tui Teka. In 1952, aged 15, he ran away to join a circus in Australia. A lone Māori entertainer, he was cast in the role as noble savage, giving him his first exposure to Australian audiences who appreciated his form of contemporary musical comedy.[40] He toured the Royal Easter shows in Australia.[41] Here he learned the trade of the entertainment industry, forming the Māori Troubadours, who were the first Māori showband to usher in the Māori showband era.[42]

The Māori Hi-Five formed in 1959, spearheading the showband brand in Australia, Europe and the United States, where Walt Disney was so impressed by their talent and skill that he signed them to

The Māori Hi-Five travelled the world in the 1950s and 1960s performing their brand of cabaret, a mixture of Māori culture, popular music and comedy. Many of these popular Māori showbands toured and settled in Australia, where they raised their families.

Ans Wetra, photographer, c.1963, Auckland, Te Papa Collection his company. The Māori Hi-Quinns, the Quin Tikis (who also went to America), the Māori Volcanics, the Māori Kavaliers, the Māori Castaways and others, helped form a (close-knit) Māori showband community in Australia, each supporting the other.[43]

The showband era began to wane in the late 1970s and many musicians furthered their careers as soloists or as smaller cabaret groups that played the Australian resort circuit, particularly in north Queensland, or at nightclubs in Sydney or on the Gold Coast. Others returned home to New Zealand to reinvent themselves. Some showband families stayed in Australia and fostered their culture through a new generation of entertainers, mostly Māori born in Australia.

In the mid-1970s, on the Gold Coast a group called the Young Polynesians was established. The members learned cultural songs and actions incorporating showband style performance, their families made costumes, and almost instantly the youth were performing live at venues such as the Iluka Motel, The Islander Motel, Tiki Village and later the Chevron Hotel, earning themselves an income.

Darren Rehu was one of the Young Polynesians and remembers the group touring New Zealand and staying at many different whānau marae. "For most of us youngsters in the party we had never been to New Zealand before, so it was a real cultural journey," he remembers. Brought up in kapa haka and surrounded by top Māori musicians of the day, Darren says that "Māori culture and music are one and the same".[44] As one of the family orientated Young Polynesians, Darren also became a child television star, performing on the Channel 9 Brisbane-based children's show *Happy Go Round* (aired on Queensland Television Station 9, 1976), from age eight until he was 13. "My sister prodded me to enter a local Gold Coast talent quest and I ended up being selected for a kids television show," he says. Music has always been Darren's passion; he has played on a range of different albums, and performed in bands and theatrical roadshows in Australia, England and New Zealand.

In the mid-1980s Darren returned to New Zealand and played the Auckland music circuit with popular jazz/funk band 358s. He has performed on Whirimako Black's Album *Hohou Te Rongo* (2002) and Max Stowers' album *Malaga* (2002), and has played backing for the stage productions of *Jesus Christ Superstar* and *The Lion King* in Australia. He and his wife Karin shifted to the United Kingdom in 2005 for employment and travel reasons, taking up residence

Nuki Waaka (second from the right), of Ngāti Pukeko, was one of the original leaders of the Māori Volcanics. He lived much of his later life in Sydney. Here he celebrates his 60th birthday in 1992 at the Point Chevalier RSA, Auckland, with fellow musicians, whānau and friends. From back left: Ricthie Russell, Golan Waaka, Bradford Haami, Rufus Rehu, Nuki Waaka and Darren Rehu. Darren was raised in the Young Polynesians on the Gold Coast under Nuki but lives in England nowadays working as a session and touring musician.

Couresy of Bradford Haami

alongside the more than 8000 other Māori living there. "When we left I really felt like I was being torn from the land," Darren says. Karin is a primary school teacher and Darren has continued his career as a musician, playing on a range of albums and with numerous bands and live shows, such as the Luther Vandross Tribute show in London in 2015 and 2016.

More recently he has made contact with his home marae at Awahou, connecting with his biological father's people of Ngāti Rangiwewehi. "Our plan is to return home one day, we are still very much drawn home — it's something that hits you when you get older," he says. Maintaining their commitment to their culture is something they believe in, which is why they have placed their daughter Ava into the Ngāti Rānana kōhanga reo in London.

Not-so-lucky country?

Statistics show the majority of Australia-based Māori are working in construction or in labour-based employment and many have succeeded in this arena (see Markie Bishop profile later in this chapter). Māori have climbed the ladder of success in other areas, especially in team sports such as rugby union and rugby league, which the NRL are keen to build on, as well as in individual sports. Stewart Simpson, previously of Kawerau/Whakatāne, shifted to Australia to play rugby, but became the manager for the national Australian beach volleyball team. Dannielle Harte of Ngāti Maru was born in Australia. She excelled not only on the Australian sporting stage but also internationally. Dannielle's mother, Prue Drady, is from the Wātene family Mātai Whetu marae near Thames, and since 1961 has lived in Australia where she raised her family. Dannielle became one of Australia's top squash players on the international circuit, ranking World Number 2 woman player of 1991, and winning the Australian Open in 1996, and the 1998 World Open Pro-AM Sydney tournament. She later established the first squash and fitness academy at the Emirates Golf and Country Club in Dubai.[45] Today she lives between Sydney and Dubai, teaming up with husband Phil Harte to run Harte International Events Management. More recently, she has begun managing an international lifestyle and travel magazine called *Classic Lifestyle*.

Migrant Māori living in Australia have had to grapple with the notion of changing citizenship. Currently, half of all New Zealand-born Māori who arrived prior to 1971 are Australian citizens. However, since 2001 the number of Māori taking up Australia citizenship has decreased dramatically due to a change in legislation. New Zealand citizens arriving into Australia have had the freedom to work in Australia through a non-protected Special Category Visa, but with new immigration laws New Zealanders cannot access social security and other employment opportunities unless they obtain permanent residence.[46] This did not change the earlier Trans-Tasman Travel Agreement, but New Zealanders are now no longer treated as 'residents' under the Social Security Act. As a result, they are denied access to a range of government and social security services, including denial of access to post-school study loans.[47] In May 2017 the Australian government announced higher-education cuts and changes, including a decision to stop subsidising enrolments by New

Zealand citizens from the start of 2018. According to a Radio New Zealand report, this move will see New Zealand students pay triple the amount (a jump from $7000 to $24,000) to study in Australia, but student loans would be made available to them. It is believed this would see expat New Zealanders send their children back to New Zealand for tertiary education.[48] For many Māori who migrated to Australia after 2001, permanent residence will never be a viable option.[49]

However, for many who settled in Australia prior to this date, residency became an important issue, leading to many considering permanent residency. In 2011 only 16.6% of Māori migrants living in Australia had Australian citizenship.[50] Dr Tahu Kukutai, associate professor at the National Institute of Demographic and Economic Analysis Waikato University, said in an Australian news article that Māori have alarmingly low rates of citizenship in Australia — it became difficult for New Zealanders to attain citizenship under the 2001 law changes — and says this is an issue "because there's a very large portion of Māori in Australia who are contributing to the tax base, but have no rights". She wrote, "It's not that Māori are singled out. This is the way indirect discrimination works." For Dr Kukutai, understanding not only the reasons people migrate but the impact mass migration will have on Māori culture remains a significant issue.[51]

Maintaining Māori identity has challenged Māori living in Australia, who have attempted to counter this by using the same community-building strategies that urban Māori migrants applied in the main centres of mid-twentieth century Aotearoa.[52] Building a marae to facilitate Māori cultural practice in the main centres, such as Sydney or Melbourne, and in Queensland has been an ongoing conversation that began in the late 1970s. Whānau gatherings, kapa haka training and organised wānanga have had to revert to using rented community centres, churches or private homes to hold gatherings. Despite 40 years of effort to build or find a space, there are still no Māori-owned community centres or marae in Australia.

Primarily the obstacles of pan-tribalism, governance in Australia, funding and the viability of running a facility have hindered the progress of establishing a marae. As well, seeking permission from the tangata whenua for establishing roots is an issue that Māori know needs to be resolved. People have been adamant not to trample on the mana of the Aboriginal community, something often overlooked.[53]

There has been some movement in this area, where local Aboriginal tribes have given consent for local Māori to build a marae-type complex. In contrast to this, other contentions over Māori activities without full Aboriginal tribal blessing eventuated in an Aboriginal-Māori reconciliation ceremony at Sydney's Blue Mountains in 2000. There, an array of tribal leaders rubbed red soil into the skin of Māori to offer an open door to their country.[54]

Probably the largest hindrance to Māori building a marae or seeking local government funding is the notion "we're not from here".[55] For some the community centre scenario is more acceptable, whereas marae and carvings are not: 'they don't belong on this land'. For others the marae is considered essential for future Māori generations who are putting down roots in Australia. These sentiments were common tensions for many Māori who shifted to the main centres in New Zealand: many elders believed that to build would mean planting roots in a land that wasn't theirs, and most were planning to return back-home.

In reality, for many the return home never happened and generations of their descendants still live in the cities, having to perform the traditional customs of gathering and mourning and

The Ham whānau of the Gold Coast and the Tipene whānau of Alice Springs celebrate Christmas together on the Gold Coast in Australia, 2016.

Courtesy of Bradford Haami

burying their dead either at their homes or on local pan-tribal marae. These issues are also relevant to Māori living in Australia.

On the Gold Coast, in 1983 when famous Māori musician Anzac Te Oka passed away, there was no marae to receive the people for his tangi. The Gold Coast Rugby Union Club opened their doors as suitable premises to lay his body in state. The rugby club was a stronghold for many Kiwi-Māori players who identified with Anzac's career as a spearhead of the Māori showband takeover in Sydney in the early 1960s.[56] The local Gold Coast council allowed the Te Oka family only three hours to hold his body in state, which went against custom.[57] Māori in Australia are still holding tangihanga in their backyards or in their air-conditioned homes, and usually only for one night.

Other tangihanga have been held at church premises such as the Church of Te Wairua Tapu in Redfern, which eventually had to be discontinued due to unsuitable parking, the overwhelming numbers attending and the small koha amounts laid down.[58] The rising number of tūpāpaku returning from Australia was a key reason for opening Te Mānukanuka o Hoturoa marae at Auckland International Airport in 2006. Te Arikinui Dame Te Atairangikaahu supported this joint venture between Tainui and Auckland International Airport Limited. One of the objectives was to give overseas deceased returning home a dignified return and to provide a place of comfort for bereaved families who arrive to receive their deceased relations.[59]

Having a designated Māori burial site has been an issue for many; to be buried in Australia is to plant roots and for some this isn't an option. For most they have no other option. The local council gifted a burial site to Māori in the Sydney suburb of Rookwood. Recently the council sold the gifted area and some families were forced to exhume their dead. Many whānau were unable to shift the remains of their deceased loved ones. A building now stands on that former burial ground.[60]

The notion of an Australian marae to hold tangihanga and practise culture is still a dream to be realised. Groups such as the Māori Aroha Co-operative Society, Te Iwi Māori and Te Aranganui in Sydney were established to raise a Māori community centre, but a lack of funds means they have been unable to fulfil their mandate.[61] Recently, the Sydney-based group Ngā Uri-o-Rahiri's development plans for a marae were put on hold as a West Sydney council sought to consult the public further because of residents' concerns about the project.[62] One unique situation is the Poi Turaki whare in Newcastle, where local Māori have been given access to the vacant Tomago Bowling Club since 2002. Here, they autonomously facilitate gatherings, wānanga and tangihanga. This became a key gathering place for Māori in New South Wales, but this situation is still only temporary.[63]

More recently, a leadership group from Marae Melbourne visited Hoani Waititi marae and Te Whānau o Waipareira to seek knowledge and strategic help to build a marae in Melbourne. The Marae Melbourne project has been in the making for 30 years, motivated by the need to provide support for whānau Māori in Melbourne and to address the growing number of social issues experienced by Māori families.[64]

Here for good or bad

One Māori collective from the Gold Coast, led by kaumātua Wi Wharekura (one of the original members of the Howard Morrison Quartet), are planning to build a multi-cultural marae-based community called The Polynesian Cultural Village. The local Logan Council and the government are fully supportive of investing in a venture to uphold the identity of new migrant Māori and Pacific communities in this part of Australia.[65] With the steady growth of Māori and Pacific migrants living in the suburbs of Coomera, Goodna and Logan, it is recognised that there is a need to create a community centre with cultural identity at its core to cater for the needs of the Māori/Pacific youth explosion. Having a cultural base is essential to curtailing issues of growing youth crime and low school pass rates of Māori children in Queensland. The local council, the Ministry of Education and the government see a need to support the local community to raise levels of progress for Māori.[66]

Kaumātua Wi has lived in Australia off and on for over 50 years. In 2017, at the request of the local community, he agreed to sit on the current executive as the President/Founder and Public Officer for the proposed Polynesian Cultural Village.[67] Kaumātua Wi was initially concerned about how hard it is to establish a marae based on tupuna from the whenua that is strong enough to hold the community together in a foreign land.[68] New entrepreneurial thinking and the creation of a new kawa is what he believes is needed in this place and time for this kaupapa.[69] The executive, which includes iwi and New Zealand community heavyweights and local Australian community leaders, is careful to move slowly and with due diligence on this wider Polynesian kaupapa, to look at all areas of communal and tribal support including education, social support, financial management, trade and training, marae protocol, and future-proofing for sports academies and employment. "It's a total necessity for our people here, it's got to be a product that is needed that bad and attracts people," Wi says.

In her article about establishing marae in Australia, Mamari Stephens quotes Tā Mason Durie from his 2009 Paerangi lectures. He said, "This was bound to happen" and commented it was "likely that overseas marae will be part of a worldwide network of marae".[70] Stephens understands the need for these etablishments but cautions her people to "be wary of transplanting our notions of being tangata whenua to the whenua of others, and risk wreaking yet another layer of colonisation upon those home peoples. We must never forget who we are. And we must never forget who we are not."[71]

Extended whānau support and whanaungatanga are identified as essential core values for Māori communities. If these are diminished, it has been demonstrated to have disastrous implications for the Māori family unit. Anecdotal evidence shows Māori whānau, in particular youth, are at risk, particularly in environments where parents are working hard and are often in transient and remote employment. Often there is no whānau support close at hand. Additionally, despite the desire for many to distance themselves from the gang, drug and alcohol element in New Zealand, the Jake and Beth Heke lifestyle still prevails and other social ills such as suicide and crime are almost inescapable. The gang element has shifted to Australia; a chapter of the Black Power has set up in southern Queensland.[72] For others, Australia just doesn't work, causing families to become 'stuck', even 'starving', unable to move forward or even to return home. This reflects the need for community marae-based centres to instil identity and strong engagement with more mainstream social services and Māori services intervention. These facilities are nearly non-existent for whānau living in Australia.[73]

On the whole most Māori see their shift to Australia as a positive move with lucrative benefits of affordable housing and better wages, and while they are far away from their cultural cradle and possibly losing engagement with their roots, many believe "the material gain in Australia outweighs the cultural deficit".[74] Nevertheless, cultural commitment to te Reo Māori and the cultural development of whānau is still important. The growing popularity of kapa haka tends to be the place Māori "most often turn to when seeking out their culture in Australia".[75] Most towns with more than 100 Māori tend to have a kapa haka team. Joining kapa haka groups, performing at Māori festivals and celebrating Waitangi Day (in Perth, more than 7000 people attend the latter every year) shows a determination to keep something of their familiar Aotearoa culture alive for the next generation.

According to Tahu Kukutai and Shefali Pawar's demographic report on Māori living in Australia, with an estimated one in five Māori living outside of Aotearoa and one in three of those Māori now born in Australia, they confer that it is no longer tenable to ignore the implications of a growing global Māori diaspora.[76] The issues of identity retention, socio-economic position and the maintenance of home connections will be strong considerations for the future as whānau in Australia try to reconcile their upbringing and obligations back-home.

For policymakers such as Te Puni Kōkiri, 'realising Māori potential' and assisting Māori to 'succeed as Māori' in 'whatever pursuit they choose' are factors they must actively consider for the large growing population of Māori living abroad, but particularly in Australia.[77] For iwi organisations and other Māori entities, it is no longer viable to ignore the rapid and 'sizeable diaspora' of whānau migrating to Australia. Knowing the circumstances, needs and aspirations of Māori living in Australia and abroad, as well as understanding insights into the conditions of living on the Red Land, is paramount to maintaining meaningful connections and networks with their kin. Various iwi organisations such as Waikato Raupatu Trustee Company and the Rongowhakaata Charitable Trust are already engaging with their people in Australia.

Returning home to Aotearoa from Australia has emotional and employment implications. Māori in Australia are more set on returning to New Zealand than professional Kiwis. Many Māori begin to feel the pull of the land and make the transition back, often to offer newfound skills or to secure rights to tribal land shares or to take up positions within the tribes. Many whānau return every year to maintain home relationships and cultural connections, particularly during the Christmas and New Year holidays. One reason for this has been for the sake of the children and offering them a more culturally focused upbringing.

Australian-born Māori children under 15 in New Zealand rose from 1113 in 1986 to 2859 in 2001.[78] More recently there has been a decline in the number of New Zealanders in Australia and 14,760 people have returned.[79] According to a Bay of Plenty report on Māori returning home to New Zealand in the near future, there are challenges to receiving this population home for education and employment reasons. The report revealed that Māori may return in large numbers from Australia to the Bay of Plenty for a number of reasons, including recent legislative restrictions (since 2001), financial reasons, trade work opportunities in Auckland and Christchurch, and family lifestyle flexibility.[80] It is estimated 4476 Māori who moved to Australia after 2001 are likely to return home between 2014 and 2024. In this group it is proposed there will be young males with low levels of education and skills, and older people ready to retire.[81] Whatever the movement of Māori whānau between countries, connectivity with 'home' is an unpredictable dilemma to overcome. The increase of social media combined with affordable and regular trans-Tasman air travel has created multiple opportunities to connect with and keep in touch with home-based whānau and the activities at the tribal homelands. One kaumātua, who has many whānau living in Australia, believes the continuation of kōrero between families living abroad and those at home is essential to maintaining strong viable cultural and whānau links.[82] As the proverb goes: Ko te kai o te rangatira, he kōrero (The food of chiefs is talk).

Bishop Whānau, Australia

Markie Bishop Jr (far right) with his wife Rachel and their children, Teina, Jayme, Kyran and Mia, Sydney, 2015.

Courtesy of Bishop whānau

Originally from Whanganui, Rena and Mark Bishop made the shift to Sydney in 1972. Forty-five years later they have retired to a waterfront unit in Surfers Paradise. "Australia has been good to us," the couple declare.

Rena is from the Waitai family. Her father, Heketa Waitai, was chief composer for Wiremu Tahupotiki Ratana's brass band, and wrote the original Ratana bandmarch. The family lived in the town of Whanganui where, Rena says, "there was little culture and no reo — I never heard the reo spoken in our neighbourhood". She left school at 15 and worked in a factory by day and as a cleaner at Whanganui hospital by night.

Rena married Mark Bishop, who was from the Moke whānau but was brought up as a whangai to the Bishop whānau of Raetihi. Mark worked at the freezing works as a meat grader and was a musician in the evenings. He played at all the major dance balls in Whanganui and also sat as the drummer for Rena's father's band. Mark was hardly ever home.

Rena felt the impetus to shift as there was no work at home and no way she could see to move forward. With her son Markie, she shifted to Sydney in 1972, telling no one where she was going. At the time the Trans-Tasman Travel Agreement between New Zealand and Australia had just been formalised and allowed people freedom of movement between the two countries.[83]

Rena arrived in Sydney with Markie, a little bit of money, and a strong determination to survive. Markie says, "Mum found a job and worked. You just need the right attitude. There was no certainty here. But when Mum managed to find a property for us to stay, she began to search for employment by reading the papers and knocking on doors." Rena was offered a delivery driver job almost immediately. She also sewed to supplement her income. Markie was placed in a new school and was the only Māori in his class at the time.

Rena found living and working in a foreign land with no whānau challenging, but she was determined to make it work. Prices were better for everything and there were better opportunities. Later that year, husband Mark Senior joined his family in Sydney. He had to give away his music for the family, finding employment at a local butcher shop. "It wasn't hard to find work and to reach the top in Australia," says Mark Snr.

For years Rena was a delivery driver of car parts, which took her all around Sydney. She got to know the city and its people intimately. She also worked in a hotel, helping to run the books. Despite never being a drinker, she soon began running pubs, showing a talent for management.

Whanganui whānau followed the Bishops to Australia. "We'd bring my sister's whānau over and now they all live here," Rena says. Soon there was an enclave of 30 Māori from Whanganui living on the Cronulla coast. When the whānau realised none of the locals would dive for food, they began to harvest paua, lobster and kina. "Most Māori living in Cronulla came through our home, then through someone else then someone else," Rena remembers. "Half of Whanganui came here." Hundreds of Māori families have transitioned to Australia through the Bishop home. During a visit home to Whanganui, Rena and Mark Snr became whāngai parents to Mark's Snr's sister's son, Wilfred Nahona, who returned to Australia with them.

Now that they were permanently living on foreign ground, keeping Māori culture alive in their lives became important. Local Māori whānau soon created the Cronulla Māori Culture Group. When people heard about the group, other Māori families rushed to join. When the children's local Aussie Rules football team needed to raise funds, a hangi was served, meat was raffled and the youth culture group performed at the club, raising more funds in one night of entertainment than the club had at a single event over the previous 30 years.

A run-a-thon between Brisbane and Sydney was organised to raise funds and advertise the 1979 Māori festival. A 12-man team was assigned to run the marathon between the two cities and included Markie and his cousin Wilfred. Markie was 15 at the time. He ran 78 kilometres over two days and nights. On reaching Government House in Sydney, the runners were met by Sydney's mayor Frank Preacher, and welcomed with special awards. This was the opening of the inaugural Sydney Māori Festival. The event set the scene for the Bishop family's involvement in kapa haka and other forms of entertainment/performing arts for many years to come.

In the 1980s the Bishop whānau shifted to the Gold Coast. Mark Snr says 90% of the venues on the Gold Coast had resident Māori musicians performing. Markie and Wilfred joined the Young Polynesians, who performed on Monday nights at the Chevron Lounge in Surfers Paradise, where Mark Snr had become the manager. There were Māori nightclub owners, builders, rugby communities, surfies, partygoers, church congregations, businessmen, homeowners, cleaners and street kids all living on the Gold Coast. It was a fast-growing and transient migrant Māori population, in which the Bishop whānau easily found their place.

When a managerial position came up at the Aitutaki Resort in the Cook Islands, Mark Snr and Rena decided to apply. They eventually shifted the whole family to the Cook Islands. "After a few years in Aitutaki, we moved back to Sydney," Mark Snr says. Mark, Rena and Markie upskilled themselves in hotel management and found themselves running separate hotel businesses in Sydney. Both of these hotels were held up by burglars. Markie was accosted, tied up and had a gun pointed at his head, while his business was ransacked. He shifted out of that business and later established Shire Scaffolding. Today it is a highly successful business.

"A lot of the Māori guys that I employed from New Zealand are good workers. Māori have a pretty good reputation among Aussies, who see them as tough, reliable and kind," Markie remarks. "We have a strong presence, we're masculine and loving as well — we offer certainty, that's why Australian women like Māori," he laughs.

Markie lives in Carringbah, Sydney, with his Australian wife Rachel and their three children. He is part of the group of second-generation Māori migrants, a generation that makes up 30% of all Māori living in Australia. Markie sees Australia as his permanent home and doesn't envisage returning to New Zealand to live. "I'm proud of New Zealand and being Māori, but I'll live here in Australia forever. I became an Australian citizen for my family's sake in 2012. I made decisions around family. I would love to bring my kids to New Zealand as there is little education about their culture here to let them experience it. I've got them greenstone necklaces, 'chur bro' t-shirts, and we follow the All Blacks hard — that's it," he says. For many Māori, such as Rena and Mark Snr, being around their children, mokopuna, and now great-grandchildren is paramount — wherever the kids are, the grandparents are not far away.

Mark Snr and Rena have retired to Surfers Paradise. Before this they lived in Coomera, south of Brisbane, a region with a large and growing Māori-Pacific population. Both Mark and Rena sit on a new executive body alongside well-known international entertainer and kaumātua Wi Wharekura, who lives nearby, with a mission to build a marae-based community called the Polynesian Cultural Village. It is envisaged that it will be a multi-generational community that can maintain the identities of the local Māori and Polynesian youth in these urban societies, a place of belonging that will provide culture, social care, training and employment.

Chapter 12 | **Hokinga ki te Kāinga**

Returning Home

Rural-urban distribution surveys recorded between 1981 and 1991 showed the percentage of Māori living in urban centres of 30,000 or more people rose by 1% to 82%, of which 74% were in major cities, 7% in secondary urban centres and 14% in minor urban areas.[1] However, between 1986 and 1991 the direction of movement changed slightly, with Māori families leaving the urban centres for smaller cities and towns or rural localities. Unsure whether this really could be regarded as 'return migration', New Zealand demographers recognised Māori families were returning to their tribal areas.[2]

From 1986 the migration flow in and out of the cities equalised, revealing a higher mobility rate among Māori than the New Zealand non-Māori population.[3] While there was a high outflow of people from Auckland to Northland, the Bay of Plenty attracted many people from all other urban centres. According to age, young adults tended to move to Auckland, Wellington, Canterbury and Otago for tertiary education, training and jobs, while families and the elderly tended to move to more provincial localities.[4] There wasn't one specific cause for "Māori going back home", but a number of factors were at play. Economics, the high cost of living and the preference for the 'quiet' life away from the hassle of the city were coupled with a period of growing cultural and tribal consciousness, all of which influenced return migration.[5]

> They had gone to the cities, worked and raised their families, and now, in their later years, with their families established in the cities, they were home again, where they wanted to be.[6]

The urge to return home ranged from feeling a call to re-connect to one's iwi identity, to represent whānau in the affairs of the hapū or iwi, or to help care for an ill or dying whānau member. The pull was sometimes spiritual.

For Melissa Williams, returning back-home is just part of a cycle, a life-course transition.[7] Māori migrated out of the city centres, leaving many of their whānau in the urban centres. The city remained important to them and the Māori communities left behind increased and thrived in many different ways. While many urban Māori had lost their back-home connection during the 1960s and 1970s, the first wave of Māori migrants to the city were never completely detribalised but "adapted their tribal outlooks to the urban environments".[8] These families adapted to the local urban 'community whakapapa' that incorporated other tribal Māori as well as non-Māori in a specific region or suburb.[9] Distance and busy lives became hindrances to maintaining links back home. Some families chose to send one (or more) of their children home to live with elders or attend rural schools to maintain a whānau presence in the rural regions.

Maintaining cultural commitment or cultural stability became strongly associated with the challenge of continuing personal and inter-generational connections to tribal home places. For some, staying connected to their homelands meant attending every tangi in their tribal territories to ensure their faces were consistently seen.[10] Travelling between Auckland and far-off tribal territories such as the tribal regions of Ngāti Awa in the Eastern Bay of Plenty, or even further to East Coast Ngāti Porou, to attend tangi and iwi-related gatherings was a serious commitment. Personal obligation associated with one's whakapapa and iwi often meant supporting the home people. This dual lifestyle has become common for Māori families strongly linked to their iwi and also for those who are re-orientating themselves with their roots.

In her study on Panguru, Melissa Williams described three features for city migrants that allowed them to adjust their perceptions and connections to back-home. These are the ability to access news and knowledge about Panguru; the ability to return back-home; and the strengthening of home ties as migrants entered their twilight years.[11] While many migrated away from their papakāinga knowing very little of their tribes and their histories, Williams points out that the constant conversation and news passed on by extended families and new city migrants helped whānau develop and retain better understandings of the Panguru geography, their whakapapa and perceptions of back-home.[12] Most long-term migrants maintained a physical relationship with Panguru, which in turn "expanded migrants' knowledge" of the kāinga.[13] Return trips to provide Auckland market resources for local marae, and to help fundraise for home initiatives were made easier by the upgrade of roading in the 1970s.[14] Those reaching their twilight years became more appreciative of homeland narratives and with the increased awareness of their mortality, they saw the significance of return migration, something Williams sees as a natural part of one's "life-course".[15]

Jim Ranginui returns to Te Kuha Tarewa marae at Tuai, Waikaremoana, with his daughters Emily Ranginui and Marcia Ranginui Charlton.

Courtesy of the Ranginui whānau

It was with age and life experience that Panguru migrants began seriously evaluating their lifetime achievements, their connections to Panguru, their children's connections, what the future might bring and the satisfaction that returning back-home could provide.[16]

While many had "escaped the area [back-home] to find themselves",[17] years later many began to look back-home to remind themselves who they were. It must be said here, looking back home to maintain or rejuvenate identity is not an easy process for many whānau or individuals. The Māori identity spectrum is broad, stretching between those who know and maintain their connections to iwi and those who can never attain their true identity back-home. Generally speaking, while some can walk between the urban and iwi worlds with ease there are many who were adopted, some as whāngai, who have been denied access to their true identity and simply do not know their biological roots. Tracing their whakapapa is difficult. Another category on this spectrum are those who purposely choose not to re-engage or even speak about their iwi affiliations due to the memory and pain of past abusive experiences back-home. Added to this is the non-acceptance by biological iwi-based whānau of the descendants of those members who were abused, kicked out or cast out as black sheep. All of these common circumstances exist in both the urban and rural environment. Generational trauma at this extremity of the identity spectrum has produced generations who are denied their whakapapa and a place in the iwi landscape. So often these whānau have carved a life for themselves as best as they can, but need reconciliation processes in place to be able to find and engage back-home.

Those who have migrated home often returned to a place with a lack of public amenities, public transport and appropriate medical services. Returning also brought to the surface old land disputes, family feuds, old jealousies and tribal contentions. Inter-whānau frictions occurred when returning migrants' occupation rights to land with multiple owners or to the family homestead were contested. Often the home lifestyle of the past had changed enormously to what the older generation remembered. While the environment and the landscape may not have changed, in many cases the modern lifestyle could be alien when compared to what the old people were expecting. The same social ills of the city were also prevalent in the rural regions.

Pare Keiha and Paul Moon wrote about the extent to which the modern industrial-technical city with its capital activity envelops the countryside. The result is expressed in the reality that some Māori communities remaining on their traditional lands are still subject to almost as many of the same forces of urbanisation as those who actually relocated to the cities.[18]

Tangi and home

For many, particularly the elderly, the wish to return home to be buried in their original whānau urupa is often the fulfilment of a deep longing to one day return back-home. It also sends a reminder to whānau to 'come home'. This has been cause for emotional tension for a younger generation who desire the best comforts for their elders in the city, close to them and to better amenities. However, the desire to go back-home and reaffirm identity at an old age, and to die at home, usually proves more powerful than the physical or medical barriers presented by the shift.

The idea that 'where you come from, you go back to' is strong for Māori. However, it is also a common statement that "it's better to go back home walking than in a box".[19]

Carrying a whānau member's tūpāpaku (corpse) home to their tribal marae for the tangihanga (funerary ritual) was the norm for first-generation migrants. Families in the city created whānau clubs where funds were deposited over time to cover the costs of travelling home and burial. Lack of finance made this journey prohibitive for others.[20] Friction over the decision to bury a loved one in the city often arose — many frowned on the idea of being buried in foreign tribal soil.[21]

Some whānau placed their deceased on the Road Services bus as one option to transport a loved one home. In one case a deceased relative was dressed and placed on a bus to travel from Auckland to Dargaville. The family told the driver their relation was drunk and asleep. They propped him up in the back seat and accompanied him home where the haukāinga (home people) met the tūpāpaku at the station.[22]

The custom of returning deceased whānau to their tribal home continues. At times it is the first time some family members have ventured to their tribal landscape. Often the memory of the returned deceased is lost to the home people, or the deceased may have never had a living association with the land or the marae of their grandparents. Other times an urban whānau in mourning with little or no knowledge of custom are suddenly confronted by a tribal contingent at their city doorstep demanding that their deceased mother, father or grandparent should be handed to them to be buried on their marae as a mark of honour. This has created awkward moments between urban Māori and rural relatives.

One Auckland Māori funeral director's experiences and observations have taught him to be flexible when involved in a tangihanga for urban Māori, especially when transporting a tūpāpaku backhome. Besides the gang-related funerals where bodies have been stolen from hearses, fistfights have occurred, and the smashing down of the funeral chapel walls is common, there is a great ignorance of tangihanga protocol among people. Some whānau returning home know little of local marae custom or, in some cases, have never ever been on to their marae or met their relatives. Apprehension and lack of confidence among returning whānau has hindered some from setting foot on their home marae with their loved one. Some whānau have abandoned plans to return their loved one home because they are overwhelmed by their fear of the unfamiliar.[23] Those returning home fear criticism by the home folk, and also feel embarrassed by their lack of knowledge of marae protocol. The home people operate in these situations out of aroha and obligation for their whanaunga, but they are sometimes disappointed at the demands of city whānau who fail to contribute financially, help clean the marae, or often never return home to reciprocate the honour.

In fulfilling the desire of whānau to return their family member home, it is common for Māori funeral directors to research the tribal origin of the whānau and make arrangements with the haukāinga to receive the tūpāpaku and the mourning family. Sometimes information about the tribal connections of the deceased is incorrect, making it difficult for the whānau to find the correct iwi, hapū or marae that needs to be contacted.[24] A lack of city whānau support systems or kaumātua have seen funeral directors become driver, embalmer, cultural advisor, kai-kōrero, negotiator between warring families, entertainer, minister and sometimes gravedigger.[25] There is a sense of fear of criticism by the home folk, and embarrassment felt by urban whānau often lacking in knowledge of marae protocol.

There are also those elders who have no desire to return home in their twilight years. Te Waka Huia leader Bub Wehi's father left instructions that when he passed he was to be buried in Māngere with his daughter. As his body lay in state at Te Tira Hou marae at Panmure, Bub and his elders waited for the whānau of Waioweka to arrive to demand his body be returned home. Bub remembers:

> Sure enough the people from Waioweka did arrive with the idea of returning my father's body to his Whakatōhea tribal papakāinga. With the strong resolve of our whānau and elders John Tūrewi and Dan McGarvey, we managed to offset our relations' plans with some witty oratory and negotiation; the pangs of aroha for my mother, now having to live alone, grew strong. It flashed through my mind how much I needed to move a little closer to her, even if it meant leaving Waihīrere; a devastating thought. Perhaps the writing was on the wall.[26]

This situation partially led to Bub and his whānau leaving Waihīrere that same year to live in Auckland.[27]

Ike Samuels, a well-known Ngāti Haua kaumātua, left New Zealand to work as a missionary in Papua New Guinea in 1965. He had no intention of returning home to Rukumoana marae near Morrinsville to be buried. He informed his whānau that he would give his land shares and tribal inheritance to his siblings as he wasn't returning.[28] He wanted to live, die and be buried in Papua New Guinea. However, the whānau returned to New Zealand as Ike's wife Mary was unwell.[29] Ike worked as a minister, a builder and a kaumātua for Auckland's mental health sector, eventually passing away in Auckland. He was buried on his home marae at Rukumoana. Ike's return to New Zealand and his burial here has allowed his children and mokopuna to forge a stronger working relationship with the haukāinga.[30]

The tamariki return

A younger generation of urban-born Māori who had little connection with their tribal family roots were influenced by the resurgence of Māori culture and iwi development, which began in the 1980s. A study in 2000 of return migration to the Mangakahia Valley in Northland concluded that the Māori renaissance and the era of iwi development had influenced the return of many whānau.[31]

Manuhuia Barcham reviewed a series of informal interviews with

33 whānau members from the Ngāti Kahungunu tribe who had returned to their tribal roots. His review revealed that the participants wished to be a part of the cultural regrowth of the tribe and desired to "get in touch with my Māori side", and to allow the children access to their Māori identity.[32] Despite a lack of employment opportunities in the region, the participants had made the choice to stay for cultural reasons, not those of economy. Barcham further states the return migration of urban Māori was a significant factor in the regrowth of the powerbase for the Māori tribal institutes.[33]

In a survey of Tūhoe who migrated to the Waikato region, most said they were hoping to return to Tūhoe lands to assist with social, educational and employment ventures, but primarily to find employment. However, they could see little chance of this occurring in the current state of poor employment prospects in rural New Zealand.[34] Most considered retiring back-home and wishing to die there, even if it meant leaving their Waikato-raised children.[35]

Many whānau members have been met with open arms by their home cousins while others have been confronted with a wall of opposition and suspicion. The traditional divide between the 'te noho roa' (those who have stayed home) and the 'te pikopiko haere' (those who have wandered away)[36] is exemplified in the traditional metaphor of those who maintain the garden-land as opposed to those who 'go wandering' — or those who maintain the ahi kaa (burning home fire), in contrast to those who abandon their fires to become ahi mataotao (extinguished cold fires). The process of returning home is akin to an individual or a whānau having to rekindle their ahi mataotao (extinguished fire). While whakapapa kin links to an area are unquestioned by locals, living on the land and being actively involved in the life of the community or tribe is seen as essential to flaming the ahi kaa. Crossing the cultural threshold between those who continued to live on the land and those who are returning has a pronounced process, made more so by the cultural renaissance and the contention for recognition of rights to Treaty settlements. These two spectrums have morphed into a rhetoric about "real Māori" verses "urban Māori", to prove or assert one's authenticity as Māori.[37]

The divide between those who move away and those who stay home is reflected in the behaviour of home-based family marking migrating whānau members as strangers or claiming them as not 'one of us'. Linda Nikora noted the positive and negative consequences for Tūhoe migrants to the Waikato, who were saddened at the way the people back home treated them differently, while others came to the realisation that those back home lived in a "restricted world".[38] For some who travelled home from the city for occasional visits, "it was like you were an outcast".[39] One Auckland kuia shared how things changed once she moved away from home.

> 'You got comments like who do you think you are? You are up yourself and your talking has changed, your clothes. Your dress style has changed, your hair. What are you doing wearing those kind of shoes? So yes it [the relationship] did change. And straight away they thought you were rich … it was not only from your immediate whānau, it was from the rest of your whānau as well, the extended whānau. They looked at you and if you had a flash car, you know, where'd you get the money? You must have stolen that. So it was quite negative so sometimes you just didn't feel like going home because of that.[40]

Names such as Ngāti Taone (townie tribe), Ngāti Pākehā (Pākehā tribe) or toto haurua (half-caste) are thrown at visiting or returning whānau by the home relatives, as are other sarcastic remarks about only turning up for holidays or not participating in the marae kitchen. Some suspicious cousins have claimed their outsider relatives as "always needing something"[41] or returning home only to search for their "piece of land".[42] Some who have returned home with a university degree have been met with resistance and an instruction that they should not 'think you can come back here and tell us what to do'. These attitudes have bred unfortunate suspicions about city Māori, who are often assumed to be 'richer than us' or 'lazy workers' and somehow superficial.

Dame Whina Cooper returned to Panguru for the opening of a new whare hui at Waipuna marae in 1983, after years on the road for the Māori Women's Welfare League and stationed in Auckland, and her reception was one of optimism. Melissa Williams records that Panguru had lost much of its population and land over the preceding decades, and deserved the respect for keeping the home fires burning.

> Regardless whether you returned home from Auckland after digging drains for 40 years or after 30 years' representing Māoridom and becoming the 'Mother of the Nation', it made no difference — you were now just one of many other whanaunga

who could either use their collective efforts to make Panguru a better place or put more pressure on community energies and amenities as a disengaged bystander.[43]

Finding acceptance among the home people can take time and effort. Drinking the locals under the table was one urban Māori woman's experience of initiation into being accepted back to her home-based marae whānau.[44] Whakapapa links whānau to a region, but it does not mean you are accepted easily into the fold. Being consistently present at hui, working in the kitchen, mourning at tangi, supporting the hapū and iwi and practising home-based culture is what knits a community together. Weaving one's whānau back into the threads of the extended family, hapū and iwi and finding the place to fit takes humility and the development of new relationships.

Manuhuia Barcham noted that 26% of all Māori who identified as being Māori in the 1996 census gave no iwi affiliation, making it hard to identify with iwi and difficult for any return-migration. Even with a high number of respondents to the freephone iwi helpline established by Te Ohu Kaimoana (Treaty of Waitangi Fisheries Commission), many still had no way of achieving contact.[45] Links for those who had never lived in the places of return,[46] or have no land or immediate whānau left in the region to connect with, have had to be established through genealogical research by second-generation Māori.

On the home front, there are those hapū and iwi who have openly called their city relatives to come home to learn the reo of the kāinga, understand the ways of the hapū and fill in the gaps on the marae. Small rural kāinga had few left to sit on their paepae as orators, or even to run the kitchens and perform the obligatory functions of hospitality when visitors arrived at the marae. The past depopulation of tribal regions is exemplified in the proverbial statement 'e rite ana ki te inanga e rere ana i Ōmutu' (like the flight of the whitebait during Ōmutu).[47] This saying describes a natural phenomenon where inanga-whitebait are seen repeatedly lifting out of the water en-masse at the height of their migratory season, as they disappear up the river estuary on the Ōmutu lunar day of the Māori calendar.[48] Creative orators on the marae used this metaphor to describe the devastating exodus of their families leaving the papakāinga-village environment for the urban centres.[49] The ramifications of this are still being felt today.

One small rural marae only had one kuia left to karanga, whaikōrero and cook the kai for a tangi.⁵⁰ Elders at another papakāinga are few and are all over the age of 70. They have been left to dig the graves of departed relations as the young people have left the region and only return sporadically.⁵¹ Kaumātua Kōhiti Kōhiti of Te Murumurunga marae at Te Whaiti made an emotional plea on Māori Television in mid-2017 for the people of Ngāti Whare to return home as their reo was dying and there was no one left to run the marae.⁵² On the other side of the Urewera ranges at Tāneatua, prominent Tūhoe personality Tame Iti and his son Toi Iti are involved in transforming the once-depressed Tāneatua township to attract people back home to the haukāinga.⁵³ Some elders proclaim, "Change will not happen in their rural communities until the people from the cities come home."⁵⁴

Papakāinga

Returns are dependent on good planning in order to cope with rural or small-town conditions. Some whānau have returned back-home under challenging circumstances, while others have delayed their return until the conditions were right, or when the resources to build are available.⁵⁵ More recently, the growth of papakāinga housing schemes where tribal land owned by many has been made available for development, providing a further incentive for some urban whānau to return home. On 29 July 2016, *Te Kaea* (Māori Television news) ran a story on the papakāinga housing project at Te Kōpua at Raglan. There, affordable housing has been made available for whānau from Tainui-a-Whiro. It is a scheme many ancestors of the area had fought for over many years. The land was originally confiscated by the Crown for use as an airstrip during World War II. After the war the land was contested by Tuaiwa Rickard and others, who fought to have the land returned to Māori hands. Today, after much wrangling, and at the completion of stage one of the Te Kōpua 3B2 papakāinga housing scheme, three families have moved into the homes built on that land. The vision for the homes is that families will move back on to their lands to maintain the ahikā (fires) and bring life back to the hapū.⁵⁶

Te Aro Pā Papakāinga scheme in Wellington provides homes for 14 families in a central cityscape at Greta Point, close to the original Te Aro Pā site where their Te Ati Awa ancestors once lived. The original inhabitants of the 1.6 ha pā, which is strategically positioned in the central city, were pressured by settlers to shift to Polhill Gully near the Ōwhiro landfill, and near Island Bay to land that was later

The Te Aro Pā Papakāinga Housing project at Greta Point on Wellington's waterfront provides homes for a number of local Te Ati Awa families.
Courtesy of Bradford Haami

taken as a racecourse.[57] Polhill Gully proved too expensive to develop and was chemically contaminated. Eventually Greta Point was established as a precious site for a symbolic papakāinga and the land was made available to the 1000-strong Te Aro Pā descendants.[58]

One tribal trust decided to build a papakāinga housing scheme outside of their own tribal boundaries in an urban environment. The Aorangi Tribal Trust Board of Takapau felt their beneficiaries would be better served by building houses for them in the Hastings area close to their places of employment. In 1970 the Aorangi Trust, from the rural village of Takapau, had the foresight to purchase land in Waipatu near Hastings with the support of the local Ngāti Hawea tribe. The Aorangi Trust has created a papakāinga of eight homes for their families on this land. Historically, these Waipatu lands were originally purchased after a small compensation was paid by the New Zealand government to the trust for the wrongful taking of 7200 acres (2914 hectares) of land in the Aorangi Block, near the current township of Takapau, in the 1850s. Aorangi was once the original home of Ngāi Te Kikiri-o-te-rangi, Ngāi Tahu-makaka-nui and Ngāi Toroiwaho people. In 1952, a century later, Ngāi Tahu accepted

£50,000 as compensation for the loss of land use over 100 years. This amount was less than one-fifth of the land value in the 1850s. The land purchased with these funds at Waipatu was originally used by the Aorangi Trust as a market garden. Today, eight homes have been built on 3.4 hectares of that land, with the remaining whenua currently scheduled for development into more papakāinga homes.[59]

Similar papakāinga housing schemes are emerging throughout New Zealand, playing a key role in encouraging Māori families, locally and city based, to return and take up residence on their whānau tribal lands. These initiatives, supported by current Māori land policies, are the manifestation of the dreams of ancestors who wished to see their descendants return home.

For kaumātua Ngāmaru Raerino, returning home to his mother's people at Awahou on Lake Rotorua was a move made for his spiritual and mental well-being. He had spent nearly 40 years away from his birthplace at Te Teko in the tribal territory of Ngāti Awa. He has worked in a variety of vocations and he is well-known for his knowledge of Māoritanga. Ngāmaru worked in Rotorua, Wellington and Auckland as a Māori Affairs Social Welfare Officer for 15 years. He was active in the affairs of his Ngāti Awa kin at Mataatua marae in Auckland, and entered the academic world at Auckland Institute of Technology (now Auckland University of Technology) as a tutor and lecturer, completing his thesis on Māori Epistemology. Education became an essential aspect of life for Ngāmaru and his children. He has been a staunch advocate for te Reo Māori and tikanga and was involved in the Māori film and television world as a producer, actor, story consultant and translator. In 2008 he and his wife Diane decided they would make

Ngāmaru Raerino at Ngā Wai o Horotiu Marae, Auckland University of Technology. Ngāmaru spent nearly 40 years living and working in the urban environment, until he and his family decided to retire back to his mother's lands at Awahou on Lake Rotorua in 2008.

Courtesy of Pūrākau Productions Ltd

a permanent move to retire to Awahou in Rotorua, among his Ngāti Rangiwēwehi relatives on his mother's side. Ngāmaru speaks of his time in the city:

> I think going to the city afforded my kids the appreciation of a diverse range of culture, people and education for the betterment of their own well-being and economically. I was strong in creating the awareness that they are Māori and they need to appreciate another lens to look at life. So there was ample Western teaching but their Māori teaching was to a certain extent wider but not as deep. The only way the kids got it was through me. I had strong Māori ties. The children were exposed to the people from home. They weren't deprived of their culture. We had a place in Rotorua that we were able to get away from the urbanisation and appreciate the idyllic surroundings of Awahou and Te Teko.[60]

Ngāmaru and Diane's eldest son Steve lives in Australia and he hasn't maintained ties back-home as much. Their other children, Maea, Kimi, Heddel and Te Awaroa, have all maintained their Māori identity and their haukāinga cultural roots despite spending years in the city. Prior to shifting to Awahou, Ngāmaru wasn't looking to move as he was happy being involved in a variety of interesting work in Auckland. "Auckland kept me alive," he says. He reflects on the shift to Awahou:

> I always regarded Te Teko as home, te wāhi tapahia toku pito [the place where my umbilical cord was cut], but now I look at Awahou as home now, with Ngāti Rangiwewehi. I haven't broken ties to Te Teko as I'm still the chairman of the marae at Tūteao with Ngā Maihi. Outside of Awahou I'm reasonably well known in Ngāti Awa and the outer Māori circles, but here in Awahou among my mother's people, they didn't really know me.[61]

Ngāmaru has lived at Awahou with his family and several mokopuna for over six years. As far as he is concerned, it has taken the people that long to accept him into the community. Being an academic and being raised in another tribe territory have been barriers to his acceptance.

> I had an interesting conversation with some of the elders here who said change would not happen in the communities until the people from the cities come home. Small communities look inward but outsiders returning home have more outward-looking world views — this would bring good change. I look at things in a more expansive way these days and try not to get too tied up in the minor arguments in the village.⁶²

Because of his deep knowledge of reo and tikanga, there is a tendency to be tested. People tried to 'catch him out', he says.

> There is a passive hostility towards the educated pūkenga (knowledgeable ones). I'm usually the last person the people come to about Māori culture. People are either too shy or scared of me or they see me as the ngārara (lizard, an outsider). A prime example is in the area of whaikōrero. The paepae here is weak and not as strong as it should be because the speakers are complacent and have not increased their body of knowledge.⁶³

For Ngāmaru, moving home was more than a change in a physical reality, it was about maintaining well-being. "Returning home for me was all about my own spiritual and mental well-being and to take stock of what I have been doing over the years. You can't do that in a foreign or alien place. My physical well-being can live anywhere but I find my spiritual well-being needed to be grounded to the whenua of my ancestors."⁶⁴ A devout follower of Te Kooti and a practising Ringatū, Ngāmaru sees Awahou as a special place of seeing to which Te Kooti made reference. "Nā Te Kooti te kī ana kei roto i te awa o Te Awahou e takoto ana ngā kōrero tapu ki roto (Te Kooti said that within Awahou the sacred talks are held)," Ngāmaru reflects. For this reason Awahou, with its beautiful lake vistas, holds a special place in the hearts of the whānau who refer to it as 'the homestead'.⁶⁵

The return home is a continuation of a life cycle: some left the region knowing one day they would return, others stayed to maintain the home fires. Some believe pathways for the city whānau to return home should be made easy, while others say returning back-home should be made with respect for the home people. As one kaumātua put it, "Me hoki ki te kāinga engari, kāua hoki whakaputa kōrero, hoki whakaiti (You should return home but don't be a know-all, return home with humility)."⁶⁶

The Raerino whānau gather for a baptismal ceremony
at the Awahou Stream in 2016.
Courtesy of the Raerino whānau

Perhaps a fitting final statement to share on returning home comes from Hirini Moko Mead. In speaking of Ngāti Awa in the Bay of Plenty, he made a call in 1990 for the tribe to overcome the dislocation of its population, most of whom lived outside their tribal territory. He commented that "our little octopus must stretch its tentacles outwards to draw in our people towards the centre".[67] He continued, saying:

> In drawing our people towards the tribal centre, we must also find ways of removing any feelings of threat that the people at home might experience. They kept the home fires going, they protected the ahi-ka while we enjoyed careers, full employment and opportunities in the outside world. How do we include everyone, without threatening the iwi kāinga? In the end it is not our feelings or our egos that are of paramount importance to our development as a tribal people. What is important is the iwi, that it survives and develops.[68]

Roger Maaka, Takapau, Central Hawke's Bay

After many years away from his papakāinga, Dr Roger Maaka has returned home to live at his beloved Takapau, Central Hawke's Bay, 2016.
Couresy of Bradford Haami

Roger Maaka returned home permanently to Takapau in 2009/2010 after being away from his birthplace for more than 50 years. He has taken a role in the civil activities of his Ngāti Kahungunu people and is the current chairman of Te Taiwhenua o Tamatea tribal governance board in central Hawke's Bay, which incorporates nine local district marae. "I always held the view that Takapau was my home and I was always going to return here," he says. "For Māori who were raised in the tribal regions the urge to return is very strong, it's a genuine desire by many to return to their tribal origins."

Roger was the first of the Maaka children in his whānau to be born at a hospital, to his mother Matangihau Ellers and father Aritaku 'Markie' Maaka. He and his sister Elizabeth were raised in Takapau, a settlement of approximately 500 residents. Markie worked as a labourer at the Lake Whatuma Lime Works after he was married and stayed there until he died in 1969.

The whānau lived in a new Māori Affairs home in Takapau and Roger attended Takapau Primary and Central Hawke's Bay College at Waipukurau. The strong Māori women in his life steered him towards an education. Grandmother Annie Maaka (nee Haberfield) was Ngāi Tahu from the South Island, and she laid the foundation, while his mother Matangihau followed suit. "My mother was very education-orientated and my sister and I were encouraged to go and get an education. I rebelled against it and joined the army," Roger says.

At age 17 Roger visited the recruitment office in Waipukurau and signed up for military service. He was stationed at Waiouru and then at Burnham for training. He spent 20 years in the New Zealand Army, which included tours of duty in Borneo, South Vietnam (twice), a two-and-a-half-year stint in Singapore, and seven years in the most elite combat unit of the New Zealand Defence Force, the Special Air Service (SAS). It was during these years Roger married Gina (Ngāti Porou) and the couple had two daughters, Hirani and Matariki. Roger's last post was in Christchurch. The Maaka whānau settled there permanently, and the last of their children, Jorgette, was born.

Roger took his discharge from the army in Christchurch and purchased a rubbish disposal business. He joined a local Māori Anglican karakia group and became a parishioner. This led him into the ministry, attending community events and tangihanga, as well as beginning university. Always interested in whakapapa and the Māori language, at the age of 43 he studied at the Department of Māori Studies at Canterbury University. He became immersed in Māori academia. His army teaching experience was acknowledged and the head of department asked him to assist in teaching. He was contracted to the department, and was eventually employed as its head.

In his community life and during the devolution and retribalisation period of the 1980s, Roger was drawn to gather Ngāti Kahungunu people in Christchurch to find a way to reconnect with home. He became involved in the establishment of Te Rūnanga o Ngāti Kahungunu ki Waitaha (Ngāti Kahungunu Council of Canterbury) in response to the political landscape of devolution and Treaty settlements, but more to fulfil the desire to reconnect to back-home. His summation that the government of the day was trying to manipulate Māori identity motivated him to study the plight of Māori moving to the city and retribalisation.

In 1994 he produced a paper on this kaupapa, "The New Tribe: Conflicts and Continuities in the Social Organization of Urban Māori," published in *The Contemporary Pacific Journal*. Roger's doctorate thesis at Canterbury University, published in 2003 and entitled *Perceptions, Conceptions and Realities: A Study of the Tribe in Māori Society in the Twentieth Century* was the product of many years of studying the detailed state of Māori iwi identity over a 100-year period. The thrust of his thesis was to track how traditional tribal identity had changed over 100 years. He also demonstrated that the modern structure of whānau, hapū and iwi had been politically reconstructed by government policy to become the basis of retribalisation and contemporary tribal organisations, but that this construct was irrelevant to the 80% of Māori living in cities. From a wider perspective, he says, "There is a mythology that indigenous people somehow belong in remote places but in reality they are flocking to the cities. If we're in the city, then somehow we're not indigenous or Māori. But the reality of the urbanisation of indigenous people is a growing phenomenon we must deal with."

Roger served on the Waitangi Tribunal from 1996 until 2011, with an interest in the Waitangi Tribunal Claim Wai 262 for intellectual property rights. However, after a research sabbatical in Canada studying urbanisation among the indigenous people here and in the Yukon, he took a position at the University of Saskatchewan, Canada, where he was a professor and Head of Department for Native Studies. He spent six years in Canada producing findings that have contributed to policy development and bringing about positive change for indigenous peoples. During this period he undertook research as part of collaborative international studies, led research teams in Canada and New Zealand and provided qualitative research expertise on several global research studies and research panels.

This led to collaborative publications such as *The Politics of Indigeneity* (2005), which reflected on the increasing organisation of indigenous people challenging Canadian and New Zealand colonial structures.

In 2009 Roger was appointed the Dean of the Eastern Institute of Technology and was the professor for Māori and Indigenous Studies. In 2010 he purchased a home in Takapau and, with his daughter Jorgette, he began to re-establish himself at the place he was raised.

"As the years went by my father died and my mother moved back to Wairarapa. I had less of a link to Takapau," he says. "When my Aunty Nancy died, she was the last of the family link here in Takapau. When we used to come back to Takapau, it was usually for a quick drive around the streets and then moving on again."

His heart has always been with Takapau but moving back to the papakāinga had its challenges. "I wasn't sure how I would fit in as I was in my sixties and most of my generation had passed on. There were few Māori my age here and those who were here from primary school days were now grandparents. I remember being in the pub and meeting a woman who was the granddaughter of a man I was at primary school with," he reflects.

Roger has returned to a rural village where there are no shops, no pub, no doctors and no petrol stations. "The stuff we had on tap in the provincial towns and cities is just not here anymore, they are more 30 minutes away." Returning home has meant fitting in to local life again. "Some things are the same but many things from the old papakāinga days are very, very different. It's not the papakāinga I remember but I have reclaimed it, and I have to work it out. Even though I whakapapa here I'm the stranger among the locals, so I had to fit in." A lot of the issues of gangs, theft and crime, often thought of as city problems, are also in the papakāinga, he says.

"Returning home is not a cake walk. If you don't have property or any surviving relations back in the papakāinga, these are challenging factors to consider. I'd think it's a very small percentage of those who migrate home, perhaps far less than 5% who take the serious move to make that shift and do it," Roger comments. Since he returned to Takapau, all of his daughters and their children have returned to the region to settle. One daughter, Matariki, lives in the Aorangi Trust papakāinga housing scheme in Hastings. "I took my daughters around all of Takapau and then the following week my sister brought her whānau and we did the journey again, taking our descendants to all the key places where our ancestors lived that they shouldn't forget," he says. "It was my attempt to get our kids interested again and to link them to the whenua. They don't want to attend big hui in marae with one person speaking from the front for hours."

Roger has made a concerted effort to become more involved in contributing to local civil activities and especially to those of his Ngāi Tahu-makakanui tribal links in Takapau. He wears his robes as a local minister for Sunday services. As he says, "The marae is poorly attended, people don't naturally go to the marae but the rugby club or the RSA are more relevant. We have a labour shortage for digging graves at the urupa and the hotshots for the paepae speakers don't live in the papakāinga but in the cities."

He concludes, "We must find ways of organising our iwi-ness to become relevant to the younger generation. We need to make pathways that are comfortable for both those urban whānau wishing to return and the people of the papakāinga who live here as well."[69]

Chapter 13

Iti Oneone Hou

The New Morsel of Soil

Pan-tribal (mātāwaka) urban Māori communities are a reality in the towns, cities and now overseas in Australia — a force that cannot be ignored or set aside. Māori have made the cities and towns their homes and have lived outside of their tribal locales for generations, but have not necessarily forgotten their iwi roots. This is a unique reality that has contested and expanded the boundaries of what it means to be Māori.

'Being Māori' or more specifically being tribal, as kaumātua like Māori Marsden and John Rangihau have declared, is the direct result of having Māori whakapapa and living in a Māori community grouped by iwi and hapū; an upbringing in a traditional, tribal community-fostered identity and world view.[1] In this environment, the essential aspects of ritual and Māoritanga as a cultural framework for life were passed on. This traditional identity is comprised of "ancestral connections through whakapapa or genealogy, combined with access to ancestral land as tūrangawaewae, bound together by the ancestral language, te Reo Māori".[2]

While these attributes are the essential building blocks of an iwi Māori identity, it does not necessarily fit the mould of a new generation of urban Māori whose families have lived in the city environment for up to 70 years. They are a pan-tribal population that has expanded the traditional mores of Māori society into the urban space. This includes drawing in non-kin relationships to the 'community whakapapa' and not having an ancestral connection to the land they dwell on.

Dr Mason Durie claims a "secure identity" for the future is not only the privilege of rural or tribal Māori, but it is also prevalent with urban Māori who are confident Reo speakers and have good access to marae and to whānau.[3] That identity in the current national and global environment is hard to hold without a strong resolve. Securing a strong Māori identity must compete daily with whānau dynamics engulfed by economic, health and social disparities, sometimes by the influence of drugs, poverty, homelessness and housing shortages. The priorities of families living in these conditions outweighs their affiliations to iwi activities and other urban-based cultural activities, presenting significant challenges for iwi and government agencies. The majority of the Māori population are now an urban-dwelling people. It must be asked, what are the iwi and government obligations to these populations? Where do mātāwaka urban Māori and their associated authorities fit into the bigger scheme of future Māori and iwi development?

Boys spontaneously dancing at a West Auckland sports festival.
Courtesy Te Whānau o Waipareira

Urban identity

This particular narrative of urban Māori history and experience does not set out to answer these questions, but to highlight the circumstances and tensions that are still current, and which have created adaptations of traditional societal mores that now influence Māori and New Zealand lifestyles. The push of poverty and unemployment and the pull of work, money and pleasure in a political atmosphere of assimilation and integration policies drew thousands of Māori to the provincial towns and larger cities, where over three-quarters of the Māori population settled outside their rural tribal territories. The family profiles included in this publication show the diversity of Māori settlement journeys and experiences living in the city. Some lost access to their tribal roots while others retained their identity. All of these whānau may live an urban life and choose to stay where they are, but on the whole they all desire to maintain or retain their Māori and their iwi identity, while continuing to live out the core values of being Māori.

Urban Māori didn't completely become Pākehā, as assimilation polices of the past aimed to create, nor did they lose desire for

A local kapa haha team perform at a function organised by Te Whānau o Waipareira.
Courtesy Te Whānau o Waipareira

community. Matua Hakiaha, a criminologist and a strong tribal advocate who has lived in West Auckland for many years, has vivid memories of the strong tikanga values that have existed in this community: "The Māori community here is a cohesive cultural community. Whenever there was a tangi you'd see the community pull together. I remember going to a tangi at Te Atatū and I sat watching people back up their cars and all sorts of kai. That's what reminded me of my marae upbringing at Poroporo where we had a two-acre potato garden and a huge vegetable patch that all went to the people. Seeing food rolling out of the boots of people's cars: that's when I knew this Māori community was alive and well. Sports days, kapa haka and tangihanga are the three areas I use as a barometer on the health of Māori community and Te Atatū was a healthy Māori community. They knew how to meet people in need."[4]

Urban Māori enclaves transformed themselves into strong community collectives and affiliates of organisations such as the Māori Women's Welfare League, the Māori Wardens and Māori Committees. Church organisations, work-based whānau, sports collectives, marae committees and urban marae, cultural clubs and various Kāhui Kaumātua councils all sought the betterment of the social and cultural aspects of urban Māori lives. Many of these groups were birthed out of the foresight of elders who sought to adapt, adjust and recreate their culture in a city landscape, not only for the current needs of the people but also for an envisioned new future. They also signalled the beginnings of permanent lives in urban territories and the connection to non-kin-based community whakapapa, where unrelated whānau became aunts, uncles and cuzzies. This permanency meant people purchased their own homes and built urban marae.

Dr Ranginui Walker spoke of urban marae as a powerful cultural statement essential to the transplantation of culture into the urban milieu.[5] The conceptual boundaries of the traditional marae and the notion of tūrangawaewae were expanded in the adaptation process. The urban marae provides a physical structure for mātāwaka Māori to connect and increase their iwi knowledge by accessing whakapapa links and whanaungatanga with iwi members.[6] They are natural places for Māori language to be spoken[7] and have often given rise to total immersion schools. Tangihanga are held on these marae now rather than at private homes, garages and community halls, and the contest over returning a tūpāpaku home to the iwi or burying the deceased in the city is still very common.[8]

These Māori collectives were also the forerunners to the Urban Māori Authorities, which demonstrated the people's determination to accept circumstances and make the city their home. The establishment of tribal rūnanga and the outsourcing of government agency services to non-profit organisations stimulated the development of the Urban Māori Authorities. They competed with iwi and hapū organisations over both the allocation of Treaty settlement assets and benefits, and access to government funding to serve the needs of pan-tribal Māori city dwellers. Successive governments considered iwi as the only preferred vehicle for Treaty settlements and future Māori development; urban Māori communities and other pan-tribal communities needed to look like iwi to receive funding or to fully participate in the affairs of Māori development.

This applied not only to city-dwelling Māori collectives but also to historical pan-tribal communities in the tribal regions. One pertinent case was the settlement process for the past grievances of the sacking of the pan-tribal community of Parihaka. The people of Parihaka were unable to enter into full Treaty settlement negotiations with the Crown because they were not an iwi or a whakapapa-related authority. During the early stages of the Taranaki Iwi Treaty settlement process, dissent occurred between Parihaka and Taranaki iwi because registration as a beneficiary of the claims was based on whakapapa and did not recognise Parihaka's unique situation. Taranaki iwi and Parihaka subsequently resolved their issues, with Taranaki refusing to settle with the Crown until the government recognised the uniqueness of the Parihaka situation. This resulted in the recognition of Parihaka's autonomy and the resultant negotiations with the Crown.

It was by special agreement between Parihaka and the Crown that a special advisory group was established — Kawe Tutaki. This group made several recommendations that laid the foundations for a reconciliatory way forward, leading to a Compact of Trust, an agreement influenced by the unique relationship forged between Tūhoe and the Crown. This Compact — a type of heads of agreement — was approved and signed in 2016.[9] This unique reconciliation proposal was formalised at an apology ceremony at Parihaka on 9 June 2017. The Legacy Statement signed on that day was formulated by the Parihaka people and was entitled Te Kawanata ō Rongo or the Deed of Reconciliation.

Despite the Waitangi Tribunal recognising urban Māori as

having Article Two Treaty rights, tribal leaders have continued to challenge those rights.[10] Some of those tensions have been amicably sorted between matāwaka and mana whenua, but the debate continues. Today, urban authorities provide an iwi environment for those who are unable to trace their whakapapa links or those who choose to live in an urban context. They provide social, educational and business services for anyone within a designated area promoting the idea of Urban Māori Proud. Urban authorities are complex units underpinned by contestable government contracts, which makes them highly vulnerable to changes in policy and budget reviews. The continual contestability between urban and iwi authorities and health providers for central Government funds has created concerns about the lack of collaboration and the future critical dependence on the state.[11] Brian Easton estimates in "Māori Meets More Market" that the trickle-down of benefits to whānau from iwi settlements is still very slow.

> While the Treaty settlements to the iwi may be a vital part of settling some long-standing grievances, they do little to enable the bulk of the Māori population to catch up with the national averages. This is especially true given that the corporates are much more rural-based than the majority of the Māori population.[12]

Any spending cuts would, Easton believes, cause significant struggles for Māori community organisations and service providers.

The tension between iwi and urban realities still poses a challenge for many Māori. Iwi who oppose the urban authorities have yet to resolve their obligations to their own people in the city centres and the logistics needed to accomplish that task. Looking at a few iwi demographics, we are able to see where iwi members are living. According to the 2013 census one in seven people living in New Zealand were Māori of which 98.2% were born in Aotearoa.[13] Ngāpuhi, New Zealand's largest tribe, numbered 125,601 (2013 Census), of which 50,000 lived in Auckland. New Zealand's second-largest tribe were Ngāti Porou at 71, 049 (2013 Census), with 16.9% dwelling in Gisborne, 18.5% in Auckland, 15.7 in Wellington, and 48.9% of their iwi population living elsewhere in New Zealand. It is estimated 30,000 Ngāti Porou also live overseas, primarily in Australia.[14] Ngāi Tahu, the largest iwi group in the South Island, represented 1% of the New Zealand population and 8.2% of the Māori population with 54,819 members. An estimated 50% of Ngāi Tahu live in the three main urban centres of Auckland, Wellington and Canterbury, and 1341 abroad (2016).[15]

If the majority of the iwi members who live outside of their tribal regions do not return home or engage with their tribal connections, how do iwi take responsibility for their own? In saying that, there are iwi who are moving to cater for the needs of their iwi membership outside the tribal regions via taura here groups and collaborations with the Urban Māori Authorities. One iwi to step forward is Te Iwi o Ngāti Kahu Trust, who have been based in South Auckland for the past 30 years providing advocacy, housing support, kaumātua assistance and the strengthening of their tribal communities in Tāmaki-makaurau. It is the only group of Te Rūnanga o Ngāti Kahu members to operate outside its own tribal rohe based in Northland.[16]

In 2017 the Waikato-Tainui iwi group announced the expansion of its Mokopuna Ora programme into Papakura, South Auckland, in partnership with Oranga Tamariki Ministry, as part of its responsibility and commitment for the care of the tribe's children. Fourteen thousand Waikato-Tainui members are based in urban Auckland. Of its 68 marae, 18 are within the wider Auckland region. The new partnership seeks to cater for the needs of Tainui mokopuna in South Auckland, where the highest number of children in Oranga Tamariki Ministry's care are of Tainui descent.[17]

For mātāwaka whānau living in the provincial regions, local iwi are having to consider how to engage them in the spirit of whanaungatanga. According to a 2015 demographic report on tangata whenua in the Western Bay of Plenty region around Tauranga, the largest mātāwaka residents here besides mana whenua are Ngāpuhi and Te Arawa followed by Waikato, Tairawhiti and then Kai Tahu. With no mātāwaka marae in the region and the local council's obligation to cater for all Māori, these demographics give good reason for local iwi to begin conversations about how to engage with mātāwaka or not.[18] Another example is the central Hawke's Bay town of Waipukurau that supports a mātāwaka Māori community that settled here for employment in shearing, farming or at the freezing works. Some of these families have been in Waipukurau for three generations. Waipukurau lies within the tribal territory of Ngāti Kahungunu called Te Taiwhenua o Tamatea, a district of eight iwi marae and one mātāwaka marae (Waipukurau Community Marae).[19]

Dr Roger Maaka, chairman of Te Taiwhenua o Tamatea district, is a strong advocate for inclusion and finding ways to engage mātāwaka in the conversations of the local area. Amidst the tensions between iwi recognition and a mātāwaka presence, he believes iwi authorities and Treaty settlements should not forego core Māori values of aroha, manaakitanga and whanaungatanga. Making decisions whether to exclude or include the mātāwaka communities in the cultural and political dynamics of these districts is something local iwi will have to grapple with, if not presently, then in the very near future.

The place of urban Māori has challenged notions of Māori tribal citizenship, leading to reconstruction of identity based on cultural association and socio-economic realities rather than solely by kin relationship and whakapapa. Paul Meredith writes how this has caused the expansion of the "boundaries of belonging" and the emergence of "new citizens".[20] He says that the citizenship of urban Māori did not arise from "abstract theoretical reflection but from the voices, visions and the material realities of those who have been marginalised in the construction of Māori citizenship".[21] He further cites the demographics of the Māori citizenry in 2000, which revealed that despite return migration to the rural regions, eight out of ten Māori were still living in urban centres with populations of 30,000 or more.

For Meredith, iwi and urban groups need to come to terms with the notion of 'co-existence' rather than the opposing 'either/or'. He reiterates how the main intention for Māori should be building better communities for all Māori that are either tribal or pan-tribal according to the way Māori live today.[22] To achieve this, he suggests considering new forms of negotiated relationships that are "multi-dimensional, strategic, and that serve the needs of the present Māori citizenry". He concludes: "It's not a matter of 'easier said than done', but instead a matter of 'it has to be done'."[23]

Similarly, Manuhuia Barcham suggests adopting mechanisms that would allow the social reality of urban Māori communities and their authorities to be seen as complimentary to iwi and vice-versa. He describes the adaptation of indigenous social institutions to the pressures of social change as a reality and argues that new 'indigenous' social institutions should not be viewed as any less authentic.[24] The disruption of communities shifting away from the papakāinga due to internal and external forces led to adaptation. Urbanised Māori were forced to examine what they needed to do to survive this disruption.

This self-examination led to innovation and the growth of a strong resilience; they survived by recreating a cultural paradigm for living in new urban environments.

Tūrangawaewae in the city

One group to represent a new paradigm of being Māori in an urban environment is Ngā Tūmanako (literally, the hopes and aspirations), a kapa haka team from Glen Eden, Auckland. This kapa haka team, which entered the 2017 Te Matatini performing arts festival, represents a generation of Māori raised on an urban marae in a total immersion kura, who are confident in their own identity either in an iwi or city setting. Formed in 2006, the group gathers past students of the kōhanga reo and kura kaupapa immersion school at Hoani Waititi marae, and is made up almost entirely of Māori members who were raised in the city. The name Ngā Tūmanako derives from the name of the wharenui at Hoani Waititi, and represents the aspirations of the marae founders for their mokopuna to be raised on a marae and in the customs of their ancestors while living in the city.

Reikura Kahi and her brother Kawariki Morgan are the current female and male leaders of Ngā Tūmanako. Reikura reflects: "What my grandmother [Letty Brown] and a lot of other Māori whānau did here is create a home, a village for themselves and their tamariki and for us. They worked hard so we could grow up on a marae and reaffirm our identity and it absolutely worked for us, because we were able to retain our reo and our tikanga and grew up like you would have on a rural marae."[25]

Reikura recognises her tribal links but claims Hoani Waititi as her marae and West Auckland as her home. "It's absolutely hard living in the city and holding on to your roots, which are for me Tainui, Ngāti Porou, Ngāti Hine, Te Whānau a Apanui and a little bit of Te Arawa too," she says. "We were heavily Waikato, and we also travelled to the coast because my Nan Letty is strongly Ngāti Porou. But because the coast is so far away from Auckland, it was probably only twice a year we went to the coast, three times if we were lucky. For me, at that time it didn't matter where we were brought up, but as an adult I feel like I missed out being Tainui, Ngāti Porou and Ngāti Hine because I wasn't brought up there, essentially."

Residency in the tribal regions and strong community association back home have often been confronting issues for Reikura. "Back home they know who your parents are, but because you're not living there or attending all their hui, you're somehow not part of them. On Hoani Waititi I never feel that way," she says. "My grandmother never saw it as an issue: she always said you will always be Ngāti Porou, or Dad would say you'll always be Tainui." But she believes she has gained in another sense. "I was absolutely fortunate to have been brought up in an urban environment in the city and on a marae," she reiterates.[26] Whānau and Māori communalism were paramount to her family; it was something they never lost living in an urban setting. "When we started off, we were living in the garage and Nan was in the main house with her kids, and my mum bought the house next door and then my aunty bought the [other] house next door and now I live across the road. When you go to your haukāinga everybody lives close together because we all want to see each other, we all want to fight each other, we all want to be with each other, we share our tamariki with each other … we're recreating our Nan's village back

Reikura Kahi and her children (from left) Te Rangihoua, Waiheke and Rereiao.
Courtesy of Reikura Kahi

in Te Araroa now. It's about being close to your whānau, we can't operate without each other," she admits.

As a youngster Reikura was exposed to the impacts of city living and witnessed the whānau disconnections that the urban environments created. Her grandmother operated a halfway house for homeless people on Hopetoun Street in Auckland Central, and also a reo teaching centre. "There was a girl who was violated in the park behind the house so my Nan looked after her and opened the doors to her house for all the street kids. Nan was there for ten years, then she shifted to Point Chev where she created a kōhanga reo at the mental health unit at Manawanui marae at Carrington. We all worked at the kōhanga mopping the floors, looking after kids; that was the life she created for us. Community work serving the people and the children were important to her."

Reikura's own schooling at Hoani Waititi embedded an unshakeable sense of Māori identity. "I always say to everybody I grew up on that marae. I knew all the kaumātua on that marae, I knew the whakairo and tukutuku on that marae, and I worked in that kitchen since I was at kura. Hoani Waititi is like being at the pā at Waahi, surrounded by houses. And that's exactly how I was brought up on an urban pā, essentially right in the heart of Glen Eden."

Ngā Tūmanako performing at the Tāmaki-makaurau senior kapa haka regional competitions in Auckland.

Courtesy of Ngā Tūmanako

Establishing Ngā Tūmanako kapa haka team allowed ex-students of the kura and their families to stay together as a collective. "We all went through Te Rōpū Manutaki, Te Waka Huia, Manu Huia and other local kapa haka teams, but we created this group to maintain our relationships with each other. Kapa haka has become that place where you can be together as Māori and maintain and reaffirm your identity and your culture," she declares. Rehearsals have been held on members' marae throughout the country so the team could meet wider tribal whānau, make connections and learn the histories of those areas. "We support ourselves because we don't have an iwi we affiliate with to access tribal trust board monies. We'd go for sponsorship from community grants, Radio Wātea or Te Puni Kōkiri, a t-shirt factory or whatever."

Māori performing arts is a traditional institution that crosses over the boundaries of iwi and urban. Thousands of school students and adults participate in kapa haka today not only as an expression of being Māori but also as a form of receiving and transferring cultural knowledge. It has become one of the largest and most popular arenas of Māori cultural growth to emerge over the last 30 years.[27] Kapa haka originates in the ancient traditions of the aural/oral Māori society and has survived the colonial reconstruction of the Māori world. Traditional performing arts have also adopted other styles of composition and music, taking new aspects of modern song and dance and incorporating them into the repertoire of Māori song and dance. Kapa haka became an essential vehicle for the revitalisation of Reo and identity, as well as fundraising, competition, international ambassadorship and tourism-related employment.

Kapa haka is a focal point for urban Māori in maintaining a connection to 'being Māori'. Reikura believes it is essential for the retention and survival of te Reo Māori, tikanga and Māori identity, particularly for urban Māori. Ngā Tūmanako represent a new generation of urban Māori who are articulate in their own culture and language, can mix easily in a city environment, are strong believers in knowing and maintaining their iwi links, and are able to walk anywhere in the world with their identity intact.

"We wish the same for our children," says Reikura. "We have reinforced the importance of their Māori identity and asserting that in everything they do: sport, kura or travelling anywhere. Their identity would be number one and having a sense of overall well-being. That dictates what we do, who we are and what we participate in, especially in an urban setting where we are surrounded by the Pākehā world everywhere — we like to create purely Māori-speaking environments for our families in everything we do." Reikura is a strong advocate for maintaining that collective Māori community and the identity instilled in them by their elders. Ngā Tūmanako and similar rōpū to emerge in this environment are a powerful demonstration of the flowering of the dreams of elders who sought to keep the culture alive for the next generation.

Keeping the fires burning

Not all of this current generation of mātāwaka urban Māori had the privilege of being raised in Reikura's environment. While opportunities for whānau to enter this setting have increased over the years, modern circumstance, choice and economics have negatively influenced the maintenance of cultural commitment and participation, something the urban authorities work towards remedying. Timing has also played an influential role, with many missing the opportunity to enter the reo immersion world because it did not exist at the time. There are families who have siblings who were fortunate enough to enter the worlds of the kōhanga and the kura kaupapa and those who were born too early. For some the divide between the non-reo speaking siblings and those who speak the reo is noticeable.[28] Despite these situations the recent revitalisation of culture has kept the interest in reo, culture and identity high. Perhaps one indicator of the desire by Māori to maintain their identity is seen in the results of *Te Kupenga 2013*, a report of Māori well-being. The survey showed 70% of Māori participants believed being involved in Māori culture was important.[29] It also found 71% of respondents knew their ancestral marae, while 11% had never been to their own marae. The report also revealed that 60% of Māori desired more contact with their marae in the preceding 12 months, but encountered significant obstacles to returning — principally cost, distance and transport.[30]

Paramount in this age is the need to look beyond the iwi/urban scenario: to create a Māori cultural identity that equips people to move seamlessly between iwi and urban contexts, and stays intact where Māori people live. In part this is future-proofing the sustainability of healthy families, particularly for a growing youth population. Māori accounted for 14% of the total New Zealand population in 2001; it is predicted that by 2051 the Māori ethnic population will almost double in size to be close to a million, or 22% of the total New Zealand population. Significantly, an estimated 33% of all children in the country will be Māori. Additionally, the Māori population over 65 will increase from 3% (1996) to 13% (2051) of the total Māori population as life expectancy lengthens.[31] By then Māori in the working-age group (15 to 64 years) will have grown to 85% of the Māori population.

Developing the capacity of whānau for caring, creating wealth, future planning, the inter-generational transfer of knowledge and skill, and the wise management of whānau estates is vital for the transformational shifts that will be necessary for Māori to navigate through the next 20 years.[32] Creating self-sufficient families who can fulfil specific roles within their whānau to sustain their cultural identity is a vision Te Whānau o Waipareira sees as essential for the future. These roles include whānau as carriers of culture, gateways into Te Ao Māori, models for lifestyle, guardians of the environment, access points to community and economic units.[33] Whanaungatanga (connection and relationship) is a key value for maintaining whānau and cultural commitment, particularly in an urban environment. If anything, the lack of communication, gathering and particularly distance is considered to be death to connection and whanaungatanga.

Commenting on the place of technology as a solution, Dr Mason Durie says:

> Abrupt transitions left many urban migrants effectively divorced from Te Ao Māori. But communication technology has telescoped the concept of distance to such an extent that Māori in London or Los Angeles, who are living lifestyles quite different from relatives in Wairoa and Whāngarei, might still be able to participate in Te Ao Māori, enjoy the legacy to which they are entitled, and contribute to the ongoing transmission and development of Māori heritage.[34]

The spread of social media, combined with affordable and regular transport throughout New Zealand and across the Tasman, has created multiple opportunities to stay in touch with home-based whānau and the activities at the tribal homelands. The manner in which data and technology are enabling the development of virtual marae, Facebook groups and newsgroups is already enabling whānau,

Boys playing rugby at an Urban Authority sports festival in West Auckland.
Courtesy Te Whānau o Waipareira

hapū and iwi gatherings for those separated by distance. Staying connected either to a mātāwaka, taura here or iwi community is a key message for Māori well-being.

For iwi and mātāwaka communities all around the country, events like tribal festivals, pā wars, sports events, Treaty of Waitangi celebrations and hui-a-tau (annual tribal meetings) are all designed to gather the local and urban tribal members to celebrate their iwitanga (tribalness) or their urban Māori identity. One significant event on the calendar since the 1970s is Te Hui Ahurei o Tūhoe, the Tūhoe Festival held every two years. Maintaining links back to Tūhoe for those living outside the tribal districts is important to the iwi, considering only an estimated 20% of Tūhoe people live in the tribal district.[35] Looking back, a 1958 survey of migrants from Ruatahuna in the Urewera National Park, who moved elsewhere to seek employment, found the majority of these Tūhoe families shifted no more than 100 kilometres away to places like Te Whaiti, Ruatoki, Murupara, Kāingaroa, Rotorua or Gisborne. Most moved to places where other family were already established. Over the years Tūhoe families settled further afield in Wellington, the Waikato and

Auckland.³⁶ The Tūhoe Festival started 40 years ago when Auckland- and Wellington-based Tūhoe people competed against each other in Rotorua in a game of rugby.³⁷ Since then the gathering has grown to encompass other sports like netball and golf as well as kapa haka, debates in the reo and a battle of the bands. But as festival committee chairman Paora Kepa says, it is more an opportunity for cousins to meet and just be Tūhoe. The festival seeks to bring the iwi together to celebrate and maintain its traditions.³⁸

Urban events can have a similar impact. The Waitangi Day celebrations at Hoani Waititi marae over the past four years have hosted prime ministers and other national and international personalities, while organising free concerts for the West Auckland community. The 2017 event attracted almost 30,000 people to the marae. Waitangi at Waititi brings together relations from many iwi and hapū, and also opened the doors for people of all ethnicities to experience Māori culture.

Without the intentional encouragement and persistent pulling together of earlier generations, particularly by early migrant Māori leaders, the cultural commitment and identity that currently exists, and still has a way to progress, could have been lost. That same 'intentionality' was crucial for voyaging ancestors and navigators, who set off remembering their point of origin and envision a path forward to a new destination. The journey into the unknown must have been a harrowing experience.³⁹ On reaching Aotearoa the ancestors had to adapt from a tropical heritage to a temperate world and then cope with "the major ecological changes that they themselves generated in their adopted land, all within a space of a few hundred years."⁴⁰

Implanting the wānanga of knowledge into the new landscape meant adaptation and adjustment, even of their own cosmological creation narratives. Previously unknown birds such as the huia, the moa and the tui were entered into an evolving tribal cosmology. When Māui killed tunanui (great eel) in the Pacific traditions for seducing his sister Hina, the great eel's head was buried in the earth and grew to produce the coconut tree. Because this tree and its nut did not survive in Aotearoa, the name and the narrative were adapted into the new Aotearoa environment: his head and other slithery body parts were thrown into the waters and produced a number of eel-like species found only in New Zealand. Similarly, language too was adjusted to cater for new marine life, flora and fauna.

More importantly, ancestors carried the iti oneone i kapua mai

Sports teams provide good opportunities for Māori youth to meet and build community.
Courtesy Te Whānau o Waipareira

Hawaiki (the small morsel of soil carried in the hollow of the hand from Hawaiki) as a symbol of identity and intellectual memory to implant in new lands as a mauri — a life-force.[41] This implanting, along with the naming of landscapes, enabled the people to draw upon everything that Hawaiki could offer them in the new space. Tradition also speaks of return journeys back to Hawaiki, although this was primarily to obtain special resources needed for the new land the ancestors had now settled in.

Implanting that blueprint of Hawaiki and nourishing a new Māori identity needs a new envisioned future that may very well mean carrying a more mobile iti oneone hou — a new morsel of soil — into the future. In today's technological age, a new envisioning is required. For Dr Mason Durie, this "future visioning" will depend on the ability to look beyond the immediate realities of economic, social and domestic crises "in order to engage in vigorous imagining".[42] Durie says these crises could easily be seen as offering little hope for the future. He reflects on a time where it was hard to imagine a young generation of Māori fluent in their own language or thousands of Māori learners as comfortable online as they are offline.[43] He poignantly says, "The vicissitudes of today should not be allowed to obscure the prospects of tomorrow."[44]

Looking to the future and allowing for diversity among Māori, Durie offers a Māori paradigm that encompasses Māori values and aspirations for a new contemporary Māori world.[45] The following core attributes that contribute to 'being Māori' should be recognised as a determinant of future Māori well-being:

o identifying as Māori
o being part of a Māori network or collective
o participating in Te Ao Māori, and enjoying a closeness with the natural environment
o celebrating the use of Māori language
o possessing some knowledge of custom and heritage
o participating as a whānau member
o having access to Māori resources.[46]

Anchoring the next generation with a traditional and adaptable world view, infused with these attributes, would allow families to be able to walk comfortably between their iwi and urban worlds, not as one or the other. They would be equipped with the capability to recognise and overcome the challenges of future economic, social, technological and climate changes. With the experiences learned by many who have walked the path of culture retention, revitalisation and adaptation, we are obliged to prepare the next generation to maintain their cultural identity and to carry Māori aspiration to new horizons, but remembering to return home often and to recognise the place of mana whenua wherever they might be. We must pass on the iti oneone hou — a new morsel of soil — embedded within it the seeds of ngā tūmanako; the dreams and aspirations of the elders and the knowledge to equip our descendants with the freedom to adapt, remap and encode their worlds with Māori ideals, meanings and purposes.

Renata Whānau, Wellington

Kelly Renata and his whānau, originally from Waikaremoana, have lived in Awakairangi (the Hutt Valley) for four generations. Back row: Rachel Renata (nee Batty), Matt Renata, Janine Renata, Michael Renata, Jessie Renata (nee Rhind). Front row: Danielle Renata, Hunsa Renata (nee Ranchhod), Esme Renata, Kelly Renata, Cali Renata.

Courtesy of the Renata family

Four generations of the Renata family have lived in the Hutt Valley. Kelly Maynard Renata shares how he came to the Wellington region at the age of seven when his parents Luckie and Beverley Renata relocated their family from Waikaremoana. He grew up in Te Awakairangi (Lower Hutt), met his wife Hunsa Ranchhod, had four children and now boasts mokopuna.

Kelly remembers how his grandmother Mere Hema used to see and talk to spirits all the time, and how his father always feared that world. "Often my father Luckie was left alone by himself for weeks on end as his parents joined shearing gangs on faraway farms," Kelly says. Luckie was able to find employment as a linesman around the Tuai district, and one of his uncles helped him to apply for a transfer with the electric company in Wellington. "There was more money in Wellington than just planting kumara and corn in the gardens. It was his opportunity to wash his hands from life in Tuai. As far as he was concerned, there were no good memories there for him," Kelly shares.

"I remember going to the shop at Ruatahuna to get some chippies. That was the day we were leaving home, but we didn't realise we were going for good." Kelly remembers. Luckie took up employment with the New Zealand Electrical Department at Haywards Substation on Haywards Hill, the main switching point for Wellington and the North Island link to the Cook Strait power transmission lines. The Renata family began their life in the city in a company house at Haywards village. After three days in their new house, Kelly and his sister were dressed and ready to catch the bus to Manor Park Primary School. Kelly was overwhelmed by all the white kids on the bus who only spoke English (white kids back in Tuai spoke te Reo Māori, but no one did here). It was an intimidating new world and Kelly didn't want to leave the house.

Kelly always heard his father declare how it was better to be a Pākehā in this world. Living in Wellington, Kelly stopped hearing his dad speak the reo for many years. "He also didn't like education as he thought it was a waste of time, yet he still wanted his children to be educated," Kelly claims. The suburb they lived in was filled with Pākehā families whom the Renata family slowly got to know well. There were two other Māori families in the village they lived in, the Hovelle and the Putaranui whānau. "Haywards was a very communal place," Kelly says.

The family joined Māwai Hakona, a local culture club associated with Ōrongomai marae. Kelly's father had helped lay the electrical lines to the marae, so the family joined and the kids became part of the junior and intermediate sections of the club. The Renata family were part of Māwai Hakona for five years before the novelty wore off for Kelly.

The New Zealand Electrical Department (NZED) crew worked well together, Kelly infers, but the pressure to 'do as the Romans do' brought alcohol into the family. "With work finishing at 5 p.m. and the public bar closing at 6, working men guzzled down as much alcohol as they could before closing time. You'd think it was the Grand National horse race," Kelly says. Both Māori and Pākehā crews rushed to get their fill. It was the alcohol that lost Luckie his position with NZED.

The whānau shifted to Wainuiomata because the houses were cheaper. "We bought it outright," Kelly remembers. His father found work at a factory near Seaview where they made car batteries. Later Kelly supported his father cleaning at night to supplement their income, while his mother Beverley (nee Puohotaua) worked as a teacher. "Dad eventually went full-time cleaning," Kelly says.

"We lost all whānau orientation when we came to the city," Kelly believes. The whānau never went home much at all, he laments, and socialising with others wasn't their norm. "Dad wasn't a marae person. Both our parents didn't want us to live in that marae world. It got to the point my sister didn't even believe she was Māori." The prevailing idea that learning the Pākehā way was deemed the only way to survive was detrimental, Kelly believes. The gardening, hunting and rugby aspects of their Tuai culture continued in their lives, as did the boil-up as a staple part of their diet. The ocean was considered tapu so Kelly's father never went near it. "In some ways we never lost our identity but in other ways we became good Pākehā. We lost being Māori."

Kelly was sent to Hāto Paora College in Feilding after a recruitment drive by Māori schools. He eventually returned home to work in the post office and to continue alongside his dad cleaning. "Everyone wanted to be a factory worker because the money was good. Office work was considered a lower-earning position," he says. "There were a lot of gangs in the area as well. I witnessed one gang initiation of getting the bash and that just wasn't me."

Snide comments about being Māori and being associated with gangs or being urbanised affected Kelly. "I wish I was brought up on the marae to learn Māori and retain that history. I would have preferred us shifting from home when I was 18, but I know why Dad came down here," Kelly reflects. "Being urban Māori means being raised in a concrete jungle and not knowing where we come from. I lost a lot due to the shift — I lost my self-worth." Kelly met Hunsa Ranchhod at the post office and the two married and had a family of four: Matthew, Janine, Michael and Danielle.

Kelly's son Matthew says, "I've come from a messy upbringing where being Māori wasn't really valued. Instead I got into drugs, drinking and bad relationships, I could have been in the gangs," he confirms. "I had a youth worker support me and help me to re-assess my views to become a better person. With faith and love, a cycle of violence and dysfunction was broken, and I want to pass that on. It takes a village to raise a child, so we need to get the village working again."

Matthew currently works for the Hutt Youth Workers Network and oversees the youth development sector. Matthew and his wife Rachel, who is Māori-Japanese, want to make a difference to the deterioration and dysfunction in Lower Hutt whānau, as well as the fatherlessness and neglect of youth in the city suburbs. With around 900 youth workers in the Hutt Valley and 160 youth agencies, Matthew's role is to co-ordinate and try to synergise these networks for the betterment of the youth community.

Matthew has been a youth worker since 2008 and has witnessed the deterioration in whānau who don't really know who they are. "It's difficult to hold on to hope as I continue to see the slow deterioration of relationships within the whānau and family units. Men don't know how to be good husbands, fathers or brothers. No one has really taught them. They don't know who they are or how to be. With the introduction of 'P' and 'legal highs' it's getting worse. I've seen my young people living on two-minute noodles, tomato sauce and white bread, dressing themselves and going to school, trying to survive because dad isn't home. He reckons he doesn't have time as he's working to make a living, but when he's finished work he heads over to his girlfriend's and spends most of his time there. A lot of our young Māori are brought up in harsh conditions. So then as a teenager, my young person, he becomes a dad, but nobody has really taught him how to be a dad. He ends up having a second child but soon splits with his girlfriend and the cycle goes on. How do we break that cycle?" he asks.

Identity is a huge issue in the lives of the youth Matthew comes across. "We have kids in our community who can tell you the whole life story of Superman, his whakapapa and his secrets, yet they can't name their own ancestors. Some of them have no identity, no home, no tūrangawaeawe, no placement of bones, and we're just creating lives of no identity and no hope. They live lives on auto-pilot, suffering from inter-generational amnesia," Matthew says.

At the age of 27 he went on the hunt for his own whakapapa identity and had to bypass his immediate family to do it. The knowledge didn't live in his own close family. "I was scared to make that move." He travelled north to Waimā, Tokomaru Bay to trace his whakapapa. He knew no one but met relations who greeted him openly and explained the Renata whānau origins. He found how the family had originated from Tikapa, then shifted to Waimā and were 'whāngaied' into Ruatahuna before ending up in Waikaremoana. Their original family name was Huihui. "It was foreign territory for me and it didn't feel like the home I knew, but I felt connected," he says.

"No one in our family was interested in this. Working, making money and the immediate challenges of life have become more important than whakapapa. It was hard for my koro to come to terms with it all," he laments. "I felt ripped off. We had no reo for starters, just basic English with a bit of swearing — that was our language and only tiny, tiny bits of our history were passed on. A whole new city life took over. We lost tikanga."

The faith aspect of the Renata family's life has been crucial to the reclaiming of their Māori identity. They have survived the city, but at the cost of having to fit the mould of the urban world. Matthew concludes: "We are having to work a lot harder with our whakapapa, reo and tikanga to accomplish reclaiming our identity as a whole family. Years ago we wouldn't have even thought this way."

Endnotes

Acknowledgements
1. Vincent O'Malley, Bruce Stirling and Wally Penetito (eds), *The Treaty of Waitangi Companion, Māori and Pakeha from Tasman to Today*, Auckland, Auckland University Press, 2010.
2. Atholl Anderson, Judith Binney, and Aroha Harris. *Tangata Whenua — An Illustrated History*, Wellington, Bridget Williams Books, 2015, p. 343.
3. Ibid.

1. Ngā Heke Māori: Māori Migration
1. Geoff Irwin and Carl Walrond, "When Was New Zealand First Settled? — The Date Debate," *Te Ara — the Encyclopedia of New Zealand*, 2008, http://www.teara.govt.nz/en/when-was-new-zealand-first-settled/page-1.
2. H. Beattie, "Traditions and Legends. Collected from the Natives of Murihiku,. Part VIII", *Journal of the Polynesian Society* 27, no. 107 (1918), 137–61.
3. Rawiri Taonui. "Polynesian Oral Traditions," in Howe, K.R. (ed.), *Vaka Moana — Voyages of the Ancestors, The Discovery and Settlement of the Pacific*, Auckland, David Bateman Ltd, 2006, p. 35.
4. Atholl Anderson, Judith Binney, and Aroha Harris. *Tangata Whenua — An Illustrated History*, Wellington, Bridget Williams Book, 2015, p. 21.
5. According to *Mataatua* and *Takitimu* traditions, dreams and visions helped lead the navigators to new settlements. While aboard the *Mataatua*, the ancestor Irakewa passed on a dream to his whānau to settle at a place with a cave at the mouth of the river. Ruawharo, the tohunga aboard *Takitimu*, was informed by a parent's dream that he should settle in the new land where the whales beached.
6. Hirini Moko Mead, *The Ngati Awa Federation of Tribes, Bay of Plenty, New Zealand*, Whakatane, New Zealand, The Ngati Awa Trust Board, 1984, p. 8. See also, Sidney Moko Mead, *Landmarks, Bridges and Visions, Aspects of Māori Culture*, Wellington, Victoria University Press, 1997.
7. Anderson et al., op. cit., pp 30–31.
8. Ibid, p. 106.
9. Mutu Kapa, "The Kaitaia Drains", *Journal of the Polynesian Society* 33, no. 131, 1924, pp. 223–25.
10. Ngāi Tahu in the South Island also derive their ancestry from Ngāti Kahungunu. See Rawiri Te Maire Tau, *Ngā Pikitūroa o Ngāi Tahu*, Dunedin, Otago University Press, 2003, pp. 156–59.
11. Angela Ballara, *Iwi, The Dynamics of Māori Tribal Organisation from c.1769 to c.1945*, Wellington, Victoria University Press, 1998, pp. 138–39.
12. Melissa Matutina Williams, *Panguru and the City, Kāinga Tahi, Kāinga Rua An Urban Migration History*, Wellington, Bridget Williams Books, 2015, p. 41.
13. Bradford Haami, *Pūtea Whakairo, Māori and the Written Word*, Wellington, Huia, 2004, p. 36.
14. Ballara, op. cit., p. 138. See also Hirini Moko Mead, *Tikanga Māori, Living by Māori Values*, Wellington, Huia, 2003, pp. 169–70.

15. Rawiri Te Maire Tau & Atholl Anderson (eds), *Ngāi Tahu, A Migration History, The Carrington Text*, Wellington, Bridget Williams Books, 2008, p. 20.
16. Ibid, p. 21.
17. Ibid, p. 21.
18. Te Ahukaramū Charles Royal, *Kāti au i kōnei; He Kohikohinga i ngā Waiata a Ngāti Toarangatira, a Ngāti Raukawa*, Wellington, Huia, 1994, p. 17.
19. Miria Pōmare, "Ngāti Toarangatira — Migration from the North", *Te Ara — the Encyclopedia of New Zealand*, Ministry of Culture and Heritage, 2005, http://www.teara.govt.nz/en/-toarangatira/page-2.
20. Te Ahukaramū Charles Royal, op. cit., pp. 19–20.
21. Ballara, op. cit., pp. 154–55.
22. Danny Keenan, *Te Whiti o Rongomai and the Resistance of Parihaka*, Wellington, Huia, 2015, p. xxvi.
22. Kennedy Warne, "Why Wasn't I Told?", *New Zealand Geographic*, December 2016, p. 77.
23. "Parihaka o neherā, o nāianei, Parihaka — Past and Present", Caritas Aotearoa New Zealand, Parihaka Schools Resource, The Catholic Agency for Justice, Peace and Development, 2015), p. 5. See http://www.caritas.org.nz/sites/default/files/Parihaka%20teachers%20booklet%20with%20worksheets%20WEB.pdf.
24. Warne, op. cit., pp. 77–79. See Revelation 21:2–7 for a description of the 'new Jerusalem'.
25. Kelvin Day (ed.), *Contested Ground, Te Whenua i Tohea, The Taranaki Wars 1860–1881*, Wellington, Huia, 2010, p. 245.
26. Ranginui Walker, *Ka Whawhai Tonu Matou, Struggle Without End*, Auckland, Penguin Books, 1990, p. 183.
27. Keith Newman, *Ratana Revisited; An Unfinished Legacy*, Reed Publishing (NZ) Ltd, Auckland, 2006, p. 104.
28. Ibid, p. 62.
29. Walker, 1990, op. cit., p. 183.
30. Roger C.A. Maaka, "Perceptions, Conceptions and Realities, A Study of the Tribe in Māori Society in the Twentieth Century", Unpublished Thesis for Doctor of Philosophy in Political Science, University of Canterbury, 2003, p. 87.
31. Anderson et al., op. cit., p. 304.
32. Ranginui Walker, 1990, op. cit., p. 197.
33. Rawiri Taonui, "Māori Urban Protest Movements" in *Huia Histories of Māori, Ngā Tāhuhu Kōrero*, Wellington, Huia, 2012, p. 233.
34. Brian Easton, "Māori Meets Market", unpublished presentation, 2016, p. 2.
35. Ranginui Walker, "Māori People since 1950" in *The Oxford History of New Zealand*, 2nd edition, Auckland, Oxford University Press, 1992, p. 500. See Hunn, LL.M., J.K., *Report on The Department of Maori Affairs*, Wellington, 24 August 1960, p. 19.
36. Anderson et al., op. cit., p. 343.
37. Ibid. See also Rawiri Taonui, "Māori Urban Protest Movements" op. cit., p. 233.
38. Williams, op. cit., p. 32.
39. Paul Meredith, "Urban Māori as 'New Citizens', The Quest for Recognition and Resources", paper presented to the Revisioning Citizenship in New Zealand Conference, University of Waikato, February 2000, p. 3.
40. Manuhuia Barcham, "The Challenge of Urban Māori, Reconciling Conceptions of Indigeneity and Social Change," *Asia Pacific Viewpoint* 39, no. 3, December 1998, 303–14, p. 303.
41. Ibid, p. 304.
42. Paul Meredith, "Urban Māori — Urbanisation," *Te Ara — the Encyclopaedia of New Zealand*. http://www.teara.govt.nz/en/urban-maori/page-1, accessed 2 October 2016.
43. Tania Rangiheuea, Urban Māori" in Malcolm Mulholland and Veronica Tawhai (eds), *Weeping Waters, The Treaty of*

Waitangi and Constitutional Change., Huia, Wellington, 2010, p. 189.
44. Meredith, op. cit., p. 3
45. See note 50 for chapter one in Melissa Matutina Williams, op. cit., p. 263
46. Ranginui Walker, "Māori People since 1950", op. cit., p. 500.
47. Ibid.
48. Paul Meredith, "Urban Māori — Urbanisation", op. cit., accessed 13 January 2017.
49. Megan C. Woods, "Integrating the Nation, Gendering Māori Urbanisation and Integration 1942–1969". Unpublished Thesis, Doctor of Philosophy in History, University of Canterbury, 2002, pp. 353–54.
50. Walker, "Māori People since 1950", op. cit., p. 501.
51. Ibid.
52. Bronwyn Dalley and Gavin McLean (eds), *Frontier of Dreams, The Story of New Zealand*, Auckland, Hodder Moa, 2005, p. 329.
53. See respective profiles for Steve Hutana (chapter 5) and Anaru Roberts (chapter 6).
54. Walker, "Māori People since 1950", op. cit., p. 501.
55. Ibid.
56. Interview with Rereata Makiha, Auckland, August 2016.
57. Williams, op. cit., p. 181.
58. Ibid, p. 32.
59. Meredith, op. cit.
60. Erin Keenan, "Māori Urban Migrations and Identities, 'Ko Ngā Iwi Nuku Whenua', A Study of Urbanisation in the Wellington Region during the Twentieth Century", Unpublished Thesis for PhD, Victoria University, 2014, p. 32. https,//core.ac.uk/download/pdf/41338859.pdf, accessed November 2016.
61. Walker, "Māori People since 1950", op. cit., p. 519.
62. Taonui, "Māori Urban Protest Movements", op. cit., p. 233.
63. Pae Keiha and Paul Moon, "The Emergence and Evolution of Urban Māori Authorities, A Response to Māori Urbanisation", *Te Kaharoa* 1 (2008), pp. 1–17.
64. Barcham, op. cit., p. 308.
65. Williams, op. cit., p. 37.
66. Ian Poole, *Te Iwi Maori, A New Zealand Population, Past, Present and Future*, Auckland, Auckland University Press, 1991, p. 133.
67. Anderson et al., op. cit., p. 343.
68. Tahu Kukutai, "Contemporary Issues in Māori Demography" in *Māori and Social Issues*, vol. 1, Wellington, Huia, 2011, p. 37.
69. Mason Durie, *Te Mana, Te Kawanatanga, The Politics of Māori Self-Determination*, Auckland, Oxford University Press, 1998, p. 55.
70. A comment by John Tamihere in Dale Husband, "John Tamihere, I've had to keep fighting my Way". Website media release. *E-Tangata A Māori and Pasifika Sunday Magazine*, March 2013. https,//e-tangata.co.nz/news/john-tamihere-ive-had-to-keep-fighting-my-way/arts.
71. Hineani Melbourne, *Maori Sovereignty, The Maori Perspective*, Auckland, Hodder Moa Beckett, 1995, p. 13.

2. Te Au o Te Awa: The River Current

1. Ranginui Walker, *Ka Whawhai Tonu Matou Struggle Without End*, Auckland, New Zealand, Penguin Books, 1990, pp. 64-65.
2. Melissa Matutina Williams, *Pangaru and the City, Kāinga Tahi, Kāinga Rua An Urban Migration History*, Wellington, New Zealand, Bridget Williams Books, 2015, p. 41.
3. Graham Butterworth, "A Rural Maori Renaissance? Maori Society and Politics 1920 to 1951", *Journal of the Polynesian Society* 81, no. 2, 1972, p. 161, http://www.jps.auckland.ac.nz/document?wid=4415&page=0&action=null, accessed February 2017.

4. Michael King, *Whina*, Auckland, New Zealand, Hodder and Stoughton, 1983, p. 166.
5. Interview with Kathrine Christensen (nee Anania), December 2016, Paptoetoe, Auckland.
6. Interview with Rereata Makiha, September 2016, Auckland.
7. Interview with Kelly Renata, September 2016, Lower Hutt.
8. Joan Metge, *A New Maori Migration, Rural and Urban Relations in Northern New Zealand*, London, England, The Althone Press, 1964, pp. 131–32, cited in Ranginui Walker, "Māori People since 1950," in *The Oxford History of New Zealand*, 2nd ed, Auckland, New Zealand, Oxford University Press, 1992, p. 501.
9. Bradford Haami, *Pūtea Whakairo, Māori and the Written Word*, Wellington, Huia, 2004, p. 23
10. Erin Keenan, "Māori Urban Migrations and Identities, 'Ko Ngā Iwi Nuku Whenua', A Study of Urbanisation in the Wellington Region during the Twentieth Century", Unpublished PhD, Victoria University, 2014. https,//core.ac.uk/download/pdf/41338859.pdf, accessed November 2016, p. 105.
11. Butterworth, op. cit., p. 161.
12. Ibid.
13. Brian Easton, "The Maori Urban Migration," Published paper, Brian Easton website, 23 August 2012, https,//www.eastonbh.ac.nz/2012/08/the-maori-urban-migration/, accessed February 2017.
14. Butterworth, op. cit., p. 161.
15. Ranginui Walker, *Ka Whawhai Tonu Matou*, op. cit., p. 196.
16. "1928, Apirana Ngata; Land and Community." originally published October 1928. *New Zealand Herald*, website article, nzherald.co.nz, http://www.nzherald.co.nz/new-zealand-herald-150-years/news/article.cfm?c_id=1503278&objectid=11140564. Accessed February 2017.
See also M.P.K. Sorrenson, "Ngata, Apirana Turupa," *Te Ara — the Encyclopedia of New Zealand, The Dictionary of New Zealand Biography*, Wellington, New Zealand, New Zealand Government, n.d., http://www.teara.govt.nz/en/biographies/3n5/ngata-apirana-turupa, accessed February 2017.
17. Michael King, *The Penguin History of New Zealand*, Albany, New Zealand, Penguin Books, 2003, p. 474.
18. Bronwyn Dalley and Gavin McLean (eds), *Frontier of Dreams, The Story of New Zealand*, Auckland, New Zealand, Hodder Moa, 2005, p. 326.
19. H. Belshaw, "Maori Economic Circumstances" in *The Maori People Today, A General Survey*, Wellington, New Zealand, New Zealand Institute of International Affairs and New Zealand Council for Educational Research, 1940, pp. 182–228.
20. Ibid, p. 193.
21. "The Maori Race", *The Auckland Star*, LXVI, no. 269, 13 November 1935, p. 20. See Erin Keenan, op. cit., p. 120.
22. See Williams, op. cit., pp. 40–41.
23. Atholl Anderson, Judith Binney, and Aroha Harris. *Tangata Whenua — An Illustrated History*, Wellington, Bridget Williams Book, 2015, p. 311.
24. "The Maori Urban Migration." Published paper. Brian Easton website, 23 August 2012. https,//www.eastonbh.ac.nz/2012/08/the-maori-urban-migration/. Accessed February 2017.
25. Ibid, p. 2.
26. Gibson Campbell, "Urbanization in New Zealand", *Demography 10*, no. 1, February 1973, p. 78.
27. King, *Whina*, op. cit., p. 112.
28. Ibid, p. 112.
29. Ibid, p. 113. See also Williams, op. cit., p.42.
30. Brian Easton, "The Maori Urban Migration", op. cit., p. 78.

31. King, *The Penguin History of New Zealand*, op. cit., p. 474.
32. Roger C.A. Maaka, "The New Tribe, Conflicts and Continuities in the Social Organization of Urban Maori", *The Contemporary Pacific*, University of Hawaii Press, Fall 1994, p. 314.
33. Claudia Orange, "An Exercise in Maori Autonomy, The Rise and Demise of the Maori War Effort Organisation", *New Zealand Journal of History* 21, no. 1, 1987, 156–72, pp. 158–59.
34. Ibid, p. 160.
35. Taonui, "Māori Urban Protest Movements", op. cit., p. 232. See also Orange, op. cit., p. 162, and Butterworth, op. cit., p. 186. Butterworth states 23,000 Māori were mobilised for the war effort.
36. Orange, op. cit., p. 162.
37. A letter by Paikea to Prime Minister Peter Fraser in 1943. Cited in Orange, op. cit., p. 162.
38. Dalley and McLean (eds), op.cit., p. 297.
39. Patricia Grace, Irihapeti Ramsden, and Jonathan Dennis, *The Silent Migration, Ngāti Poneke Young Māori Club, 1937–1948*, Wellington, Huia, 2001, p. 173.
40. Orange, op. cit., p. 161
41. Ibid, p. 161.
42. Nancy M. Taylor, *The Home Front Volume II*, Wellington, Historical Publications Branch, 1986, p. 682.
43. Heeni Wharemaru and Mary Katharine Duffie, PhD, *Heeni, A Tainui Elder Remembers*, Harper Collins Publishers, 1997, p. 120.
44. *The Press*, 20 August, p. 6, in Megan C. Woods, "Integrating the Nation, Gendering Māori Urbanisation and Integration, 1942–1969", Unpublished Thesis for Doctor of Philosophy in History, University of Canterbury, 2002, pp. 185–186.
45. Woods, op. cit., p. 185.
46. Deborah Montgomarie, *The Women's War, New Zealand Women 1939–45.*, Auckland, Auckland University Press, 2001, p. 98–99. In Woods, op. cit., pp. 185–186.
47. Butterworth, op. cit., p. 16.
48. Aroha Harris, "Concurrent Narratives of Māori Integration in the 1950s and 60s", *Journal of New Zealand Studies*, no. 6/7, 2008, 139–55, p. 142.
49. Ibid, p. 142.
50. Dalley and McLean (eds), op. cit., p. 297.
51. Walker, "Māori People since 1950", op. cit., p. 500.
52. Manuhuia Barcham, "The Challenge of Urban Maori, Reconciling Conceptions of Indigeneity and Social Change", *Asia Pacific Viewpoint* 39, no. 3, December 1998, p. 312, also see note 3.
53. Metge, op. cit., p. 251.
54. The Awhitu whanau of Taumarunui and the Eruera family came to the city for the childrens' health needs in 1932 and in the 1950s respectively.
55. Interview with Hoko Ria of Gisborne in 2016 at Christchurch. Also, Waipareira Research file 4-CHO4.
56. Interview with Kelly Renata, 2016, at Wellington.
57. "Submission to the Māori Affairs Select Committee on the Ngāti Porou Claims Settlement Bill. Affdavit of Tokorua Barney Te Kani In The Waitangi Tribunal Wai 272", New Zealand Parliament, 2009, pp.18–20, https,//www.parliament.nz/resource/en-nz/49SCMA_EVI_00DBHOH_BILL10537_1_A194716/ae30b282903493ce2f18340b2a286820c88412fe. Accessed in May 2017.
58. New Zealand Government. *New Zealand Census of Population and Dwelling, 1976*, 1976, p. 10
59. Keenan, op. cit., p. 138–39. See https://core.ac.uk/download/pdf/41338859.pdf.
60. Te Hira Henderson, "Koraua; Anaru Kingi", HD, *Koraua*, Auckland, Māori Television, 8 February 2017. Accessed March 2017.

61. Keenan, op. cit., p. 28.
62. Ibid, p. 124.
63. Ibid, pp. 102–103.
64. "Helping the Maoris, Hutt Meeting House A Useful Purpose", *Evening Post*, 7 February 1936.
65. Ibid.
66. Ibid.
67. Ibid.
68. Ibid.
69. Grace, et. al., op. cit., pp. 1, 53.
70. Keenan, op. cit., p.106. See also Patricia Grace et al., ibid
71. Grace, et al., op. cit., pp. 7–13, 84–85.
72. Ibid, p. 177.
73. Ibid, p. 2.
74. 'Helping the Maoris', *Evening Post*, op. cit., p. 13.
75. Walker, "Māori People since 1950," op. cit., p. 500.
76. Murray Groves, "Maori Young Leaders Conference, 1959," *The Journal of the Polynesian Society* 68, no. 3, 1959, pp. 244–246.

3. Tūranga Hou: A New Standing Place

1. Jenny Carlyon and Diana Morrow, *Urban Village, The Story of Ponsonby, Freeman's Bay, and St Mary's Bay*, Glenfield, Auckland, Random House, 2008, p. 206.
2. Ibid.
3. Ibid, pp. 207–208.
4. Ibid, p. 211.
5. Ibid, p. 208.
6. Melissa Matutina Williams, *Panguru and the City, Kāinga Tahi, Kāinga Rua An Urban Migration History*. Bridget Williams Books, Wellington, 2015, p. 89.
7. Ibid, p. 248.
8. Ibid, pp. 208–210.
9. Keenan, Erin. "Māori Urban Migrations and Identities, 'Ko Ngā Iwi Nuku Whenua', A Study of Urbanisation in the Wellington Region during the Twentieth Century." Unpublished PhD, Victoria University, 2014. https,//core.ac.uk/download/pdf/41338859.pdf. Accessed November 2016, p. 175
10. Interview with Kathrine Christensen, December 2016, Papatoetoe, Auckland.
11. Melissa Matutina Williams, *Panguru and the City, Kāinga Tahi, Kāinga Rua An Urban Migration History*. Wellington, Bridget Williams Books, 2015, p. 89.
12. Bronwyn Dalley and Gavin McLean (eds). *Frontier of Dreams, The Story of New Zealand*. Auckland, Hodder Moa, 2005, p. 329.
13. Ibid.
14. Malcolm McKinnon (ed.), Barry Bradley, and Russell Kirkpatrick, *Bateman New Zealand Historical Atlas Ko Papatuanuku e Takoto Nei*, David Bateman Ltd, Albany, New Zealand, 1997.
15. Keenan, op. cit., p. 211.
16. Williams, op. cit., p. 103. See chapter 4, note 14 on p. 271.
17. Dan Morrow, "Tradition and Modernity in Discourse of Māori Urbanisation," *Journal of New Zealand Studies*, no. NS18, 2014, pp. 85–105.
18. Ibid. p. 87.
19. Ibid, p. 88.
20. Ibid, p. 88
21. Ibid, p. 90.
22. Ibid, pp. 92–93. See also J.K. Hunn, LL.M., "Report on The Department of Māori Affairs", Wellington, 24 August 1960, p. 15.
23. J.K. Hunn, LL.M., op. cit., p. 16. See also Jock Phillips, "The New Zealanders — Bicultural New Zealand," *Te Ara — the Encyclopedia of New Zealand*, Wellington, Ministry of Culture and Heritage, updated 2015 2005), http://www.teara.govt.nz/en/the-new-zealanders/page-12.
24. Atholl Anderson, Judith Binney, and Aroha Harris. *Tangata Whenua — An Illustrated History*, Wellington, Bridget Williams Books, 2015, p. 347.

25. Ranginui Walker, "Māori People since 1950," in *The Oxford History of New Zealand*, 2nd edition, Auckland, Oxford University Press, 1992, p. 501.
26. Ibid, p. 501.
27. Morrow, op. cit.
28. Dalley and McLean, op. cit., p. 310.
29. Ibid.
30. Anderson et al., op. cit., p. 345.
31. Anne Salmond, *Eruera, The Teachings of a Māori Elder Eruera Stirling*, Penguin Books, Auckland, 2005, p. 188.
32. Hiwi Tauroa and Pat Tauroa, *Te Marae, A Guide to Customs and Protocols*, Reed Books, Auckland, 1986, p. 166.
33. Williams, op. cit., p. 86.
34. Ibid, p. 84.
35. Megan C. Woods, "Integrating the Nation, Gendering Māori Urbanisation and Integration, 1942–1969", Unpublished Thesis for Doctor of Philosophy in History, University of Canterbury, 2002, pp. 353–54.
36. Ibid, pp. 162–70.
37. *Parliamentary Debates (Hansard)*, Vol. 268, 1948, p. 241.
38. Woods, op. cit., pp. 166–67.
39. Ibid.
40. Interview with the Anania family, December 2016, Auckland.
41. Interview with Rereata Makiha, December 2016, Auckland.
42. Interview with the Anania family, December 2016, Auckland.
43. Walker, "Māori People since 1950," op. cit., p. 502.
44. *Te Ao Hou The New World Magazine*, "Girls Come to the City," September 1961, p. 29.
45. Ibid, pp. 29–31.
46. Ibid, p. 62.
47. Walker, "Māori People since 1950", op. cit., p. 502.
48. Dalley et al., op. cit., pp. 326–27.
49. Lily (L.M.) George, "Tradition, Invention, and Innovation, Multiple Reflections on an Urban Marae", Unpublished Doctorate of Philosophy in Social Anthropology, Massey University, 2010, p. 179.
50. Walker, "Māori People since 1950", op. cit., p. 500.
51. Michael King and W.H. Oliver (ed.), "Between Two Worlds" in *The Oxford History of New Zealand*, 1st edition, Wellington, Oxford University Press, 1981, p. 299.
52. James Belich, *Paradise Reforged, A History of New Zealanders from the 1880s to the Year 2000*, Auckland, Allen Land and Penguin Press, 2001, p. 474.
53. Williams, op. cit., p. 103.
54. Ibid, p. 106.
55. Ibid, p. 102.
56. Ibid, p. 166.
57. Marrow, op. cit., p. 94.
58. Williams, op. cit., p.105.
59. Ibid, pp. 107–108.
60. Interview with Poata Eruera, March 2017, Auckland. From his experience he explained how tribal banter was common.
61. Interview with Wynn Anania, December 2016, Auckland.
62. Anne Salmond, *Hui A study of Māori Ceremonial Gatherings.* A.H. & A.W. Reed, Wellington, New Zealand, 1975, p. 86.
63. Carlyon and Morrow, op. cit., p. 248.
64. Anderson et al., op. cit., p. 344; see also Salmond, *Hui*, op. cit., p. 197.
65. Personal comment by Kathrine Anania, December 2016, Auckland.
66. Anderson et al., op. cit., p. 344.
67. Salmond, *Hui*, op. cit., p. 86.
68. Personal comment by Rereata Makiha, December 2016, Auckland.
69. John Dix, "The Gluepot," *Audio Culture The Noisy Library of New Zealand Music*, Wellington, Audio Culture, October 2014, http://www.audioculture.co.nz/scenes/the-gluepot. Accessed January 2017.
70. Ibid.
71. Carlyon and Morrow, op. cit., p. 216.
72. Ibid, pp. 217–21.

73. Ranginui Walker, *Ka Whawhai Tonu Matou, Struggle Without End*. Penguin Books, Auckland, 1990, p. 198.
74. Ibid, p. 501.
75. *Sunday News*, "Ōtara; City without a Soul", 25 June 1967.
76. Ranginui Walker, "The Social Adjustment of Māori to Urban Living in Auckland", Unpublished Doctorate of Philosophy, University of Auckland, 1970, p. 38.
77. Ibid, pp. 39–43.
78. Ibid, p. 46.
79. Ibid, p. 51.
80. Tapu Misa, "Ōtara — the First Polynesian Suburb," nzherald.co.nz, 28 August 2010, http://www.nzherald.co.nz/nz/news/article.cfm?c_id=1&objectid=10667583.
81. Ibid.
82. Walker, "The Social Adjustment of Māori to Urban Living in Auckland", op. cit., p. 369.
83. Ibid, p. 80–85.
84. Ibid, p. 113.
85. Ibid, pp. 114–15.
86. Ibid, p. 513.
87. Ibid, p. 514.
88. Ibid, p. 516. See also Dan Morrow, op. cit., p. 97.

4. Akoranga Mahi-ā-rehe: Trade Training

1. Woods, Megan C. "Integrating the Nation, Gendering Māori Urbanisation and Integration, 1942–1969." Unpublished Thesis for Doctor of Philosophy in History, University of Canterbury, 2002, p. 187.
2. *Appendices to the Journal of House of Representatives*, 1948, G-9, p. 10.
3. Ibid, 1953, G-9, pp.11–12.
4. Atholl Anderson, Judith Binney, and Aroha Harris. *Tangata Whenua — An Illustrated History*, Wellington, Bridget Williams Books, 2015, p. 346.
5. Hill, Kim. "Tame Iti, Activist and Artist." *Saturday Morning with Kim Hill*. Radio New Zealand, Auckland, 12 November 2016. http://www.radionz.co.nz/national/programmes/saturday/audio/201823561/tame-iti-artist-and-activist.
6. "Young Maori Become Skilled Tradesmen", *Te Ao Hou The New World Magazine*, 1966, p. 7. http://teaohou.natlib.govt.nz/journals/teaohou/issue/Mao55TeA/c7.html.7.
8. "Whairawa/Economy", Website, *Te Runanga o Ngāti Porou*, 2014, http://www.ngatiporou.com/nati-story/our-korero/whairawa-economy. Accessed February 2017.
9. Williams, Melissa Matutina, *Panguru and the City, Kāinga Tahi, Kāinga Rua An Urban Migration History*. Wellington, Bridget Williams Books, 2015, pp. 90–92.
10. Ibid, p. 91.
11. Woods, op. cit., p. 189.
12. Interview with Colin Campbell, August 2016, Auckland.
13. Ibid.
14. Wharemaru, Heeni, and Duffie, Mary Katharine, PhD, *Heeni, A Tainui Elder Remembers*. Harper Collins Publishers, Auckland, 1997, p. 120.
15. Ibid, p.121.
16. Ibid.
17. Interview with Terry Ryan, December 2016, Christchurch.
18. Woods, op. cit., p. 184.
19. Wharemaru and Duffie, *Heeni*, op. cit., p. 123.
20. Norman Gill, *Mission Accomplished, The Establishment of the Christchurch Methodist Mission*, Christchurch, Christchurch Methodist Mission, 1991, p. 49.
21. Ibid.
22. Ibid.
23. Ibid.
24. Woods, op. cit., p. 188.
25. Ibid.
26. Ibid.
27. Interview with Terry Ryan, 1 December 2016, Christchurch. Norman Gill, op. cit.

28. Interview with Hokowhitu Ria, 1 December 2016, Christchurch.
29. Woods, op. cit., pp. 20–30.
30. Interview with Hokowhitu Ria, op. cit.
31. Ibid.
32. Ibid.
33. Gill, op. cit., p. 50.
34. Ruku Wainohu speaks in Norman Gill, op. cit., p. 50.
35. Terry Ryan interview at http://rehuamarae.co.nz/history/.
36. Mike McRoberts, "White Sheep Wairoa Documentary", *Documentary New Zealand*, New Zealand, Television New Zealand, 2000. https://www.youtube.com/watch?v=_uhdxTDspoo.
37. Gill, op. cit., p. 51.
38. Interview with Terry Ryan, op. cit., and confirmed by email 2 February 2017.
39. Gill, op. cit., p. 52.
40. Interview with Terry Ryan, op. cit.
41. Ibid.
42. Ibid.
43. Erin Keenan, "Māori Urban Migrations and Identities, 'Ko Ngā Iwi Nuku Whenua', A Study of Urbanisation in the Wellington Region during the Twentieth Century." Unpublished PhD, Victoria University, 2014. https://core.ac.uk/download/pdf/41338859.pdf. Accessed November 2016.
See "Table 7. Population of Statistical Divisions and Urban Areas, 1966 and 1971 Census," New Zealand Census Population and Dwellings, n.d.
44. Melissa Williams, op. cit., p. 90.
45. *United Maori Mission 1936–1986 Jubilee Book*, United Maori Mission Inc, 1987, p. 6.
46. Ibid, p. 5.
47. Ibid, p. 18.
48. Ibid, p. 17.
49. Ibid, p. 18.
50. Ibid.
51. Eldson Craig, "Gillies, Heppy and Shelley, The Story of Three Mission Hostels", *Te Ao Hou The New World Magazine*, August 1957, p. 38.
52. Ibid, p. 39.
53. Ibid.
54. Ibid.
55. "Young Maori Become Skilled Tradesmen," op. cit., p. 8.
56. Crain, op. cit.
57. McRoberts, op. cit.
58. Interview with Kathy Eruera, 2016.
59. Interview with Norm Dewes, 6 March 2017, Christchurch.
60. Terry Ryan interview, "Inspiring Māori Leadership in Trades", 14 December 2014.
61. Interview with Roger Maaka, August 2016, Takapau.
62. "Inzone", Inzone Education Foundation, Auckland, 2014. http://www.inzoneeducation.org.nz/who-we-are. Accessed October 2016.
63. Barry and the boys loved Bill, he was a mentor to them. When Bill died he lay at Rehua marae. Twenty boys carried him home to Tasmania for final burial.

5. Te Whakahiato: The Rise of the Collective

1. Interview with Ella Henry, February 2017, Auckland.
2. Harris, Aroha, "Concurrent Narratives of Māori Integration in the 1950s and 60s". *Journal of New Zealand Studies*, no. 6/7, 2008, p. 146.
3. Ibid.
4. Interview with Poata Eruera in March 2017 at Glen Eden, Auckland. Apparently his father walked outside on Sunday morning to pick up his axe to go to work on a rā tapu (sacred rest day). He found an owl on his axe, which he took as an omen. He knew something would happen and this was the day his daughter was injured. He made a promise to God to serve him if his daughter lived. She woke out of her coma and he became a Rātana minister.

5. Ibid.
6. Waipareira Research Files, interview 4, CH04, 2017.
7. Interview with Poata Eruera, March 2017 at Glen Eden, Auckland. *Bonanza* ran from 1959 to 1973.
8. "Leadership Conference at Auckland", *Te Ao Hou The New World Magazine*, December 1963, p. 33. http://teaohou.natlib.govt.nz/journals/teaohou/issue/Mao45TeA/c14.html. Accessed April 2017.
9. Arapera Blank, "One Two Three Four Five" in Erik Schwimmer (ed.), *The Maori People in the Nineteen Sixties*. Blackwood & Janet Paul Ltd, Auckland, 1968, p. 95. This phrase is found in the Ngāti Porou waiata, "Po! Po!". See *Nga Moteatea*, song 38 or *Te Ao Hou*, no. 53, 1965, pp. 19–21.
10. John Harre, "Maori-Pakeha Intermarriage," in Schwimmer, Erik (ed) *The Maori People in the Nineteen-Sixties*. Blackwood & Janet Paul Ltd, Auckland, 1968, pp. 120–21.
11. Interview with Ngamaru Raerino, 2006, Auckland. His father, from Te Teko, made this comment when Ngamaru contemplated marrying Diane, a Pākehā woman from the South Island. Ngamaru and his wife Diane married and had four children of their own, and fostered many others.
12. Ranginui Walker, "Māori People since 1950" in *The Oxford History of New Zealand*, 2nd edition, Oxford University Press, Auckland, 1992, p. 502.
13. Ibid.
14. Roger Maaka, "The New Tribe, Conflicts and Continuities in the Social Organization of Urban Māori", *The Contemporary Pacific*, University of Hawaii Press, Fall 1994.
15. Harris, op. cit., p. 142.
16. Graham Butterworth, "A Rural Maori Renaissance? Maori Society and Politics 1920 to 1951", *Journal of the Polynesian Society* 81, no. 2, 1972, p. 189.
17. Ranginui Walker, *Ka Whawhai Tonu Matou, Struggle Without End*. Penguin Books, Auckland, 1990, p. 202.
18. Butterworth, op. cit., p. 189.
19. Atholl Anderson, Judith Binney, and Aroha Harris. *Tangata Whenua — An Illustrated History*, Wellington, Bridget Williams Books, 2015, p. 341.
20. Hine Poa, Hine Poa, Haki and Adam Langford oral history interview, online recording. No. 2 of two volumes. Recollect Upper Hutt City Library Heritage Collections. Wellington, 2016. http://uhcl.recollect.co.nz/nodes/view/25438.
21. Ranginui Walker, "The Social Adjustment of Maori to Urban Living in Auckland", Unpublished Doctorate of Philosophy, University of Auckland, 1970, p. 317–19.
22. Ibid, p. 319.
23. Ibid, p. 321.
24. Ibid.
25. Michael King, *Whina, A Biography of Whina Cooper*. Hodder & Stoughton, Auckland, 1983, p. 176.
26. Ibid. p. 176.
27. Walker, "The Social Adjustment of Maori to Urban Living in Auckland", op. cit., p. 202.
28. King, *Whina*, op. cit., p. 177.
29. Ibid, pp. 184–85.
30. Richard Hill, *Māori and the State, Crown Māori Relations in New Zealand/Aotearoa 1950–2000*, Victoria University Press, Wellington, 2009, pp. 123–24. See http://nzetc.victoria.ac.nz/tm/scholarly/tei-HilMaor-t1-body-d6-d3.html. Accessed April 2017. According to some sources the wardens or watene were the brainchild of Princess Te Puea at Turangawaewae marae.
31. Anderson et al., op. cit., p. 336.
32. Augie Fleras, "Maori Wardens And The Control Of Liquor Among The Maori of New Zealand." *Journal of the Polynesian Society* 90, no. 4, 1981, pp. 495–513.
33. Walker, "The Social Adjustment of Maori

34. to Urban Living in Auckland", op. cit., p. 347.
34. Ibid, p. 351.
35. Interview with Darlene Evans (nee Raharaha), September 2016, Auckland. Darlene's father was the founder.
36. Walker, "The Social Adjustment of Maori to Urban Living in Auckland", op. cit., p. 349.
37. Interview with Darlene Evans (nee Raharaha), September 2016, Auckland.
38. Ibid.
39. Walker, "Māori People since 1950", op. cit., p. 504.
40. Walker, "The Social Adjustment of Maori to Urban Living in Auckland", op. cit., p. 354–55
41. Ann Parsonson, "Herangi, Te Kirihaehae Te Puea." *Te Ara —the Encyclopedia of New Zealand*. From the *Dictionary of New Zealand Biography*, n.d. Accessed 9 February 2017.
42. Bradford Haami, *Ka Mau Te Wehi Taking Haka to the World; Bub and Nen's Story*, Ngāpō and Pīmia Wehi Whānau Trust, Auckland, 2013, pp. 14–15.
43. Williams, op. cit., p. 172.
44. *Te Waka Huia*, series documentary, Letty Brown interview, 2016. Kawariki Morgan, director, 21 August 2016. https,//www.youtube.com/watch?v=tJ8l83xuQ2A. Additional information from Reikura Kahi, granddaughter of Letty.
45. Anderson et al., op. cit., p. 351.
46. Ibid.
47. Williams, op. cit., p. 172.
48. *Te Waka Huia*, series documentary, op. cit. Sir Pita Sharples said this was the first time a doctorate had been conferred on a persona at Hoani Waititi marae.
49. *Te Whanau, A Celebration of Te Whanau o Waipareira*, Te Whānau o Waipareira, Waitakere City, Auckland, 2001, p. 12.
50. Leona Bresnehan, "Hoani Waititi Marae", *Insight '81*. Radio New Zealand National Programme, Wellington, 1981, ref. no. 24673, Sound Collection. Accessed April 2017.
51. Interview with Evelyn Taumaunu , April 2017, Te Atatū North, Auckland.
52. Hoani Waititi Celebrates Milestone." *Te Karere News Website*, 20 April 2015. http://tvnz.co.nz/te-karere-news/hoani-waititi-marae-celebrates-milestone-6294751.
53. Findlay McDonald and Ruth Kerr (eds), *West, The History of Waitakere*. Random House, Auckland, 2009, p. 166.
54. *Te Whānau o Waipareira Report. WAI 414, Waitangi Tribunal Report.* Waitangi Tribunal Report. Wellington, GP Publications, 1998, p. 37.
55. Bresnehan, op. cit.
56. *Te Whanau, A Celebration of Te Whanau O Waipareira*, op. cit., p. 83.
57. Paul Tapsell, "Marae and Tribal Identity in Urban Aotearoa/New Zealand." *Pacific Studies* 25, no. 1/2, June 2002, p. 157.
58. McDonald, op. cit., p. 210.
59. Naumaiplace Ltd, "Hoani Waititi Marae," website article, 2007, http://www.naumaiplace.com/site/hoaniwaititi/home/welcome/.
60. *Te Whanau, A Celebration of Te Whanau O Waipareira*, op. cit., p. 82.
61. *Te Whānau o Waipareira Report. WAI 414*, op. cit., p. 40.
62. Ibid, p. 37. Evidence of Tai Nathan.
63. Ibid.

6. Tau Whare: Laying Down Roots
1. Ranginui Walker, *Ka Whawhai Tonu Matou, Struggle Without End*, Penguin Books, Auckland, 1990, p. 210.
2. Paul Tapsell, "Marae And Tribal Identity In Urban Aotearoa/New Zealand", *Pacific Studies* 25, no. 1/2, June 2002, p. 142.
3. Lily (L.M.) George, "Tradition, Invention, and Innovation, Multiple Reflections on an Urban Marae", Doctorate of Philosophy in Social Anthropology, Massey University, 2010, p. 173.

4. Tapsell, "Marae and Tribal Identity", op. cit., p. 143.
5. Jennifer Lee, "The Second Great Migration", website article, *Post Colonial Web*, n.d., http.//www.postcolonialweb.org/nz/maorijlg5.html. Accessed May 2017.
6. Ranginui Walker, "Marae, A Place to Stand" in King, Michael (ed), *Te Ao Hurihuri The World Moves On; Aspects of Maoritanga*. 1st Edition. Hicks Smith & Sons Ltd, Wellington, 1975, p. 27.
7. Ibid, p. 28.
8. Ranginui Walker, "Māori People since 1950" in *The Oxford History of New Zealand*, 2nd edition, Oxford University Press, Auckland, 1992, p. 500.
9. Manuhuia Barcham, "The Challenge of Urban Maori, Reconciling Conceptions of Indigeneity and Social Change". *Asia Pacific Viewpoint 39*, no. 3, December 1998, p. 305.
10. Ranginui Walker, *Nga Tau Tohetohe*, Penguin Books, Auckland, 1987, p. 147.
11. Ibid, p. 148.
12. Ibid, pp.145–46.
13. Ibid, p. 146.
14. Ibid. See also, *Awataha Marae Project* (booklet), Auckland, 1987.
15. Interview with Rereata Makiha, August 2016, Auckland.
16. Melissa Williams, *Panguru and the City, Kāinga Tahi, Kāinga Rua An Urban Migration History*. Wellington, Bridget Williams Books, 2015. pp. 103–104.
17. Walker, *Ka Whawhai Tonu Matou, Struggle Without End*, op. cit., pp. 200–201.
18. Williams, op.cit., p. 120.
19. "Auckland's Community Centre", *Te Ao Hou The New World Magazine*, September 1962, p. 26. http://teaohou.natlib.govt.nz/journals/teaohou/issue/Mao40TeA/c13.html.
20. Walker, "Māori People since 1950", op. cit., pp. 506–507.
21. Anne Salmond, *Eruera; The Teachings of a Māori Elder Eruera Stirling*. Penguin Books, Auckland, 2005, p. 197.
22. Williams, op. cit., p. 120.
23. Ibid.
24. Interview with Wi Wharekura, January 2017, Gold Coast, Australia.
25. Salmond, *Eruera*, op. cit., p. 197.
26. Interview with Wi Wharekura, op. cit.
27. "Auckland's Community Centre," *Te Ao Hou*, op. cit., p. 26. http://teaohou.natlib.govt.nz/journals/teaohou/issue/Mao40TeA/c13.html.
28. Ibid, pp. 25–29.
29. Walker, *Ka Whawhai Tonu Matou, Struggle Without End*, op. cit., p. 200.
30. Interview with Matua Hakiaha, October 2017, Auckland.
31. Melissa Williams, op. cit., p. 122. The centre was eventually supplanted in the 1970s by new urban marae, closer to where Māori lived in suburban Auckland. The centre was eventually demolished in the late 1990s.
32. Salmond, *Ererua*, op. cit., p. 197.
33. Ibid, p. 200.
34. I.H. Kawharu, "Urban Immigrants and Tangata Whenua" in Erik Schwimmer (ed.), *The Maori People in the Nineteen Sixties, a Symposium*, Blackwood & Janet Paul Ltd, 1968, p. 181.
35. Ranginui Walker, *Ngā Pepa a Ranginui The Walker Papers; Thought-Provoking Views On The Issues Affecting Māori and Pākehā*. Penguin Books, Auckland, 1996, p. 50.
36. John C.M. Cresswell, *Maori Meeting Houses of the North Island*, PCS Publications, Auckland, 1977, p. 27.
37. Walker, "Marae, A Place to Stand", op. cit., p. 29.
38. Cresswell, *Maori Meeting Houses of the North Island*, op. cit., p. 27.
39. Walker, *Ka Whawhai Tonu Matou Struggle Without End*, op. cit., p. 201. The trustees of the marae were Te Arikinui Dame Te Atairangikaahu and two members of the tangata whakamahana (people who keep the marae warm) whare are the land-owning family.

40. "Submission in Response to the Auckland Law Reform Bill, Third Reading, Statutory Māori Board," Parliamentary Report, New Zealand, n.d., p. 2, https,//www.parliament.nz/resource/mi-nz/49SCAGL_EVI_00DBHOH_BILL9729_1_A34597/dc313f6332a3789ad98c426d28b1768db3a365fd. Accessed February 2017.
41. "He Rerenga Korero 1982", Ngā Hau E Whā Marae Part 1 of 2, audio. Ngā Taonga Sound & Vision, Wellington, 1982, Ref. no. 47482. Interview with Anaru Piripi.
42. Ibid, interview with Peter Heal.
43. Maraea Rakuraku, "Marae in the South Island". Radio interview. Te Ahi Kaa. Wellington, Radio New Zealand, March 2017. http://www.radionz.co.nz/national/programmes/teahikaa/audio/201837551/marae-of-the-south-island. Accessed December 2016.
44. Ibid, interview with kaumātua Mike Kaui.
45. "Te Runanga o Nga Mata Waka Incorporated," website, n.d. http://maatawaka.org.nz/.
46. Interview with Roger Maaka, August 2016, Takapau.
47. "Establishment of Kirikiriroa Marae," website article, Kirikiriroa Marae, 2017. http://kirikiriroamarae.com/Who.
48. Williams, op. cit., p. 168.
49. Walker, "Marae, A Place to Stand," op. cit., p. 32.
50. "Tatai Hono, Tying Us Together," in *Anglican Taonga, Telling The Stories of the Anglican Church in Aotearoa, NZ and Polynesia*, 2017, 2005, http://anglicantaonga.org.nz/News/Tikanga-Maori/Tatai-Hono. Accessed February 2017. The name of the house was given by Reverend Hone Kaa.
51. Walker, "Marae, A Place to Stand", op. cit., p. 29.
52. Ibid, p. 33.
53. Ranginui Walker, *Nga Tau Tohetohe*, Penguin Books, Auckland, 1987, pp. 146–47.
54. Tania Ka'ai, "The Role of Marae in Tertiary Education Institutions." *Te Kaharoa* 1, 2008, p. 193.
55. Ibid, p. 193.
56. Ibid, p. 201.
57. George, op. cit., Figure 44, p. 160.
58. Kawharu, "Urban Immigrants and Tangata Whenua", op. cit., pp. 175–76.
59. Natacha Gagne, *Being Māori In The City, Indigenous Everyday Life In Auckland*, University of Toronto Press, Toronto, 2013, p. 101.
60. Tapsell, "Marae and Tribal Identity", op. cit., p. 146. Kawharu states in his 1968 articles that "some nameless public servants reduced the meeting-house to ashes and offered six shillings per square foot, the demolition value, as compensation.
61. Walker, "Marae, A Place to Stand", op. cit., p. 505.
62. Ibid, p. 147.
63. Ibid, p. 145.
64. Williams, op. cit., p. 30.
65. Rawiri Taonui, "Ngāti Whātua Facts and Figures." *Te Ara — the Encyclopedia of New Zealand*, 2005. http://www.teara.govt.nz/en/ngati-whatua/page-5; Statistics New Zealand. "Auckland City (Census 96) (1996 Census of Population and Dwellings)", in *Statistics New Zealand, Tatauranga Aotearoa*, www2.stats.govt.nz/domino/external/pasfull/pasfull.nsf/web/Brochure+Auckland+City+(Census+96)+1996+Census+of+Population+and+Dwellings?open.
66. Tapsell, "Marae and Tribal Identity", op. cit., p. 149.
67. Megan C. Woods, "Integrating the Nation, Gendering Māori Urbanisation and Integration, 1942–1969", Unpublished Thesis for Doctor of Philosophy in History, University of Canterbury, 2002, note 194, p. 269.

7. Whakatū Marae: The Urban Marae

1. Ranginui Walker, *Ngā Pepa a Ranginui The Walker Papers; Thought-Provoking Views On The Issues Affecting Māori and Pākehā*. Penguin Books, Auckland, 1996, p. 51.
2. Megan C. Woods, "Integrating the Nation, Gendering Māori Urbanisation and Integration, 1942–1969". Unpublished Thesis for Doctor of Philosophy in History, University of Canterbury, 2002, p. 261.
3. Norman Gill, *Mission Accomplished, The Establishment of the Christchurch Methodist Mission*. Christchurch Methodist Mission, Christchurch, 1991, p. 49.
4. Ibid, p. 52.
5. Interview with Terry Ryan, 1 December 2016, Christchurch.
6. Woods, "Integrating the Nation", op. cit., p. 262.
7. Ibid.
8. Interview with Dr Terry Ryan. Maraea Rakuraku, "Māori Trade Training, its History and Future", radio interview, *Te Ahi Kaa*, Radio New Zealand, 14 December 2014, Auckland. http://www.radionz.co.nz/audio/player?audio_id=20160871.
9. Woods, "Integrating the Nation", op. cit.
10. Ibid, pp. 265–68.
11. Ibid, note 194, p. 269.
12. Interview with Terry Ryan, op. cit.
13. Ibid.
14. Christchurch City Libraries, *Rēhua Marae Te Whatu Manawa Māoritanga o Rēhua*, Rēhua marae 50th anniversary pamphlet. http://christchurchcitylibraries.com/TiKoukaWhenua/RehuaMarae/RehuaMaraeAnniversaryPamphlet.pdf.
15. Interview with Terry Ryan, op. cit.
16. "History of Māori Trade Training", website video article, *Rehua Marae History*, 2017. http://rehuamarae.co.nz/history.
17. Kimiora Raerino, "He Tirohanga O Ngāti Awa Uri Taone Mō Ngā Āhuatanga Māori — An Urban Ngāti Awa Perspective on Identity and Culture." Unpublished Master of Arts, Auckland University of Technology, 2007, p. 19.
18. Ibid, p. 20.
19. Te Hira Henderson, "Koraua; Anaru Kingi." HD. *Koraua*. Auckland, Māori Television, February 2017. Accessed March 2017.
20. Interview with Ngamaru Raerino of Ngāti Awa, February 2017, Rotorua.
21. Henderson, "Koraua; Anaru Kingi", op. cit. Also, Interview with Ngāmaru Raerino, February 2017, Rotorua.
22. Interview with Ngāmaru Raerino, February 2017, Rotorua.
23. Raerino, "He Tirohanga O Ngāti Awa Uri Taone Mō Ngā Āhuatanga Māori", op. cit., pp. 20–21.
24. Hirini Moko Mead, *Tikanga Māori, Living by Māori Values*. Wellington, New Zealand, Huia, 2003, p. 218.
25. Raerino, "He Tirohanga O Ngāti Awa Uri Taone Mō Ngā Āhuatanga Māori", op. cit., p. 21.
26. Ibid, p. 20.
27. Ibid, p. 86.
28. NZSC minutes, 21 April 1975, cited in Lily George, "Tradition, Invention, and Innovation, Multiple Reflections on an Urban Marae". Unpublished Doctorate of Philosophy in Social Anthropology, Massey University, 2010, p. 181 of 179–97.
29. George, "Tradition, Invention, and Innovation", op. cit., p. 189.
30. *Awataha Marae Project* (booklet), Auckland, 1987.
31. George, "Tradition, Invention, and Innovation", op. cit., p. 191.
32. Mihingarangi Forbes, "Locals Complain North Shore Marae 'Hijacked.'" Radio New Zealand. November 2016. http,//www.radionz.co.nz/news/te-manu-korihi/317622/locals-complain-north-shore-marae-'hijacked'. http,//teipuwhakahauaa.co.nz/uploads/gillies/2006/632_Gillies2006.pdf. Accessed April 2017.

33. George, "Tradition, Invention, and Innovation", op. cit., pp. 193, 210.
34. Ibid, p. 218.
35. Interview with Raewyn Harrison, Northcote, Auckland, May 2017.
36. Forbes, "Locals Complain North Shore Marae 'Hijacked.'", op. cit.
37. Rachel Clarke, "Marae Plans Move Forward", *North Shore Times*, December 2015, http://stuff.co.nz/Auckland/local-news/north-shore-times/74479741/marae-plans-move-forward.
38. *Awataha Marae, He Marae Iwi Kore He Maumau He Iwi Marae Kore Maumau*, Te Raki Paewhenua Kōmiti Māori, April 2017.
39. Interview with Raewyn Harrison, Northcote, Auckland, May 2017.
40. *Awataha Marae, He Marae Iwi Kore He Maumau He Iwi Marae Kore Maumau*, April 2017.
41. Ibid.
42. Patricia Grace, Irihapeti Ramsden, and Jonathan Dennis. *The Silent Migration, Ngāti Pōneke Young Māori Club, 1937–1948*. Wellington, Huia, 2001, p. 59.
43. Gavin McLean, "Pipitea Marae, Wellington (1980).", New Zealand History website, updated 2013. https,//nzhistory.govt.nz/media/photo/pipitea-marae.
44. Mary McEwen, *Te Oka — Pākehā Kaumātua; The Life of Jock McEwen*. Riveresco Trust, Wellington, 2016, pp. 30–31.
45. McLean, "Pipitea Marae", op. cit.
46. Margaret Smiler comment in Patricia Grace et al., *The Silent Migration*, p. 79.
47. Keenan, p. 161.
48. McEwen, *Te Oka*, op. cit., p. 32.
49. Ibid, p. 241.
50. McLean, "Pipitea Marae", op. cit.
51. "Pipitea Marae & Function Centre," Website, (n.d.), http://www.pipiteamarae.co.nz/.
52. McEwen, *Te Oka*, op. cit., p. 252.
53. Hariata Jasper, *Hariata Jasper Oral History Interview*, online recording, Wellington, 2000, 1–5. http://archives.uhcc.govt.nz/nodes/view/16021.
54. McEwen, *Te Oka*, op. cit., p. 252.
55. Māwai Akona was the original name of the cultural group. It was renamed Māwai Hakona, which was the original name of a local stream. See also Jasper, *Hariata Jasper Oral History Interview*, op. cit.
56. Jasper, *Hariata Jasper Oral History Interview*, op. cit.
57. McEwen, *Te Oka*, op. cit., p. 254.
58. Jasper, *Hariata Jasper Oral History Interview*, op. cit.
59. McEwen, *Te Oka*, op. cit., p. 256.
60. Ibid, p. 255.
61. Ibid, p. 256.
62. "Ōrongomai Marae." Website. *Recollect Upper Hutt Library Heritage Collections*, 2017–2011. http://archives.uhcc.govt.nz/nodes/view/16021.
63. Findlay McDonald & Ruth Kerr (eds), *West, The History of Waitakere*. Random House, Auckland, 2009, p. 209. See Jenny Bol Jun Lee, "Marae-a-Kura; Tracing the Birth of Marae in Schools." *Te Māori I Ngā Ara Rapu Mātauranga — Māori Education*, no. Set 2 (2012), 3–11.
64. Manukia, Claire, "Whare Akoranga", website, Green Bay High School, 2014. See About Us/Facilities/Whare Akoranga. http://www.greenbayhigh.school.nz/whare-akoranga/.
65. McDonald and Kerr, *West*, op. cit.
66. Ibid.
67. Personal comment by the author, who worked on this television feature film.
68. Jenny Bol Jun Lee, "Marae-a-Kura:, op. cit., p. 4. New marae-a-kura are being regularly built. In 2015, the author attended the opening of the newly-built Te Waipuna o te Mātauranga marae at Waitakere College in Henderson, West Auckland. The marae was built close to the road for practical reasons,

but also to accentuate the diversity of the school and the value of Māoritanga.

8. Ngā Piki me ngā Heke: Highs and Lows

1. Brian Easton, "Māori Meets Market", unpublished presentation, 2016.
2. Richard Hill, *Maori and the State, Crown Māori Relations in New Zealand/Aotearoa 1950–2000*. Victoria University Press, Wellington, 2009. http,//nzetc.victoria.ac.nz/tm/scholarly/tei-HilMaor-t1-body-d6-d3.html. Accessed April 2017, p. 17.
3. "Māori Welfare Officers Meet The Minister," *Te Ao Hou The New World Magazine*, November 1973, p.14, http://teaohou.natlib.govt.nz/journals/teaohou/issue/Mao74TeA/c6.html.
4. Ibid.
5. Ibid.
6. Melissa Matutina Williams. *Panguru and the City, Kāinga Tahi, Kāinga Rua An Urban Migration History*. Bridget Williams Books, Wellington, 2015, p. 215.
7. Atholl Anderson, Judith Binney, and Aroha Harris. *Tangata Whenua — An Illustrated History*, Wellington, Bridget Williams Books, 2015, p. 366.
8. Paul Meredith, "Urban Maori as 'New Citizens', The Quest for Recognition and Resources," paper presented to the Revisioning Citizenship in New Zealand Conference, University of Waikato, February 2000, p. 4.
9. Marama Muru-Lanning, *Tupuna Awa; People and Politics of the Waikato River*, Auckland University Press, Auckland, 2016, p. 100. See Ralph Piddington, "Emergent Development and 'Integration,'" in Erik Schwimmer (ed.),*The Maori People in the Nineteen-Sixties*.
10. Meredith, op. cit., p. 4.
11. Te Whānau o Waipareira. *Te Whānau, A Celebration of Te Whānau O Waipareira*. Waitakere City, Auckland, 2001, p. 12.
12. Department of Social Welfare, "Puao-Te-Ata-Tu (Day Break) The Report of the Ministerial Advisory Committee on a Māori Perspective for the Department of Social Welfare." Wellington, Department of Social Welfare, June 1986, p. 15.
13. Ibid, p. 8.
14. Ibid, p. 15.
15. Interview with Ngāmaru Raerino, December 2016, Rotorua.
16. Ibid.
17. *Te Whānau o Waipareira Report. WAI 414, Waitangi Tribunal Report*. Waitangi Tribunal Report, GP Publications, Wellington, 1998, p. 35.
18. Interview with Rereata Makihi, September 2016, Auckland.
19. Ibid.
20. Jenny Carlyon and Diana Morrow. *Urban Village; The Story of Ponsonby, Freeman's Bay, and St Mary's Bay*. Random House, Auckland, 2008, p. 249.
21. Interview with Maria Tia, daughter of Anne Tia, April 2017, Auckland.
22. Carlyon and Morrow, op. cit., pp. 249–51.
23. Ibid, pp. 251–54.
24. Ibid, pp. 254–55.
25. Interview with Maria Tia, op. cit.
26. Ranginui Walker, "The Social Adjustment of Maori to Urban Living in Auckland." Unpublished Doctorate of Philosophy, University of Auckland, Auckland, 1970, p. 284.
27. Augie Fleras, "Maori Wardens And The Control Of Liquor Among The Maori of New Zealand." *Journal of the Polynesian Society* 90, no. 4, 1981, p. 503.
28. Ibid, p. 504.
29. Ibid, p. 506.
30. Ibid. Also a personal comment also to author by Steve Hutana, 2016, Auckland. His father saw the local public bar, where he'd meet his kin six nights a week, as his marae.
31. Megan Cook, "Māori Smoking, Alcohol

and Drugs — Tūpeka, Waipiro Me Te Tarukino — Māori Use of Alcohol." Website article. *Te Ara — the Encyclopedia of New Zealand*, September 2013. http,//www.teara.govt.nz/en/maori-smoking-alcohol-and-drugs-tupeka-waipiro-me-te-tarukino/page-2. Accessed April 2017.
See the 1874 petition against alcohol at Appendix to the Journals of the House of Representatives, 1874, session I, J-01, http://atojs.natlib.govt.nz/cgi-bin/atojs?a=d&d=AJHR1874-I.2.2.6.1&e=-------10--1------2%22grog+is+the+cause%22—

32. Cook, op.cit.
33. *New Zealand History Nga korero a ipurangi o Aotearoa.* "'Six o'clock swill' begins." Website article. 2 December 1917. https,//nzhistory.govt.nz/the-six-oclock-swill-begins.
34. Ibid.
35. Fleras, op. cit., p. 514.
36. Waipareira Research Files, interview 4, CH04, 2017.
37. Marten Hutt, *Te Iwi Maori Me Te Inu Waipiro, He Tuhituhinga Hitori, Maori and Alcohol, A History*. Wellington, Health Services Research Centre for Kaunihera Whakatupato Waipiro o Aotearoa/Alcohol Advisory Council of New Zealand (ALAC), 1999, p. 76.
38. Ibid, pp. 76–77. See Mihi Edwards, *Mihipeka, Time of Turmoil. Nga Wa Raruraru.* Penguin, Auckland, 1992, p. 67.
39. Hutt, op. cit., pp, 76–77. See Alan Duff, *Once Were Warriors*, Tandem Press, Auckland, 1991, p. 48.
40. Personal comment to the author by an interviewee, 13 October 2016, Auckland. The interviewee wished to remain anonymous.
41. Hutt, op. cit., p 78.
42. Interview with Jason Hotere, April 2017, Henderson, Auckland. Jason is a counsellor at St Peter's College, Auckland City, who was born in Auckland, raised in Avondale. The Hotere family are originally from Mitimiti. Alcohol, aggression and abuse were prevalent in his family for the previous three generations. After the war his uncles (war veterans) and father migrated to Auckland for 'big money and bright lights'. Jason remembers much of his father's pay-packet would be spent on alcohol and his mother had to work two jobs to keep the home running. Jason saw alcohol as a consequence of colonialism that has fuelled the fires of underlying family issues. Being labelled 'urban Māori' was a label Jason always despised.
43. Interview with Evelyn Taumanu, 9 April 2017, Te Atatū North, Auckland.
44. *Te Whānau o Waipareira Report, WAI 414*, op. cit., p. 35.
45. Cook, op. cit.
46. Rawiri Taonui and Greg Newbold, "Māori Gangs", in McIntosh, Tracey and Mulholland, Malcolm (eds), *Māori And Social Issues*. Huia, Wellington, 2011, p. 212.
47. Jarrod Gilbert, *Patched, The History of Gangs in New Zealand*, Auckland University Press, Auckland, 2013, p. 12.
49. Taonui and Newbold, op. cit., p. 211.
49. Interviews with Wynn Anania and Poata Eruera, March 2017; who witnessed this world in Auckland.
50. Interview with Wynn Anania, the originator of the Head Hunter gang, December 2016, Glen Innes, Auckland
51. Gilbert, op. cit., p. 45.
52. *Te Whānau o Waipareira Report, WAI 414*, op. cit., p. 35–36.
53. Isaac Tuhoe and Bradford Haami, *True Red; The Life of an Ex-Mongrel Mob Gang Leader*, True Red, Auckland, 2007, pp. 7–8.
54. Ibid, p. 8.
55. Ibid, p. 10.
56. Ibid, pp. 10–11
57. Taonui and Newbold, op. cit., p. 218.
58. Ibid, p. 209.

59. Rawiri Taonui, , "Māori Urban Protest Movements" in Danny Keenan, *Huia Histories of Māori, Ngā Tāhuhu Kōrero*, Huia, Wellington, 2012, p. 235.
60. Aroha Harris, *Hīkoi, Forty Years of Māori Protest*. Huia, Wellington, 2004, p. 24.
61. Ibid, pp. 24–25.
62. Interview with Poata Eruera, March 2017, Auckland.
63. Taonui, "Māori Urban Protest Movements", op. cit., p. 237.
64. Ibid, p. 238.
65. Hana O'Regan, "The Fate of the Customary Language Te Reo Māori 1900 to the Present" in Danny Keenan, *Huia Histories of Māori Nga Tāhūhū Korero*, Huia, Wellington, 2012, p. 304.
66. Mason Durie, "Māori Health Transitions 1960–1985" in Danny Keenan (ed), *Huia Histories of Māori Nga Tahuhu Korero*, Huia, Wellington, 2012, p. 267.
67. Ibid, p. 268.
68. Ibid, p. 272.
69. Mason Durie, "The Treaty of Waitangi and Health Care" in *New Zealand Medical Journey*, no. 102, 1989, p. 284.
70. Stephanie Knight, *Auckland Hospital Racism Intervention Project, A History*. Race Relations Office and Auckland Hospital Board, 1989, p. 5.
71. Phone interview with ex-Auckland Area Health Board member Heather Thompson, 22 June 2015. Heather said Principle Nurse Mary Hackett (nee Futter) was a key advocate for creating a culturally sensitive understanding to hospital treatment of Māori patients.
72. Knight, op. cit., p. 5.
73. Interview with Karena Way, December 2014, Auckland.
74. Amohaere G. Ngaropo, B.J. Anderson and K. Way, "Te Whānau Atawhai, A New Zealand Model For Supporting Indigenous Families With Children in Intensive Care." Unpublished presentation, 1990, p. 3.
75. Interview with Amohaere Tangitū (Judith Ngaropo), April 2016, Whakatane.
76. Ibid, May 2015, Whakatane.
77. Nursing Council of New Zealand. "Cultural Safety Guidelines, the Treaty of Waitangi and Māori Health in Nursing Education and Practice." http://pro.healthmentoronline.com/assets/Uploads/refract/pdf/Nursing_Council_cultural-safety11.pdf.
78. Te Whānau Atawhai, "Te Whānau Atawhai, A New Initiative in Health Provision." 1993, p. 1.
79. Te Whānau Atawhai, "Steps into the Future. Te Whānau Atawhai Developments to the Year 2000." February 1992, Te Whānau Atawhai Archive, p. 9.
80. "Te Whānau Atawhai', op. cit., p. 9.
81. Interview with Amohaere Tangitū (Judith Ngaropo), April 2016, Whakatane.
82. Martin Johnston, "Exclusive, Man Who Fled Mental Health Found Dead — Inquiry Plea," *nzherald.co.nz*, 27 October 2016. http://www.nzherald.co.nz/nz/news/article.cfm?c_id=1&objectid=11736463.
83. Ibid.

9. Iwitanga Hou: Retribalisation

1. Roger Maaka, "The New Tribe, Conflicts and Continuities in the Social Organization of Urban Māori." *The Contemporary Pacific, University of Hawaii Press*, Fall 1994, pp. 311–336, see p. 315.
2. Annemarie Gillies, *Kia Taupunga Te Ngākau Māori; Anchoring Māori Health Workforce Potential*. Doctorate of Philosophy, Massey University, 2006. http://teipuwhakahauaa.co.nz/uploads/gillies/2006/632_Gillies2006.pdf, pp. 77–78. See also *Te Whānau o Waipareira Report. WAI 414, Waitangi Tribunal Report*. Waitangi Tribunal Report. Wellington, GP Publications, 1998, p. 41.
3. *Te Whānau o Waipareira Report. WAI 414*, op. cit., p. 42. See also Atholl Anderson,

Judith Binney, and Aroha Harris. *Tangata Whenua — An Illustrated History*, Wellington, Bridget Williams Books, 2015, pp. 372–73.
4. Interview with Evelyn Taumaunu, April 2017, Te Atatu Peninsula, Auckland.
5. Ibid.
6. "In Brief". Website article, Te Whānau o Waipareira, no date, http://www.waipareira.com/about.
7. *Te Whānau o Waipareira Report. WAI 414*, op. cit., p. 43.
8. Ibid, pp. 41–42.
9. Atholl Anderson et al., op. cit., p. 372. See also "In Brief," op. cit.
10. Te Whanau o Waipareira. *Te Whanau A Celebration of Te Whanau O Waipareira*. Waitakere City, Auckland, 2001, p. 13.
11. Ibid, p. 13.
12. Ibid, p. 1. See also Atholl Anderson et al., op. cit., p. 373.
13. Dale Husband, "John Tamihere, I've Had to Keep Fighting My Way," website media release, *Te Whānau O Waipareira*, March 2013. http://www.waipareira.com/news/calendar/2016/3/.
14. Ibid.
15. Ibid.
16. Te Whanau o Waipareira. *Te Whanau A Celebration of Te Whanau O Waipareira*, op. cit., p. 94.
17. *Te Whānau o Waipareira Annual Report 2014–2015*, Auckland, 2015, p. 4.
18. Atholl Anderson et al., op. cit., p. 373.
19. Roger C.A. Maaka, op. cit., p. 317.
20. Manuhuia Barcham, "The Challenge of Urban Māori, Reconciling Conceptions of Indigeneity and Social Change." *Asia Pacific Viewpoint* 39, no. 3 (December 1998), 303–14, p. 306.
21. Hirini Moko Mead, *Tikanga Māori Living by Māori Values*, Wellington, Huia, 2003.
22. Ibid, p. 227.
23. Mason Durie, *Ngā Tini Whetū, Navigating Māori Futures*, Wellington, Huia, 2011, p. 143.
24. Roger C.A. Maaka, "Perceptions, Conceptions and Realities, A Study of the Tribe in Māori Society in the Twentieth Century" (Unpublished Thesis for Doctor of Philosophy in Political Science, University of Canterbury, 2003), p. 174.
25. Ibid.
26. Annemarie Gillies, op. cit., p. 75
27. Steven Webster, "Māori Retribalization and Treaty Rights to the New Zealand Fisheries," *The Contemporary Pacific*, University of Hawaii Press 14, no. 2 (2002), 341–76, pp. 351–52.
28. Ibid, p. 352.
29. Ibid.
30. Ibid.
31. Michael King, *The Penguin History of New Zealand*. Albany, New Zealand, Penguin Books, 2003, p. 484.
32. Elizabeth Rata, *A Political Economy of Neotribal Capitalism*, New York, Lexington Books, 2000, pp. 41–45.
33. Steven Webster, op.cit., p. 342.
34. Roger C.A. Maaka, op. cit., pp. 311–336, in particular p. 311.
35. Ibid, p. 311.
36. Ranginui Walker, "Te Karanga A New Beginning," Metro, February 1992, p. 128.
37. Roger C.A. Maaka, 2003, ibid., pp. 153–54. Maaka recalls Te Okenga Huata's bigger vision to unify all the tribes associated with the *Takitimu* canoe.
38. Roger C.A. Maaka, 2003, Ibid, pp 153-154.
39. Roger C.A. Maaka, 2003, Ibid, p. 158.
40. Roger C.A. Maaka, 1994, Ibid, p. 311.
41. Roger C.A. Maaka, 1994, Ibid, p. 321.
42. Roger C.A. Maaka, op. cit., p. 322.
43. Roger C.A. Maaka, op. cit., p. 323.
44. Te Rūnanga O Nga Maata Waka Incorporated, Website/About Us, no date, http://maatawaka.org.nz/. Also, Personal comment to the author by Norm Dewes, 6 April 2017, Nga Hau e Whā Marae, Christchurch.
45. Roger C.A. Maaka, "Perceptions,

Conceptions and Realities, A Study of the Tribe in Māori Society in the Twentieth Century." Unpublished Thesis for Doctor of Philosophy in Political Science, University of Canterbury, 2003, p. 164. The date of the rūnanga's establishment is also mentioned in Emily Spink, "Queens Birthday Honours Takes Māori Advocate by Surprise," *The Press*, June 2016, http://www.stuff.co.nz/the-press/news/80615786/queens-birthday-honour-takes-maori-advocate-by-surprise.
46. Roger C.A. Maaka,1994, op. cit., p. 325.
47. Ibid, pp. 327–28.
48. Ibid, p. 327.
49. Roger C.A. Maaka, 2003, op. cit., p. 167.
50. Ibid, p. 167.
51. Ibid, p. 168.
52. Ibid, p. 171.
53. Interview with Norm Dewes, 6 April 2017, Ngā Hau e Whā marae, Christchurch.
54. Ibid.
55. Roger, C.A. Maaka, 2003, op. cit., p. 171.
56. Personal comment to the author by Norm Dewes, 6 April 2017, Nga Hau e Whā Marae, Christchurch. In this interview with Norm, he said, "We put our hand up at a special meeting to say that we were prepared to take on the difficulties that were inherent in this marae to try and restore it to a position of sustainability and credibility. They were in a crisis situation and that's well known. We took on that mission and that's what it's been and it's ongoing. We were the only community group to put up our hand … So we agreed and signed a contract with the trustee as the manager of the marae. We determine the management of the marae."
57. Personal comment to the author by Norm Dewes, 6 April 2017, Nga Hau e Whā Marae, Christchurch.
58. Tina Law, "Christchurch Marae Hosts New Temporary Workers Village," *The Press*, February 2016, http://www.stuff.co.nz/the-press/business/the-rebuild/77171269/Christchurch-marae-hosts-new-temporary-workers-village. Also, Interview with Norm Dewes, op. cit.
59. Tania Rangiheuea, "Urban Māori". In Malcolm Mulholland and Veronica Tawhai, Veronica (eds), *Weeping Waters, The Treaty of Waitangi and Constitutional Change*. Huia, Wellington, 2010, p. 194.
60. Richard Hill, "Ngā Whakataunga Tiriti – Treaty of Waitangi Settlement Process — The Waitangi Tribunal and Negotiated Settlements." Te Ara, The Encyclopedia of New Zealand, Wellington, Ministry of Culture and Heritage, 20 June 2012. http://www.teara.govt.nz/en/nga-whakataunga-tiriti-treaty-of-waitangi-settlement-process/page-3.
61. Michael King, op. cit., p. 501.
62. Richard Hill, op. cit., pp. 254–55
63. Tania Rangiheuea, op. cit., p. 194.
64. Michael King, op. cit., p. 502.
65. Richard Hill, op. cit., p. 255.
66. Tania Rangiheuea, op. cit., p. 194.
67. Norm Dewes, "Formation As An Urban Authority". Audio interview on Te Rūnanga O Nga Matawaka Incorporated website, no date. http://maatawaka.org.nz/about-nga-maata-waka/.
68. Yvonne Tahana, "Straight-Talking Dame Recalls Humble Origins," *Nzheraland.co.nz*, 7 June 2010, http://www.nzherald.co.nz/nz/news/article.cfm?c_id=1&objectid=10650239.
69. Tania Rangiheuea, op .cit., p. 195.

10. Mana Mātāwaka: The Urban Authorities

1. Paul Meredith, "Urban Maori as 'New Citizens', The Quest for Recognition and Resources," paper presented to the Revisioning Citizenship in New Zealand Conference, University of Waikato, February 2000, p. 9.
2. John Tamihere, "Urban Māori Court Victory Over Iwi." Website article. Te

Whānau o Waipareira, 2016, http://www.waipareira.com/news/urban-maori-court-victory-over-iwi. Accessed April 2017.
3. Meredith, op. cit., p. 9.
4. Tania Rangiheuea, "Urban Māori" in Mulholland, Malcolm and Tawhai, Veronica (eds), *Weeping Waters, The Treaty of Waitangi and Constitutional Change*. Huia, Wellington, 2010.
5. Ibid, p. 195.
6. Cited in Rangiheuea, op. cit., p. 196.
7. Evidence statements cited in Roger Maaka, 2003, Ibid, pp. 178-187.
8. Rangiheuea, op. cit., p. 196.
9. "High Court Judgement on Te Pūtea Whakatupu Trust." Website article. Te Ohu Kaimoana, 19 July 2016. http,//teohu.maori.nz/media-release/2016/19.07.16-High-Court-Judgement-on-Te-Putea-Whakatupu-Trust. Accessed May 2017.
10. "Urban Maori Fight Iwi Over Fisheries." Website article. Te Whānau o Waipareira media release, 3 June 2015. http,//www.waipareira.com/news/urban-maori-fight-iwi-over-fisheries. Accessed April 2017.
11. Ibid.
12. Ibid.
13. Ibid. Also, "High Court NUMA Decision Media Release", Te Ohu Kaimoana The Māori Fisheries Trust website, 2016. http://teohu.maori.nz/media-release/2016/High_Court_NUMA_Decision.pdf. Accessed May 2017.
14. Tamihere, op. cit.
15. Hineani Melbourne, *Maori Sovereignty The Maori Perspective*. Hodder Moa Beckett, Auckland, 1995, p. 113.
16. Nick Smith, "Award for Faithful Servant to His People." nzherald.co.nz., 2000. http,//www.nzherald.co.nz/nz/news/article.cfm?c_id=1&objectid=13695. Accessed April 2017. See also Te Whanau o Waipareira *Te Whanau, A Celebration of Te Whānau o Waipareira*. Te Whānau o Waipareira, Waitakere City, Auckland, 2001, pp. 137–38
17. *Te Whānau o Waipareira Report. WAI 414, Waitangi Tribunal Report*. Waitangi Tribunal Report. Wellington, GP Publications, 1998, p xxiii. See also evidence cited in Roger C.A. Maaka, "Perceptions, Conceptions and Realities, A Study of the Tribe in Māori Society in the Twentieth Century". Unpublished Thesis for Doctor of Philosophy in Political Science, University of Canterbury, 2003, p. 197.
18. *Te Whānau o Waipareira Report. WAI 414*, op. cit., p. xxiii.
19. Ibid, p. 2.
20. Atholl Anderson, Judith Binney, and Aroha Harris. *Tangata Whenua — An Illustrated History*, Wellington, Bridget Williams Books, 2015, p. 394. *Te Whānau o Waipareira Report. WAI 414*, op. cit., pp. 208–209.
21. Rangiheuea, op. cit., p. 198.
22. Ibid, p. 199.
23. *Te Whānau o Waipareira Report. WAI 414*, op. cit., p. 3.
24. Anderson et al., op. cit., p. 394. *Te Whānau o Waipareira Report. WAI 414*, op. cit., pp. 3, 76, 174.
25. Anderson et al., op. cit., p. 394. See *Te Whānau o Waipareira Report. WAI 414*, op. cit., pp. 77–80, 225, 226, 235.
26. *Te Whānau o Waipareira Report. WAI 414*, op. cit., p. 243.
27. Ibid.
28. Ibid, pp. 244–45.
29. Ibid, p. 244.
30. I. Tūpara, unpublished thesis, p. 125; cited in Roger C.A. Maaka, op. cit., p. 196.
31. *Te Whānau o Waipareira Report. WAI 414*, p. 6.
32. Rangiheuea, op. cit., p. 199.
33. Ibid, p. 200.
34. See MUMA report in *Te Whānau o Waipareira Annual Report 2010–2011*. Auckland, 2011.
35. Rangiheuea, op. cit., p. 200.
36. http://www.muma.co.nz/about-us. See also

Anderson et al., op. cit., p. 392. MUMA Manukau Urban Māori Authority, "Our Whanau Our Future." Website article, n.d.
37. Anderson et al., op. cit., p. 409.
38. Mason Durie, *Ngā Tini Whetū; Navigating Māori Futures* (Wellington, Huia, 2011, p. 26
39. Atholl Anderson et al., op. cit., p. 409.
40. Mason Durie, *Ngā Tini Whetū — Navigating Māori Futures*. Huia, Wellington, 2011, p. 27.
41. See MUMA report in *Te Whānau o Waipareira Annual Report 2010–2011*, op. cit.
42. Ibid.
43. New Zealand Parliament, "Mangere Electorate Profile Data." Electorate Profile Data. New Zealand Parliament, June 2015. https,//www.parliament.nz/en/mps-and-electorates/electorate-profiles/electorate-profiles-data/document/DBHOH_Lib_EP_M%C4%81ngere_Households/m%C4%81ngere-households. Accessed April 2017.
44. Waatea TV, "Waatea Television," You Tube, Waatea TV website, 2017, https,//www.youtube.com/channel/UC1PVrafYKLbNWhW6pnSjjyg. Accessed April 2017.
45. Radio New Zealand, "Charter School Opens for Business." Website article, 5 March 2015. http://www.radionz.co.nz/news/te-manu-korihi/267773/charter-school-opens-for-business. Accessed April 2017.
46. Kirikiriroa Marae, "Establishment of Kirikiriroa Marae." Website article, 2017. http://kirikiriroamarae.com/Who.
47. Rangiheuea, op. cit., p. 201.
48. *Te Whanau A Celebration of Te Whanau o Waipareira*, op .cit., p. 45.
49. Ibid, p. 47.
50. Ibid, op. cit., p. 67. See also *Te Whānau o Waipareira Annual Report 2010–2011*, op. cit.
51. *Te Whanau A Celebration of Te Whanau o Waipareira*, op. cit., p. 68.
52. Husband, Dale, Husband, Dale, "John Tamihere, I've had to keep fighting my way". Website media release, *E-Tangata A Maori and Pasifika Sunday Magazine*, March 2013. https,//e-tangata.co.nz/news/john-tamihere-ive-had-to-keep-fighting-my-way/arts. Accessed May 2017.
53. John Stokes, "Tamihere Back in Charge at Waipareira," *New Zealand Herald*, 15 April 2006. http://www.nzherald.co.nz/nz/news/article.cfm?c_id=1&objectid=10377533.
54. Husband, op. cit.
55. *Te Whānau o Waipareira Annual Report 2010–2011*, op. cit.
56. Ibid, CEO report.
57. Te Whānau o Waipareira, "Waipareira on the Cutting Edge of Technology." Website media release. Te Whānau o Waipareira, 16 May 2012. http,//www.waipareira.com/news/waipareira_on_the_cutting_edge. Accessed April 2017.
58. *Te Whānau o Waipareira Annual Report 2010–2011*, op. cit.
59. Te Whānau o Waipareira, "Strategic Plan." Website article. Te Whānau o Waipareira, 2017 2013.www.waipareira.com. Accessed May 2017.
60. Te Whānau o Waipareira, "Wai-Research." Website article. Te Whānau O Waipareira Media Release, n.d. http,//www.waipareira.com/wai-research.html. Accessed May 2017.
61. Te Whānau o Waipareira, *Te Whānau o Waipareira Annual Report 2013–2014*, Auckland, 2014, p. 6.
62. Te Puni Kōkiri Realising Māori Potential, "Why Whānau Ora," website article, 8 February 2017. https,//www.tpk.govt.nz/en/whakamahia/whanau-ora/why-whanau-ora/.
63. Te Whānau o Waipareira, "Urban Māori Proud" in *Te Whānau o Waipareira Annual Report 2015–2016,* Auckland, 2016, p. 25.
64. Ibid, p. 4.

65. Te Ohu Kaimoana, "High Court NUMA Decision Media Release", op. cit., paragraph 12.
66. Husband, op. cit.
67. "Our Vision." Website article. Nga Ngaru Rautahi Aotearoa National Urban Authority Inc., 2016. http://www.ngangaru.com/about/.
68. Nga Ngaru Rautahi Aotearoa National Urban Authority Inc., "Meet Our Board Members," website article, 2016, http://www.ngangaru.com/about/.
69. Adam Dudding, "Parish Pumped, How Destiny Church Is Struggling." *Sunday Star Times*, 2013. http://www.stuff.co.nz/life-style/life/8968824/Parish-pumped-How-Destiny-Church-is-struggling. Accessed May 2017.
70. Peter Lineham, *Destiny; The Life and Times of a Self-Made Apostle*. Penguin Books, Auckland, 2013.
71. Bradford Haami, *The River of the Water of Life A Biography of Ihaka "Ike" Samuels*. 2nd Edition. Auckland, Ike Samuels Whānau Trust, 2016, pp. 41–42.
72. Lineham, op, cit., p. 213.
73. Ibid, p. 175.
74. Cited in ibid, p. 213.
75. Ibid, p. 214.
76. Adam Bennett, "Destiny Church Receives Govt Funding". nzherald.co.nz, 8 June 2011, http://www.nzherald.co.nz/nz/news/article.cfm?c_id=1&objectid=10730987.
77. Dudding, "Parish Pumped" op. cit.
78. Destiny Church, "Man Up Conventions." Website article, n.d. https,//www.destinychurch.org.nz/manupnz. Accessed May 2017.
79. Interview with Duane Evans, a member of Destiny Church, April 2017, Auckland.
80. Craig Hoyle, "Gangs Help 'Build' Destiny Church." *Waikato Times*, 18 April 2017. https,//www.pressreader com/new-zealand/waikato-times/20170418/281547995764044. Accessed April 2017..
81. Ibid.
82. Lineham, op. cit., p. 183.
83. Interview with Matua Hakiaha, January 2017, Auckland.
84. Personal comment to the author by Cortez Olsen, December 2016, Auckland.
85. *Te Whānau o Waipareira Annual Report 2014–2015*, p. 18.
86. Ibid, p. 19.
87. Ibid.
88. Pae Keiha and Paul Moon, "The Emergence and Evolution of Urban Maori Authorities, A Response to Maori Urbanisation". *Te Kaharoa* 1, 2008., 1–17, p. 14.
89. Keiha and Moon, op. cit., p. 15.
90. *Te Whanau A Celebration of Te Whanau o Waipareira*, op. cit., p. 135.

11. Noho Tāwāhi: Māori in Australia

1. Sidney M. Mead, "The Latest Maori Migration." *Te Kaunihera Maori The Official Organ Of The New Zealand Maori Council*, autumn issue, 1969, p. 45.
2. Paul Hamer, *Māori in Australia, Ngā Māori i te Ao Moemoeā*. Te Puni Kokiri Ministry of Māori Development and Griffiths University, Australia, June 2007, see Executive Summary.
3. Ibid, pp. 9, 15.
4. Mead, op. cit., p. 45.
5. Ibid.
6. Hamer, op. cit., p. xii.
7. Ibid, p. xi.
8. Ibid, p. 36.
9. Ibid.
10. "Submission in Response to the Auckland Law Reform Bill, Third Reading, Statutory Maori Board." Parliamentary Report, New Zealand, n.d. https,//www.parliament.nz/resource/mi-nz/49SCAGL_EVI_00DBHOH_BILL9729_1_A34597/dc313f6332a3789ad98c426d28b1768db3a365fd. Accessed February 2017.
11. Tahu Kukutai and Shefali Pawar, "A Socio-Demographic Profile of Māori

Living in Australia". National Institute of Demographic and Economic Analysis (NIDEA), University of Waikato, Hamilton, June 2013, p. 34.
12. Ibid, pp. 7–8.
13. Ibid.
14. Nicole Pryor, "Maori in Oz, Living the Good Life." *The Dominion Post*, 2013. http://www.stuff.co.nz/national/8937746/Maori-in-Oz-Living-the-good-life. Accessed December 2016.
15. Mead, op. cit., p. 49.
16. Ibid, pp. 49–51.
17. Ibid, p 53.
18. Hamer, op. cit., pp. 43, 45, 416.
19. Ibid, p. 41.
20. Interview with Graeme Taiaroa, 31 December 2017, Ipswich, Brisbane, Australia.
21. Interview with Stewart Simpson, December 2016, Reedy Creek, Australia.
22. Interview with Grenville Ham, August 2016, Whakatane.
23. Sylvia Varnham O'Regan, "Is the Maori-Australian Dream All Its Cracked up to Be?" SBS News, 22 May 2014. http://www.sbs.com.au/news/article/2014/03/21/maori-australian-dream-all-its-cracked-be. Accessed November 2016.
24. Ibid.
25. Hamer, p 45.
26. Ibid, p. 60.
27. Ibid, p 55.
28. Ibid, p. 56.
29. Mares, Peter. "Comment, New Zealand's 'Bondi Bludger' and Other Australian Myths." SBS News, 11 February 2014. http://www.sbs.com.au/news/article/2014/02/11/comment-new-zealands-bondi-bludger-and-other-australian-myths?cx_navSource=related-side-cx#cxrecs_s. Accessed November 2016.
30. "Ngā Māori i Te Ao Moemoeā Māori in Australia", website media release fact sheet, Te Puni Kōkiri Ministry of Māori Development, December 2013, https,//www.tpk.govt.nz/en/a-matou-mohiotanga/demographics/maori-in-australia-fact-sheet. See also Kukutai and Pawar, op. cit., p. 11.
31. Kukutai and Pawar, op. cit., p. 11.
32. Ibid, p. 13.
33. Ibid, p. 39.
34. Interview with Sheana Ham, December 2016, Alice Springs, Gold Coast, Australia.
35. David Waretini Karena, "Maori Showbands a Tribute to Danny Robinson." Master of Arts, Waikato Institute of Technology, 2009. http://researcharchive.wintec.ac.nz/523/1/2009_Maori_showbands_Whanau_for_Archives_version.pdf. Accessed December 2016.
36. Ibid, p. 7.
37. Ibid, p. 5.
38. Ibid.
39. Ibid, p 6.
40. Ibid, p. 16.
41. Interview with Wi Wharekura, December 2016, Gold Coast, Australia.
42. Karena, op. cit., p 16.
43. Ibid, p 23.
44. Interview with Darren Rehu, 17 December 2016, by Skype between New Zealand and the United Kingdom.
45. "Dannielle Harte," *Harte International*, 2016, http://www.harteinternational.com/danielle-harte/.
46. Kukutai and Pawar, ibid, p. 9.
47. Mares, op. cit. Also, "Ngā Māori i Te Ao Moemoeā Māori in Australia", website media release fact sheet, Te Puni Kōkiri Ministry of Māori Development, December 2013, https,//www.tpk.govt.nz/en/a-matou-mohiotanga/demographics/maori-in-australia-fact-sheet, p. 3.
48. John Gerritsen, Gerritsen`, John, "Cost of Study in Australia to Triple for NZers." New Zealand/Politics. Radio New Zealand, 3 May 2017. http://www.radionz.co.nz/news/national/329917/cost-of-study-in-

australia-to-triple-for-nzers. Accessed June 2017.
49. Mares, op. cit.
50. Ibid, p. 10.
51. Varnham O'Regan, op. cit.
52. Atholl Anderson, Judith Binney, and Aroha Harris. *Tangata Whenua — An Illustrated History*, Wellington, Bridget Williams Books, 2015, p. 415.
53. At the landing of the inaugural Air New Zealand flight to Cairns in 1989, the celebrities on board, including Prime Minister Helen Clark, were welcomed on to the tarmac by a small Māori kapa haka group. Some of the Māori passengers on that flight, including the author, were concerned that proper protocol should have the local Aboriginal tribe welcome the New Zealand contingent. A local Aboriginal tribal team from Cairns were on this flight after visiting New Zealand, but they were ushered off the plane through customs, while the New Zealanders were taken to the tarmac to a Māori powhiri. Speaking with the Māori kapa haka team afterwards about this issue, they said they were paid a fee to perform.
54. Personal comment to author by John Dawson, CEO of YWAM International and David Moko of Auckland, December 2016. This was a ceremony that took place at the third World Christian Gathering of Indigenous People at the Blue Mountains in 2000. It was here Māori leaders thanked the Aboriginal community for opening the door to their people and caring for dead ancestors in their whenua.
55. Hamer, op. cit., p. 77.
56. Interview with Anzac te Oka Jnr, 5 January 2017, Gold Coast.
57. Ibid.
58. Hamer, op. cit., p 88.
59. See 'Beginnings' Auckland Airport web, http://www.airportmarae.co.nz/beginnings.php and also Paul Hamer, ibid, pp. 88–89.
60. Interview with Mark Bishop snr at Gold Coast, Dec 2016.
61. Hamer, op. cit., p. 82.
62. "Australia's First Marae Put on Hold." Newshub, Media Works TV. 16 December 2016. http://www.newshub.co.nz/world/australias-first-marae-put-on-hold-20150 12412. Accessed December 2016.
63. Hamer, op. cit., p. 85.
64. Talisa Kupenga, "Plans for First Marae in Australia Under Way", *Te Kaea News*, Auckland New Zealand, Māori Television, 15 June 2016, http://www.maoritelevision.com/news/regional/plans-first-marae-australia-underway.
65. Interview with Wi Wharekura, 30 December 2016, Gold Coast, Australia.
66. Interviews with Mark and Rena Bishop and Wi Wharekura, December 2016, Gold Coast, Australia.
67. Wharekura, Wi, "Wi Wharekura — Polynesian Cultural Village." Facebook page, 23 January 2016. https,//www.facebook.com/permalink.php?story_fbid=1233682933314903&id=499160920100445. Accessed January 2017.
68. Interview with Wi Wharekura, January 2017, Gold Coast, Australia.
69. Ibid.
70. Mamari Stephens, "And There He Lies, Ever, Ever, the Manuhuri", *E-Tangata A Māori and Pasifika Sunday Magazine*, 20 June 2017, https,//e-tangata.co.nz/news/and-there-he-lies-ever-ever-the-manuhuri.
71. Ibid.
72. Interview with Stewart Simpson, op. cit.
73. Hamer, op. cit., pp. 149–51.
74. Ibid, p. xiii.
75. Ibid, p. 106.
76. Kukutai and Pawar, op. cit., pp. 7, 13.
77. Hamer, op. cit., p. 2.
78. Ibid, p. 153.
79. Integrity Professionals, "Invest Bay of Plenty — Māori Migration." Rotorua Lakes Council, 26 June 26 2014. http://

www.rotorualakescouncil.nz/our-city/
SmartFutures/Documents/Maori-
migration.pdf. Accessed December 2016.
80. Ibid, p. 2.
81. Ibid.
82. Anderson et. al, op. cit.
83. Interview with Matua Hakiaha, December 2016, Auckland.

12. Hokinga ki te Kāinga: Returning Home

1. Whetū Weratā, "Māori Demographic Trends", *Social Policy Journal of New Zealand Te Puna Whakaaro*, no. 3, December 1994, https,//www.msd.govt.nz/about-msd-and…/03-maori-demographic-trends.html. Accessed May 2017.
2. Ibid.
3. Manuhuia Barcham, "The Politics of Māori Mobility." In *Population Mobility and Indigenous People in Australasia and North America*. Routledge Taylor & Francis Group, London and New York, 2004, p. 171.
4. Weratā, op. cit.
5. Linda Waimarie Nikora, Bernard Guerin, Mohi Rua and Ngahuia Te Awekotuku, "Moving Away From Home, Some Social Consequences for Tūhoe Migrating to the Waikato", in *New Zealand Population Review* 30 (2004), p. 95. See also Ulrike Pia Andres, "Return Migration and Māori Identity in a Northland Community". Unpublished thesis for Doctorate of Philosophy, University of Auckland, 2011, pp. 45–48. https,//researchspace.auckland.ac.nz/bitstream/handle/2292/6985/02whole.pdf?sequence=2. Accessed April 2017.
6. Atholl Anderson, Judith Binney, and Aroha Harris. *Tangata Whenua — An Illustrated History*, Wellington, Bridget Williams Books, 2015, p. 372.
7. Melissa Matutina Williams. , *Panguru and the City, Kāinga Tahi, Kāinga Rua An Urban Migration History*. Bridget Williams Books, Wellington, 2015, pp. 224, 226.
8. Anderson et al., op. cit., p. 372.
9. Interview with the Taumaunu family, April 2017, Te Atatū North, Auckland.
10. Personal comment to author by Vapi Kupenga of Ngāti Porou, 2001, Auckland. She and others constantly returned to Ngāti Porou from Auckland to maintain their links.
11. Williams, op. cit., p. 221
12. Ibid, p. 222.
13. Ibid, p. 223.
14. Ibid.
15. Ibid, p. 224.
16. Ibid.
17. Ibid.
18. Pare Keiha and Paul Moon, "The Emergence and Evolution of Urban Maori Authorities, A Response to Maori Urbanisation," *Te Kaharoa* 1, 2008, pp. 6–7.
19. Williams, op. cit., p. 232.
20. Ibid, p. 230.
21. Ibid.
22. Personal comment to author by Dr Mere Roberts, April 2017, Auckland.
23. Interview with Te Hira Henderson, April 2017, Auckland.
24. Ibid.
25. Ibid.
26. Bradford Haami, *Ka Mau Te Wehi Taking Haka to the World; Bub and Nen's Story*. Ngāpō and Pīmia Wehi Whānau Trust, Auckland, 2013, p. 131.
27. Ibid, pp. 131–32.
28. Bradford Haami, *The River of the Water of Life A Biography of Ihaka "Ike" Samuels*. 2nd Edition. Ike Samuels Whānau Trust, Auckland, 2016, p. 69.
29. Ibid, pp. 127–28.
30. Personal comment to author by Paul Samuels, April 2017, Auckland.
31. Andres, op. cit., p. 47.
32. Barcham, op. cit., p. 177.
33. Ibid.

34. Nikora et al., op. cit., p. 107.
35. Ibid.
36. See full proverb in Bradford Haami, *Dr Golan Maaka Māori Doctor*, Tandem Press, North Shore City, Auckland, 1995, p. 41.
37. Natacha Gagne, *Being Māori In The City, Indigenous Everyday Life In Auckland*. University of Toronto Press, Toronto, 2013, pp. 71, 79.
38. Nikora et al., op. cit., p. 100.
39. Waipareira Research Files, interview 4, CH04, 2017.
40. Ibid.
41. See testimony of Fiona in Gagne, op. cit., p. 67.
42. A comment the author has heard expressed at rural whānau gatherings.
43. Williams, op. cit., p. 232–34.
44. Personal comment to author by Sandra Richmond, 31 March 2017, Auckland. Sandra lives in Auckland but her whānau are originally from the Eastern Bay of Plenty.
45. Barcham, op. cit., p. 178.
46. Andres, op. cit., p. 46.
47. Wiremu Tawhai, *Living By The Moon; Te Maramataka a Te Whanau-A-Apanui*, Huia, Wellington, 2013, pp. 38–39.
48. Ibid.
49. Ibid.
50. Personal comment to author by Siosi Tofi, 26 November 2016, at Auckland.
51. Interview with Roger Maaka, August 2016, Takapau, Hawke's Bay.
52. Oriini Kaipara, "The Lonely Paepae." Magazine item. Native Affairs. Auckland, New Zealand, Māori Television, 30 May 2017. https,//www.maoritelevision.com/news/latest-news/native-affairs--lonely-paepae. Accessed June 2017.
53. Justine Murray, "Transforming Tāneatua." Radio interview. Te Ahi Kaa. Wellington, New Zealand, Radio New Zealand National Programme, 14 May 2017, 17'40"–18'15". http://www.radionz.co.nz/national/programmes/teahikaa/podcast.
54. Interview Ngāmaru Raerino, December 2016, Rotorua.
55. Williams, op. cit., p. 236.
56. Mania Clarke, "Whānau Move into Te Kopua Papakāinga." Te Kaea. Te Kopua, Raglan, Māori Television, 29 July 2016. http://www.maoritelevision.com/news/latest-news/whanau-move-te-kopua-papakainga. Accessed 15 December 2016.
57. Hank Schouten, "New Homes for Te Aro Pa Descendants." *The Dominion Post*. 18 October 2014. http://www.stuff.co.nz/dominion-post/business/commercial-property/10632789/New-homes-for-Te-Aro-Pa-descendants. Accessed December 2016.
58. Ibid.
59. Aroha Treacher, "Homes for Whanau Are Now Ready in Hastings." *Hawke's Bay Today*. 24 November 2015. http://www.nzherald.co.nz/hawkes-bay-today/property/news/article.cfm?c_id=1503451&objectid=11546736. Accessed December 2016. See also "Professor Roger Maaka — Aorangi Māori Trust." Video recording. He Toa Takitini; Our Strength is in Unity, 2017. http://www.hetoatakitini.iwi.nz/twkd2rm1/. Accessed April 2017.
60. Interview with Ngāmaru Raerino, December 2016, Rotorua.
61. Ibid.
62. Ibid.
63. Ibid.
64. Ibid.
65. Ibid.
66. Interview with Matua Hakiaha, January 2017, at Auckland.
67. Sidney Moko Mead, *Landmarks, Bridges and Visions, Aspects of Māori Culture*, Victoria University Press, Wellington, 1997, pp. 262–63.
68. Ibid.
69. Interview with Roger Maaka, op. cit.

13. Iti Oneone Hou: The New Morsel of Soil

1. Kimiora Raerino, "He Tirohanga O Ngāti Awa Uri Taone Mō Ngā Āhuatanga Māori An Urban Ngāti Awa Perspective on Identity and Culture". Unpublished Master of Arts, Auckland University of Technology, 2007, p. 24.
2. Ibid.
3. Mason Durie, "*Mauri Ora The Dynamics of Māori Health*", Oxford University Press, Melbourne, 2001, p. 56.
4. Personal comment to author by Matua Hakiaha, December 2016, Auckland.
5. Ranginui Walker, *Ka Whawhai Tonu Matou, Struggle Without End*. Penguin Books, Auckland, 1990, p. 201.
6. Raerino, op. cit., p. 19.
7. Ibid, p. 18.
8. At a recent tangihanga attended by the author in Auckland, the tūpāpaku, born and bred in the city, was relentlessly contested for by northern relatives, who sought to return the body to the original papakāinga. The deceased had relayed his wishes to kaumātua that he was to be buried in the city, close to immediate family. The dispute between two iwi and the urban whānau over the tūpāpaku reflected that the tensions between iwi and urban whānau are still present in Māori lives.
9. "Reconciliation Kawe Whakamua Process Update Report II". Parihaka Papakāinga Trust, 2016. http://parihaka.maori.nz/home/wp-content/uploads/C-Reconciliation-Kawe-Whakamua-Process-Update-II.pdf. Accessed June 2017.
10. Tania Rangiheuea, "Urban Māori". In Malcolm Mulholland and Veronica Tawhai, Veronica (eds), *Weeping Waters, The Treaty of Waitangi and Constitutional Change*. Huia, Wellington, 2010, p. 203.
11. Durie, op. cit., p. 149.
12. Brian Easton, "Māori Meets Market", unpublished presentation, 2016, p. 39.
13. "2013 Census QuikStats about Māori," *Stats NZ Tatauranga Aotearoa*, March 2017, http://www.stats.govt.nz/Census/2013-census/profile-and-summary-reports/quickstats-about-Māori-english/population.aspx.
14. Ibid.
15. "Ngāi Tahu Research," Website article, *Ngāi Tahu Research*, 2016, https,//www.ngaitahuresearch.co.nz/population/. Accessed June 2017.
16. "Our History." Website article. Te Iwi O Ngāti Kahu Trust He Pou Ora, n.d. http://tionk.co.nz/history/. Accessed May 2017.
17. Leo Hogan, "Mokopuna Ora Expands into Tāmaki Makaurau", Maori Television Online News Team, Auckland, 7 June 2017, https://www.maoritelevision.com/news/regional/mokopuna-ora-expands-tamaki-makaurau. Accessed 7 June 2017.
18. SmartGrowth Maori and Tangata Whenua Iwi Demographics, 6 August 2015, Beca Ltd, 2015, pp. i, ii, 6. https,//www.smartgrowthbop.org.nz/media/1091/a-action-11c1-maori-demographics.pdf. Accessed 7 June 2017. Also personal comment to author by Shadrach Rolleston of Ngāi Te Rangi, 17 June 2017, Cambridge.
19. Personal comment to the author by Roger Maaka at Takapau, Hawke's Bay, 2017.
20. Paul Meredith, "Urban Maori as 'New Citizens', The Quest for Recognition and Resources," paper presented to the Revisioning Citizenship in New Zealand Conference, University of Waikato, February 2000, p. 14.
21. Ibid, p. 17
22. Ibid, p. 19.
23. Ibid, p. 20.
24. Manuhuia Barcham, "The Challenge of Urban Maori, Reconciling Conceptions of Indigeneity and Social Change". *Asia Pacific Viewpoint 39*, no. 3, December 1998, 303–314, p. 311.

25. Personal comment to author by Reikura Kahi, April 2017, Auckland.
26. Interview Reikura Kahi, ibid.
27. Bradford Haami, *Ka Mau Te Wehi Taking Haka to the World; Bub and Nen's Story*. Ngāpō and Pīmia Wehi Whānau Trust, Auckland, 2013, p. 7.
28. Personal comment to author by Mia Henry-Teirney at Auckland, January, 2017.
29. Stats NZ Tatauranga Aotearoa, "Māori Cultural Well-Being in 2013 — Poster." Website report. *Stats NZ Tatauranga Aotearoa*, 6 May 2014. http://www.stats.govt.nz/browse_for_stats/people_and_communities/maori/te-kupenga/cultural-wellbeing-poster.aspx. Accessed May 2017.
30. Stats NZ Tatauranga Aotearoa, infographic, "Ngā Huarahi Ki Te Marae, Māori Connecting to Their Ancestral Marae 2013-Infographic." Website report. *Stats NZ Tatauranga Aotearoa*, 2015. http://www.stats.govt.nz/browse_for_stats/people_and_communities/maori/te-kupenga/connect-ancestral-marae-infographic.aspx. Accessed May 2017.
31. Mason Durie, *Ngā Tini Whetū — Navigating Māori Futures*. Huia, Wellington, 2011, p. 305.
32. Mason Durie, *Mauri Ora,* op. cit., pp. 146–49.
33. Te Whānau o Waipareira, Te Whānau o Waipareira Annual Report 2010–2011, Auckland, New Zealand, 2011.
34. Mason Durie, *Nga Tai Matatu — Tides of Maori Endurance*. Oxford University Press, Melbourne, Australia, 2005, p. 3.
35. Joanne O'Brien, "Thousands Expected for Tūhoe Festival." Website article. Radio New Zealand, 24 March 2016. http://www.radionz.co.nz/news/regional/299793/thousands-expected-for-tuhoe-festival. Accessed May 2017.
36. Malcolm McKinnon (Ed), Barry Bradley, and Russell Kirkpatrick, *Bateman New Zealand Historical Atlas Ko Papatuanuku e Takoto Nei*. David Bateman Ltd, Albany, New Zealand, 1997, plate 91.
37. Ibid.
38. Ibid.
39. Ibid, plate 10. See the computer simulation showing ten waka sailing from Rarotonga to Aotearoa with five finding their target.
40. K.R. Howe, *"The Quest For Origins,"* Penguin Books, Auckland, 2003, p. 182.
41. The author has known a number of people who carry a small capsule of soil from their homelands with them wherever they travel. Soldiers in the Māori Battalion carried soil from their home to overseas as a comfort and to remember who they were. Others, such as the author's grandfather, carried a steel pātītī (short-handled axe) that belonged to his warrior ancestor, Whangataua. After his death this symbol of the ancestors' lineage was returned to the whānau and handed to a nephew, who now also carries this pātītī with him.
42. Durie, *Ngā Tini Whetū*, op. cit., p. 7.
43. Ibid, p. 8.
44. Ibid.
45. Ibid, p. 151.
46. Ibid.

Bibliography

Interviews

Kathrine Anania, Wynn Anania and May Johnson, Papatoetoe, Auckland, December 2016.
Wynn Anania, Henderson, Auckland, February 2017.
Barry Baker, Christchurch, December 2016.
Mark and Rena Bishop, Gold Coast, Australia, December 2016.
Mark Bishop Junior, Sydney, Australia, November 2016.
Seth Barrett, Henderson, Auckland, December 2016.
Colin Campbell, Otorohanga, December 2016.
John Dawson, Auckland, December 2016.
Norm Dewes, Christchurch, March 2017.
Kathy Eruera, Papakura, December 2016.
Poata Eruera, Auckland, March 2017.
Darlene Evans, Henderson, Auckland, September 2017.
Duane Evans, Auckland, May 2017.
Grenville and Sandra Haami, Auckland, December 2017.
Matua Hakiaha, Henderson, Auckland, October and December 2016.
Sheana Ham, Gold Coast, Australia, December 2016.
Dannielle Harte, Gold Coast, Australia, January 2017.
Raewyn Harrison, North Shore, Auckland, May 2017.
Te Hira Henderson, Auckland, April 2017.
Ella Henry, Avondale, January 2017.
Mia Henry-Teirney, Auckland, January 2017.
Jason Hotere, Henderson, Auckland, April 2017.
Steve Hutana, Henderson, Auckland, November 2016.
Reikura Kahi, Henderson, Auckland, March and April 2017.
Vapi Kupenga, Mt Eden, Auckland, March 2001.
Roger Maaka, Takapau, Hawke's Bay, August 2016.
Rereata 'Ral' Makiha, Rānui, Auckland, September 2016.
Lianne Marshall, Pakuranga, Auckland, 2017.
Jessie Matthews, Henderson, Auckland, April 2017.
David Moko, Auckland, January 2016.
Cortez Ohlsen, Henderson, Auckland, December 2016.
Margaret Pritchard, Henderson, Auckland, April 2017.
Ngamaru Raerino, Awahou, Rotorua, December 2016 and February 2017.
Mere Raharaha, Panmure, September 2016.
Jim Ranginui, Hamilton, April 2017.
Darren Rehu, London–Auckland, December 2016.
Kelly Renata, Hutt Valley, September 2016.
Matthew Renata, Wellington, February 2017.
Hokowhitu Ria, Christchurch, December 2016.
Sandra Richmond, Henderson, Auckland, March 2017.
Anaru Roberts, Henderson–Panmure, January 2017.
Mere Roberts, North Shore, Auckland, April 2017.
Shadrach Rolleston, Cambridge, June 2017.
Judy Rudolph, Henderson, Auckland, January 2017.

Pauline Rudolph, Kaikohe, March 2017.
Terry Ryan, Christchurch, 1 December 2016.
Paul Samuels, Auckland, April 2017.
Stewart Simpson, Reedy Creek, Gold Coast, Australia, December 2016.
Anzac Te Oka Junior, Gold Coast, Australia, January 2017.
Graeme Taiaroa, Ipswich, Brisbane, Australia, December 2016.
Lorraine Taogaga, Henderson, Auckland, December 2016.
John Tamihere, Henderson, Auckland, May 2017.
Amohaere Tangitū, in a series of interviews at Whakatāne, between 2015 and 2017.
Taumaunu whānau, Te Atatū North, Auckland, April 2017.
Maria Tia, Henderson, Auckland, April 2017.
John Te Morenga, Wellington, November 2016.
Siaosi Tofi, Mt Albert Auckland, November 2016.
Karena Way, Mt Eden, Auckland, November 2014.
Wi Wharekura, Gold Coast, Australia, January 2017.

Published works

Anderson, Atholl, Binney, Judith and Harris, Aroha, *Tangata Whenua — An Illustrated History*. Bridget Williams Books, Wellington, 2015.
"Awataha Marae; He Marae Iwi Kore He Maumau He Iwi Marae Kore Maumau." Te Raki Paewhenua Kōmiti Māori Pamphlet, April 2017.
Awataha Marae Project. Auckland, 1987.
Awatere, Arapeta, and Awatere, Hinemoa (eds), *Awatere; A Soldier's Story*. Huia, Wellington, 2003.
Ballara, Angela, *Iwi, The Dynamics of Māori Tribal Organisation from c.1769 to c.1945*. Victoria University Press, Wellington, 1998.
Barcham, Manuhuia, "The Challenge of Urban Maori, Reconciling Conceptions of Indigeneity and Social Change". *Asia Pacific Viewpoint 39*, no. 3, December 1998, pp. 303–314.
——, "The Politics of Māori Mobility." In *Population Mobility and Indigenous People in Australasia and North America*. Routledge Taylor & Francis Group, London and New York, 2004.
Beattie, H., "Traditions and Legends. Collected from the Natives of Murihiku. Part VIII". *Journal of the Polynesian Society 27*, no. 107 (1918), pp. 137–61.
Belich, James, *Paradise Reforged, A History of New Zealanders from the 1880s to the Year 2000*. Allen Land and Penguin Press, Auckland, 2001.
Belshaw, H., "Maori Economic Circumstances" in *The Maori People Today*, *A General Survey, 182–228*. New Zealand Institute of International Affairs and New Zealand Council for Educational Research, Wellington, 1940.
Biggs, Bruce, "The Maori Language Past and Present" in Schwimmer, Erik (ed.), *The Maori People in the Nineteen-Sixties*. Blackwood & Janet Paul Ltd, Auckland, 1968.
Blank, Arapera, "One Two Three Four Five" in Schwimmer, Erik (ed.), *The Maori People in the Nineteen Sixties*. Blackwood & Janet Paul Ltd, Auckland, 1968.
Bol Jun Lee, Jenny, "Marae-a-Kura; Tracing the Birth of Marae in Schools." *Te Māori i Ngā Ara Rapu Mātauranga — Māori Education*, Set 2 (2012), pp. 3–11.
Campbell, Gibson, "Urbanization in New Zealand". *Demography 10*, no. 1, February 1973.
Carlyon, Jenny, and Morrow, Diana, *Urban Village; The Story of Ponsonby, Freeman's Bay, and St Mary's Bay*. Random House, Auckland, 2008.
Costello, John, *Howard, The Life and Times of Sir Howard Morrison*. Moa Beckett Publishers Ltd, Auckland, 1992.
Craig, Eldson, "Gillies, Heppy and Shelley. The

Story of Three Mission Hostels". *Te Ao Hou The New World Magazine*, August 1957.

Cresswell, John C.M., *Maori Meeting Houses of the North Island*. PCS Publications, Auckland, 1977.

Dalley, Bronwyn, and McLean, Gavin (eds), *Frontier of Dreams, The Story of New Zealand*. Hodder Moa, Auckland, 2005.

Day, Kelvin (ed.), *Contested Ground, Te Whenua i Tohea; The Taranaki Wars 1860–1881*. Huia, Wellington, 2010.

Dieffenbach, Ernst, *Travels in New Zealand (1843)*, Vol. II. New Zealand, Capper Press (reprint), Christchurch, 1974.

Duff, Alan, *Once Were Warriors*. Tandem Press, Auckland, 1991.

Durie, Mason, *Mauri Ora The Dynamics of Māori Health*. Oxford University Press, Melbourne, Australia, 2001.

——, *Nga Tai Matatu — Tides of Maori Endurance*. Oxford University Press, Melbourne, Australia, 2005.

——, *Ngā Tini Whetū — Navigating Māori Futures*. Huia, Wellington, 2011.

——, "Te Aka-Matua — Keeping Maori Identity." In *Mai i Rangiatea*. Auckland University Press, Auckland, 1997.

——, *Te Mana, Te Kawanatanga, The Politics of Māori Self-Determination*. Oxford University Press, Auckland, 1998.

——, "The Treaty of Waitangi and Health Care" in *New Zealand Medical Journey*, no. 102, 1989.

Durie, Mason, "Maori Health Transitions 1960–1985" in Keenan, Danny (ed.), *Huia Histories of Māori Nga Tahuhu Korero*. Huia, Wellington, 2012.

Edwards, Mihi, *Mihipeka, Time of Turmoil. Nga Wa Raruraru*. Penguin, Auckland, 1992.

Fleras, Augie, "Maori Wardens And The Control Of Liquor Among The Maori of New Zealand." *Journal of the Polynesian Society* 90, no. 4, 1981.

Gagne, Natacha, *Being Māori In The City, Indigenous Everyday Life In Auckland*. University of Toronto Press, Toronto, 2013.

George, Lily (L.M.), "Tradition, Invention, and Innovation, Multiple Reflections on an Urban Marae". Unpublished Doctorate of Philosophy in Social Anthropology, Massey University, 2010.

Gilbert, Jarrod, *Patched, The History of Gangs in New Zealand*. Auckland University Press, Auckland, 2013.

Gill, Norman, *Mission Accomplished, The Establishment of the Christchurch Methodist Mission*. Christchurch Methodist Mission, Christchurch, 1991.

Gillies, Annemarie, "Kia Taupunga Te Ngākau Māori; Anchoring Māori Health Workforce Potential." Doctorate of Philosophy, Massey University, 2006.

"Girls Come to the City" in *Te Ao Hou The New World Magazine*, September 1961.

Grace, Patricia; Ramsden, Irihapeti and Dennis, Jonathan, *The Silent Migration, Ngāti Poneke Young Māori Club, 1937–1948*. Huia, Wellington, 2001.

Groves, Murray, "Maori Young Leaders Conference, 1959." *The Journal of the Polynesian Society* 68, no. 3, 1959.

Haami, Bradford, *Dr Golan Maaka Māori Doctor*. Tandem Press, North Shore City, Auckland, 1995.

——, *Ka Mau Te Wehi Taking Haka to the World; Bub and Nen's Story*. Ngāpō and Pīmia Wehi Whānau Trust, Auckland, 2013.

——, *Pūtea Whakairo, Māori and the Written Word*. Huia, Wellington, 2004.

——, *The River of the Water of Life A Biography of Ihaka "Ike" Samuels*. 2nd Edition. Ike Samuels Whānau Trust, Auckland, 2016.

Hamer, Paul, *Māori in Australia, Ngā Māori i te Ao Moemoeā*. Te Puni Kokiri Ministry of Māori Development and Griffiths University, Australia, June 2007.

Hamilton, A., "Fishing and Sea-Food of the Ancient Maori." *Dominion Museum Bulletin* no.2. Wellington, John McKay, Government Printer, 1908.

Harre, John, "Maori-Pakeha Intermarriage" in Schwimmer, Erik (ed.), *The Maori People in the Nineteen-Sixties*. Blackwood & Janet Paul Ltd, Auckland, 1968.

Harris, Aroha, "Concurrent Narratives of Māori Integration in the 1950s and 60s". *Journal of New Zealand Studies*, no. 6/7, 2008.

———, *Hīkoi Forty Years of Māori Protest*. Huia, Wellington, 2004.

"He Rerenga Korero 1982." Ngā Hau E Whā Marae Part 1 of 2, audio. Ngā Taonga Sound & Vision, Wellington, 1982. Ref. no. 47482.

"Helping The Maoris; Hutt Meeting House A Useful Purpose." *Evening Post*, 7 February 1936.

Howe, K.R., *The Quest For Origins*. Penguin Books, Auckland, 2003.

Hunn, LLM., J.K., *Report on The Department of Maori Affairs*. Wellington, 24 August 1960.

Hutt, Marten, *Te Iwi Maori Me Te Inu Waipiro, He Tuhituhinga Hitori, Maori and Alcohol, A History*. Health Services Research Centre for Kaunihera Whakatupato Waipiro o Aotearoa/Alcohol Advisory Council of New Zealand (ALAC), Wellington, 1999.

Isaac, Tuhoe, and Bradford Haami, *True Red; The Life of an Ex-Mongrel Mob Gang Leader*. True Red, Auckland, 2007.

Kapa, Mutu, "The Kaitaia Drains." *Journal of the Polynesian Society* 33, no. 131, 1924.

Kawharu, I.H., "Urban Immigrants and Tangata Whenua" in Schwimmer, Erik (ed.), *The Maori People in the Nineteen-Sixties*. Blackwood & Janet Paul Ltd, Auckland, 1968.

Keenan, Danny, *Te Whiti o Rongomai and the Resistance of Parihaka*. Huia, Wellington, 2015.

King, Michael, *The Penguin History of New Zealand*. Penguin Books, Albany, New Zealand, 2003.

———, *Whina*. Hodder and Stoughton, Auckland, 1983.

King, Michael, and Oliver, W.H. (ed.), "Between Two Worlds" in *The Oxford History of New Zealand*, 1st edition. Oxford University Press, Wellington, 1981.

Kingi, Te Kani, "Māori Mental Health, Past Trends, Current Issues, and Māori Responsiveness." Te Puna Hauora, Research School of Public Health, Massey University, Wellington, 2005.

Knight, Stephanie, *Auckland Hospital Racism Intervention Project, A History*. Race Relations Office and Auckland Hospital Board, 1989.

Kukutai, Tahu, "Contemporary Issues in Māori Demography" in *Māori and Social Issues*, vol. 1. Huia, Wellington, 2011.

Kukutai, Tahu, and Pawar, Shefali, "A Socio-Demographic Profile of Maori Living in Australia". National Institute of Demographic and Economic Analysis (NIDEA), University of Waikato, Hamilton, June 2013.

Lineham, Peter, *Destiny; The Life and Times of a Self-Made Apostle*. Penguin Books, Auckland, 2013.

Maaka, Roger C.A., "Perceptions, Conceptions and Realities, A Study of the Tribe in Māori Society in the Twentieth Century". Unpublished Thesis for Doctor of Philosophy in Political Science, University of Canterbury, 2003.

———, "The New Tribe, Conflicts and Continuities in the Social Organization of Urban Maori". *The Contemporary Pacific*, University of Hawaii Press, Fall 1994.

Mahuika, Nepia, "Revitalizing Te Ika-a-Maui, Maori Migration and the Nation." *New Zealand Journal of History* 43, no. 2, 2009, pp. 133–49.

McDonald, Findlay, and Kerr, Ruth (eds), *West, The History of Waitakere*. Random House, Auckland, 2009.

McEwen, Mary. *Te Oka — Pākehā Kaumātua; The Life of Jock McEwen*. Riveresco Trust, Wellington, 2016.

McKinnon, Malcolm (ed.), Barry Bradley, and Russell Kirkpatrick, *Bateman New Zealand Historical Atlas Ko Papatuanuku e Takoto Nei*.

David Bateman Ltd, Albany, New Zealand, 1997.
Mead, Hirini Moko, *The Ngati Awa Federation of Tribes, Bay of Plenty, New Zealand*. The Ngati Awa Trust Board, Whakatane, New Zealand, 1984.
——, *Tikanga Māori, Living by Māori Values*. Huia, Wellington, 2003.
Mead, Sidney M., "The Latest Maori Migration." *Te Kaunihera Maori The Official Organ Of The New Zealand Maori Council*, autumn issue, 1969.
Mead, Sidney Moko, *Landmarks, Bridges and Visions; Aspects of Maori Culture*. Victoria University Press, Wellington, 1997.
Melbourne, Hineani, *Maori Sovereignty, The Maori Perspective*. Hodder Moa Beckett, Auckland, 1995.
Meredith, Paul, "Urban Maori as 'New Citizens', The Quest for Recognition and Resources," paper presented to the Revisioning Citizenship in New Zealand Conference, University of Waikato, February 2000.
Metge, Joan, *A New Maori Migration, Rural and Urban Relations in Northern New Zealand*. The Althone Press, London, England, 1964.
Montgomerie, Deborah, *The Women's War, New Zealand Women 1939–45*. Auckland University Press, Auckland, 2001.
Morrow, Dan, "Tradition and Modernity in Discourse of Māori Urbanisation." *Journal of New Zealand Studies*, no. NS18, 2014.
Muru-Lanning, Marama. *Tupuna Awa; People and Politics of the Waikato River*. Auckland University Press, Auckland, 2016.
Taylor, Nancy M., *The Home Front Volume II*. Historical Publications Branch, Wellington, 1986.
Newman, Keith, *Ratana Revisited, An Unfinished Legacy*. Reed Publishing (NZ) Ltd, Auckland, 2006.
New Zealand Government, *New Zealand Census of Population and Dwelling, 1976*, 1976.
Nikora, Linda Waimarie; Guerin, Bernard; Rua, Mohi; and Te Awekotuku, Ngahuia. "Moving Away From Home, Some Social Consequences for Tūhoe Migrating to the Waikato." *New Zealand Population Review 30*, 2004.
O'Malley, Vincent; Stirling, Bruce; and Penetito, Wally (eds), *The Treaty of Waitangi Companion, Māori and Pākehā from Tasman to Today*. Auckland University Press, Auckland, 2010.
Orange, Claudia. "An Exercise in Māori Autonomy, The Rise and Demise of the Maori War Effort Organisation." *New Zealand Journal of History* 21, no. 1, 1987.
O'Regan, Hana. "The Fate of the Customary Language Te Reo Māori 1900 to the Present" in Keenan, Danny (ed.), *Huia Histories of Māori Nga Tāhūhū Korero*. Huia, Wellington, 2012.
Parliamentary Debates (Hansard). Volume 268, 1948.
Piddington, Ralph, "Emergent Development and 'Integration'" in Schwimmer, Erik (ed.), *The Maori People in the Nineteen-Sixties*. Blackwood & Janet Paul Ltd, Auckland, 1968.
Poole, Ian, *Te Iwi Maori, A New Zealand Population, Past, Present and Future*. Auckland University Press, Auckland, 1991.
"Puao-Te-Ata-Tu (Day Break) The Report of the Ministerial Advisory Committee on a Māori Perspective for the Department of Social Welfare." Department of Social Welfare, Wellington, June 1986.
Raerino, Kimiora, "He Tirohanga O Ngāti Awa Uri Taone Mō Ngā Āhuatanga Māori An Urban Ngāti Awa Perspective on Identity and Culture". Unpublished Master of Arts, Auckland University of Technology, 2007.
Rangiheuea, Tania, "Urban Māori" in Mulholland, Malcolm and Tawhai, Veronica (eds), *Weeping Waters, The Treaty of Waitangi and Constitutional Change*. Huia, Wellington, 2010.

Rata, Elizabeth, *A Political Economy of Neotribal Capitalism*. Lexington Books, New York, 2000.

Richards, Rhys, "Māori Names for Marine Mammals." In *Te Tuhinga* 19, 2008.

Royal, Te Ahukaramū Charles, *Kāti au i kōnei; He Kohikohinga i ngā Waiata a Ngāti Toarangatira, a Ngāti Raukawa*. Huia, Wellington, 1994.

Salmond, Anne, *Eruera; The Teachings of a Maori Elder Eruera Stirling*. Penguin Books, Auckland, 2005.

———, *Hui A Study of Maori Ceremonial Gatherings*. A.H. & A.W. Reed, Wellington, New Zealand, 1975.

Tamihere, John. *John Tamihere, Black and White*. Reed Books, Auckland, 2004.

Taonui, Rawiri, "Māori Urban Protest Movements" in Keenan, Danny (ed.), *Huia Histories of Māori, Ngā Tāhuhu Kōrero*, Huia, Wellington, 2012.

———, "Polynesian Oral Traditions" in Howe, K.R. (ed.), *Vaka Moana — Voyages of the Ancestors, The Discovery and Settlement of the Pacific*. David Bateman Ltd, Auckland, 2006.

Taonui, Rawiri, and Newbold, Greg. "Māori Gangs" in McIntosh, Tracey and Mulholland, Malcolm (eds), *Māori And Social Issues*. Huia, Wellington, 2011.

Tapsell, Paul. "Marae And Tribal Identity In Urban Aotearoa/New Zealand." *Pacific Studies* 25, no. 1/2, June 2002.

Tau, Rawiri Te Maire, *Ngā Pikitūroa o Ngāi Tahu*. Otago University Press, Dunedin, 2003.

———, "Ngai Tahu — from 'Better Dead and out of the Way' to 'To Be Seen to Belong.'" In *Southern Capital Christchurch, Towards a City Biography 1859–2000*. Canterbury University Press, Christchurch, 2000.

Tau, Rawiri Te Maire, and Anderson, Atholl (eds), *Ngāi Tahu A Migration History, The Carrington Text*. Bridget Williams Books, Wellington, 2008.

Tauroa, Hiwi, and Tauroa, Pat, *Te Marae, A Guide to Customs and Protocols*. Reed Books, Auckland, 1986.

Tawhai, Wiremu. *Living By The Moon Te Maramataka a Te Whanau-A-Apanui*. Huia, Wellington, 2013.

Taylor, Nancy M., *The Home Front Volume II*, Wellington, Historical Publications Branch, 1986.

Te Whanau, A Celebration of Te Whānau o Waipareira. Te Whānau o Waipareira, Waitakere City, Auckland, 2001.

Te Whānau o Waipareira Annual Report 2015–2016; Urban Māori Proud. Te Whānau o Waipareira, Auckland, 2016.

Te Whānau o Waipareira Report. WAI 414, Waitangi Tribunal Report. Waitangi Tribunal Report, GP Publications, Wellington, 1998.

"The Maori Race". *The Auckland Star*, LXVI, no. 269, 13 November 1935.

United Maori Mission, *United Maori Mission 1936–1986 Jubilee Book*. United Maori Mission Inc., 1987.

Walker, Ranginui. "Te Karanga A New Beginning." *Metro*, February 1992.

———, *Ka Whawhai Tonu Matou, Struggle Without End*. Penguin Books, Auckland, 1990.

———, "Māori People since 1950", in *The Oxford History of New Zealand*, 2nd edition. Oxford University Press, Auckland, 1992.

———, *Ngā Pepa a Ranginui The Walker Papers; Thought-Provoking Views On The Issues Affecting Māori and Pākehā*. Penguin Books, Auckland, 1996.

———, *Nga Tau Tohetohe*. Penguin Books, Auckland, 1987.

———, "The Social Adjustment of Maori to Urban Living in Auckland." Unpublished Doctorate of Philosophy, University of Auckland, Auckland, 1970.

———, "Te Karanga a New Beginning." *Metro*, February 1992.

Walker, Ranginui, "Marae, A Place to Stand" in King, Michael (ed.), *Te Ao Hurihuri The World Moves On; Aspects of Maoritanga*. 1st Edition. Hicks Smith & Sons Ltd, Wellington, 1975.

Waipareira Research Files, interview 4, CH04, 2017.
Warne, Kennedy. "Why Wasn't I Told?". *New Zealand Geographic*, December 2016.
Webster, Steven. "Māori Retribalization and Treaty Rights to the New Zealand Fisheries." *The Contemporary Pacific*, University of Hawaii Press 14, no. 2, 2002, pp. 341–76.
Wharemaru, Heeni, and Duffie, Mary Katharine, PhD, *Heeni, A Tainui Elder Remembers*. Harper Collins Publishers, Auckland, 1997.
Williams, Melissa Matutina, *Panguru and the City, Kāinga Tahi, Kāinga Rua An Urban Migration History*. Bridget Williams Books, Wellington, 2015.
Woods, Megan C. "Integrating the Nation, Gendering Māori Urbanisation and Integration, 1942–1969." Unpublished Thesis for Doctor of Philosophy in History, University of Canterbury, 2002.

Other sources

"1928, Apirana Ngata; Land and Community", originally published October 1928. *New Zealand Herald*, website article, nzherald.co.nz, http://www.nzherald.co.nz/new-zealand-herald-150-years/news/article.cfm?c_id=1503278&objectid=11140564. Accessed February 2017.

"2013 Census Quik Stats about Māori." *Stats NZ Tatauranga Aotearoa*, March 2017. http://www.stats.govt.nz/Census/2013-census/profile-and-summary-reports/quickstats-about-maori-english/population.aspx. Acessed June 2017.

Andres, Ulrike Pia, "Return Migration and Māori Identity in a Northland Community." Unpublished Doctorate of Philosophy, University of Auckland, 2011. https://researchspace.auckland.ac.nz/bitstream/handle/2292/6985/02whole.pdf?sequence=2. Accessed April 2017.

"Auckland's Community Centre." *Te Ao Hou The New World Magazine*, September 1962. http://teaohou.natlib.govt.nz/journals/teaohou/issue/Mao40TeA/c13.html. Accessed January 2017.

"Australia's First Marae Put on Hold." Newshub, Media Works TV. 16 December 2016. http://www.newshub.co.nz/world/australias-first-marae-put-on-hold-2015012412. Accessed December 2016.

Ballara, Angela, and Mariu, June, "Waititi, Hoani Waititi." *Te Ara — the Encyclopedia of New Zealand. The Dictionary of New Zealand Biography*, 1 April 2014. http://www.teara.govt.nz/en/biographies/5w2/waititi-hoani-retimana. Accessed August 2016.

Bennett, Adam, "Destiny Church Receives Govt Funding." nzherald.co.nz, 8 June 2011. http://www.nzherald.co.nz/nz/news/article.cfm?c_id=1&objectid=10730987. Accessed April 2017.

Bresnehan, Leona, "Hoani Waititi Marae", *Insight '81*. Radio New Zealand National Programme, Wellington, 1981. Ref. no. 24673, Sound Collection. Accessed April 2017.

Butterworth, Graham, "A Rural Maori Renaissance? Maori Society and Politics 1920 to 1951". *Journal of the Polynesian Society* 81, no. 2, 1972. http://www.jps.auckland.ac.nz/document?wid=4415&page=0&action=null. Accessed February 2017.

Calman, Ross, "Māori Education — Mātauranga — Kaupapa Māori Education." Website article. *Te Ara — the Encyclopedia of New Zealand*, 2012. http://www.teara.govt.nz/en/maori-education-matauranga/page-5. Accessed April 2017.

"Charter School Opens for Business." Website article. Radio New Zealand, 5 March 2015. http://www.radionz.co.nz/news/te-manu-korihi/267773/charter-school-opens-for-business. Accessed April 2017.

Clarke, Mania, "Whānau Move into Te Kopua Papakāinga." Te Kaea. Te Kopua, Raglan, Māori Television, 29 July 2016. http://www.maoritelevision.com/news/latest-news/whanau-move-te-kopua-papakainga. Accessed 15 December 2016.

Clarke, Rachel, "Marae Plans Move Forward." *North Shore Times*, December 2015. http://www.stuff.co.nz/auckland/local-news/north-shore-times/74479741/marae-plans-move-forward. Accessed 17 May 2017.

Cook, Megan, "Māori Smoking, Alcohol and Drugs — Tūpeka, Waipiro Me Te Tarukino — Māori Use of Alcohol." Website article. *Te Ara — the Encyclopedia of New Zealand*, September 2013. http://www.teara.govt.nz/en/maori-smoking-alcohol-and-drugs-tupeka-waipiro-me-te-tarukino/page-2. Accessed April 2017.

Dix, John, "The Gluepot." *Audio Culture The Noisy Library of New Zealand Music*. Wellington, Audio Culture, October 2014. http://www.audioculture.co.nz/scenes/the-gluepot. Accessed January 2017.

Dudding, Adam, "Parish Pumped, How Destiny Church Is Struggling." *Sunday Star Times*, 2013. http://www.stuff.co.nz/life-style/life/8968824/Parish-pumped-How-Destiny-Church-is-struggling. Accessed May 2017.

Easton, Brian, "Māori Meets More Market", unpublished presentation given 2016.

———, "The Maori Urban Migration." Published paper. Brian Easton website, 23 August 2012. https,//www.eastonbh.ac.nz/2012/08/the-maori-urban-migration/. Accessed February 2017.

Gerritsen`, John, "Cost of Study in Australia to Triple for NZers." New Zealand/Politics. Radio New Zealand, 3 May 2017. http://www.radionz.co.nz/news/national/329917/cost-of-study-in-australia-to-triple-for-nzers. Accessed June 2017.

Ka'ai, Tānia, "The Role of Marae in Tertiary Education Institutions." Te Kaharoa 1, 2008.

Keiha, Pae and Moon, Paul, "The Emergence and Evolution of Urban Maori Authorities, A Response to Maori Urbanisation". *Te Kaharoa* 1, 2008.

Kirikiriroa Marae, "Establishment of Kirikiriroa Marae". Website article, 2017. http://kirikiriroamarae.com/Who.

Forbes, Mihingarangi, "Locals Complain North Shore Marae 'Hijacked.'" Radio New Zealand. November 2016. http://www.radionz.co.nz/news/te-manu-korihi/317622/locals-complain-north-shore-marae-'hijacked'. http://teipuwhakahauaa.co.nz/uploads/gillies/2006/632_Gillies2006.pdf. Accessed April 2017.

Harte International, "Dannielle Harte", 2016. http://www.harteinternational.com/danielle-harte/. Accessed December 2016.

Henderson, Te Hira (Director), "Koraua; Anaru Kingi." *Koraua*, Auckland, Māori Television, February 2017. Accessed March 2017.

"He Rerenga Korero 1982." Audio. Ngā Hau E Whā Marae Part 1 of 2. Wellington, Ngā Taonga Sound and Vision, 1982. Ref. no. 47482. Accessed April 2017.

"High Court Judgement on Te Pūtea Whakatupu Trust." Website article. Te Ohu Kaimoana, 19 July 2016. http://teohu.maori.nz/media-release/2016/19.07.16-High-Court-Judgement-on-Te-Putea-Whakatupu-Trust.htm?utm_medium=email&utm_campaign=correction%20%20HIGH%20COURT%20JUDGMENT%20ON%20TE%20PTEA%20WHAKATUPU%20TRUST&utm_content=correction%20%20HIGH%20COURT%20JUDGMENT%20ON%20TE%20PTEA%20WHAKATUPU%20TRUST+CID_d3621907b8ab32dc9744318a920503d2&utm_source=Email%20marketing%20software&utm_term= statement %20to%20media. Accessed May 2017.

"High Court NUMA Decision Media Release", Te Ohu Kaimoana The Māori Fisheries Trust website, 2016. http://teohu.maori.nz/media-release/2016/High_Court_NUMA_Decision.pdf. Accessed May 2017.

Hill, Kim, "Tame Iti, Activist and Artist." *Saturday Morning with Kim Hill*. Auckland, Radio New Zealand, 12 November 2016.

http://www.radionz.co.nz/national/programmes/saturday/audio/201823561/tame-iti-artist-and-activist. Accessed November 2016.

Hill, Richard, *Maori and the State, Crown Māori Relations in New Zealand/Aotearoa 1950–2000.* Victoria University Press, Wellington, 2009. http://nzetc.victoria.ac.nz/tm/scholarly/tei-HilMaor-t1-body-d6-d3.html. Accessed April 2017.

———, "Ngā Whakataunga Tiriti — Treaty of Waitangi Settlement Process — The Waitangi Tribunal and Negotiated Settlements." *Te Ara — the Encyclopedia of New Zealand.* Ministry of Culture and Heritage, Wellington, 20 June 2012. http://www.teara.govt.nz/en/nga-whakataunga-tiriti-treaty-of-waitangi-settlement-process/page-3. Accessed April 2017.

"History of Māori Trade Training." Website video article. *Rehua Marae History,* 2017. http://rehuamarae.co.nz/history/. Accessed April 2017.

"Hoani Waititi Celebrates Milestone." Te Karere News website, 20 April 2015. http://tvnz.co.nz/te-karere-news/hoani-waititi-marae-celebrates-milestone-6294751. Accessed February 2017.

"Hoani Waititi Marae." Website article. Naumaiplace Ltd, 2007. http://www.naumaiplace.com/site/hoaniwaititi/home/welcome/. Accessed March 2017.

Hogan, Leo, "Mokopuna Ora Expands into Tāmaki Makaurau", Maori Television Online News Team, Auckland, 7 June 2017, https://www.maoritelevision.com/news/regional/mokopuna-ora-expands-tamaki-makaurau. Accessed 7 June 2017.

Hoyle, Craig, "Gangs Help 'Build' Destiny Church." *Waikato Times,* 18 April 2017. https,//www.pressreader.com/new-zealand/waikato-times/20170418/281547995764044. Accessed April 2017.

"Human Migration Guide." National Geographic Society. Marco Polo Expeditions, 2005. http://www.nationalgeographic.com/xpeditions/lessons/09/g68/migrationguidestudent.pdf. Accessed January 2017.

Husband, Dale, "John Tamihere, I've had to keep fighting my way". Website media release, *E-Tangata A Maori and Pasifika Sunday Magazine,* March 2013. https,//e-tangata.co.nz/news/john-tamihere-ive-had-to-keep-fighting-my-way/arts. Accessed May 2017.

"In Brief." Website article. Te Whānau o Waipareira, undated. http://www.waipareira.com/about. Accessed April 2017.

Integrity Professionals, "Invest Bay of Plenty — Māori Migration." Rotorua Lakes Council, 26 June 26 2014. http://www.rotorualakescouncil.nz/our-city/SmartFutures/Documents/Maori-migration.pdf. Accessed December 2016.

Inzone Education Foundation, "Inzone." Auckland, 2014. http://www.inzoneeducation.org.nz/who-we-are. Accessed October 2016.

Irwin, Geoff, and Walrond, Carl, "When Was New Zealand First Settled? — The Date Debate." *Te Ara — the Encyclopedia of New Zealand,* 2008, http://www.teara.govt.nz/en/when-was-new-zealand-first-settled/page-1. Accessed January 2017.

Jasper, Hariata, Oral history interview. Online recording. Wellington, 2000. "Orongomai Marae," website, *Recollect Upper Hutt Library Heritage Collections,* http://archives.uhcc.govt.nz/nodes/view/16021.

Johnston, Martin, "Exclusive, Man Who Fled Mental Health Found Dead — Inquiry Plea." nzherald.co.nz. 27 October 2016. http://www.nzherald.co.nz/nz/news/article.cfm?c_id=1&objectid=11736463. Accessed January 2017.

Kaipara, Oriini. "The Lonely Paepae." Magazine item. Native Affairs. Auckland, New Zealand, Māori Television, 30 May 2017. https,//www.maoritelevision.com/news/latest-news/native-affairs--lonely-paepae. Accessed June 2017.

Keenan, Erin, "Māori Urban Migrations and Identities, 'Ko Ngā Iwi Nuku Whenua', A Study of Urbanisation in the Wellington Region during the Twentieth Century." Unpublished PhD, Victoria University, 2014. https,//core.ac.uk/download/pdf/41338859.pdf. Accessed November 2016.

Kupenga, Talisa, "Plans for First Marae in Australia Under Way", *Te Kaea News*, Auckland New Zealand, Māori Television, 15 June 2016, http://www.maoritelevision.com/news/regional/plans-first-marae-australia-underway.

Law, Tina, "Christchurch Marae Hosts New Temporary Workers Village." *The Press*. February 2016. http://www.stuff.co.nz/the-press/business/the-rebuild/77171269/Christchurch-marae-hosts-new-temporary-workers-village. Accessed April 2017.

"Leadership Conference at Auckland", *Te Ao Hou The New World Magazine*, December 1963. http://teaohou.natlib.govt.nz/journals/teaohou/issue/Mao45TeA/c14.html. Accessed April 2017.

Lee, Jennifer. "The Second Great Migration". Website article. *Post Colonial Web*, n.d. http://www.postcolonialweb.org/nz/maorijlg5.html. Accessed May 2017.

"Man Up Conventions". Website article, n.d. https,//www.destinychurch.org.nz/manupnz. Accessed May 2017.

"Mangere Electorate Profile Data", Electorate Profile Data. New Zealand Parliament, June 2015. https,//www.parliament.nz/en/mps-and-electorates/electorate-profiles/electorate-profiles-data/document/DBHOH_Lib_EP_M%C4%81ngere_Households/m%C4%81ngere-households. Accessed April 2017.

Manukia, Claire, "Whare Akoranaga." Green Bay High School website. 2014. About Us — Facilities — Whare Akoranga. http://www.greenbayhigh.school.nz/whare-akoranga/. Accessed January 2017.

"Māori Cultural Well-Being in 2013 — Poster." Website report. *Stats NZ Tatauranga Aotearoa*, 6 May 2014. http://www.stats.govt.nz/browse_for_stats/people_and_communities/maori/te-kupenga/cultural-wellbeing-poster.aspx. Accessed May 2017.

"Maori Welfare Officers Meet The Minister." *Te Ao Hou The New World Magazine*, November 1973. http://teaohou.natlib.govt.nz/journals/teaohou/issue/Mao74TeA/c6.html. Accessed April 2017.

Mares, Peter, "Comment, New Zealand's 'Bondi Bludger' and Other Australian Myths." SBS News, 11 February 2014. http://www.sbs.com.au/news/article/2014/02/11/comment-new-zealands-bondi-bludger-and-other-australian-myths?cx_navSource=related-side-cx#cxrecs_s. Accessed November 2016.

McLean, Gavin,. "Pipitea Marae, Wellington, 1980." Website, updated 2013. https,//nzhistory.govt.nz/media/photo/pipitea-marae. Accessed February 2016.

McRoberts, Mike, "White Sheep Wairoa Documentary." Documentary New Zealand. New Zealand, Television New Zealand, 2000. https,//www.youtube.com/watch?v=_uhdxTDspoo. Accessed April 2017.

Meredith, Paul, "Urban Māori — Urbanisation." *Te Ara — the Encyclopedia of New Zealand*. http://www.teara.govt.nz/en/urban-maori/page-1. Accessed 2 October 2016.

Misa, Tapu, "Otara — the First Polynesian Suburb." nzherald.co.nz. 28 August 2010. http://www.nzherald.co.nz/nz/news/article.cfm?c_id=1&objectid=10667583. Accessed March 2017.

Murray, Justine, "Transforming Tāneatua." Radio interview. Te Ahi Kaa. Wellington, New Zealand, Radio New Zealand National Programme, 14 May 2017. http://www.radionz.co.nz/national/programmes/teahikaa/podcast. Accessed June 2017.

"Ngā Huarahi Ki Te Marae, Māori Connecting to Their Ancestral Marae 2013-Infographic." Website report. *Stats NZ Tatauranga Aotearoa*, 2015. http://www.stats.govt.nz/

browse_for_stats/people_and_communities/maori/te-kupenga/connect-ancestral-marae-infographic.aspx. Accessed May 2017.

"Ngā Māori i Te Ao Moemoeā Māori in Australia", website media release fact sheet, Te Puni Kokiri Ministry of Māori Development, December 2013, https,//www.tpk.govt.nz/en/a-matou-mohiotanga/demographics/maori-in-australia-fact-sheet. Acccessed November 2016.

"Ngāi Tahu Research." Website article. *Ngāi Tahu Research*, 2016. https,//www.ngaitahuresearch.co.nz/population/. Accessed June 2017.

Nursing Council of New Zealand, "Cultural Safety Guidelines, the Treaty of Waitangi and Maori Health in Nursing Education and Practice", 2011. http://pro.healthmentoronline.com/assets/Uploads/refract/pdf/Nursing_Council_cultural-safety11.pdf. Accessed March 2017.

Ngaropo, Amohaere G., B.J. Anderson and K. Way, "Te Whānau Atawhai, A New Zealand Model For Supporting Indigenous Families With Children in Intensive Care." Unpublished presentation, 1990, p. 3.

O'Brien, Joanne, "Thousands Expected for Tūhoe Festival." Website article. Radio New Zealand, 24 March 2016. http://www.radionz.co.nz/news/regional/299793/thousands-expected-for-tuhoe-festival. Accessed May 2017.

O'Regan, Sylvia Varnham, "Is the Maori-Australian Dream All Its Cracked up to Be?" SBS News, 22 May 2014. http://www.sbs.com.au/news/article/2014/03/21/maori-australian-dream-all-its-cracked-be. Accessed November 2016.

"Orongomai Marae." Website. Recollect Upper Hutt Library Heritage Collections, 2011. http://archives.uhcc.govt.nz/nodes/view/16021. Accessed February 2017.

"Our History." Website article. Te Iwi O Ngāti Kahu Trust He Pou Ora, n.d. http://tionk.co.nz/history/. Accessed May 2017.

"Our Vision." Website article. Nga Ngaru Rautahi Aotearoa National Urban Authority Inc., 2016. http://www.ngangaru.com/about/.

"Our Whanau Our Future". Website article. MUMA Manukau Urban Maori Authority, n.d. http://www.muma.co.nz/about-us. Accessed April 2017.

"Parihaka and Negotiations with the Crown", Parihaka — Past, Present and Future, 2015. http://parihaka.maori.nz/parihaka-reconciliation-process/. Accessed June 2017.

"Parihaka O Neherā, O Nāianei, Parihaka — Past and Present", Caritas Aotearoa New Zealand, Parihaka Schools Resource, The Catholic Agency for Justice, Peace and Development, 2015. http://www.caritas.org.nz/sites/default/files/Parihaka%20teachers%20booklet%20with%20worksheets%20WEB.pdf. Accessed January 2017.

Parsonson, Ann, "Herangi, Te Kirihaehae Te Puea." *Te Ara — the Encyclopedia of New Zealand*. From the *Dictionary of New Zealand Biography*, n.d. Accessed 9 February 2017.

"Petition of Haimona Te Aoterangi and 167 Others." *Appendix to the Journals of the House of Representatives* Session I, J-01, 18 August 1874. http://atojs.natlib.govt.nz/cgi-bin/atojs?a=d&d=AJHR1874-1.2.2.6.1&e=-------10--1------2%22grog+is+the+cause%22--. Accessed April 2017.

Phillips, Jock, "The New Zealanders — Bicultural New Zealand." *Te Ara — the Encyclopedia of New Zealand*. Ministry of Culture and Heritage, Wellington, updated 2015 (2005). http://www.teara.govt.nz/en/the-new-zealanders/page-12. Accessed March 2017.

"Pipitea Marae & Function Centre". Website, n.d. http://www.pipiteamarae.co.nz/. Accessed February 2017.

Poa, Hine, Hine Poa, Haki and Adam Langford oral history interview. Online recording. No. 2 of two volumes. Recollect Upper Hutt City Library Heritage Collections. Wellington, 2016. http://uhcl.recollect.co.nz/

nodes/view/25438. Accessed December 2016.
Pomare, Miria, "Ngāti Toarangatira — Migration from the North". *Te Ara — the Encyclopedia of New Zealand*, Ministry of Culture and Heritage, 2005. http://www.teara.govt.nz/en/ngati-toarangatira/page-2. Accessed January 2017.
"Professor Roger Maaka — Aorangi Māori Trust." Video recording. He Toa Takitini; Our Strength is in Unity, 2017. http://www.hetoatakitini.iwi.nz/twkd2rm1/. Accessed April 2017.
Pryor, Nicole, "Maori in Oz, Living the Good Life." *The Dominion Post*, 2013. http://www.stuff.co.nz/national/8937746/Maori-in-Oz-Living-the-good-life. Accessed December 2016.
"Quick Biz Stats". Website article. *Te Rūnanga O Ngāti Porou*, 2014. http://www.ngatiporou.com/nati-biz/doing-business-ngati-porou/quick-biz-stats. Accessed June 2017.
Rakuraku, Maraea, "Maori Trade Training Its History and Future." Te Ahi Kaa. Auckland, Radio New Zealand, 14 December 2014. http://www.radionz.co.nz/audio/player?audio_id=201823561. Accessed December 2016.
——, "Marae in the South Island". Radio interview. Te Ahi Kaa. Wellington, Radio New Zealand, March 2017. http://www.radionz.co.nz/national/programmes/teahikaa/audio/201837551/marae-of-the-south-island. Accessed December 2016.
"Reconciliation Kawe Whakamua Process Update Report II". Parihaka Papakāinga Trust, 2016. http://parihaka.maori.nz/home/wp-content/uploads/C-Reconciliation-Kawe-Whakamua-Process-Update-II.pdf. Accessed June 2017.
Schouten, Hank, "New Homes for Te Aro Pa Descendants." *The Dominion Post*. 18 October 2014. http://www.stuff.co.nz/dominion-post/business/commercial-property/10632789/New-homes-for-Te-Aro-Pa-descendants. Accessed December 2016.

"'Six O'clock Swill' Begins 2 December 1917." Website article. New Zealand History Nga Korero a Ipurangi O Aotearoa, 25 January 2017. https,//nzhistory.govt.nz/the-six-oclock-swill-begins. Accessed April 2017.
SmartGrowth Maori and Tangata Whenua Iwi Demographics, 6 August 2015, Beca Ltd, 2015, pp. i, ii, 6. https,//www.smartgrowthbop.org.nz/media/1091/a-action-11c1-maori-demographics.pdf. Accessed 7 June 2017.
Smith, Nick, "Award for Faithful Servant to His People." nzherald.co.nz., 2000. http://www.nzherald.co.nz/nz/news/article.cfm?c_id=1&objectid=13695. Accessed April 2017.
Sorrenson, M.P.K., "Ngata, Apirana Turupa", *Te Ara — the Encyclopaedia of New Zealand. The Dictionary of New Zealand Biography*. Wellington, New Zealand Government, n.d. http://www.teara.govt.nz/en/biographies/3n5/ngata-apirana-turupa. Accessed February 2017.
Spink, Emily, "Queens Birthday Honours Takes Maori Advocate by Surprise." *The Press*. June 2016. http://www.stuff.co.nz/the-press/news/80615786/queens-birthday-honour-takes-maori-advocate-by-surprise. Accessed April 2017.
Stephens, Mamari, "And There He Lies, Ever, Ever, the Manuhuri", *E-Tangata A Māori and Pasifika Sunday Magazine*, 20 June 2017, https,//e-tangata.co.nz/news/and-there-he-lies-ever-ever-the-manuhuri.
Stokes, John, "Tamihere Back in Charge at Waipareira." *New Zealand Herald*. 15 April 2006. http://www.nzherald.co.nz/nz/news/article.cfm?c_id=1&objectid=10377533.
"Strategic Plan." Website article. Te Whānau o Waipareira, 2017 2013.www.waipareira.com. Accessed May 2017.
"Submission in Response to the Auckland Law Reform Bill, Third Reading, Statutory Maori Board." Parliamentary Report, New Zealand, n.d. https,//www.parliament.nz/resource/mi-nz/49SCAGL_EVI_00DBHOH_

BILL9729_1_A34597/dc313f6332a3789ad98c426d28b1768db3a365fd. Accessed February 2017.

"Submission to the Māori Affairs Select Committee on the Ngāti Porou Claims Settlement Bill. Affidavit of Tokorua Barney Te Kani In The Waitangi Tribunal Wai 272." New Zealand Parliament, 2009. https,//www.parliament.nz/resource/en-nz/49SCMA_EVI_00DBHOH_BILL10537_1_A194716/ae30b282903493ce2f18340b2a286820c88412fe. Accessed May 2017.

"Table 7. Population of Statistical Divisions and Urban Areas, 1966 and 1971 Census." New Zealand Census Population and Dwellings, n.d.

Tahana, Yvonne, "Criticism Cut Me Deep, Says GC's Creator." nzherald.co.nz. April 2013. http://www.nzherald.co.nz/entertainment/news/article.cfm?c_id=1501119&objectid=10876063. Accessed December 2017.

——, "Straight-Talking Dame Recalls Humble Origins." nzherald.co.nz, 7 June 2010. http://www.nzherald.co.nz/nz/news/article.cfm?c_id=1&objectid=10650239. Accessed April 2017.

Tamihere, John, "Urban Māori Court Victory Over Iwi." Website article. Te Whānau o Waipareira, 2016. http://www.waipareira.com/news/urban-maori-court-victory-over-iwi. Accessed April 2017.

Taonui, Rawiri, "Ngati Whātua Facts and Figures." Website. *Te Ara — The Encyclopedia of New Zealand*, 2005. http://www.teara.govt.nz/en/ngati-whatua/page-5. Accessed February 2017.

"Tatai Hono, Tying Us Together". *Anglican Taonga, Telling The Stories of the Anglican Church in Aotearoa, New Zealand and Polynesia*, 2017, 2005. http://anglicantaonga.org.nz/News/Tikanga-Maori/Tatai-Hono. Accessed February 2017.

"Te Runanga O Nga Maata Waka Incorporated." Website. About Us, n.d. http://maatawaka.org.nz/. Accessed April 2017.

"Te Runanga O Nga Maata Waka Incorporated." Website, n.d. http://maatawaka.org.nz/. Accessed April 2017.

"Te Runanga O Nga Maata Waka Incorporated." Audio. Formation As An Urban Authority, undated. http://maatawaka.org.nz/about-nga-maata-waka/. Accessed April 2017.

"Te Runanga O Nga Maata Waka Incorporated." Audio. The Formation of Te Runanga O Nga Maata Waka, undated. http://maatawaka.org.nz/about-nga-maata-waka/. Accessed April 2017.

"Te Runanga O Nga Maata Waka Incorporated." Audio. The Definition and Philosophy of Nga Maata Waka, undated. http://maatawaka.org.nz/about-nga-maata-waka/. Accessed April 2017.

Te Whānau Atawhai, "Te Whānau Atawhai, A New Initiative in Health Provision." 1993.

Te Whānau Atawhai, "Steps into the Future. Te Whānau Atawhai Developments to the Year 2000." February 1992, Te Whānau Atawhai Archive.

"Te Whānau o Waipareira Annual Report 2010–2011." Auckland, Te Whānau o Waipareira, 2011. file,///C,/Users/Bradford/Downloads/Te_Whanau_O_Waipareira_Annual_Report_2010-11.pdf. Accessed May 2017.

"Te Whanau o Waipareira Annual Report 2014–2015." Auckland, Te Whānau o Waipareira, 2015. Accessed April 2017.

"Te Whatu Manawa Māoritanga o Rehua." Website, 2017. http://rehuamarae.co.nz/history/te-whatu-manawa-maoritanga-o-rehua/. Accessed January 2017.

"The City Rail Link — Ngati Te Ata Waiohua Maori Values Assessment for Auckland Transport," October 2012. https,//at.govt.nz/media/1168412/aeeappendix6culturalvalues.pdf. Accessed January 2017.

Treacher, Aroha, "Homes for Whanau Are

Now Ready in Hastings." *Hawke's Bay Today*. 24 November 2015. http://www.nzherald.co.nz/hawkes-bay-today/property/news/article.cfm?c_id=1503451&objectid=11546736. Accessed December 2016.

"Urban Maori Fight Iwi Over Fisheries". Website article. Te Whānau o Waipareira media release, 3 June 2015. http://www.waipareira.com/news/urban-maori-fight-iwi-over-fisheries. Accessed April 2017.

"Waatea Television". You Tube. Waatea TV Website, 2017. https://www.youtube.com/channel/UC1PVrafYKLbNWhW6pnSjjyg. Accessed April 2017.

"Waipareira on the Cutting Edge of Technology". Website media release. Te Whānau o Waipareira, 16 May 2012. http://www.waipareira.com/news/waipareira_on_the_cutting_edge. Accessed April 2017.

"Wai-Research." Website article. Te Whānau o Waipareira Media Release, n.d. http://www.waipareira.com/wai-research.html. Accessed May 2017.

Waretini Karena, David, "Maori Showbands a Tribute to Danny Robinson." Master of Arts, Waikato Institute of Technology, 2009. http://researcharchive.wintec.ac.nz/523/1/2009_Maori_showbands_Whanau_for_Archives_version.pdf. Accessed December 2016.

Wereta, Whetu, "Māori Demographic Trends." *Social Policy Journal of New Zealand Te Puna Whakaaro*, no. 3, December 1994. https://www.msd.govt.nz/about-msd-and.../03-maori-demographic-trends.html. Accessed May 2017.

"Whairawa/Economy". Website, Te Runanga o Ngati Porou, 2014. http://www.ngatiporou.com/nati-story/our-korero/whairawa-economy. Accessed February 2017.

Wharekura, Wi, "Wi Wharekura — Polynesian Cultural Village." Facebook page, 23 January 2016. https://www.facebook.com/permalink.php?story_fbid=1233682933314903&id=499160920100445. Accessed January 2017.

"Why Whānau Ora". Website article. Te Puni Kokiri Realising Māori Potential, 8 February 2017. https://www.tpk.govt.nz/en/whakamahia/whanau-ora/why-whanau-ora/. Accessed April 2017.

"Young Maori Become Skilled Tradesmen", *Te Ao Hou The New World Magazine*, 1966. http://teaohou.natlib.govt.nz/journals/teaohou/issue/Mao55TeA/c7.html. Accessed August 2016.

Index

Alcohol   26, 40, 46–47, 57, 60, 99–100, 137–41, 150–52, 190, 195, 211, 256
Anania whānau   45–48, 50–51, 55–56
Auckland   19–21, 23–27, 29, 31, 33–34, 37, 41, 44–47, 49–51, 53, 55, 58–67, 69, 75–78, 83–84, 88–100, 102–116, 118–23, 127, 130, 133–37, 140–41, 145–48, 150–53, 155–58, 165, 169, 174, 178–83, 186–88, 191–92, 194–97, 200, 204–205, 209, 213, 217–19, 221–23, 225, 229–30, 240, 242–43, 245, 247, 252
Auckland Maori Community Centre   24, 44, 59, 60, 83–84, 92–94, 103–104, 107, 114, 136–37
Auckland University of Technology   25, 192, 229
Australia   26, 67, 99, 115, 198–216, 230, 237, 242
Awataha marae   120–23

Baker, Barry   79–81
Bishop whānau   214–16
Buck, Te Rangihiroa Sir Peter   32, 52

Carroll, Sir James   32, 123
Christchurch   26, 41, 66, 69, 70–73, 75, 77, 79–81, 108, 111–12, 116–17, 129–31, 162–67, 181–82, 187, 194, 200, 213, 234
Cooper, Dame Whina   35, 86, 88, 99, 189, 225

Department of Māori Affairs   21, 23, 40, 52–53, 55, 59, 67–69, 71–72, 77, 79–80, 86, 88, 104, 112, 119, 121, 131, 133, 136–37, 140–41, 151, 155–56, 158–59, 161, 163–65, 169, 172–73, 196, 229, 233
Department of Social Welfare   134–36, 156, 164, 178–79, 229

Destiny Church   187–89
Drugs   26, 96, 137, 140–41, 151–52, 188, 190, 192, 198, 211, 238, 257
Dunedin   41

Edwards, Mihipeka   37, 139

Gangs   26, 47–48, 102, 132, 136, 140–43, 152, 188, 190, 198, 211, 222, 235, 257
Gisborne   21, 34, 40–41, 52, 73, 129–31, 242, 251

Hamilton   37–38, 66, 70, 108, 110, 131, 133, 165, 171–73, 181–83, 194
Hastings   40, 108, 172, 228, 235
Hawaiki   13–14, 253
Heke, Hone   32
Henare, Sir James   101, 123
Henry, Ella and Mia   25–28, 82–83
Hoani Waititi marae   60, 65, 92–97, 99, 108, 112, 115–16, 134, 156, 178, 180, 186, 196, 210, 245–47, 252
Hokianga   35, 43, 45, 109
Hospitals   26–27, 44, 46–47, 83, 88, 113, 131, 146–50, 152, 192, 214, 233
Hutana whānau   98–100

Invercargill   40, 181
Iti, Tame   143, 227

Kahi, Reikura   245–49
Kāhui Kaumatua Council   27, 146, 148, 240
Kākāriki marae   127–28
Kapa haka   80, 91, 96, 114, 130–31, 195–96, 204, 207, 212, 215, 239–40, 245, 247–48, 252
Kapiti Island   16
Kauri gum   30, 35

Index

Kawhia 15
Kīngitanga 17, 89, 108, 194
Kōhanga reo 27, 93, 96, 115, 118, 120, 126–27, 145, 155, 205, 245, 247, 249

Land Wars 16, 33
Lange, David 95
London 27, 115, 205, 250

Maaka, Dr Roger 17, 77, 161–62, 164, 233–36, 244
Manukau Urban Māori Authority (MUMA) 48, 169, 176, 181–83
Māori Affairs Trade Training programme 23, 66–81, 112, 172
Māori Battalion, 28th 36, 40, 59, 71, 114
Māori Hi-Five 60, 105, 203
Māori Party 115, 182
Māori War Effort Organisation (MWEO) 36–38, 39, 85–86
Māori Women's Welfare League 38, 52, 55, 59, 65, 85, 86, 88, 92, 94, 98, 104, 114, 121, 125, 136–37, 155–56, 194, 196, 225, 240
Marshall, Lianne 150–53
Mataatua marae 107, 118–20, 229
Mātauranga 127, 145, 173
Metge, Joan 21, 32
Morrison, Howard 60, 105, 203, 210

Napier 34, 108
Ngāi Tahu 15, 72, 74, 108, 110–12, 117–18, 131, 143, 162–63, 165–68, 199, 228, 233, 236, 242–43
Ngāpuhi 63, 107, 113–14, 121, 150, 199, 242–43
Ngata, Sir Apirana 19, 32–34, 36, 52, 101, 114, 123
Ngāti Awa 107, 118–20, 218, 229–30, 232
Ngāti Kahungunu 108, 143, 162–67, 199, 224, 233–34, 243
Ngāti Pōneke 37, 43–44, 86, 91, 103, 108, 123–25
Ngāti Porou 69, 92, 94–95, 114, 166, 169, 175, 199, 218, 234, 242, 245–46
Ngāti Raukawa 16, 86

Ngāti Whātua 104, 111–12, 146, 184
Ngā Aho Whakaari (Māori in Film and Television) 27
Ngā Hau e Whā National Marae 108, 166–67
Ngā Tamatoa 143–44
Ngā Tūmanako 93, 95–96, 245, 247–49

Ōrongomai marae 91, 108, 125–27, 256
Ōtara 21, 26–27, 61–63, 87–88, 90–91, 106, 109, 156

Papakāinga 16, 18, 22, 34, 35, 65, 100, 111, 115, 135–36, 219, 223, 226–29, 233, 235–36, 244
Parihaka 16–17, 187, 241
Pendennis Māori Girls' Hostel 39, 56
Pipitea marae 123–25
Pōmare, Lady Miria 44, 123
Pōmare, Sir Māui 32, 38
Princess Te Puea 38, 70–71, 75, 89, 118
Prince Tui Teka 60, 203

Ranginui, Jim 171–73, 219
Rātana 17–18, 70, 89–90, 104–105, 117, 136, 187
Reeves, Sir Paul 20, 95
Rehua marae 77, 81, 112, 116–17
Renata whānau 32, 255–58
Ria, Hokowhitu 129–31
Roberts, Anaru 113–15
Rotorua 21, 34, 40, 71, 110, 135, 229–30, 232, 251–52
Rudolph family 64–65

Sharples, Dr Pita 94–96, 134, 146, 178, 180, 189, 196
South Africa 26–27

Tainui 63, 70, 119, 173, 175, 209, 227, 243, 245–46
Taumaunu whānau 89, 155, 194–97
Tamihere, John 48, 156, 169, 174, 176, 178–81, 184–86
Taranaki 16, 42, 187, 241

Tātai Hono marae   91, 109
Tauranga   14, 243
Te Kanawa, Kiri   60, 105
Te Puea marae   106–107, 110–11
Te Rāhui Wahine Hostel   38, 70
Te Tira Hou marae   107, 114, 118, 223
Te Whānau Atawhai   148–49
Te Whānau a Apanui   66, 92, 245
Te Whānau o Waipareira Trust   24, 27, 48, 96–97, 155–58, 167, 169, 174, 176, 178–80, 183–86, 189–94, 196–97, 210, 239, 250
Tokomaru Bay   98–100, 113–14, 258
Treaty of Waitangi   37, 143–44, 146–47, 158, 165, 168–69, 178–79, 224, 226, 241–42, 251
Tūhoe   107, 114, 118, 142–43, 150, 171–73, 224, 227, 241, 251–52

United Māori Mission (UMM)   20, 67, 75–78
Urewera   31, 171, 227, 251

Victoria University   110, 115, 128

Waikato Institute of Technology   110, 173
Wairarapa   14, 115, 162, 235
Waitangi Day   96, 214, 251–52
Waitangi Tribunal   97, 144, 168, 175, 178–79, 234, 241
Waitematā Tribal Executive   59, 104
Waititi, Hoani   93, 95–96, 106
Walker, Dr Ranginui   61–63, 85, 90, 102, 109, 146, 162, 240
Wellington   21, 25, 32, 34, 36–39, 41–43, 51, 56, 61, 66–69, 75, 77, 87, 91, 103, 108, 117, 123–24, 128, 130, 133, 135, 141, 145, 159, 165, 172–73, 182, 217, 227–29, 242–43, 251–52, 255–56
Whanganui   21, 34, 214–15
Whāngarei   21, 52, 250
Williams, Melissa   24, 30, 54, 58, 92, 218, 225
World War I   36
World War II   18–19, 36, 38, 66, 72, 108, 136–37, 227

Young Māori Leaders' Conference   44, 102